'Quality peace is the only kind of peace that meets the true needs of those who have experienced the devastating effects of civil war. In this wide-ranging volume, expert researchers probe what can make quality peace effective and lasting.'
—**Michael Doyle**, *Columbia University, USA*

'*Understanding Quality Peace* gives us a new, useful concept by which to assess both peace agreements and post-war societies. The volume will be helpful to students and policymakers seeking to conceptualize and analyze sustainable peace. It answers a need to go beyond the "negative peace" of minimal stability, but not to unrealistically expect "positive peace" of egalitarian, wealthy consolidated democracy in places like Somalia and Haiti.'
—**Charles T. Call**, *American University, USA*

'This volume deepens our insights into the conditions after a peace agreement in civil wars. It takes up factors that that are proven to be conducive for preventing war recurrence. By analyzing five crucial dimensions in global work as well as through cases studies it focuses on the qualities that are required for sustaining peace. Thus, this book specifies the state of the art, stimulates further research and gives directions for peace making.'
—**Anna Jarstad**, *Umeå University, Sweden*

'Based on decades of empirical evidence, clear case studies, and a well-rounded theoretical understanding the editors and authors in this volume break new ground that helps us transcend the binary notion of negative or positive peace. *Understanding Quality Peace* gives us an excellent platform, engaging for the practitioner and the theorist, that helps us shift toward evidence-based approaches to peacebuilding in the aftermath of war.'
—**John Paul Lederach**, *Professor Emeritus, Kroc Institute, University of Notre Dame, USA*

UNDERSTANDING QUALITY PEACE

This book provides an analytical framework for understanding how the concept of quality peace can be used to evaluate post-conflict peacebuilding, using social science, statistics, and case studies.

Including contributions from over 20 researchers and practitioners, it argues that the quality of the peace in a post-conflict state relates to the extent to which peace accords are implemented, the agreed-upon mechanism for the non-violent resolution of the conflict, and the available social space for civil and political actors. To arrive at the concept of 'quality peace', the authors evaluate the existing literature and identify a lack of a satisfactory means of measuring outcomes, and consequently how these might be researched comparatively. The volume problematizes the 'quality peace' concept as a way to understand the origins of armed conflict as well as problems deriving from the conflict dynamics and the need for social, political, and economic changes in the post-conflict periods.

The book emphasizes five dimensions as crucial for quality peace in a post-accord society. Negotiations and agreements not only aim at avoiding the return of war but also seek to: (1) promote reconciliation, (2) develop mechanisms for resolving future disputes, (3) provide for reliable security, (4) open economic opportunities for marginalized segments of the population, and (5) generate space for civil society. These five dimensions together provide for quality peace after war. They are studied in the context of internal armed conflicts in which multiple parties have signed a peace agreement.

This book will be of great interest to students of peace and conflict studies, civil wars, global governance, security studies, and International Relations in general.

Madhav Joshi is Research Associate Professor and Associate Director of the Peace Accords Matrix project at the Kroc Institute for International Peace Studies, University of Notre Dame, USA.

Peter Wallensteen is Professor of Peace and Conflict Research, Uppsala University, Sweden, and University of Notre Dame, USA. He is editor/author of many books, including, recently, *Understanding Conflict Resolution* (4th edition, 2015), *Quality Peace: Peacebuilding, Victory and World Order* (2015), and *Regional Organisations and Peacemaking* (co-editor, Routledge 2014).

Security and Conflict Management
Series Editors:
Fen Osler Hampson
Carleton University, Canada
Chester Crocker
Georgetown University, Washington DC
Pamela Aall
United States Institute of Peace, Washington DC

This series will publish the best work in the field of security studies and conflict management. In particular, it will promote leading-edge work that straddles the divides between conflict management and security studies, between academics and practitioners, and between disciplines.

Recently published titles:

Human Security in Turkey
Challenges for the 21st Century
Edited by Alpaslan Özerdem and Füsun Özerdem

Understanding Complex Military Operations
A Case Study Approach
Edited by Karen Guttieri, Volker Franke and Melanne A. Civic

Regional Organisations and Peacemaking
Challengers to the UN
Edited by Peter Wallensteen and Anders Bjurner

International Mediation Bias and Peacemaking
Taking Sides in Civil Wars
Isak Svensson

Conflict Management in International Missions
A Field Guide
Olav Ofstad

International Multiparty Mediation and Conflict Management
Challenges of Cooperation and Coordination
Siniša Vuković

Mediation of International Conflicts
A Rational Model
Lesley G. Terris

Understanding Quality Peace
Peacebuilding after Civil War
Edited by Madhav Joshi and Peter Wallensteen

UNDERSTANDING QUALITY PEACE

Peacebuilding after Civil War

Edited by
Madhav Joshi and Peter Wallensteen

LONDON AND NEW YORK

First published 2018
by Routledge
2 Park Square, Milton Park, Abingdon, Oxon OX14 4RN

and by Routledge
711 Third Avenue, New York, NY 10017

Routledge is an imprint of the Taylor & Francis Group, an informa business

© 2018 selection and editorial material, Madhav Joshi and Peter Wallensteen; individual chapters, the contributors

The right of the editor to be identified as the author of the editorial material, and of the authors for their individual chapters, has been asserted in accordance with sections 77 and 78 of the Copyright, Designs and Patents Act 1988.

All rights reserved. No part of this book may be reprinted or reproduced or utilised in any form or by any electronic, mechanical, or other means, now known or hereafter invented, including photocopying and recording, or in any information storage or retrieval system, without permission in writing from the publishers.

Trademark notice: Product or corporate names may be trademarks or registered trademarks, and are used only for identification and explanation without intent to infringe.

British Library Cataloguing-in-Publication Data
A catalogue record for this book is available from the British Library

Library of Congress Cataloging-in-Publication Data
Names: Joshi, Madhav, editor. | Wallensteen, Peter, 1945– editor.
Title: Understanding quality peace : peacebuilding after civil war /
edited by Madhav Joshi and Peter Wallensteen.
Description: Abingdon, Oxon ; New York, NY : Routledge, 2018. |
Series: Security and conflict management | Includes bibliographical references and index.
Identifiers: LCCN 2017039627| ISBN 9781138307674 (hbk : alk. paper)
| ISBN 9781138307681 (pbk : alk. paper) | ISBN 9781315142470 (ebk)
Subjects: LCSH: Peace-building. | Transitional justice. | Truth commissions. | Civil society. | Democratization. | Civil war.
Classification: LCC JZ5538 .U535 2018 | DDC 303.6/4—dc23
LC record available at https://lccn.loc.gov/2017039627

ISBN: 978-1-138-30767-4 (hbk)
ISBN: 978-1-138-30768-1 (pbk)
ISBN: 978-1-315-14247-0 (ebk)

Typeset in Bembo and Stone Sans
by Florence Production Ltd, Stoodleigh, Devon, UK

In memory of John Darby

CONTENTS

List of figures xii
List of tables xiii
List of contributors xiv
Preface by Madhav Joshi and Peter Wallensteen xvii
List of acronyms xix

Introduction 1

1 Understanding quality peace: introducing the five dimensions 3
   Madhav Joshi and Peter Wallensteen

PART I
Post-war security 27

2 Peace implementation and quality peace 29
   Terrence Lyons

3 Same peace—different quality? The importance of security equality for quality peace 44
   Louise Olsson

PART II
Governance 59

4 Governance and negotiations: whose quality standards? 61
   Roger Mac Ginty

5 Quality peace in post-civil war settings: the role of local institutions 75
   Jenny Guardado, Leonard Wantchekon, and Sarah Weltman

PART III
Economic reconstruction — 91

6 Business on the Frontlines — 93
   Viva Ona Bartkus

7 Peace processes, economic recovery, and development agencies — 108
   Achim Wennmann

PART IV
Reconciliation and transitional justice — 119

8 Factoring transitional justice into the quality peace equation — 121
   David Backer

9 The challenges of reconciling tradition with Truth and Reconciliation Commission processes: the case of Solomon Islands — 135
   Karen Brounéus and Holly L. Guthrey

10 Reconciliation and quality peace — 148
   Alexander Dukalskis, Laura K. Taylor, and John Darby

PART V
Civil society — 161

11 Is civil society needed for quality peace? — 163
   Thania Paffenholz

12 Civil society and quality peace: what happened in El Salvador? — 178
   Richard Jones

PART VI
Case studies — 195

13 Quality peace in Cambodia: 20 years after the Paris Peace Agreement — 197
   Kheang Un

14 El Salvador 20 years later: successful democratization but
   questionable peace   212
   Dinorah Azpuru

15 Quality peace: a Northern Ireland case study   235
   Colin Knox

16 Mozambique: a credible commitment to peace   257
   Carrie Manning and Chipo Dendere

Conclusion   **275**

17 Developing quality peace: moving forward   277
   Peter Wallensteen and Madhav Joshi

Index   *285*

FIGURES

5.1	Distribution of *intrastate* conflict termination by type: 1946–2009	80
14.1	Authority trends in El Salvador: 1946–2010	215
14.2	Selected governance indicators in El Salvador: 1996–2012	218
14.3	Economic growth rates in El Salvador: 2000–2010	224
15.1	Civil society in Northern Ireland	239
15.2	Security-related incidents	244
15.3	Relations between Catholics and Protestants	249
15.4	How much has NI Assembly achieved?	252

TABLES

3.1	December 1975–September 1999	50
3.2	September 1999–March 2006	52
5.1	Peace agreements with local provisions: 1989–2005	82
5.2	Local and cultural provisions by type of conflict	82
5.3	Peace agreements with power-sharing provisions: 1989–2005	83
5.4	*Probit* analysis of the effect of local provisions on violence outbreak	84
5.5	Basic *probit* analysis of the effect of local governance on recurrence of violence within 5 years	87
5.6	Governance and violence	90
14.1	Indicators of regime type in El Salvador, 1990 vs. 2012	214
14.2	Electoral results for the FMLN, 1994–2012	216
14.3	Turnout in presidential elections in El Salvador, 1984–2009	216
14.4	World Bank governance indicators for El Salvador, 1996 vs. 2012	217
14.5	Post-accord homicides in El Salvador, 1993–2012	219
14.6	Most important problem in El Salvador, 1991–2012 (in percentages)	220
14.7	Perceptions about the rule of law and legitimacy of institutions in El Salvador, 1991–2012	222
14.8	Cross-time selected socio-economic indicators for El Salvador	225
15.1	Key economic indicators	241
15.2	Confidence in PSNI's ability to provide a service for all people of NI	244

CONTRIBUTORS

Dinorah Azpuru is Associate Professor of Political Science at Wichita State University in Kansas, USA.

David Backer is currently Associate Research Professor and Assistant Director of the Center for International Development and Conflict Management at the University of Maryland, USA.

Viva Ona Bartkus is Associate Professor of Management at the University of Notre Dame, USA.

Karen Brounéus is Senior Lecturer, Director of Studies at the Department of Peace and Conflict Research, Uppsala University, Sweden.

John Darby was Professor of Comparative Ethnic Studies at the Kroc Institute for International Peace Studies and Director of Peace Accords Matrix (PAM) project at the University of Notre Dame, USA (deceased on June 2, 2012).

Chipo Dendere is Derrick K. Gondwe Visiting Scholar and Visiting Assistant Professor of Africana Studies at the Gettysburg College, Pennsylvania, USA.

Alex Dukalskis is Assistant Professor in the School of Politics and International Relations at the University College Dublin, Ireland.

Jenny Guardado Rodriguez is Assistant Professor at the School of Foreign Service at the Georgetown University, USA.

Holly L. Guthrey, Ph.D., is a Research Fellow at the Hugo Valentin Centre, Uppsala University, Sweden.

Richard Jones is currently Deputy Regional Director for Global Solidarity and Justice for Catholic Relief Services, Latin America and Caribbean Regional Office.

Madhav Joshi is Research Associate Professor and Associate Director of the Peace Accords Matrix at the Kroc Institute for International Peace Studies, University of Notre Dame, USA.

Colin Knox is Emeritus Professor at Ulster University and Professor of Public Policy at Nazarbayev University, Kazakhstan.

Terrence Lyons is Associate Professor at the Institute for Conflict Analysis and Resolution, and co-director of the Center for Global Studies at George Mason University, USA.

Roger Mac Ginty is Professor of Peace and Conflict Studies at the Humanitarian and Conflict Response Institute (HCRI) and the Department of Politics at the University of Manchester, UK.

Carrie Manning is Professor and Chair of the Department of Political Science at the Georgia State University, USA.

Louise Olsson, Ph.D., from Uppsala University, Sweden, Senior Researcher at the Peace Research Institute Oslo (PRIO) and Senior Advisor on Women, Peace and Security and Gender Mainstreaming at the Folke Bernadotte Academy (FBA), Sweden.

Thania Paffenholz is Senior Researcher at the Graduate Institute Geneva, Geneva, Switzerland.

Laura K. Taylor is Assistant Professor in the School of Psychology at Queen's University, Belfast, UK.

Kheang Un is Associate Professor of Political Science and Assistant Director of the Center for Southeast Asian Studies at the Northern Illinois University, USA.

Peter Wallensteen is Senior Professor of Peace and Conflict Research, Uppsala University, Sweden (since 2012), previously holding the Dag Hammarskjöld Chair at Uppsala University (1985-2012), and the Richard G. Starmann, Senior Research Professor of Peace Studies at the Kroc Institute for International Peace Studies, University of Notre Dame, USA (since 2006).

Leonard Wantchekon is Professor in the Politics department and associated faculty in the Economics department at Princeton University, USA.

Sarah Weltman is currently a Ph.D. student in the Economics Department at Harvard University, USA.

Achim Wennmann is Researcher at the Graduate Institute Geneva and an Executive Coordinator of the Geneva Peacebuilding Platform, Geneva, Switzerland.

PREFACE

Since the end of the Cold War peace processes, peace agreements, and peacebuilding have become central in ending wars and constructing lasting security. This can be witnessed in the number of peace agreements as well as the rise in mediators, civil society organizations (CSOs) engaged in peace work and the establishment of the Mediation Support Unit within the United Nations. These peacemaking efforts have led to the reversal in the mode of conflict terminations that negotiated outcomes now are more frequent than victories. In lights of new trends in conflict termination and roles for various actors in the peace process, the quality and quantity of research has made remarkable headway to identify conditions that constitute the key factors in sustaining durable peace. The current volume brings together scholars and practitioners at the forefront of these efforts to focus on the quality of the peace that follow the end of war. In this book and two accompanying volumes the notion of Quality Peace is presented and elaborated.

This initiative is the result of a collaboration formed at the Kroc Institute for International Peace Studies, University of Notre Dame, Indiana, USA. It began in 2006 when John Darby, Professor of Comparative Ethnic Conflict at the Kroc Institute, and Peter Wallensteen, Richard G. Starmann Sr. Research Professor of Peace Studies at the Kroc Institute and Dag Hammarskjöld Professor of Peace and Conflict Research at Uppsala University in Sweden began to cooperate on the idea of systematically studying the implementation of peace agreements. John had started to develop a matrix for teaching purposes. It would potentially allow researchers and practitioners to compare the terms of peace agreements and whether these terms were implemented. With funding from the United States Institute of Peace, the Peace Accords Matrix (PAM) began collecting data and developed its own website. Peter was then the leader of the UCDP at Uppsala University, Uppsala, Sweden. In addition to containing detailed information on armed conflicts around the world, UCDP also had collected systematic information on peace agreements and there were obvious synergies between the projects. As the collaboration continued to grow, Erik Melander, Deputy Director of the UCDP, and Madhav Joshi, Associate Director of PAM, joined the team.

A central puzzle that the researchers considered was how to describe post-war periods that were conducive for lasting peace between former belligerents. The team settled for the term Quality Peace, by which it aimed to identify the specific conditions in the post-accord environment that were the most conducive to a durable peace that also met basic human values. The project received support from the National Science Foundation to elaborate the notion of quality peace and develop tools for measuring the quality of peace. The Kroc Institute also provided substantial financial support for this endeavor.

A workshop was convened at the Kroc Institute in November 2010 including leading scholars and experienced peace practitioners, who agreed to contribute to the development of the concept. At a follow-up conference in May 2012, 15 papers were presented. Five factors were identified that were explored through analysis and case studies of processes that had lasted more than a decade. These factors include post-war security, governance, economic reconstruction, reconciliation and transitional justice, and civil society. These contributions have now been converted into the book chapters of this volume, primarily edited by Madhav Joshi and Peter Wallensteen. The editors have added their own introductory remarks and final comments on the future of the concept of Quality Peace.

Apart from those mentioned above, our colleagues R. Scott Appleby, John Paul Lederach, Hal Culbertson, Robert Johansen, George Lopez, and David Cortright at the Kroc Institute for International Studies have provided important input to intellectual debate throughout this project. We are thankful for encouragements, constructive comments, and suggestions from anonymous reviewers that we found helpful in the manuscript revision processes. We are also thankful to Samuel J. Nicholas, Lucy Dunderdale, and Audrey Faber who provided excellent assistance during several rounds of revisions.

We dedicate this volume to our colleague John Darby who continued to follow the project and hoped to join the conference in May 2012, although his health was deteriorating. He finally had to decline, but sent the participants an encouraging message. He passed away just a month later. John insisted that the study of peace accords should be useful for both researchers and practitioners. Indeed, it is and PAM already has a role in ongoing peace processes. Also, many of the contributors to this volume come from the world of practice, adding important insights to the academic contributions.

Notre Dame/Uppsala
Madhav Joshi and Peter Wallensteen
The Editors

ACRONYMS

ANC—African National Congress (South Africa)
ARENA—Alianza Nacional Republicana
BLDP—Buddhist Liberal Democratic Party
CAVR—Commission for Reception, Truth and Reconciliation in Timor-Leste
CBO—Community-Based Organizations
CCM—Christian Council of Mozambique
CDD—Community-Driven Development
CDR—Community-Driven Reconstruction
CEDE—Center for Democracy and Development
CONARA—National Commission for Restoration of Areas
COPAZ—Comisión Nacional para la Conslidación de la Paz
COVAFGA—Cooperative de Valorisation des Fruites de Gakenke
CPA—Comprehensive Peace Agreement
CPDN—National Debate for Peace (El Salvador)
CPP—Cambodian People's Party
CRPs—Community Reconciliation Processes
CSC—Supervision and Control Commission (Mozambique)
CSO—Civil Society Organization
DDR—Disarmament, Demobilization, and Reintegration
DUP—Democratic Unionist Party
ECCC—Extraordinary Chamber in the Court of Cambodia
ECOWAS—Economic Community of West African States
EISA—Electoral Institute for Sustainable Democracy in Africa
EU—European Union
FMLN—Farabundo Martí National Liberation Front
Frelimo—Front for Liberation of Mozambique
FUNCINPEC—*Front uni national pour un Cambodge indépendant, neutre, pacifique et coopératif*

FUSADES—The Salvadoran Foundation for Economic Development
GDP—Gross Domestic Product
GPA—General Peace Agreement (Mozambique)
HET—Historical Enquiries Team (in Northern Ireland)
ICC—International Criminal Court
ICTY—International Criminal Tribunal for the Former Yugoslavia
IDPs—Internally Displaced Persons
IMF—International Monetary Fund
INTERFET—International Force in East Timor
IUDOP—University Institute for Public Opinion
LPC—Liberia Peace Council
NATO—North Atlantic Treaty Organization
NEC—National Electoral Commission
NGO—Non-Governmental Organization
ODA—Overseas Development Assistance
OHR—Office of the High Representative
OREC—Organization for Conflict Resolution
PAM—Peace Accords Matrix
PCNAs—Post-Conflict Needs Assessments
PNC—National Civilian Police
PPA—Paris Peace Agreement
PRIO—Peace Research Institute Oslo
PRK—People's Republic of Kampuchea
PSNI—Police Service of Northern Ireland
RAMSI—Regional Assistance Mission to Solomon Islands
RENAMO—Mozambique National Resistance Movement
RUF—Revolutionary United Front
SICA—Solomon Islands Christian Association
SIT—Social Identity Theory
SoC—State of Cambodia
SSR—Security Sector Reform
TPA—Townsville Peace Agreement
TRC—Truth and Reconciliation Commission
UCDP—Uppsala Conflict Data Program
UK—United Kingdom
ULIMO—United Liberation Movement of Liberia for Democracy, divided into two factions of ULIMO-J and ULIMO-K
UN—United Nations
UNAMET—United Nations Mission in East Timor
UNDP—United Nations Development Program
UNITA—National Union for the Total Independene of Angola
UNMISET—United Nations Mission of Support in East Timor
UN OCHA—United Nations Office for the Coordination of Humanitarian Assistance

UNOMOZ— United Nations Operation in Mozambique
UNOTIL—United Nations Office in Timor-Leste
UN SRSG—United Nations Special Representative of the Secretary General
UNTAC—United Nations Transitional Authority in Cambodia
UNTAET—United Nations Transitional Administration in East Timor
URNG—La Unidad Revolucionaria Nacional Guatemalteca
US—United States
USAID—United States Agency for International Development
ZANU—Zimbabwe African National Union

Introduction

1
UNDERSTANDING QUALITY PEACE

Introducing the five dimensions

Madhav Joshi and Peter Wallensteen

The question of the quality of peace relates to how wars end. In this volume we focus on the situation after peace agreements in civil wars and ask how to understand the qualities of the resulting peace. This partly includes the danger of the recurrence of war, but also other qualities for the society as a whole. This focus is necessary as the peacebuilding experiences vary in remarkable ways over cases. Some recent examples make this clear.

In 2016, Nepal celebrated the tenth anniversary of the Comprehensive Peace Agreement (CPA) between the government and the Maoist rebel party. Since the agreement in 2006, Nepal abolished the monarchy, made a transition to a federal state, and consolidated this in a new constitution that came into effect on September 20, 2015, guaranteeing representation of women and indigenous minorities in the local, state, and federal levels as well as in civil services. Despite these landmark achievements, the post-CPA governments have lacked a coherent policy of economic reconstruction. Civil war victims from both sides were still looking for truth, reconciliation, and admissions of guilt. During the subsequent 10 years, nine different governments formed, with three headed by the Maoist rebel party.

A different, but still troubling, development can be found in El Salvador. After the 1992 agreement with the Farabundo Martí National Liberation Front (FMLN), El Salvador's democracy has seen increased trust and legitimacy of state institutions, including the armed forces. State practices of human rights have improved in El Salvador. However, two decades after the end of the civil war, drug-related violence has increased exponentially, threatening to undermine these reforms.

A further example is the case of Cambodia, where successful post-war recovery and economic growth have contributed to the consolidation of a one-party regime with widespread corruption. A similar situation can be identified in Sudan after the 2005 agreement with the Sudan People's Liberation Movement (SPLM). The 2005 agreement provided the foundation for the creation of South Sudan; however, the newly independent country has never been able to break out of post-war cycles of violence, despite multiple rounds of negotiations and strong support from the international community.

As these cases make clear, the fate of societies after civil war does not follow a linear logic that establishes the requirement for quality peace. According to the PAM at the University of Notre Dame's Kroc Institute, more than 80 percent of the 31 countries that negotiated a CPA between 1989 and 2012 were no longer fighting an armed conflict as of 2016. While the absence of war is the most common phenomenon observed in these post-war countries, the quality of the ensuing peace—as indicated by the examples just mentioned—is marked by varying degrees of social, political, and economic contradictions. How can we capture such differences in the quality of the peace in post-armed conflict settings? Here we want to address this question from what we term a Quality Peace perspective by focusing on the post-settlement process of changes that are taking place at the state, community, and individual levels.

Recent years have seen a significant growth of research into the success or failure of peace processes in ending wars. This is parallel to a growing interest among researchers to identify factors related to successful peacebuilding, and locating examples of quality peacebuilding practice. While scholars are still searching for general explanations of peacebuilding success, peace duration, or armed conflict recurrence (see Doyle and Sambanis 2000, 2006; Walter 2002; Paris 2004, 2010; Richmond 2006; Hartzell and Hoddie 2007; Quinn et al. 2007; Kreutz 2010; Mac Ginty 2010; Joshi and Mason 2011, Wallensteen 2015a), there are also practical experiences that enrich the discussion. The Truth and Reconciliation Commission (TRC) in South Africa was one such precedent-setting experience that deepened the discussion on key issues related to victims, truth, justice, and reconciliation in post-agreement context. There was also the reconstruction of armed forces in Mozambique and significant socio-economic reforms written into the El Salvador peace accords, two of the important civil war agreements of the 1990s. Certainly, the role of international (military) intervention has been widely discussed since the events in the Balkans, and more recently, in the cases of Libya, Ivory Coast, Syria, Ukraine, and Yemen. These experiences, as well as contemporary research, have developed insights that have been adopted by negotiators in peace processes.

Despite the emergence of these new conclusions and insights, we have observed that there is a lack of an agreed-upon framework for what constitutes the success or failure of peace efforts beyond the absence of war. An exception is the Höglund and Kovacs (2010) study that proposes a "peace triangle" framework by emphasizing the status of armed conflict issues, the armed actors' conflict behavior and societal attitudes toward conflict. According to Höglund and Kovacs, peace differs from one post-negotiated settlement case to another depending on where things fall in this triangle. This goes beyond the notion of "no war" as a measure of the situation after a negotiated settlement, but it is still static in its view. The peace triangle assists in categorizing the *type* of peace of post-war countries, but it does not help to explain the causes of the variety of peace. Therefore, we offer the Quality Peace framework for conceiving post-war strategies that are not only useful to explain the recurrence of war, but also explore the conditions necessary for a quality and sustainable peace. In a way, we advance the research from Höglund and Kovacs (2010), respond to the calls of Regan (2014) and Diehl (2016) to directly engage the issue of peace and its causes, and deepen the prior work of Wallensteen (2015a).

While a vast debate has focused on concepts such as peace duration and armed conflict recurrence as a framework for success or failure (see Licklider 1995; Walter 2002; Hartzell and Hoddie 2007; Quinn et al. 2007; Kreutz 2010; Joshi and Mason 2011, Wallensteen 2015a), these notions do not account for the significant changes a post-conflict society may undergo following years of armed conflict experiences and peace negotiations. Peace agreements, which mean that the parties have agreed on a framework for changes in the post-war period, often lead to high expectations. Such agreements are intended to institutionalize peace following the tenuous conditions in the immediate aftermath of armed conflict.

Certainly, agreeing to an accord demonstrates an important commitment by the signatories. However, peace treaties are often brittle, especially when not all key issues are addressed (see Joshi and Quinn 2015). Disagreements that lead to war and its effects result in dozens of issues that are interconnected, sometimes in unpredictable ways. Peace processes can also be fragile when all stakeholders are not represented in the negotiation process (Höglund and Kovacs 2010). Groups on the outside of the negotiation process are not likely to take any responsibility for adhering to accords, and may even actively try to counter their implementation (this has been known as "spoiler behavior" (Stedman 1997) a term that can be questioned, (see Höglund 2008) but still a phenomenon to be alert to). This means that the efficacy of a peace process and of peace accords, to a large degree, rests on the success of implementing the agreed-upon provisions. Thus, we argue that the quality of the changes in a post-accord state is directly related to the extent to which peace accords are implemented as well as the agreed mechanism for the non-violent resolution of the armed conflict, and the social space available for civil and political actors.

This volume explores five dimensions that are both theoretically and empirically necessary for quality peace in a post-accord society. When belligerent parties commit themselves to a negotiated settlement to end armed conflict, they also consent in principle to the implementation of the agreement. Here we argue that successful building of peace through accords does not only aim at avoiding the return of war but also seeks to: (1) provide for reliable security provisions through security sector reforms, (2) develop mechanisms for resolving disputes related to access to power and resources through governance reforms, (3) contribute to rebuilding and opening of economic opportunities for marginalized segments of the population, (4) promote reconciliation, and (5) generate space for civil society to hold government accountable as well as provide goods and services to citizens when necessary. In this volume, we analyze these five dimensions within the context of internal armed conflicts in which multiple parties have signed a peace agreement. In this Introduction, we will clarify the composition of the book and its contents, and explain how these five dimensions emerged as particularly crucial for quality peace.

Peacebuilding research in a post-Cold War world

There have been remarkable advances in peace research on the topic of peacebuilding since the end of the Cold War. Moving beyond the initial conceptualization of successful peacebuilding in terms of settlement of deadly armed conflicts and the promotion of liberal democracy (Doyle and Sambanis 2000), scholars have construed the definition of peacebuilding success in terms of (1) success in avoiding armed conflict recurrence/recidivism, (2) addressing the root causes of armed conflict, (3) democratization and state-building, and (4) economic recovery (Call 2008). By defining peacebuilding success only in terms of armed conflict reoccurrence, Walter (2004) found that 36 percent of civil wars had recurred between 1945 and 1996; whereas Joshi and Mason (2011) demonstrated that 48 percent of cases experienced armed conflict recurrence between 1945 and 2005. Licklider's study (1995) of negotiated settlements between 1945 and 1993 suggested that only half of all negotiated settlements lasted beyond 5 years; other analysts found that most of them lasted for only 3.5 years. This reflects an earlier generation of studies that, necessarily, rested on data from the Cold War period, where global rivalry may have determined the likelihood of armed conflict recurrence more so than the quality of war endings. Thus, we can see that more recent research on civil war termination indicates that the most likely outcome of a civil war in the post-Cold War period is a negotiated settlement (Wallensteen 2015a). In the post-Cold War period, governments have managed to win approximately 28 percent of all major civil wars, with the remaining 52 percent resolved through negotiated settlement, and 19 percent ending in rebel victory.[1] If minor armed conflicts settled after 1990 are taken into account, the percentage of civil war conflicts ending in a negotiated settlement increases to 90 percent. As a matter of fact, 183 peace agreements in 50 different countries were signed between 1989 and 2011; but, 68 of those accords failed as violence resumed between the same dyads (Högbladh 2011; also see Kreutz 2013). If efficacy of peace accords is to be used as an indication of peacebuilding, the success rate is almost 63 percent (i.e. 115 agreements). If only Comprehensive Peace Accords are measured, in which all major issues are up for negotiation and all major actors are involved, 25 out of 34 armed conflicts (75 percent) did not recur (see Joshi and Darby 2013; Joshi et al. 2015). Using armed conflict recurrence to explain peacebuilding success, however, does not help us to understand how the Rwandan, Cambodian, or East Timorese societies are different from those in South Africa, El Salvador, or Nepal. The qualities of peace found in these countries vary considerably, and that is why additional dimensions have to be introduced.

If peacebuilding success is more than simply avoiding armed conflict recurrence, and, instead is about addressing the root causes of the armed conflict, Paris' (2004) data suggests only a 22 percent success rate. Among the 11 cases selected in his study, United Nations (UN) peacebuilding operations rendered a successful result only in Namibia and Croatia. Furthermore, these were not typical civil wars (Wallensteen 2015a). It can safely be argued that many countries failed to address basic armed conflict causes in their post-war policies. As the PAM demonstrates, few post-civil war societies emerging from signed peace accords have faithfully and successfully implemented socio-economic and other rights-related provisions (Lee et al. 2016). Still, are these to be regarded as failures of the entire peacebuilding enterprise? If peace in the form of non-recurrence of war is holding in these countries without addressing the root causes of the armed conflict, then what accounts for the outcomes in these countries?

By using the criteria of armed conflict non-recurrence, shared sovereignty, and requiring a minimal measure of political participation, Doyle and Sambanis found a 31 percent rate of peacebuilding success between 1945 and 1999 in their analysis of 121 civil wars. Their critique is focused on following the slow implementation of agreed disarmament measures—the Disarmament, Demobilization, and Reintegration (DDR) process—which, often extends for several years once the implementations begin. Given that most civil war incidents occur in developing countries under authoritarian or semi-democratic regimes, it would be unrealistic to assume these societies would emerge as functioning democracies in the immediate aftermath of armed conflict. By assuming post-civil war states would make gradual progress toward democracy after the termination of the civil war, Joshi (2010: 841–842) reported that a transition toward democracy occurred in 72 percent of cases (92 of 125) between 1946 and 2005. The survival of these transitions, however, depends on the inclusive political process of adopting a parliamentary and proportional-representation system, which avoids the predicament of winner-take-all elections (Joshi 2013). Further, Wallensteen (2015a) reports a much higher rate of democratization in cases of peace agreements than victory. The high rate of transitioning toward democracy, however, is related to the requirement of post-armed conflict elections, which is often negotiated as part of the armed conflict settlement in the post-Cold War period. Indeed, a Joshi et al. (2014) study found that 26 of 34 CPAs between 1989 and 2012 had provision for elections or electoral reforms. However, the tendency of international actors to promote electoral democracy does not necessarily suggest that the states emerging from armed conflict are functionally capable of actually developing democratic institutions. This is often what is associated with the notion of "liberal" peacebuilding, meaning a concern for political and human rights, but giving less attention to economic and social dimensions of peacebuilding (Paris 2004; Joshi et al. 2014). For successful peacebuilding, Ghani and Lockhart (2009: 124–166) suggest ten core functions or capacities of states, ranging from administrative control to market formation.[2] While societies trying to move forward in the post-war period find challenges to achieve or restore many of these functional capabilities of the state, holding elections to identify a new ruler of the country can be a prescription for further instability. In many instances, by election time, former rebels—as well as the militarized state—remain militarily mobilized, as was the case in Angola and Cambodia in the 1990s. In other instances, there remains fear of violence, which trumps the electoral preferences of voters, as was the case in Liberia in 1997 (Lyons 2004). These examples indicate that the non-recurrence of violence and the presence of electoral participation are not sufficient indicators for peacebuilding success. The peace and the minimal level of democratic governance achieved in a post-accord period might not be sustained when the state machinery struggles to function. At the same time, the state needs to be reformed to gain legitimacy with the parts of the population that supported the rebels. Thus, the state needs policies that address basic issues, such as access to government services, economic resources, and land. As such, liberal peace is not enough. Strategies of peace need to involve more comprehensive approaches including a diverse set of actors and settlement mechanisms to move away from armed conflict.

Post-civil war states that gain a functional capability may also be more likely to see economic recovery. Unfortunately, most civil war states tend to fall into a continued pattern of downward economic trends (Collier 2003; Fearon and Laitin 2003). In fact, 73 percent of the world's population of the lowest income societies have experienced or are still experiencing civil war (Collier 2008). Collier suggests stagnation or decline in economic growth proportionately increases the likelihood of civil war onset. Walter (2004) further argues that a dire economic situation makes former combatants more willing to engage in renewed armed conflict. But, economic recovery does not suffice as a primary condition for successful peacebuilding. For peacebuilding to be successful, it is also important to understand how economic opportunities are created, and whether people in post-armed conflict economies have reasonably equal economic opportunities.

As this suggests, scholars and practitioners have developed and tested new theories as to what constitutes successful peacebuilding. While the typically used criteria seems very attractive, they are still operating on the macro-level and do not adequately help to determine whether civilians in the post-accord states are experiencing meaningful changes in their lives and communities (Richmond 2006; Mac Ginty 2010). The concept of Quality Peace introduced in this volume, therefore, attempts to engage the research and policy communities in evaluating peacebuilding by using the aforementioned five different dimensions for understanding and explaining changes brought at the state, community, and individual levels after armed conflict terminates.

What is quality peace?

Recently, there is a tendency on the political level to search for peaceful measures beyond the mere absence of war. This means that notions of "sustainable peace" as well as "to promote peaceful and inclusive societies" are part of the UN discourse, notably for the implementation of the 16th of the 17 Sustainable Development Goals.[3] This makes emerging peacebuilding research on the successes and failures of peace processes particularly relevant. However, there are few studies evaluating the successes and failures of peace processes from the perspective of implementing peace agreements (i.e., Stedman et al. 2002; Bekoe 2003, 2005; Darby and Mac Ginty 2008; Jarstad and Nilsson 2008; Joshi and Quinn 2017). There are even fewer comparing these outcomes to those of victory (Wallensteen 2015a). This may explain why much of the debate focuses on a few indicators, such as power-sharing and peacekeeping. Peace accords have not been used to evaluate and determine the outcome of peace processes, and therefore there is still not a clear understanding of why some agreements have been operative while others have failed. Obviously, there is even less insight into what constitutes failure, or even how to define success in peace processes. The 2012 report of the UN General-Secretary on mediation presented the idea of "quality peace agreement" for mediators involved in peace processes (United Nations General Assembly 2012). The report defines the "quality" of a peace agreement in terms of maintaining mediation support beyond the peace agreement that definitely ends violence, and provide a foundation for peace, justice, and reconciliation. Furthermore, the "quality peace agreement" is one that provides for mechanisms to address tensions during the implementation process, and garner external support without undermining national ownership. These criteria are useful for mediators. When effectively applied during the negotiation phase they could help to arrive at an agreement that is more viable. Also, mediation and external support during the post-agreement period would further assist in the implementation process. It does not indicate whether quality peace would actually follow once a "quality peace agreement" is negotiated. We still lack a satisfactory means of measuring outcomes, and consequently how they might be researched comparatively. To a varying degree, many recent and ongoing peace processes have components of quality peace agreements, but these criteria do not help to understand why some of them have produced a more satisfactory outcome beyond the non-recurrence of armed conflict.

We suggest that the outcome must be measured beyond "negative pace" or the absence of violence. One way is to use the positive peace concept presented by Galtung (1969), and assess whether it would be more suitable for measuring peacebuilding success. For Galtung, "positive peace" is the absence of structural or latent violence by the state where social injustices are undone. Manifestations of structural violence, social injustice, or cultural violence are outcomes from attempts on the part of one actor, normally the state, to maintain the *status quo* (Galtung 1969: 184; 1990). It seems reasonable that successful peacebuilding involves institutional reforms aimed to address the causes of cultural and structural violence or causes of social injustices. Nevertheless, the conceptualization of positive peace as absence of structural violence or social justice and inclusion makes the positive peace concept a governance issue, which is conceptually too limited to evaluate peacebuilding in the aftermath of armed conflict. Governance provides important metrics for evaluating peacebuilding success, but it is not the only defining criteria to evaluate success and failure.

As a start, we define quality peace in terms of whether the objectives of the peace process are achieved. Darby and Mac Ginty (2008) suggested that the notion of a peace process should be inclusive of all major issues and actors and that the involved parties would use bargaining or negotiation as a means of achieving their social, political, and economic objectives, as opposed to military means. Thus, the signing of a peace accord regarding constitutional or political frameworks would not in itself constitute a successful peace process. This is not the end, but rather the beginning of building peace. According to Darby and Mac Ginty, the "conflict will continue to have to be managed through the implementations and institutionalization of the accord" (2008: 4). As such, peace processes may last for several years, allowing former belligerent groups to agree on accommodation, achieve socio-political and economic inclusion, and rebuild fractured infrastructure and community relations. After signing a formal agreement to end armed conflict, a post-war state is expected to progress toward quality peace where social, economic, and political changes at the individual, community, and state levels are gradually but systematically fulfilled through the implementation of the accord. This means that the actual implementation of an accord has important bearings on our conceptualization of quality peace, not just the negotiated settlement. The pace of implementation tells the analysts, as well as the parties, when the parties should be expected to move forward to accomplish the elements of quality peace, rather than expecting peace to commence immediately after the signing of an accord (see Höglund and Kovacs 2010). Peace can be tenuous in the short and medium terms as parties continue negotiating issues related to the implementation of accords, such as reforming institutions or enacting socio-economic policies (Sisk 2009; Joshi and Darby 2013; Joshi and Quinn 2017). In a positive way, one might expect that the differences among belligerent groups would diminish, and the resulting quality of peace would be observed in significant social, economic, and political changes that were never experienced before at the individual, societal, and state levels. Our quality peace conceptualization is based on the notion of successful peace processes that bring social, political, and economic changes in post-accord society and make peace more durable by, not only systematically addressing the commonly understood root causes of the armed conflict, but also, addressing the armed conflict-caused problems such as security issues and issues related to governance. This is in line with the findings from a systematic comparison of peacebuilding and victory outcome in all types of armed conflict: respect of human dignity as well for security needs is basic. So is the expectation that peaceful conditions will also prevail for the foreseeable future (Wallensteen 2015a). At the same time, it will be possible to point to setbacks and decisions that move away from achieving such a quality peace and serve, instead, as early warning signs.

For almost all societies emerging from armed conflict, achieving quality peace can be a very difficult task as many attributes that constitute quality peace are difficult to achieve at reasonable levels even after several years of settlement. In fact, the dimensions and criteria we have outlined to evaluate quality peace can be very difficult to find, even in societies that have not experienced deadly armed conflicts. The higher standard for quality peace, however, is the ultimate goal, and therefore, the journey is most important for societies transitioning from war to peace.

Dimensions and criteria of evaluating quality peace

In this volume, we are moving beyond the type of research and policy that emphasizes the non-recidivism of armed conflict, and toward a notion of quality peace that incorporates social, economic, and political changes in societies emerging from armed conflict. In doing so, we are also mindful of the importance of issues that are either armed conflict-induced or that become more salient after armed conflict. If lack of economic opportunities or access to markets and resources are one of the causes of the armed conflict, economic reconstructions are the way to address gaps in economic opportunities in the post-accord periods. Economic reconstruction requires considerable attention in war-to-peace transitions, whether mentioned in the peace accord or not. Similarly, self-governance issues for marginalized ethnic or minority groups can be one of the causes of the armed conflict; but even if no animosity existed between groups, the armed conflict, irrespective of the outcome, may have produced mistrust and hatred between ethnic groups. Giving all sides access to political power could address the self-governance issue, but this may also require reconciliation to rebuild fractured relations. As a step toward quality peace in societies emerging from violent armed conflicts, this volume proposes five dimensions that we posit will determine the quality of the resulting peace. These dimensions are security after armed conflict, negotiations and governance, economic reconstruction, transitional justice and reconciliation, and civil society.

Post-war security

Issues of security after armed conflict are critical and have the ability to derail the peace process in the short term; in the long term they could be detrimental to the quality of peace. Security concerns are particularly acute among demobilized groups because demobilization often leaves a group feeling vulnerable to surprise attack from the state (Walter 2002; Fortna 2004). Therefore, unbiased peacekeeping can alleviate security concerns and allow the parties to agree to a settlement (Walter 1997, 2002). The deployment of peacekeeping, however, does not guarantee security improvement in post-accord states. Even after parties to the armed conflict agree on the terms of settlement and use democratic processes to resolve their differences, violence often continues in many forms, and threatens the success of the peace process (see Stedman 1997; Darby 2001, 2006). Spoilers from the rebel group, as well as from the governing elites, can sabotage the peace process and undermine the prospects for peace. Post-accord security issues can emerge when belligerent parties sign the agreement, under domestic and international pressure, yet have no intention of implementing it (Höglund and Zartman 2006). Such a disingenuous signing of the accord can lead to the failure of the peace process (Höglund and Zartman 2006: 18; see also Stedman 1997; Darby 2001; Sisk 2006). In other instances, however, peace accords are signed with the assumption that spoilers can exist, as in Northern Ireland's peace process between 1972 and 1993 (Mac Ginty 2006). Groups outside the peace process could also use violence to attempt to amplify their voice. Factions inside the peace process may turn to violence for further bargaining or as a way to exit the peace agreement (Stedman 1997; Darby 2001; Zahar 2006; Sisk 2009). However, empirical evidence suggests the violence enacted by groups not included in the peace process does not affect the commitment of signatories (Nilsson 2008). So far, empirical research regarding security issues focuses on demobilizing parties and the emergence of spoiler groups, problems that are suggested to be managed through external security guarantees. While such external security guarantees may help secure peace, the quality of peace achieved can be diminished as a result of what evolves during the transition period. In the post-armed conflict phase, disarming and demobilizing combatants before initiating an electoral process helps to ensure quality of representation and governance. Similarly, societies emerging from violent armed conflict face security challenges, such as civilians' perception of the security forces and the equal distribution of security, particularly for men and women.

In their respective chapters, Terrence Lyons and Louise Olsson examine post-armed conflict security issues as one of the dimensions of quality peace. By suggesting that peace accords may preserve mistrust and polarization among signatories, Lyons indicates that quality peace does not come from signing an accord. He emphasizes strengthening and nurturing of "weak agreements" during the implementation phase to create incentives for insurgents and military regimes to transform themselves into political actors. During the armed conflict period, insurgents and the state develop a pattern of militarized governance, as the use of force is perceived to be the only effective means of establishing control over the population. The implementation of an accord would, therefore, have to respond to the incentives and opportunities of wartime governance while operating alongside institutions that provide very different incentives due to political competition in peacetime. In other words, quality peace remains weak when institutions preserve wartime incentives derived from the use of force after the signing of an accord. Therefore, ensuring quality peace requires the demilitarization of armed groups by the time elections identify political winners and losers. For peace to be sustained, the losers, then, must place their trust in the quality of institutions and remain committed to the benefits of political competition rather than the possible gains from warfare incentives.

While Lyons concludes his chapter by emphasizing the peace implementation process and the patterns of behaviors of political actors in the transition period, Louise Olsson puts forth "security equality" as a benchmark for evaluating quality peace. By conceptualizing "security equality" from a gender perspective, Olsson suggests women are less protected than men from all forms of violence; therefore, there is variation in the "quality" of "peace" experienced by men and women. Such discrepancies in security equality become an acute issue in societies emerging from armed conflicts. Women are as vulnerable as their male counterparts to lethal violence, but women also find themselves sexually abused in rebel military camps and by state institutions during armed conflict. Women's security situation does not improve after peace agreements because their security needs are not systematically evaluated and, therefore, women are not given relevant forms of protection for their security. By examining lethal and non-lethal violence, Olsson suggests women are more likely to be the target of non-lethal violence that mostly takes place in private spheres and, therefore, is not publically discussed. Olsson provides empirical support from her Timor-Leste case study and urges the importance of incorporating gender specific considerations in peacebuilding works. The understanding and provision of security should be gender sensitive, which is an unexplored dimension of quality peace. Lyons' chapter is primarily focused on demilitarizing the political process in post-accord states while Olsson is more concerned with women feeling secure in post-armed conflict societies by realigning the distribution of security. While these two chapters evaluate different aspects of security issue, both agree on the contribution of security to quality peace in post-agreement period.

Governance

Governance issues have recently gained more currency in civil war onset and recurrence studies. The indicators are often debatable, however. For instance, much of the governance literature relies on natural resources being correlated with poor governance which then connects to civil war onset (Murshed 2002; de Soysa 2002; Fearon and Laitin 2003; Ross 2004). Very few studies have tried to explore how governance would help to explain peacebuilding success. Joshi and Mason (2011) found that larger, more inclusive governing coalitions may enhance peace duration by providing opportunities for others to gain access to political power and resources; however, they have not specifically focused on governance issues in their analysis. In another related study, Joshi (2013) suggests that post-civil war states that adopt a parliamentary and proportional governance system experience more sustainable transitions toward democracy. These two studies also provide insights on the role of institutions in fostering peacebuilding success in post-armed conflict states. While inclusive institutions may contribute to the duration of peace, inclusive institutions also tend to have various constraints. Walter (2015) finds that the strengths and weakness of institutions—measured in terms of rule of law—determines the likelihood of civil war recurrence. As a matter of fact, social justice that Galtung (1969) relates to positive peace cannot be secured in the absence of rule of law.

The governance explanations offered so far, however, have tended to focus on overall outcomes, which suggests a top-down approach. The explanations tend to prefer state-level institutions and fixate the analysis on recurrence of armed conflict. Such an approach ignores the role of local actors and institutions and their interactions with international actors. Quality peace in post-civil war states does not tend to trickle down from external interveners when local actors and institutions are not included on issues of governance. It is for this reason that in his chapter, Roger Mac Ginty provides a lens of "hybridity" as a way of understanding the dynamic nature of peace processes and post-conflict environments in which peace agreements are implemented. He finds that current approaches of evaluating peacebuilding are as technocratic, and therefore, uncreative, unimaginative, non-innovative, and predisposed toward the success and failure heading. Instead, he presents the "hybridity" concept as more inclusive by incorporating international and local actors, as well as structures and networks in the shaping of the peace process and peacebuilding outcomes. The factors keep influencing each other with top-down and bottom-up approaches and practices. For Mac Ginty, different forms of governance are simply the outcomes of different types, or phases, of negotiations. Formal inter-party negotiations in a peace process often produce a written peace agreement—a set of rules that governs issues related to institution building, good governance, distribution of economic opportunities, and security sector reforms. Success of these formal rules and structures, however, requires adherence and public acceptance across diverse territories and populations. Therefore, governance success or failure cannot be measured at the center without examining variance at the local level. At the micro-level, people and communities are likely to work with informal institutions, suggesting a need to develop different measures for success or failure.

The importance of local actors and institutions is also highlighted in Jenny Guardado, Leonard Wantchekon, and Sarah Weltman's chapter. By advancing the importance of local institutions for quality peace in post-armed conflict period, Guardado and her colleagues examine peace agreements signed between 1989 and 2005 and explore whether local governance provisions in the agreements contribute to durable peace. In their analysis, Guardado et al. find that the inclusion of local governance provisions in peace agreements significantly reduces the recurrence of armed conflicts. In fact, they find that the effect is more significant than the inclusion of power-sharing arrangements, security arrangements or arrangements for general elections. While Guardado et al. focus on local governance and how it contributes to quality peace by providing space for political actors at the local level, Mac Ginty also suggests that these issues should be accounted for in our understanding of quality peace in post-civil war states.

Economic reconstruction

Because the lack of economic well-being remains the main cause of armed conflicts (Fearon and Laitin 2003; Collier 2003), economic reconstruction should be a priority in the post-armed conflict period. Post-civil war states find themselves with two distinct but interrelated economic challenges: first, reconstructing ravaged and mismanaged war-economics into functioning market economies and, second, creating economic opportunities for the deprived segment of the population and uplifting the potential for economic growth (Castillo 2008). For these reasons, Castillo recognizes that the post-war societies undergoing economic reconstructions require a very different multilateral international framework. The *World Bank Development Report* had the theme of Conflict, Security, and Development and also pointed to the special needs after a protracted civil war, not least providing employment (World Bank 2011). To consolidate peace, Castillo suggests creating jobs, stabilizing the economy and seeking investment and growth (Castillo

2008: 29). Job creation is a short-term policy objective, while sustainable growth and poverty alleviation are long-term objectives. Quality peace can be enhanced by mobilizing local and international economic resources that provide employment opportunities and setting up post-war societies for sustainable economic growth.

In this volume, Achim Wennmann and Viva Ona Bartkus, each present fresh perspectives on the economic reconstruction dimension of quality peace. Development agencies play a key role in economic reconstruction, but usually, require the formal ending of hostilities through a peace process before initiating their work. Challenging the dominant approach adopted by international development agencies, Wennmann suggests involving development agencies in the peace process to assist in developing better economic reconstruction policies. Wennmann argues that the development agencies' war termination requirement serves to sideline the economic development and reconstruction agendas. Peace processes, Wennmann suggests, are development concerns; through their involvement, development agencies can play an important role in strengthening quality peace. Development agencies can also advocate for the placement of economic issues (i.e., short-term and long-term economic needs assessments) in peace negotiations and help to establish consensus on economic issues among stakeholders.

Contrary to Wennmann's focus on the role of development actors and economic recovery, Bartkus brings business perspectives and emphasizes the role of business in laying the foundation for quality peace. By including examples from post-war Bosnia, Lebanon, Mindanao in the Philippines, Rwanda, and Uganda, she suggests wealth creation as the only mechanism for breaking the cycle of armed conflict and underdevelopment. Building on experiences from field studies, she highlights how local entrepreneurs can create job opportunities, mobilize local resources, and provide avenues for various ethnic groups to interact. However, war often leads to lower levels of inter-ethnic trust, which can pose obstacles to making sensible business decisions, expanding businesses, or recruiting former combatants. Bartkus argues that business helps to create peace from below. Local entrepreneurs, business communities, and multinationals can contribute substantially to mobilizing local resources and, thus, create equal economic opportunities for all, including former combatants and ethnic minorities.

Reconciliation and transitional justice

Regardless of how armed conflict is resolved, societies coming out of such conflict are faced with transitional justice and reconciliation issues. Transitional justice and reconciliation literature, especially following the seminal South Africa's TRC, has mapped out how transitional justice contributes to democracy by promoting reconciliation (Gibson 2006) and improving prosecutions of human rights violations (see Kim and Sikkink 2010; Olsen et al. 2010). A transitioning society needs to find a precarious equilibrium in which perpetrators are held accountable, but opportunities for restorative justice are not eliminated. Finding this balance is important for promoting accountability, socio-economic and political justice and reconciliation (see Lambourne 2008). Transitional justice mechanisms, including the establishment of commissions to find the truth about victims and perpetrators, may bring a sense of justice, help victims and loved ones of victims find closure, and impact human rights and democratic practices in the aftermath of armed conflict. The way transitional justice mechanisms are addressed in the peace process substantially influences the quality of peace.

In this volume, David Backer provides a rich theoretical debate on the various dimensions of transitional justice and their impact on quality peace. He explains that transitional justice mechanisms should aim to eliminate the capacity for violence. Such a goal requires both truth commissions and reparations programs. While justice components are often prioritized by human rights organizations, justice itself does not serve a society in transition if the risk of impunity is not mitigated by promoting reconciliation and social harmony. In his chapter, Backer questions whether transitional justice is required to achieve quality peace and whether justice needs to be pursued promptly, or if quality peace should come first. For Backer, quality peace promotion in post-armed conflict society depends on whether transitional justice processes contribute to political, social, and economic development, or, whether they only aim to address the needs and interests of victims. Backer concludes with a cautionary note, warning that transitional justice processes can become a weapon to advance the political interests of certain political parties, leaders, or ethnic groups.

While Backer focuses on transitional justice issues, the second chapter on this issue, by Alexander Dukalskis, Laura K. Taylor, and John Darby, maintains that reconciliation can impact peace at international, state, and intergroup levels. By suggesting divergent reconciliation processes at each level, they identify four key aspects of reconciliation to explain quality peace. Similar to Backer's emphasis on victims' needs and interests, Dukalskis et al. suggest including victims, if they choose to participate, in reconciliation processes in order to avoid the manipulative influence of powerful political actors. Symbols are a critical component of effective reconciliation and promoting common activities and sports for the divided community may help the reconciliation process. Such symbols and activities should also promote intergroup reconciliation if they bring joint identities, trust, forgiveness, and positive future orientation. Finally, Dukalskis et al. propose to use inter-generational approaches to address the lingering effects of political violence after the settlement of armed conflict.

While the transitional justice or reconciliation processes are recognized, more generally, as important catalysts for much-needed reconciliation by Backer and Dukalskis et al., Karen Brounéus and Holly L. Guthrey use a case study to focus exclusively on transitional justice issues in the Solomon Islands. By exploring the historical cause of armed conflict and the complex TRC in the Solomon Islands, Brounéus and Guthrey point out the importance of local consultation in the creation and implementation of the TRC. The Western way of prosecuting wrongdoers often dominates TRC processes; and TRCs tend to ignore the context of armed conflict, cultural norms, and the needs of victims. Ignoring local context, culture, and concerns of victims often leads to disconnects between the TRC process and the victims, which diminishes quality peace. Backer and Dukalskis et al. acknowledge that transitional justice and reconciliation are very sensitive topics; similarly, Brounéus and Guthrey, from their case study of the Solomon Islands, suggest the promotion of quality peace requires being sensitive to the participation of victims and adopting local traditions and culture in the TRC process. Brounéus and Guthrey's emphasis on victims and local tradition in the TRC process is in fact close to Mac Ginty's emphasis on the importance of local communities and informal institutions during peace process, and the type of governance emerging from that process.

Civil society

Societies emerging out of armed conflict are left with low levels of trust that further increase societal divisions. Civil society is hampered in promoting societal cohesion because civil society tends to shrink during armed conflict (see Paffenholz and Spurk 2006). This has important implications for the liberal peace argument.

One of the main critiques of the liberal peace argument in peacebuilding research is its reliance on Western models and its failure to pay sufficient attention to local conditions and approaches (see Chandler 2004, Richmond 2006, Mac Ginty 2008 and 2010 among others). Studies have indicated the importance of inter-ethnic networks and interactions to understand patterns of ethnic violence and peace (see Darby 1986; Varshney 2001). Other studies have highlighted the contribution of civil society actors in negotiating settlements, related to the fact that armed conflict situations are likely to generate concerted civil society mobilization (Wanis-St. John and Kew 2008; Marchetti and Tocci 2009). Nilsson (2012) found a higher chance of peace prevailing when civil society actors are involved in the peace process. In fact, the breakdown of peace between signatories declines by almost 64 percent when civil society actors are included in the peace process (Nilsson 2012: 258). While deeply divided societies often maintain ethnic, religious, and nationalist sentiments, such societies also maintain multi-ethnic and civic constituencies. Including civil society in a peacebuilding process brings necessary legitimacy, as local actors do not feel excluded. Local actors and civil society groups need external support in their advocacy roles and in empowering marginalized groups; however, such groups are vulnerable to the imposition of programs and activities by external actors (i.e., donor agencies and interest groups). To avoid dependence on external donors, civil society groups might come up with programs and activities that international actors are likely to emphasize and, thus, fund (Donais 2009). Nevertheless, civil society organizations (CSOs) need to be promoted, and in some instances resurrected, after deadly armed conflicts, to turn into local actors that can actively engage themselves in peace processes from a local basis. They can be instrumental in bringing the local to attention of domestic and international actors, and thus be important in rebuilding war-torn communities.

The two chapters in this section explore the civil society dimension of quality peace. Authors of the chapters suggest that a successful peace process needs to examine both the distinctive contribution of civil society to successful peacebuilding, and the consequences of excluding civil society from peace processes. Recognizing that civil society is not a homogenous actor, Thania Paffenholz highlights roles civil society can play during different phases of peace processes. She suggests that the contribution of civil society to quality peace is derived from effectiveness in performing such roles. While Paffenholz points to "functional capability" in understanding civil society's contribution to "quality peace" she also mentions other factors that support as well as hinder an effective contribution to quality peace. The factors that contribute, positively or negatively, to quality peace include: the composition of civil society itself, media performance, and the influence of external funding. In an effort to better understand quality peace, Paffenholz suggests paying attention to the context in which initiatives are born and the way such initiatives are planned and implemented by civil society.

While Paffenholz offers a conceptual definition and comparative framework for evaluating civil society contributions to quality peace, Richard Jones evaluates civil society's human rights and monitoring roles during the armed conflict and its contribution to peace negotiations and post-negotiation phases. Jones' chapter is case specific, and rests on his own experience as a peacebuilder working with the Catholic Relief Services in Central America. Nevertheless, the particular functions of civil society pointed out by Jones are very similar to what Paffenholz brings forth in her chapter. In the post-accord period, Jones points out the focus of civil society in El Salvador has shifted to elections, human rights, and privatization and, therefore, civil society has become less involved on matters such as reconciliation and social cohesion. The return of refugees and increasing gang violence tore apart the country's social fabric, and brought suffering to many communities in post-war El Salvador. After the peace agreement in 1992, Salvadorian civil society and the FMLN neglected local issues, which provided a fertile ground for an increase in gang-related violence. Jones sees a particular challenge in achieving quality peace when civil society shifts its focus in a post-accord period. His chapter suggests a sustained need for civil society to promote reconciliation and social cohesion, both at the local and national levels.

Toward a notion of quality peace

In addition to explaining the various dimensions of quality peace: post-accord security, governance, economic reconstruction, transitional justice and reconciliation, and civil society; four case studies examine each of these dimensions to further explain quality of peace. In their chapter, Carrie Manning and Chipo Dendere demonstrate that all dimensions need not be present to measure quality peace. In Mozambique, neither transitional justice and reconciliation mechanisms nor a strong civil society were in place. Rather, it was the involvement of external actors that fundamentally changed the security perceptions of formerly warring parties and influenced economic reconstruction and recovery. External guarantees also influenced governance issues as both sides remained committed to the democratic process in Mozambique.

Kheang Un's account of Cambodia's quality peace after the Paris Agreement (1991) examines all five dimensions of quality peace and suggests how a failure to provide post-agreement security blocked prospects for a neutral political environment. Instead, a patronage-based, one-party system of governance emerged. In his analysis of Cambodia, Un also identifies heavy external influence on the independent functions of civil society, and a partial failure of the tribunal to promote reconciliation. Nevertheless, Cambodia has achieved remarkable economic growth, reform, and reconstruction supported by donor countries. Un's assessment of quality peace based on the five dimensions is therefore mixed.

In her case study of El Salvador, Dinorah Azpuru reports a mixed quality peace following the 1992 peace agreement. Azpuru finds improvement on political competition and overall institutional quality, but a minimal improvement or even decline on rule of law according to the World Bank governance index. While people have more trust in political institutions and most importantly in armed forces, El Salvador suffers from a high homicide rate. In the post-accord years, significant improvement in socio-economic conditions were realized as its Human Development Index improved by almost 15 points between 1990 and 2010; but poverty, the root cause of the armed conflict, has only marginally declined. Citizens in post-accord El Salvador are more willing to participate in solving community problems and the number of church-related groups has increased significantly. While perpetrators of human rights violations were granted amnesty, the Salvadorian state recently apologized to the victims of state repression, which suggests significant progress in terms of reconciliation.

In his chapter on Northern Ireland, Colin Knox depicts a sanguine picture of quality peace realized after the Good Friday Agreement (1998). Knox assesses the growing impact of civil society, and the values they promote in post-accord Northern Ireland. Knox argues that economic success is mixed due to the recent downturn in the global economy, but Northern Ireland has achieved remarkable success in reforming its police force and there is also a reduction in the number of security-related incidents. While the trauma of "the troubles" still lingers in Northern Ireland, inter-religious reconciliation has been a great success perhaps fostered by a power-sharing and inclusive governance.

The way the five different dimensions of quality peace are evaluated in these four case studies helps to highlight that post-accord societies are very different from one another in at least two respects. First, for quality peace to be realized, all five dimensions are necessary conditions. Carrie Manning and Chipo Dendere's presentation of Mozambique appears as a deviant case where they suggest the existence of a relatively high degree of quality peace in Mozambique without an active role for civil society and without transitional justice and reconciliation mechanisms. Twenty years after the peace process, however, the former rebel party Renamo (Resistência Nacional Moçambicana) in Mozambique again resorted to armed conflict for grievances related to skewed economic opportunities, and unfair electoral laws that favored the governing party Frente de libertação de Moçambique (Frelimo) and its supporters since the 1992 General Peace Agreement. Had all dimensions that we discussed in this book been addressed in the Mozambique peace process, perhaps, we might have had a different outcome in Mozambique by now.

Second, while all five dimensions appear equal in terms of affecting quality peace, post-accord states often prioritize issues for factors related to local context and availability of resources. For example, resolving governance issues has been given precedence in all the cases studies here, but they also report varying degrees of success. Similarly, demilitarizing politics are often seen to be important early in the process, whereas security issues at the individual level, particularly women's security need, is often regarded a longer-term challenge, albeit it could be dealt with simultaneously with other forms of security-enhancing measures. This suggests that some dimensions are selected and acted upon early in the process in the post-armed conflict period. This prioritization could be related to the type of armed conflict, the completeness of the peace agreement or even the extent of involvement of external actors. Future study needs to focus on sequencing of these five dimensions and whether different orders would predict a very different quality peace outcome.

Throughout the volume, the authors have presented divergent views on quality peace with focus on different levels of analysis. Jones and Olsson focus on the individual level and the improvement of the lives of ordinary citizens. Lyons, on the other hand, suggests quality peace to be measured by the transformation of the context and the demilitarization of politics at the national level. National-level measures of quality peace are offered in the analysis of role of civil society by Paffenholz. Mac Ginty's chapter presents a multi-layered approach, dealing with external, national, and local levels. A similar level of analysis is offered by Dukalskis et al., when they emphasize reconciliation at the international, national, and intergroup level. For Wennmann, the focus is on the role of international development partners but mostly at the national level while Guardado et al., Brounéus and Guthrey, and Bartkus suggest individual and community-level measures of quality peace. These various concentrations on different levels and divergent views suggest the potential of the Quality Peace framework, not least that can be utilized to develop a global quality peace index that measures the progress of post-armed conflict society at the individual level, community level, and national level. Such a quality peace informed index could be used to understand and explain outcome of peace process by utilizing social, economic, and political indicators with interval level or longitudinal data. For example, one could be able to evaluate the relationship between the scores on a quality peace index with levels of inclusion of women and minority groups in the political process; or, with post-war economic performance as well as opportunities for citizens. Despite the divergent views on quality peace and different levels of analytical focus, contributors to this volume seem to agree that societies emerging from violent armed conflict need to see meaningful changes with respect to all the five dimensions and that these changes can, and perhaps should be, evaluated to understand society's move toward quality peace.

In conclusion, we invite readers to assess whether the five dimensions that we have selected are a valid measure for the concept of quality peace in the post-agreement setting. This approach to quality peace could be improved by including more on empowerment of discriminated groups (women, ethnic, and religious communities, for instance). Similarly, one could add more on public service delivery as another dimension. We see this as a beginning of a discussion, and where quality peace has to be a peace that includes broader political, social, and economic changes at the micro and macro (individual, community, and country) levels in the post-agreement settings. Therefore, our approach is different from the armed conflict resolution approach (see Ramsbotham et al. 2011; Wallensteen 2015b) in that we believe that our conceptualization of quality peace offers a richer context, and a potential for causal explanation. It leads to ways in which changes can be measured and compared across the countries and over time. They would help inform academics as well as the policy community on how policies can be formulated, for instance for the achievement of more peaceful societies by 2030 as is the target for the globally agreed Goal 16 of the Sustainable Development Goals that the UN General Assembly established in 2015.

Notes

1. Based on Doyle and Sambanis (2006) data calculated for this volume.
2. These ten core functions are: monopoly of the legitimate use of violence; administrative control; sound management of public finances; investment in human capital; creation of citizenship rights through social policy; formation of a market; management of public assets; effective public borrowing; investment in natural, industrial, and intellectual assets; and infrastructure service.
3. The UN Decisions in April 2016 (UNSCR 2282 and GA 70/262) use the term sustaining peace and the General Assembly in 2015 decided on the goals for 2030, including goal 16 on peaceful societies.

References

Bekoe, Dorina A. "Toward a theory of peace agreement implementation: The case of Liberia." *Journal of Asian and African Studies* 38, no. 2–3 (2003): 256–294.

Bekoe, Dorina A. "Mutual vulnerability and the implementation of peace agreements: Examples from Mozambique, Angola, and Liberia." *International Journal of Peace Studies* 10, no. 2 (2005): 43–68.

Call, Charles T. "Knowing peace when you see it: Setting standards for peacebuilding success." *Civil Wars* 10, no. 2 (2008): 173–194.

Castillo del, Graciana. *Rebuilding war-torn states: The challenge of post-conflict economic reconstruction*. OUP Oxford, 2008.

Chandler, David. "The responsibility to protect? Imposing the 'Liberal Peace'." *International Peacekeeping* 11, no. 1 (2004): 59–81.

Collier, Paul. *Breaking the conflict trap: Civil war and development policy.* World Bank Publications, 2003.

Collier, Paul. *The bottom billion: Why the poorest countries are failing and what can be done about it.* Oxford University Press, USA, 2008.

Darby, John P. *Intimidation and the control of conflict in Northern Ireland.* Syracuse University Press, 1986.

Darby, John. *The effects of violence on peace processes.* United States Institute of Peace Press, 2001.

Darby, John P. *Violence and reconstruction.* University of Notre Dame Press, 2006.

Darby, John and Roger Mac Ginty (Eds.) *Contemporary peacemaking. Conflict, peace processes and post-war reconstruction.* Second Edition. Palgrave Macmillan, 2008.

De Soysa, Indra. "Paradise is a bazaar? Greed, creed, and governance in civil war, 1989–99." *Journal of Peace Research* 39, no. 4 (2002): 395–416.

Diehl, Paul F. "Exploring peace: Looking beyond war and negative peace." *International Studies Quarterly* 60, no. 1 (2016): 1–10.

Donais, Timothy. "Empowerment or imposition? Dilemmas of local ownership in post-conflict peacebuilding processes." *Peace & Change* 34, no. 1 (2009): 3–26.

Doyle, Michael W., and Nicholas Sambanis. "International peacebuilding: A theoretical and quantitative analysis." *American Political Science Review* 94, no. 4 (2000): 779–801.

Doyle, Michael W., and Nicholas Sambanis. *Making war and building peace: United Nations peace operations.* Princeton University Press, 2006.

Fearon, James D., and David D. Laitin. "Ethnicity, insurgency, and civil war." *American Political Science Review* 97, no. 1 (2003): 75–90.

Fortna, Virginia Page. "Does peacekeeping keep peace? International intervention and the duration of peace after civil war." *International Studies Quarterly* 48, no. 2 (2004): 269–292.

Galtung, Johan. "Violence, peace, and peace research." *Journal of Peace Research* 6, no. 3 (1969): 167–191.

Galtung, Johan. "Cultural violence." *Journal of Peace Research* 27, no. 3 (1990): 291–305.

Ghani, Ashraf, and Clare Lockhart. *Fixing failed states: A framework for rebuilding a fractured world.* Oxford University Press, 2009.

Gibson, James L. "The contributions of truth to reconciliation lessons from South Africa." *Journal of Conflict Resolution* 50, no. 3 (2006): 409–432.

Hartzell, Caroline A., and Matthew Hoddie. *Crafting peace: Power-sharing institutions and the negotiated settlement of civil wars.* Penn State Press, 2007.

Högbladh, Stina. "Peace Agreements 1975–2011– Updating the UCDP Peace Agreement Dataset." In Pettersson Therése and Lotta Themnér (Eds.). *States in armed conflict 2011*, Uppsala University: Department of Peace and Conflict Research Report 99, 2012, 39–56.

Höglund, Kristine. *Peace negotiations in the shadow of violence.* Martinus Nijhoff, 2008.

Höglund, Kristine, and Mimmi Söderberg Kovacs. "Beyond the absence of war: The diversity of peace in post-settlement societies." *Review of International Studies* 36, no. 2 (2010): 367–390.

Höglund, Kristine, and I. William Zartman. "Violence by the State: Official Spoilers and their Allies." In John Darby, Ed. *Violence and reconstruction.* University of Notre Dame Press, 2006:11–31.

Jarstad, Anna K., and Desirée Nilsson. "From words to deeds: The implementation of power-sharing pacts in peace accords." *Conflict Management and Peace Science* 25, no. 3 (2008): 206–223.

Joshi, Madhav. "Post-civil war democratization: Promotion of democracy in post-civil war states, 1946–2005." *Democratization* 17, no. 5 (2010): 826–855.

Joshi, Madhav. "Inclusive institutions and stability of transition toward democracy in post-civil war states." *Democratization* 20, no. 4 (2013): 743–770.

Joshi, Madhav, and John Darby. "Introducing the Peace Accords Matrix (PAM): A database of comprehensive peace agreements and their implementation, 1989–2007." *Peacebuilding* 1, no. 2 (2013): 256–274.

Joshi, Madhav, and David T. Mason. "Civil war settlements, size of governing coalition, and durability of peace in post-civil war states." *International Interactions* 37, no. 4 (2011): 388–413.

Joshi, Madhav, and Jason Michael Quinn. "Implementing the Peace: The Aggregate Implementation of Comprehensive Peace Agreements and Peace Duration after Intrastate Armed Conflict." *British Journal of Political Science* 47, no. 4 (2017): 869–892.

Joshi, Madhav, and Jason Michael Quinn. "Is the sum greater than the parts? The terms of intrastate peace agreements and the commitment program revisited." *Negotiation Journal* 31, no. 1 (2015): 7–30.

Joshi, Madhav, Jason Michael Quinn, and Patrick M. Regan. "Annualized implementation data on comprehensive intrastate peace accords, 1989–2012." *Journal of Peace Research* 52, no. 4 (2015): 551–562.

Joshi, Madhav, Sung Yong Lee, and Roger Mac Ginty. "Just how liberal is the liberal peace?" *International Peacekeeping* 21, no. 3 (2014): 364–389.

Kim, Hunjoon, and Kathryn Sikkink. "Explaining the deterrence effect of human rights prosecutions for transitional countries 1." *International Studies Quarterly* 54, no. 4 (2010): 939–963.

Kreutz, Joakim. "How and when armed conflicts end: Introducing the UCDP Conflict Termination dataset." *Journal of Peace Research* 47, no. 2 (2010): 243–250.

Kreutz, Joakim, 2013. "Time to live: Does time heal civil war wounds?" Paper presented at the Annual Convention for the International Studies Association (ISA), San Francisco, CA, April 3–6 2013.

Lambourne, Wendy. "Towards sustainable peace and development in Sierra Leone: Civil society and the peacebuilding commission." *Journal of Peacebuilding & Development* 4, no.2 (2008): 47–59.

Lee, Sung Yong, Roger Mac Ginty, and Madhav Joshi. "Social peace vs. security peace." *Global Governance: A Review of Multilateralism and International Organizations* 22, no. 4 (2016): 491–512.

Licklider, Roy. "The consequences of negotiated settlements in civil wars, 1945–1993." *American Political Science Review* 89, no. 3 (1995): 681–690.

Lyons, Terrence. "Post-conflict elections and the process of demilitarizing politics: The role of electoral administration." *Democratization* 11, no. 3 (2004): 36–62.

Mac Ginty, Roger. "Northern Ireland: A Peace Process Thwarted by Accidental Spoiling." In Edward Newman and Oliver Richmond (Eds.). *Challenges to peacebuilding: Managing spoilers during conflict resolution*. United Nations University Press, 2006, 153–172.

Mac Ginty, Roger. "Indigenous peace-making versus the liberal peace." *Cooperation and Conflict* 43, no. 2 (2008): 139–163.

Mac Ginty, Roger. "Hybrid peace: The interaction between top-down and bottom-up peace." *Security Dialogue* 41, no. 4 (2010): 391–412.

Marchetti, Raffaele, and Nathalie Tocci. "Conflict society: Understanding the role of civil society in conflict." *Global Change, Peace & Security* 21, no. 2 (2009): 201–217.

Murshed, S. Mansoob. "Conflict, civil war and underdevelopment: An introduction." *Journal of Peace Research* 39, no. 4 (2002): 387–393.

Nilsson, Desirée. "Partial peace: Rebel groups inside and outside of civil war settlements." *Journal of Peace Research* 45, no. 4 (2008): 479–495.

Nilsson, Desirée. "Anchoring the peace: Civil society actors in peace accords and durable peace." *International Interactions* 38, no. 2 (2012): 243–266.

Olsen, Tricia D., Leigh A. Payne, and Andrew G. Reiter. "The justice balance: When transitional justice improves human rights and democracy." *Human Rights Quarterly* 32, no. 4 (2010): 980–1007.

Paffenholz, Thania, and Christoph Spurk. "Civil society, civic engagement, and peacebuilding." *Social Development Papers: Conflict Prevention and Reconstruction* 36 (2006).

Paris, Roland. *At war's end: Building peace after civil conflict.* Cambridge University Press, 2004.

Paris, Roland. "Saving liberal peacebuilding." *Review of International Studies* 36, no. 2 (2010): 337–365.

Quinn, J. Michael, David T. Mason, and Mehmet Gurses. "Sustaining the peace: Determinants of civil war recurrence." *International Interactions* 33, no. 2 (2007): 167–193.

Ramsbotham, Oliver, Hugh Miall, and Tom Woodhouse. *Contemporary conflict resolution.* Polity, 2011.

Regan, Patrick M. "Bringing peace back in: Presidential address to the Peace Science Society 2013" *Conflict Management and Peace Science*, 31 no. 4 (2014): 345–356

Richmond, Oliver P. "The problem of peace: Understanding the 'liberal peace'." *Conflict, Security & Development* 6, no. 3 (2006): 291–314.

Ross, Michael L. "What do we know about natural resources and civil war?" *Journal of Peace Research* 41, no. 3 (2004): 337–356.

Sisk, Timothy D. "Political Violence and Peace Accords: Searching for the Silver Lining." In John Darby, Ed. *Violence and Reconstruction.* University of Notre Dame Press, (2006): 121–142.

Sisk, Timothy D. *International mediation in civil wars: Bargaining with bullets.* Routledge, 2009.

Stedman, Stephen John. "Spoiler problems in peace processes." *International Security* 22, no. 2 (1997): 5–53.

Stedman, Steven J., Donald Rothchild, and Elizabeth M. Cousens (Eds.) *Ending civil wars. The implementation of peace agreement.* Lynne Rienner, 2002.

United Nations General Assembly. *Strengthening the role of mediation in the peaceful settlement of disputes, conflict prevention and resolution.* A/66/811, June 25, 2012.

Varshney, Ashutosh. "Ethnic conflict and civil society: India and beyond." *World Politics* 53, no. 3 (2001): 362–398.

Wallensteen, Peter. *Quality peace: Peacebuilding, victory and world order.* Oxford University Press, 2015a.

Wallensteen, Peter. *Understanding conflict resolution. Fourth Edition.* Sage, 2015b.

Walter, Barbara F. "The critical barrier to civil war settlement." *International Organization* 51, no. 3 (1997): 335–364.

Walter, Barbara F. *Committing to peace: The successful settlement of civil wars.* Princeton University Press, 2002.

Walter, Barbara F. "Does conflict beget conflict? Explaining recurring civil war." *Journal of Peace Research* 41, no. 3 (2004): 371–388.

Walter, Barbara F. "Why bad governance leads to repeat civil war." *Journal of Conflict Resolution* 59, no. 7 (2015): 1242–1272.

Wanis-St John, Anthony, and Darren Kew. "Civil society and peace negotiations: Confronting exclusion." *International Negotiation* 13, no. 1 (2008): 11–36.
World Bank. *World Development Report 2011: Conflict, security, and development*. World Bank, 2011.
Zahar, Marie-Joëlle. "Political violence in peace processes: Voice, exit, and loyalty in the post-accord period." *Violence and reconstruction* vol. 1, Research initiative on the resolution of ethnic conflict series. University of Notre Dame Press, 2006, 3–51.

PART I
Post-war security

2
PEACE IMPLEMENTATION AND QUALITY PEACE

Terrence Lyons

Quality peace must be built upon processes that make a return to civil war less likely. There is a rich literature on the conditions and processes that make reaching a negotiated settlement to end civil war and the provisions most likely to sustain peace (Zartman 1989; Roeder and Rothchild 2005; Toft 2009). Less often emphasized is the importance of the peace implementation stage, and its impact on facilitating the transition from war to sustainable, quality peace (Hampson 1996; Stedman 2002; Lyons 2005). All negotiated settlements are bad, to varying degrees, because mistrustful and polarized parties sign them under pressure to end humanitarian suffering and generally include what they can, leave out what cannot be settled, and gloss over differences in an effort to stop the killing. Militarized actors made powerful by violence negotiate settlements but are not the best actors to sustain quality peace. The peace implementation process, however, provides opportunities to strengthen and nurture weak agreements and to transform insurgents and military regimes into political actors so that the process is strengthened from its initial, imperfect state and has the potential to support quality peace (Hampson 1996: 3; see also: Rothstein 1999: 224). This chapter focuses on how prioritizing the demilitarization of politics early in the process provides a favorable environment for implementing a negotiated settlement and much-needed institutional reforms, which provide the foundations for quality peace in post-war countries. In many cases this process of demilitarization of politics during the peace implementation phase is more important to promoting quality peace than the provisions contained in the peace agreement.

The peace implementation process is a time of great uncertainty and risk, often characterized by security dilemmas, information failures, and difficulties in making credible commitments (Lake and Rothchild 1996; Woodward 2007; Coyne and Boettke 2009). It is a critical time of testing during which each party's perceptions of the likely behavior of others and the viability of fledging post-conflict institutions and norms are shaped. Some have emphasized how third party "guarantees" and power-sharing pacts can help parties navigate this difficult period. This chapter, however, argues that intra-party and inter-party dynamics that change the perceived feasibility of political strategies are more significant in explaining why some peace implementation processes lead to quality peace while others collapse in war recurrence.

We can assume that parties to civil war will act as rational actors and adopt strategies based on their perceptions of opportunities and likely payoffs.[1] As Shugart has argued, "decisions by regime and rebel leaders alike to seek a democratic 'exit' from a conflict are based upon rational calculations of the possibilities and limitations inherent in playing the competitive electoral game versus continuing the armed conflict" (1992). Strategies and behaviors shift as calculations of the costs of war rise and the potential benefits of peace increase. This combination of making peaceful strategies more attractive and military strategies less attractive creates what Bermeo calls a

> double challenge. On the one hand, they must raise the costs of violent competition. On the other hand, they must lower the costs of electoral competition. The probability of stable democracy is a function of both these processes and the many variables that drive them.
>
> (2003)

Peace implementation may be conceptualized as a time when parties face a choice between two archetypical strategies: (1) accepting the settlement and adopting political, often electoral, strategies; or (2) defecting from the agreement and reverting to violence and war. Parties following these different strategies are often labeled "doves" and "hawks."[2] Making an assessment of whether a "political" strategy or a "military" strategy is most likely to produce the greatest benefit is difficult during peace implementation when perceptions and expectations are particularly unsettled. Hardliners accuse moderates of betraying the cause, while the expectations of the possible benefits from peace are unrealistic and often impossible to meet. Missteps in following through on the often-ambitious and generally vague agendas stipulated in peace agreements are common and in a context of mistrust are often perceived as evidence of bad faith. In order for peace implementation to remain on track, a working majority of each party (including key constituencies with the capacity to return to war) must perceive that remaining in the process is the best strategic choice. We concur with the editors of this volume that the terms of a negotiated settlement are fundamental to moving a country from war to quality peace. However, these generally vague and sometimes contradictory terms must be prioritized, redefined, and made operational during the implementation phase. Processes to demilitarize politics during this phase therefore can transform the initial settlement into the basis for quality peace.

The first phase involves shaping pre-negotiations and negotiation strategies. A number of scholars have written about how ripeness shapes negotiations and pre-negotiations (Saunders 1985; Stein 1989; Zartman 1989; Lilja 2011). However, ripeness applies throughout the peace implementation stage as well. The specific circumstances that lead parties to perceive a hurting stalemate and hence enter into negotiations will not remain static. Perceptions will change if violence decreases and political opportunities become clearer. As the balance of power within and between parties remains unsettled, opinions will shift. Thus, the coalition within each party that supported the signing of the agreement must be held together and overcome the tendency for defection. Peace implementation therefore is a continuous process of establishing ripeness so that broad coalitions in all of the major parties continue to favor non-military strategies.

After the negotiation phase, the "demilitarization of politics" is the next phase during which the settlement is implemented. This phase is critical as its success or failure shapes the trajectory of quality peace. Demilitarization of politics shifts incentive structures in favor of peace by increasing the attractiveness of political strategies (through political party building or strengthening of electoral processes) and decreasing the feasibility of success through violence (through effective peacekeeping and through processes of demobilization and security sector reform). A critical mass on all sides of the conflict needs to be able to convince those whose commitment to peace is fragile that pursuing political strategies is better than returning to war. Some will not be convinced and will act as spoilers but so long as a sufficient number of key members of the coalitions remain persuaded of the feasibility of politics, spoilers can be managed.[3]

This chapter is organized into three main sections. The first briefly outlines a framework for understanding peace implementation as a process of transforming the institutions and patterns of governance developed during a civil war into organizations, rules, and norms that can support quality peace. The second section suggests that there are two archetypical ways of implementing peace agreements—execute blue prints or transform institutions. The third section argues that demilitarization politics can generate the incentives and opportunities that raise the perceived costs of military strategies and increase the perceived benefits of engaging in political processes.

Wartime institutions and rebel governance

Peace implementation requires the transformation of wartime actors into parties that can operate effectively in times of peace and therefore perceive political strategies as feasible. If the insurgents remain unreconstructed, then military strategies will remain attractive. Large-scale armed conflicts are sustained by the creation of alternative institutions and systems of governance that are based on fear and predation and end when new processes are put in place that lead key actors to perceive better opportunities to achieve their goals through peaceful means. Civil wars may be initiated by grievance or frustration but to become protracted and sustained for decades they require institutions that respond to the incentives and opportunities for violence, successfully mobilize and coordinate large numbers of fighters and supporters, and overcome the collective action problem (Wood 2003). Regan and Norton, for example, argue that grievance may be the "backbone" of rebellion but "resources become necessary to pay selective benefits to keep the rational rebel soldier supporting a rebellious movement and to offset government efforts to lure the rebel soldier away" (2005: 322).

Sustained violence produces norms and patterns of behavior that constitute a system of "wartime governance" and this system of governance in turn reinforces strategies of violence. Civil wars are not periods of anarchy or political vacuum but are alternative systems of governance based on fear and predation and that reward violence (see Keen 2000; Duffield 2001). Violence, rather than being an eruption of frustration and rage, may be understood in instrumental terms, as a calculated strategy to advance a goal (Gamson 1975: 81; Kalyvas 2006). Generating fear is often a cost-effective way to mobilize supporters (Mason and Krane 1989; Elwert 1999: 90).

States that are in the throes of civil war and even those that have collapsed have recognized patterns of behavior or practice around which expectations converge that shape conflict dynamics, create expectations, and therefore reinforce different military and political strategies.[4] In Somalia, for example, Menkhaus argues that an informal mosaic of business networks, religious institutions, traditional authorities, and civic groups have created patterns of behavior and "governance without government," (2007). A transition from war to peace is therefore also a transition from institutions that are suited to respond to the incentives and opportunities of wartime governance into institutions that can function effectively in response to the very different incentives of political competition in peacetime.

Models of peace implementation: blue prints or institutional transformation

Given how robust wartime institutions often become, how can they be transformed into institutions pursuing strategies consistent with quality peace? There are two broad models of peace implementation. One emphasizes the specific content of the peace agreement, international guarantees, and the implementation of the blue print specified in the settlement. This model draws attention to the importance of initial conditions and roles played by third parties to monitor and enforce the settlement. A second model focuses on the implementation process itself in the first phase and highlights flexibility and the transformations that may occur within the parties to the agreement as they move from wartime to peacetime phases. In this model, initial conditions and third parties matter less than inter- and intra-party dynamics during implementation, as the military organizations that fought the war and signed the agreement assess their options and make strategic decisions whether or not to pursue peace.

There is an extensive literature on what types of peace agreements are most likely to foster sustained peace. Fortna, for example, argues that the content of an agreement can shape incentives, reduce uncertainty, and prevent accidental violations, thereby making some agreements more durable than others (2004). Many suggest that various forms of power-sharing or political pacts are useful ways to manage the uncertainty and fear that characterize the periods of peace implementations (Karl 1990; Hartzell and Hoddie 2003; Joshi and Mason 2011). Pacts, however, ultimately rely upon other mechanisms for enforcement and do not by themselves end uncertainty or resolve the difficulty in making credible commitments (Lake and Rothchild 1996). The most recent studies suggest the contents of a peace agreement itself do not bring peace unless they are successfully implemented (Joshi and Quinn 2017).

Scholars have also investigated how third party roles in guaranteeing a peace agreement's implementation through peacekeeping have made a difference in whether or not civil war recurred. Walter (1999), among others, emphasizes third party "guarantees" as a means to overcome security dilemmas and improve prospects for successful implementation.[5] The challenge of peace, in this formulation, is how to increase monitoring so that the agreement is implemented as written. Without such support, the first model suggests, peace implementation is prone to failure and the recurrence of civil war.

The second model, however, suggests that a well-designed peace implementation process should seek to transform the context in which the warring parties operate rather than seek to implement the settlement as written. A sustainable agreement should be forward-looking and flexible enough to adjust to changes and "anticipate and devise means to cope with the issues of the future" (Holsti 1991: 353; see also Hampson 1996: 3).[6] One of the most important conditions that facilitate successful implementation is the ability to renegotiate terms peacefully as conditions change the relative power and interests of the former warring parties (Werner 1999: 919). Even a weak peace agreement will generate new opportunities and have the potential to alter the strategic calculations of parties previously engaged in conflict.

Peace implementation and the shift from military to political forms of contention tend to generate intense intra-party debate and often result in schisms and breakaway factions (Manning 2008; Lodge 2009; Orjuela 2009; Woldermariam 2011). It is common (perhaps inevitable) that at any given moment one set of leaders will be ready to make the shift while others will not. Not every member of the leadership will assess opportunities in the same way and every move toward peace strengthens some while weakening others. The fundamental shift from pursuing military strategies to electoral strategies may result from a divided leadership finally reaching a tipping point where a thin majority alters its assessments of the efficacy of the two options.

This acceptance, however, will be contingent upon a variety of factors and if circumstance and incentives change, then so can the decision to accept an agreement. The conditions that created ripeness during the ceasefire and negotiation phases will no longer be in place and new, fluid conditions favoring ongoing ripeness are needed. What is needed is a working coalition or what Pruitt calls a "broad central coalition" that represents a large enough constituency to keep the process moving forward (2007). A critical mass may accept a peace process but then revert to war if perceptions change during the peace implementation period. Even if a majority accepts the need for a new direction, spoilers who are threatened by the transition often attempt to derail the process (Stedman 1997; Darby 2001; Newman and Richmond 2006).

The peace implementation phase provides the context for testing and assessing the risks and benefits of cooperation and whether the intentions of former rivals are conciliatory or duplicitous. It is often necessary to leave key issues indeterminate in the agreement and to design some kind of contingent process such as an election to determine outcomes.[7] In many cases, parties to a conflict adopt the extreme rhetoric of total war during the conflict but shift their language and tactics (if not their goals) during the peace implementation process. During the period of peace implementation, each party will look for evidence to confirm its fears that its rival is cheating.

Given the inherent uncertainties and the high stakes, most actors will hedge their bets and assess whether complying with the agreement or defecting is the best way to stay safe and advance toward their goals. A party or a faction may decide to cooperate in a negotiated agreement for a period of time but then defect and revert to military strategies as perceived opportunities and the relative likelihood that military or political strategies will be more effective shift. Institutions endure and thrive in part by their capacity to adjust to changing contexts. A change from violence to security will compel a transformation if the organization is to remain vital. Social movements, political parties, and other organizations seek self-preservation in the first instance through strategies to meet their maintenance needs. As Zald and McCarthy argue, "organizations exist in a changing environment to which they must adapt. Adaptation to the environment may itself require changes in goals and in the internal arrangement of the organization" (1987: 122). This adaptation will be particularly challenging when the context shifts dramatically from one set of incentives and opportunities, such as war, to another, such as electoral competition.

If peace implementation therefore focuses on strict adherence to the blueprint agreed upon by the parties made powerful by the conflict, as in the first model, then post-war governance risks remaining frozen in the polarized conditions of wartime. Implementation must be a process of redefining the terms of the agreement rather than a strict, narrow interpretation of the settlement as a fixed set of commitments. A system of governance that takes a snapshot of the political topography and (mal)distribution of power at the moment of a ceasefire and seeks to make this arrangement permanent is unlikely to sustain quality peace in the long run. When seeking to build systems of governance that promote quality peace, therefore, the goal should be to create structures that can facilitate change, ensure flexibility, emphasize phased processes, and allow for institutional transformation, as in the second model. If peace is sustained, then over time the population is likely to shift its support to civilian political organizations. Some organizations will make this transition along with their constituencies while others will fail and be replaced by new ones. Institutions endure and thrive through their capacity to adjust to changing contexts (Tarrow 2011). The key to post-conflict governance, therefore, is to facilitate these organizational changes to occur through different peace process phases without derailing the agreement and returning the country to war.

Demilitarization of politics: interim institutions and transforming militias into political parties

Demilitarization of politics creates the conditions for institutional transformation that strengthens those parties capable of supporting electoral competition while weakening those geared toward armed conflict immediately in the post-agreement period. Among the key institutions are credible interim regimes (particularly electoral authorities) and transformed militias capable of operating as political parties. These processes and institutions increase and make more credible the rewards for participating in and accepting outcomes of electoral competition while simultaneously reducing the perceived benefits of violence. These two aspects are interlinked and progress on one encourages the demilitarization process in the other. For example, building effective political parties increases the prospects for demobilization, as groups perceive that they can protect their interests through political rather than military means and therefore are ready to lay down their arms. Processes to demilitarize politics simultaneously increase both the incentives and opportunities to play by the rules of non-violent electoral competition and decrease the incentives and opportunities to seek power by engaging in violence. Therefore, the demilitarization of politics involves two interrelated priorities: interim administration and transformation of former rebel groups into political parties.

Interim administration

One component of demilitarizing politics entails building interim institutions that can generate precedents and support perceptions that peaceful electoral processes can work. While interim institutions for the transition phase are negotiated in the peace agreement, translating those institutions in practice during the peace implementation phase is inherently contentious. Transitional governments must deal with critical and difficult policy issues and the processes through which such policies are made will shape the expectations of the major actors and may either inspire confidence or ignite fears. Disputes are inevitable during the transition, as the broad and often vague, if not contradictory, principles listed in the peace agreement must be made operational in a difficult atmosphere characterized by fear and distrust. As Joshi and Quinn and others suggest, a dispute resolution mechanism provides space for actors to discuss peace implementation-related disputes and reinforce cooperation without increasing the risk of exploitation from a spoiler who does not comply (2017).

Institutions based upon ongoing consultations, bargaining, and joint decision-making create a framework for continuing cooperation and encourage the development of a constituency that supports such cooperation (Kelman 1999). Such bargaining processes may change the initial design of the agreement. Parties engaged in such problem-solving processes may develop a sense of partnership (even if only tentatively and tactically) and perceive a joint interest in managing risk and marginalizing extremists and spoilers (including those within their own parties) who want to derail the peace process. These processes may or may not be enumerated in the settlement or formally institutionalized. What matters is a process of self-interested mutual adjustment of behavior that may initiate a self-reinforcing cycle of increased cooperation and confidence (Rothchild 1995; Sisk 1996; Deutsch 2006).

Interim electoral commissions that are set up in the peace implementation phase provide a particularly important opportunity to demilitarize politics by building consultative mechanisms and norms that increase perceptions that political strategies will be effective. With so much at stake, decisions on electoral plans and processes inevitably are highly contentious and electoral institutions become the focus of partisan struggles. In a context of high mistrust, parties fear that their opponents will capture the electoral commission and tilt the rules. Electoral administration that does not address the fears and mistrust of key parties, particularly recently warring and incompletely demobilized parties, may reignite conflict. If, however, collaborative institutions are developed to manage the electoral process during the transition, greater confidence in the peace process can be nurtured and the prospects for an election that promotes both peace and democracy can be enhanced (Lyons 2004). These patterns may be illustrated by comparing post-conflict elections in El Salvador (1992) and Liberia (1997).

In El Salvador, the 1991 peace accords set up the National Commission for the Consolidation of Peace (Comisión Nacional para la Conslidación de la Paz, COPAZ), a body with representation evenly split between the government and its allies and the opposition including the FMLN insurgents, with observer status for the UN and the Catholic Church. COPAZ was conceived as the major forum for verifying compliance and resolving disputes during the implementation of the peace agreements and was an important guarantee to the FMLN (Byrne 1996: 192; Fagen 1996: 219). COPAZ debated and passed implementing legislation under the peace agreement, ranging from a new electoral law to constitutional amendments that redefined the role of the armed forces. Because the commission was evenly split between the government and the opposition, "hammering out compromises became a political necessity—and a newly acquired skill for many politicians" (Montgomery 1995: 233–234).

COPAZ's structure led to slow and cumbersome decision-making, compelling endless rounds of negotiations among parties (Holiday and Stanley 1993). From the perspective of building new norms to demilitarize politics, however, such continuous discussion is a strong asset. When problems arose over the electoral system, over delays in reforming the police, or when an FMLN arms cache was uncovered after the deadline for disarmament, COPAZ was able to keep the parties talking and to keep the process moving toward elections. While the transition was uncertain, interim institutions in which they had an effective voice managed their fears of losing everything. "The course of the implementation of the accords was determined by a process of political bargaining [whereby] . . . political actors hammered out agreements and concessions on the various issues that reflected the evolving balance of power among the contending interests" (Wood 1996: 101–102). This process thereby helped support perceptions that electoral strategies were more likely to succeed than military strategies. The success of COPAZ in finding mutually acceptable solutions to many issues related to the implementation of the agreement in the early phase made other reforms possible. In the post-COPAZ period, El Salvador has significant respect for political institutions and armed forces as Azpuru finds in the companion chapter in this volume.

The Abuja II peace process in Liberia (1996–1997), in contrast, represented a much more minimal framework for a ceasefire leading to quick elections with little ongoing bargaining or attention to building effective interim institutions that could serve as the basis for longer-term peacebuilding and democratization. The interim Liberian Council of State consisted of representatives of the major warring factions along with representatives of civil society organizations but interim administration was parceled out to each of the many factions and the generally stalemated Council of State lacked the authority to coordinate. The rival parties rarely engaged in talks regarding the administration of the interim period or to build a sense of confidence in the peace process. Instead, each sought to place loyalists in key locations within the bureaucracy where they could tap into resources and patronage. Rather than engaging in political bargaining among the main Liberian parties, the West African peacekeeping force managed the process without consulting the Liberian parties or people. The peace implementation process did little to alter perceptions of rival parties' commitment to peace and elections (Lyons 1999). The Liberian Council of State was ineffective in addressing contentious issues and bringing all stakeholders together in the initial phase. While the Abuja II Accord led to a period of relative peace from 1997, civil war returned in 1999 until the Accra Peace Agreement of August 2002 was signed.

These illustrations suggest that peace implementation should emphasize creating the spaces and building opportunities for the formerly warring parties to work together in joint decision-making institutions. Continuous bargaining and regular processes of consultation may generate contentious debate and disorderly outcomes but such decision-making processes demilitarize politics more than a well-designed and efficiently implemented administration that excludes the parties. Sustainable peacebuilding relies more fundamentally on altering the perceptions and expectations of the parties. These perceptions and expectations will be shaped by their experiences during the peace implementation phase. Direct interactions, rather than third party guarantees or the formal commitments contained in the peace agreement, are more likely to shape such expectations.

Transforming militias into political parties

It is extremely difficult for insurgents and military governments that derived their power from the conflict to play the role of competing political parties in a democratic system if they remain unreconstructed and organized as they were during the period of armed violence. In the more successful cases of transition, particularly in El Salvador, Mozambique, and Nepal, processes to demilitarize politics encouraged military organizations to transform themselves into political parties able to operate effectively in an electoral context. In the less successful or failed cases, particularly Bosnia-Herzegovina, Angola, Liberia, and Tajikistan, insurgents and military regimes retained the ability to operate as military forces at the time of elections. Key leaders perceived that military strategies remained viable and either acted as spoilers or won a majority of the votes from a population still polarized by fear.

Some militias do not make the transition and fade away. Not every military organization can or should be a political party. *La Unidad Revolucionaria Nacional Guatemalteca* (URNG) in Guatemala, the political party that developed out of the insurgency, has failed to win more than a handful of seats (Allison 2009; Allison 2010). The Revolutionary United Front (RUF) in Sierra Leone collapsed as a political party but retained an institutional identity that focused on advocating for more generous assistance to ex-combatants (Richards and Vincent 2007). Under the Abuja II peace agreement, all Liberian military factions had equal representation in the interim Council of State. After the 1997 elections, however, it was clear that only Taylor's National Patriotic Party had significant support and that the others (United Liberation Movement of Liberia for Democracy—ULIMO-J and ULIMO-K, and Liberia Peace Council—LPC) were less significant (Lyons 1999). The United Tajik Opposition and the Islamist parties also played vastly reduced roles after failing to do well in the 1999 elections.

In relatively successful cases, military organizations were transformed into political parties prior to the election. For example, the transformation of the insurgent Renamo from an armed insurgency into a viable civilian political party able to play a constructive role in a multiparty electoral process was critical to the successful Mozambique peace process. After initial concerns from donors reluctant to fund a party with a particularly brutal reputation, a $19 million fund was established.[8] To fill the many posts in interim institutions, Renamo recruited new, better-educated officials who, over the period of the transition, became more influential at the expense of the old wartime leaders. The slate of parliamentary candidates in 1992 represented this younger civilian group and included few wartime leaders (Manning 2002). The ruling Frelimo party went through its own transformation. The party transformed itself from a Marxist-Leninist vanguard party into a "democratic socialist" organization that then endorsed a multiparty constitution in 1990 (Simpson 1993). It was these new political organizations that engaged in the peace implementation process and the post-conflict elections. Manning and Dendere in this volume provide more detailed accounts of Renamo's transition into a political party.

In Angola, by contrast, the National Union for the Total Independene of Angola (UNITA) did not transform itself and participated in the elections as a military organization. UNITA leader Jonas Savimbi demonstrated he was an "all-or-nothing" player and held onto his determination to accept nothing less than the presidency. Poorly designed and implemented demobilization programs, a weak UN peacekeeping operation, and UNITA's ability to tap into resources such as diamonds to rearm and remain in the field resulted in UNITA perceiving more attractive alternatives than accepting the role of loyal opposition following electoral defeat.

Demilitarization of politics may result from a combination of effective political process and effective demobilization. What matters is that leaders and rank-and-file members change expectations and perceive that they will not be vulnerable if they demobilize and disarm, rather than a precise number of soldiers reintegrated and weapons collected. When challenged that parties were hedging their bets and hiding weapons, UN Special Representative to Mozambique Ajello responded

> I know very well that they will give us old and obsolete material, and they will have here and there something hidden. I don't care. What I do is create the political situation in which the use of those guns is not the question. So that they stay where they are.
>
> (quoted in Hall 1994)

Demilitarization of politics—the process of creating perceptions that guns should stay hidden and that elections are an attractive option—can make peace implementation a phase of transformation that can support quality peace.

Conclusions: conditions for high quality peace

Sustained, quality peace necessarily builds on the key precedents, incentives, and patterns of behavior established in the peace implementation process. A settlement to end a civil war is a snap shot of power relationships and perceived alternatives among the parties made powerful by the war. Such agreements should not be regarded as strict blueprints or contracts to be implemented but as the first imperfect stage of a process to nurture peace that can create opportunities and incentives, transform powerful wartime parties, and thereby support a shift from military to political competition. The peace implementation process is often a time of significant intra-party conflict as factions that favor political and electoral strategies ("doves") contend with factions that favor military strategies ("hawks"). The outcome of these intra-party struggles is vital to the prospects for quality peace. Policies to demilitarize politics shape the incentives and provide opportunities that make the pursuit of political strategies more attractive and thereby strengthen the doves. Transforming militias into political parties and building effective interim institutions, for example, can reinforce perceptions that favor electoral strategies. These perceptions, in turn, will support those factions that support such strategies.

Successful demilitarization of politics and peace implementation provides the setting for the many difficult transitions necessary to sustain quality peace. Reconciliation, the consequences of gender-based violence, and the use of child soldiers require time for relationships to be rebuilt and trauma addressed. Security sector reform, strengthening institutions of democracy and governance, economic reconstruction, development, and so forth are all long-term processes that are predicated on getting through the difficult liminal stage between war and peace. In order to reach the phase where long-term, sustainable, and quality peace is possible it is necessary to demilitarize politics so that the institutions and patterns of governance made powerful by the civil war are transformed.

Notes

1. For criticism of applying rational choice models see Kaufman 2006.
2. Actual processes generally have elements of both; strategies and strategic calculation change over time but it is useful to think of them as alternatives for the purpose of clarifying my argument.
3. For a discussion of this with regard to the Real IRA and the Good Friday Peace Process, see Pruitt 2007.
4. Governance as used here is similar to the International Relations concept of "regime" developed by Young 1982, and Krasner 1982. For a discussion of governance and civil war see Lyons 2012.
5. Walter is categorical on this point: "If an outside state or international organization is not willing or able to provide such guarantees, the warring factions will reject a negotiated settlement and continue their war" (Walter 1999).
6. On forward-looking outcomes see Zartman and Kremenyuk 2004.
7. As Oran Young argues,

   A bargain based on contingent devices may be seized upon as a means of terminating a severe crisis. Such a bargain tends to delay the settlement of at least some of the critical issues at stake, thereby permitting a termination of the actual physical confrontation produced by a crisis (1968: 285).

8. UN Special Representative Ajello recognized that peace implementation required Renamo to become a political party and that the international community should fund this transformation: "Democracy has a cost and we must pay that cost" (Vines 1996: 146).

References

Allison, Michael E. "Opportunity Lost: The Guatemala National Revolutionary Unit (URNG)," In Bruce W. Dayton and Louis Kriesberg, Eds. *Conflict transformation and peacebuilding: Moving from violence to sustainable peace*. Routledge, 2009.

Allison, Michael E. "The legacy of violence on post-civil war elections: The case of El Salvador." *Studies in Comparative International Development* 45, no. 1 (2010): 104–124.

Bermeo, Nancy. "What the democratization literature says—or doesn't say—about postwar democratization." *Global Governance* 9, no. 2 (2003): 159–177.

Byrne, Hugh. *El Salvador's civil war: A study of revolution*. Lynne Rienner, 1996.

Coyne, Christopher J., and Peter J. Boettke. "The problem of credible commitment in reconstruction." *Journal of Institutional Economics* 5, no. 1 (2009): 1–23.

Darby, John. *The effects of violence on peace processes*. United States Institute of Peace Press, 2001.

Deutsch, Morton. "Cooperation and Competition." In Morton Deutsch, Peter T. Coleman, and Eric C. Marcus, Eds. *The handbook of conflict resolution: Theory and practice*. Jossey-Bass (2006): 23–42.
Duffield, Mark R. *Global governance and the new wars: The merging of development and security*. Vol. 87. Zed Books, 2001.
Elwert, Georg. "Markets of Violence." In Elwert et al. Eds., *Dynamics of collective violence: Processes of escalation and de-escalation in violent group conflicts*. Duncker & Humblot, 1999: 85–102.
Fagen, Patricia Weiss. "El Salvador, Lessons in Peace Consolidation." In Tom Farer, Ed. *Beyond sovereignty: Collectively defending democracy in the Americas*. Johns Hopkins University Press, 1996.
Fortna, Virginia Page. *Peace time: Cease-fire agreements and the durability of peace*. Princeton University Press, 2004.
Gamson, William A. *The strategy of social protest*. Dorsey Press, 1975.
Hall, Brian. "Blue helmets, empty guns." *New York Times Sunday Magazine* 2 (1994).
Hampson, Fen Osler. *Nurturing peace: Why peace settlements succeed or fail*. US Institute of Peace Press, 1996.
Hartzell, Caroline, and Matthew Hoddie. "Institutionalizing peace: Power sharing and post-civil war conflict management." *American Journal of Political Science* 47, no. 2 (2003): 318–332.
Holiday, David, and William Stanley. "Building the peace: Preliminary lessons from El Salvador." *Journal of International Affairs* 46, no. 2 (1993): 415–438.
Holsti, Kalevi Jaakko. *Peace and war: Armed conflicts and international order, 1648–1989*. Vol. 14. Cambridge University Press, 1991.
Joshi, Madhav, and David T. Mason. "Civil war settlements, size of governing coalition, and durability of peace in post-civil war states." *International Interactions* 37, no. 4 (2011): 388–413.
Joshi, Madhav, and Jason Michael Quinn. "Implementing the peace: The aggregate implementation of comprehensive peace agreements and peace duration after intrastate armed conflict." *British Journal of Political Science* 47, no. 4 (2017): 869–892.
Kalyvas, Stathis. *The logic of violence in civil war*. Cambridge University Press, 2006.
Karl, Terry Lynn. "Dilemmas of democratization in Latin America." *Comparative Politics* 23, no. 1 (1990): 1–21.
Kaufman, Stuart J. "Symbolic politics or rational choice? Testing theories of extreme ethnic violence." *International Security* 30, no. 4 (2006): 45–86.
Keen, David. "Incentives and Disincentives for Violence." In Mats Berdal and David Malone, Eds. *Greed and grievance: Economic agendas in civil wars*. Lynne Rienner, 2000.
Kelman, Herbert C. "Transforming the Relationship between Former Enemies: A Social-Psychological Analysis." In Robert L. Rothstein, Ed. *After the peace: Resistance and reconciliation*. Lynne Rienner, 1999.
Krasner, Stephen D. "Structural causes and regime consequences: Regimes as intervening variables." *International Organization* 36, no. 2 (1982): 185–205.
Lake, David A., and Donald Rothchild. "Containing fear: The origins and management of ethnic conflict." *International Security* 21, no. 2 (1996): 41–75.
Lake, David A., and Donald Rothchild. "Territorial Decentralization and Civil War Settlements." In Philip G. Roeder and Donald S. Rothchild. *Sustainable peace: Power and democracy after civil wars*. Cornell University Press (2005): 109–132.
Lilja, Jannie. "Ripening within? Strategies used by rebel negotiators to end ethnic war." *Negotiation Journal* 27, no. 3 (2011): 311–342.
Lodge, Tom. "Revolution Deferred: From Armed Struggle to Liberal Democracy: The African National Congress in South Africa," in Bruce Winfield Dayton and Louis

Kriesberg, Eds. *Conflict transformation and peacebuilding: Moving from violence to sustainable peace*. Routledge, 2009.

Lyons, Terrence. *Voting for peace: Postconflict elections in Liberia*. Brookings Institution Press, 1999.

Lyons, Terrence. "Post-conflict elections and the process of demilitarizing politics: the role of electoral administration." *Democratization* 11, no. 3 (2004): 36–62.

Lyons, Terrence. *Demilitarizing politics: Elections on the uncertain road to peace*. Lynne Rienner, 2005.

Lyons, Terrence. "Governance: A Security Perspective," in Joanna Spear and Paul D. Williams, Eds. *Security and development in global perspectives: A critical comparison*. Georgetown University Press, 2012.

Manning, Carrie L. *The politics of peace in Mozambique: Post-conflict democratization, 1992–2000*. Greenwood Publishing, 2002.

Manning, Carrie. *The making of democrats: Elections and party development in postwar Bosnia, El Salvador, and Mozambique*. Palgrave Macmillan, 2008.

Mason, David T., and Dale A. Krane. "The political economy of death squads: Toward a theory of the impact of state-sanctioned terror." *International Studies Quarterly* 33, no. 2 (1989): 175–198.

Menkhaus, Ken. "Governance without government in Somalia: Spoilers, state building, and the politics of coping." *International Security* 31, no. 3 (2007): 74–106.

Montgomery, Tommie Sue. *Revolution in El Salvador: From civil strife to civil peace*. Westview Press, 1995.

Newman, Edward, and Oliver P. Richmond, Eds. *Challenges to peacebuilding: Managing spoilers during conflict resolution*. United Nations University Press, 2006.

Orjuela, Camilla. "Domesticating Tigers." In Bruce Winfield Dayton and Louis Kriesberg, Eds. *Conflict transformation and peacebuilding: Moving from violence to sustainable peace*. Routledge, 2009.

Pruitt, Dean G. "Readiness theory and the Northern Ireland conflict." *American Behavioral Scientist* 50, no. 11 (2007): 1520–1541.

Regan, Patrick M., and Daniel Norton. "Greed, grievance, and mobilization in civil wars." *Journal of Conflict Resolution* 49, no. 3 (2005): 319–336.

Richards, Peter, and James Vincent. "Sierra Leone: The Marginalization of the RUF." In Jeroen de Zeeuw, Ed. *From soldiers to politicians: Transforming rebel movements after civil war*. Lynne Rienner, 2007.

Roeder, Philip G., and Donald S. Rothchild. *Sustainable peace: Power and democracy after civil wars*. Cornell University Press, 2005.

Rothchild, Donald. "Ethnic bargaining and state breakdown in Africa." *Nationalism and Ethnic Politics* 1, no. 1 (1995): 54–72.

Rothstein, Robert L. "Fragile Peace and Its Aftermath." In Robert L. Rothstein, Ed., *After the peace: Resistance and reconciliation*. Lynne Rienner, 1999.

Saunders, Harold H. "We need a larger theory of negotiation: The importance of pre-negotiating phases." *Negotiation Journal* 1, no. 3 (1985): 249–262.

Shugart, Matthew Soberg. "Guerrillas and elections: An institutionalist perspective on the costs of conflict and competition." *International Studies Quarterly* 36, no. 2 (1992): 121–152.

Simpson, Mark. "Foreign and domestic factors in the transformation of Frelimo." *The Journal of Modern African Studies* 31, no. 2 (1993): 309–337.

Sisk, Timothy D. *Power sharing and international mediation in ethnic conflicts*. US Institute of Peace Press, 1996.

Stedman, Stephen John. "Spoiler problems in peace processes." *International Security* 22, no. 2 (1997): 5–53.

Stedman, Stephen John, Donald Rothchild, and Elizabeth Cousens, Eds. *Ending civil wars: The implementation of peace agreements*. Lynne Rienner, 2002.

Stein, Janice Gross. "Getting to the table: The triggers, stages, functions, and consequences of prenegotiation." *International Journal* 44, no. 2 (1989): 475–504.

Tarrow, Sidney G. *Power in movement: Social movements and contentious politics*. Cambridge University Press, 2011.

Toft, Monica Duffy. *Securing the peace: The durable settlement of civil wars*. Princeton University Press, 2009.

Vines, Alex. *Renamo: From terrorism to democracy in Mozambique*. James Currey, 1996.

Walter, Barbara F. "Designing transitions from civil war: Demobilization, democratization, and commitments to peace." *International Security* 24, no. 1 (1999): 127–155.

Werner, Suzanne. "The precarious nature of peace: Resolving the issues, enforcing the settlement, and renegotiating the terms." *American Journal of Political Science* 3, no. 3 (1999): 912–934.

Woldemariam, Michael H. *When Rebels Collide: Factionalism and Fragmentation in African Insurgencies*. PhD dissertation. Princeton University, 2011.

Wood, Elisabeth J. "The Peace Accords and Postwar Reconstruction." In James K. Boyce, Ed. *Economic policy for building peace: The lessons of El Salvador*. Lynne Rienner, 1996.

Wood, Elisabeth J. *Insurgent collective action and civil war in El Salvador*. Cambridge University Press, 2003.

Woodward, Susan L. "Do the root causes of civil war matter? On using knowledge to improve peacebuilding interventions." *Journal of Intervention and Statebuilding* 1, no. 2 (2007): 143–170.

Young, Oran R. *Politics of force: Bargaining during international crises*. Princeton University Press, 1968.

Young, Oran R. "Regime dynamics: The rise and fall of international regimes." *International Organization* 36, no. 2 (1982): 277–297.

Zald, Mayer N., and John David McCarthy, Eds. *Social movements in an organizational society: Collected essays*. Transaction Publishers, 1987.

Zartman, William I. *Ripe for resolution: Conflict and intervention in Africa*. Oxford University Press, 1989.

Zartman, William I., and Viktor Kremenyuk, Eds. *Peace versus justice: Negotiating forward- and backward-looking outcomes*. Rowman and Littlefield, 2004.

3
SAME PEACE—DIFFERENT QUALITY?

The importance of security equality for quality peace

Louise Olsson

> [The Security Council is d]eeply concerned also about the persistent obstacles and challenges to women's participation and full involvement in the prevention and resolution of conflicts as a result of violence, intimidation and discrimination, which erode women's capacity and legitimacy to participate in post-conflict public life, and acknowledging the negative impact this has on durable peace, security and reconciliation, including post-conflict peacebuilding.
>
> (UNSCR 1888, 2009)

This chapter[1] claims that "security equality" is central for quality peace. In its essence, security equality means that different groups should be equally protected from the threats that affect their security.[2] From a gender perspective, security equality is particularly relevant because, historically, women have been systematically less protected than men when some forms of violence were consistently neglected in our understanding of what constitutes a "peaceful" society. Sexual violence and domestic violence are recognized forms in point. The central problem is, thus, that men and women may experience different degrees of "quality" of the same "peace." Protection from violence thereby becomes intertwined with the broader questions of quality peace as the security equality concept identifies central considerations for us when we conceive of "peace" in more positive—i.e., more qualitative—terms.[3] In essence, the argument is that quality peace has to encompass the notion of equal protection of men and women from the security threats that affect them respectively.

The security equality concept was originally launched to capture scholarly discussions on differences in how men and women are targeted with violence during armed conflict, what forms the violence takes, what measures are developed to enhance protection, and, more importantly, how these measures of protection are distributed between men and women (Olsson 2009). The basis for the concept was the factual problem that creating a more peaceful—i.e., less violent—situation for men did not automatically result in a more peaceful situation for women. In fact, Mary Caprioli found that traditional measures undertaken to increase security in a society—for example, by strengthening the police—might not increase women's security although it did improve men's security i.e., when security for men increased, a similar increase in women's security did not follow (Caprioli 2004). Armed conflicts involving human rights abuse or systematic sexual violence, such as those in Timor-Leste, Bosnia-Herzegovina, and the Democratic Republic of Congo, have highlighted the different forms of protection that men and women might need in order to become equally secure when peace is created. In recent years, therefore, the UN has begun to debate gender specific aspects of rule of law, Disarmament, Demobilization and Reintegration (DDR), and Security Sector Reform (SSR) processes as well as to consider how to address the problem of systematic sexual violence during armed conflict.[4] To enforce the latter, in 2010, the Office of the Special Representative of the Secretary General on Sexual Violence was created, based on the adoption of Security Council resolutions 1820(2008) and 1888(2009). International pressure to go from words to action by enforcing decisions on more equal protection of men and women has also increased substantially. For instance, both the UN operation in the Democratic Republic of Congo and the Congolese Government have received extensive criticism for not forcefully addressing the substantial systematic sexual violence conducted by military organizations and groups operating in the Kivu regions (United Nations Security Council 2012). In the Global Study conducted to evaluate the progress of implementing the Women, Peace and Security agenda 15 years after the first thematic resolution was adopted, a more forceful handling of violence and injustices that affect women became a central theme, particularly related to transitional justice (United Nations Security Council 2015).

The need to strengthen such practical work makes our elaborations of quality peace important in more ways than the theoretical. This chapter contributes to the debate on quality peace by using the concept of security equality—the distribution of protection from violence—from a gender perspective to unearth fundamental considerations. Developments in Timor-Leste from 1975 to 2006 are then employed as an empirical illustration of how men and women are affected by violence and how protection as established by international actors can be unequally distributed through the regular measures undertaken in such situations.

Why, then, would the conflict in Timor-Leste and the subsequent UN operations be particularly fruitful for increasing our understanding of security equality and quality peace? The conflict in the country affected the security of both men and women as well as mobilized them both in the struggle. The UN operations in Timor-Leste that came to assist in creating peace had a substantial impact on security as the largest operation was a transitional authority mission, acting as the state of Timor-Leste for 2.5 years. Thus, two time periods are used to contrast the security situation of both women and men. The first period, from December 1975 to mid-September 1999, displays the gender-specific situation during an enduring war. The second period, from the latter half of September 1999 to March 2006, brings out the effects for men and women of building peace with the assistance of international peace operations. The comparison makes it evident to us how we can end up in a situation where men and women experience different levels of quality of the same peace.

Security equality in quality peace

Empirically, men (as a total in a given state) have in all states the world over better access to power and other resources than women (as a total in the same given state). This observation is built on the fact that there are no states where either the gender-development index, or the gender-empowerment index, is 1.00 (that is, complete equal access to power and resources for both men and women).[5] It is only the degree of how imbalanced the access to power and resources is, that differs between countries. That is, every country has a certain degree of inequality to men's advantage. The balance can then become more equal or more unequal during the process toward peace (Olsson 2009).

The argument in this chapter is that quality peace must encompass the notion of equal protection of men and women from the security threats that affect them respectively. For the original development of the security equality concept, two observations were central: (1) both men and women are the target of violence, but of different forms; (2) in spite of this, the measures undertaken to enhance protection are not equally distributed to address all forms of violence. This becomes even more emphasized during an armed conflict and then, as Dara Cohen and Ragnhild Nordås' work indicates, continues well into the post-war period.[6] Ergo, the end of war might not mean equal peace and security for all. The problem of continued violence after war has been a focus in the broader debate on the peace concept. For example, as shown by Kristine Höglund and Mimmi Söderberg Kovacs, "peace" after armed conflict can entail various levels of violence and human rights abuse. This makes certain situations of "peace" more destructive than others (Höglund and Söderberg Kovacs 2010). Likewise, Michael W. Doyle and Nicolas Sambanis hold that the levels of residual violence need to be considered in addition to just noting the absence of conflict violence. This means that peace might fail even if war does not formally return.[7] As recognized in this research, abuse can continue against both men and women outside the confines of armed conflict. Notably, however, "women and girls" are often identified in policy and research as the main vulnerable groups. However, empirically, young males have to be considered as another "vulnerable group" as they tend to constitute the majority of those forcefully recruited, abused or killed. The concept of security equality is therefore central to the full picture of violence directed at both men and women in order to understand the importance of the distribution of protection. The aim of the concept is not to identify which group is the "most" vulnerable but rather to increase our understanding of how both men and women are vulnerable and how they can be equally protected.

Though under-researched, the empirical trend visible in the demographic balances after conflict suggests that men are mostly subjected to direct lethal conflict violence where lethal conflict violence is understood as physical violence conducted by the warring parties of the armed conflict. This is also true if civilian groups targeted with lethal conflict violence are included. Charli R. Carpenter claims that gender-stereotypical assumptions about women as the "civilian" and the "innocent peacemaker," compared to men as "culprits" and "war-makers," have taken focus away from the fact that men and boys of the civilian population are the ones with the highest risk of direct lethal conflict violence. In addition, these assumptions limit the reporting of, and protection from, many non-lethal forms of violence against men (such as rape), reporting that would shake the established assumptions about masculinity and war (Carpenter 2005). As noted by Bjarnegård et al., the strongly gendered patterns of participation and suffering defy simplistic stereotypes that assign all men to the category of combatants and all women and children to the role of victim (Bjarnegård et al. 2015). In Carpenter's view, integrating a gender perspective in the work of international agencies would thereby enable them to more effectively protect all civilians, both women and men (2005).[8] Thus, while it is likely that men will constitute the majority of victims of lethal violence, both men and women are targets of non-lethal conflict violence. Here, women are often the main targets of sexual violence and sexual abuse. Sexual violence can have long-term lethal consequences. Apart from the risk of dying from the physical long-term effects of violence, sexual violence can have a stigma attached to it—labeling the victim as being just as guilty as the perpetrator. Abused women thereby risk losing social and economic networks. This, in turn, increases the risk of further violence. In addition, abused women might, in many cases, later die from STDs, most prominently HIV/AIDS, or risk being killed by male family members, or men from their community, because rape may be considered as a loss of honor as much for the male relatives as for the abused woman (Kelly 2000; Meintjes et al. 2001). International efforts to address this form of violence have attempted to change this negative perception of the victims, both male and female.[9]

In addition to lethal and non-lethal conflict violence, a third form of violence, non-conflict violence, i.e., violence that is not conducted by the warring parties, is of relevance to understand security equality in quality peace. For example, young men are often targeted by organized crime or drawn into gang violence that can increase during the conflict and in the post-war period. However, the relevance of non-conflict violence has primarily been brought up in previous research in regard to the argument that there is limited attention given to violence taking place in the private sphere—a violence that often targets women (Venis and Horton 2002; Watts and Zimmerman 2002). What violence should be considered relevant to ensure protection from, and how to analyze it, are therefore integral parts of much feminist research. Susie Jacobs et al. argue that the, in many respects illusionary, analytical division between public and private (domestic) spheres, complicates and "hides" a majority of the violence endured by women. For understanding women's security, what goes on in the private sphere is therefore central. It is in the private sphere that many women will spend most of the conflict, and it is here that they risk becoming victims of violence, directly or indirectly caused by the conflict (Jacobs et al. 2000). Reportedly, non-conflict violence taking place in the private sphere—such as sexual violence and domestic violence—increases and becomes more severe during armed conflict. Simultaneously, research argues, such forms of non-conflict violence can become even less prioritized by relevant authorities (Kelly 2000: 59–60). Protection created in a society thereby excludes the forms of violence from which women are the main targets. In the last couple of years the international community's views of how serious this form of violence is has begun to alter. As the World Bank argued, gender-based violence causes ill-health to as many women the world over each year as all cases of malaria and traffic accidents put together (Venis and Horton 2002). In addition, feminist research claims that women are often the targets of even more violence in the post-war period than during actual armed conflict. Therefore, it is wrong to call this period "an aftermath" of conflict (Meintjes et al. 2001). With the new 2030 agenda, ending violence against women has been made a central part of a common global goal of gender equality. Hence, utilizing security equality for understanding quality peace thereby raises the important point that measures taken to enhance protection should not be too limited in scope to exclude violence of which women are the main targets.

Security equality in quality peace: the case of Timor-Leste

There are good reasons to illustrate these discussions with the case of Timor-Leste. The country had a long civil war that affected both men and women. The international peace operations shaped men and women's security and they undertook special measures to strengthen women's protection.[10]

> The fact that women and men are equally—albeit differently—affected by organized violence must be highlighted, and the complex, multi-faceted and ambivalent roles played by women and men during times of war and peace must be engaged with to avoid the perpetuation of incomplete understandings.
>
> (Hudson 2005: 162)

In 1999, Timor-Leste (until May 2002 more generally known as East Timor) had a population of about 900,000 people with very high fertility rates.[11] Timor-Leste is to a large extent a rural country, and poverty is more widespread in the rural areas than in the urban centers. The country was first colonized by Portugal in the sixteenth century and remained a Portuguese colony until 1974–1975, interrupted only by Japanese occupation during World War II. Before Timor-Leste could obtain international recognition as an independent state, it was invaded by

Indonesia in December 1975. The subsequent occupation was continuously under attack from armed Timorese groups, the largest being Fretilin. Indonesia's occupation resulted in persistent international critique. Women and men were both involved in Fretilin, which used its women's organization to mobilize women politically. Thus, women were involved in guerilla activities along with men. However, these women were formally labeled as political cadres—something that affected their ability to get veteran benefits after the war. Women and youth were a large section of the urban non-violent struggle. The majority of guerillas, however, were men. Men also constituted the absolute number of those mobilized by Indonesia for the military, police and subsequent militia groups in Timor-Leste. To these men, their wives, children, and relatives were expected by the authorities to be supportive. The reasons for men joining the Indonesian military or militia varied from forceful to voluntary (which could be either for political or economic and social benefits). The reasons why men joined also affected whether they could be demobilized into society (that is, if they were accepted back) after the conflict ended.

That end arrived rather unexpectedly. In 1999, the Indonesian regime agreed to hold a referendum to determine Timor-Leste's status within Indonesia. The terms were settled in 1999 in the 5th of May Agreements, signed by Indonesia, Portugal, and the UN. The UN, through the United Nations Mission in East Timor (UNAMET) organized the elections on August 30, 1999. Of the Timorese electorate, 78.5 percent voted in favor of independence. Both men and women voted in the elections even though the level of threat against voters was high. From September 1, and further intensified by the UN declaration of election results on September 4, there was a serious escalation of organized violence by local militias and segments of the Indonesian National Army. On September 20, the International Force in East Timor (INTERFET), led by Australia under a UN Security Council mandate, was sent in to halt the violence, organized looting, and systematic destruction of buildings and infrastructure. The United Nations Transitional Administration in East Timor (UNTAET) then received a mandate to assist Timor-Leste in establishing independence. This operation had both peace enforcement, peacekeeping and peacebuilding components in its mandate. On May 20, 2002, after being under UNTAET administration for 2.5 years, the Independent Democratic Republic of Timor-Leste was declared. UNTAET was replaced by United Nations Mission of Support in East Timor (UNMISET), which initially had an executive policing mandate (which ended May 10, 2004) but primarily provided support to the new Timorese government. In 2005, UNMISET was, in its turn, replaced by the United Nations Office in Timor-Leste (UNOTIL), which had a 1-year follow-up mandate to advise the government and support the Timorese police.

For the period used to illustrate the use of security equality for quality peace, that is 1975–2006, data and information on violence and protection in Timor-Leste is primarily descriptive. However, for pedagogical purposes, and in order to demonstrate the argument on security equality, the information can be aggregated and discussed in terms of low, medium, and high.[12] In this manner, we can obtain an overview of the levels of violence and protection that existed in the period of war, 1975–1999, and the period of peacebuilding, 1999–2006.

The period of war: 1975–1999

When war broke out in 1975, both women and men were affected and mobilized. The period of war was, however, to have different effects for women and men in terms of what forms of violence they were the targets of and what forms of protection from violence were to develop. In Table 3.1, we can observe and compare the levels of violence against men and women. For men, the risk of lethal conflict violence was generally quite high, but peaked in the initial, and concluding, parts of the conflict. Conflict violence was also high in the non-lethal form, such as torture and abuse where men were the main targets. Information on non-conflict violence is generally more difficult to find, but available sources indicate that the current high level of assault crimes against men was a legacy of the occupation and it is likely that they took place to a reasonably high degree during the period. Women were unlikely the direct targets of lethal conflict violence, even though a substantial number were killed. They were instead primarily the target of non-lethal conflict violence in the form of sexual violence, sexual slavery, rape, torture, and abuse. An exact comparison is difficult to make, but the level of violence was high enough to cause a public discussion on violence against women, a previously taboo topic. Non-conflict violence against women, in the form of sexual violence and domestic violence, was also high.

If we instead look at the level of protection in 1975 to 1999, as also portrayed in Table 3.1, the level of conflict violence (both lethal and non-lethal) was high against men, but there were some structures developed to protect those who were politically active.[13] The supportive network of the struggle was, in part, used to increase the protection to at least enable collective action and protection. However, civilian men, not working to enforce a political agenda or participating militarily in the conflict, were also targeted. There is indication of a higher degree in the level of violence directed at them because they were male, as civilian women were not the targets to the same degree. For this civilian group of men, there was no

TABLE 3.1 December 1975–September 1999[1]

	Estimated level of violence		*Estimated level of protection*	
	Men	*Women*	*Men*	*Women*
Lethal conflict violence	High	Medium	Medium-Low	Low
Non-lethal conflict violence	High	High	Low	Low
Non-conflict violence	Medium	High	Medium	Low

1. See Olsson 2009: 148–149.

protection developed and human rights abuses were a common feature of the occupation. What is interesting to note about the conflict violence against men is that it was not blamed on the victim of the abuse as we can observe for some forms of violence where women were targets.

Women were less the target of lethal conflict violence than men, but the women who participated in the conflict received less protection from developed structures. To come to terms with this, attempts were made by women's organizations to increase the protection of female participants in the pro-independence movement. This could be what Cynthia Cockburn identifies as "fighting" not only the enemy but also one's own colleagues to achieve equal protection and respect (1998: 42). For example, Fretilin's women's movement worked to improve the situation for females in guerilla groups. In addition to lethal conflict violence, women were also targeted with non-lethal conflict violence, where sexual violence was a common feature. No formal protection from non-lethal conflict violence was developed. Both for targeted civilians as well as for politically active women, sexual violence was often blamed on the victim and not solely on the perpetrator. Although the extent of the violence against women from Indonesian troops resulted in the issue of blame being brought up in way it had not been before, the result often remained as increased insecurity for abused women after the incident of violence. For example, because of the stigma, women were ostracized, leaving some abused women no choice but to turn to prostitution in order to find an income. Regarding the last form of violence, non-conflict violence, women were especially the targets of domestic violence. There was very little protection developed to handle this form of violence. For both men and women, existing state institutions were not prepared to take complaints as a means of handling non-conflict violence or to provide protection. The police were part of the apparatus to keep control of the territory and therefore the Timorese population distrusted them. As an alternative, the traditional justice system grew substantially in importance and took the place of the state justice system for most Timorese. The traditional system was male-based and gave more protection from non-conflict violence where men were the main victims. The violence that women were primarily the target of, domestic violence, was not addressed with the same weight. It was often regarded as something that was to be solved within the family, and thus not seen as a crime. The level of protection from violence for women was, thus, even lower than that for men.

The period of peacebuilding: 1999–2006

The situation of violence and protection was to alter, in some respects, when the peace process and peace operations began. INTERFET was deployed in late-September 1999 and achieved control of the territory by the end of October. In the areas secured by the peacekeeping operation, the level of conflict violence against men, both lethal and non-lethal, decreased drastically. As can be seen in Table 3.2, these forms of violence then remained reasonably low even though they peaked during short periods of time when militias made attempts to operate inside Timor-Leste, attempts that resulted in incidents of violence, foremost directed at men but also with women as victims. For men, non-conflict violence has remained mainly at a medium level, as there was a continuous presence of man-to-man violence. This took the form of riots, gang fights and other types of crime-related violence. For women, the risk of both forms of conflict violence was seriously decreased by the work of first INTERFET, and then UNTAET, peacekeeping forces. By comparison, non-conflict violence against women, primarily in the form of domestic violence, remained very high. That is, there is limited in-group variation over time for the last form of violence. In addition, negative behavior of peace-operation personnel would add a degree of non-lethal conflict violence, primarily directed against women. If we move on to consider the development of protection from violence, the peacekeeping forces, INTERFET and UNTAET, undertook measures for increased protection. A substantial part of the operation was directed to ensure the removal of conflict violence (the measures taken, in effect increased the protection of the population). As can be seen in Table 3.2, protection from non-lethal conflict violence was initially high for both men and women.

However, with cases of rape and abuse of primarily Timorese women by international staff (which the operation failed to sufficiently take measures against until very late into the operation), the level of protection that the operation provided was somewhat reduced for women. With the arrival of international police, followed by the construction of the national Timorese police force, the work to increase protection from non-conflict violence commenced. Handling violence directed against men, almost exclusively from other men, was placed on the agenda from the beginning of the operation and remained central. However, the slow build-up of the UN's civilian police, the problems of creating a new Timorese police force based on human rights standards, the competition between the new Timorese military and the new Timorese police, and two competing judicial systems limited the effectiveness of measures taken to increase protections. As the traditional justice system was often part of a patron-client relationship, this also affected the protection of the competing system for men.

TABLE 3.2 September 1999–March 2006[1]

	Estimated level of violence		Estimated level of protection	
	Men	Women	Men	Women
Lethal conflict violence	Medium-Low	Low	High	High
Non-lethal conflict violence	Low	Medium-Low	High	High-Medium
Non-conflict violence	Medium	High	High-Medium	Low-Medium

1. See Olsson 2009: 150–151.

Non-conflict violence against women taking place in the public sphere was addressed by official structures, that is, through the UN-developed institutions. Thereby it suffered from the same problems that affected men. In addition, protection against non-conflict violence that mostly affected women—domestic violence—was not automatically included in the interpretation of the mandate for UNTAET unlike the forms of violence which affected men. Domestic violence was only included in the implementation of the mandate after much local and international pressure. When the question of increasing protection from domestic violence was addressed, the focus was first on getting domestic violence recognized as a crime. Once recognized as a crime, domestic violence could be handled by the police. Even after this recognition was made in the development of the constitution and subsequent laws, domestic violence, however, continued to be accorded low priority by the police. Thus, even though the attitude toward the violence had begun to change, actual protection remained low, particularly when compared to other forms of violence.

Thus, the development of protection from conflict violence—both lethal and non-lethal—had a higher impact on men than on women because men were the targets of such violence to a higher degree than women. Concerning non-conflict violence, violence related to public crimes, such as murder, gang fights, or organized crime, were primarily addressed while protection from domestic violence remained lower. That is, much of the focus in increasing protection from non-conflict violence was directed at halting man-to-man violence. As a result, in "relational" terms, the security situation for men improved more than the security situation for women when the war phase transitioned into the peacebuilding phase. In that respect, the peace operation benefited men to a higher degree than women, who received less protection through the measures taken by the operation (as women's situation had required other measures to make their protection equal to that of men). Interestingly, and similarly to that predicted by Caprioli, the security situation for women did not automatically improve equally to that of men (2004). However, it can also be argued that women became somewhat less unequal to men from the moment that the operation started taking measures to include the handling of domestic violence. As a result, domestic violence became a crime that could be addressed by the police even though it still had lower priority than other forms of non-conflict violence. An additional difference between men and women that is particularly worth noting is the normative aspects of blame for the violence. Violence against men was usually not blamed on both perpetrator and victims, as was the case with much of the violence directed at women. For example, women victims of sexual violence or domestic violence were often stigmatized by being labeled as partly responsible for being abused.

Conclusions

This chapter has argued that the distribution of protection between groups—i.e., security equality—is central for quality peace. We cannot assume that all groups in a society automatically receive equal protection from the threats that affect them respectively when a peace is being established. As the case of Timor-Leste demonstrates with clarity, if gender-specific considerations are not consciously incorporated into the process, men might get a (disproportionately) higher degree of quality peace than women. Hence, we cannot correctly capture quality peace if it is not fine-tuned to gender differences. Ongoing efforts both to strengthen gender awareness in the handling of conflict violence and to improve the protection of women speak forcefully to the practical need for us to adopt a more in-depth understanding of what form of peace the international community actually contributes to when assisting with a resolution process. Moreover, while this chapter has argued this on a more overarching level, the same concept applies when we diverge into analyzing more specific aspects of a peace process, such as the establishment of rule of law or the implementation of a DDR, or a SSR, process.[14] While it is often the international community that has been the focus of debate, it is important to note that the Timor-Leste developments clearly display that it is both the actions of the internal actors and the international actors that affect how protection is developed and distributed between men and women. In addition, it is important not to be overly simplistic when determining how traditional measures to address violence affect women's security. Most notably, measures taken by international operations to reduce conflict violence, since the INTERFET deployment in 1999, did result in improved security for both men and women to a degree. That said, the measures taken resulted in more enhanced protection for men, i.e., were not followed by an equal enhancement in the protection for women. Initially, therefore, women's security situation became more unequal compared to that of men. Security equality thereafter improved toward the second half of the UNTAET operation as measures were taken to address the more specific threats to women's security.

Research and practice have demonstrated that the problems and opportunities identified in this chapter on Timor-Leste are not unique. Similar trends have appeared in many countries with peace operations: Kosovo, Bosnia and Herzegovina, Cambodia, Democratic Republic of Congo, and Namibia to name a few. In these countries, the behavior of the warring parties, the state, and the peace operations have had direct but different implications for men's and women's security.[15] For the UN, it is important to remember that these differences emerged regardless of whether the peace operation had a conscious approach to gender or not. However, what appears to be a general trend is that when there was a lack of gender awareness in the international operation, the result tended to be that men received an even higher degree of quality peace than women.

In conclusion, there are several relevant implications for policy and for future research that can be identified when utilizing the security equality concept in quality peace.

First, on a more basic level, it is relevant to consider how protection is distributed in a society and how unequal protection should be considered in relation to quality peace. This is central both in research and when practically contributing to building peace. Further development using security equality can, in addition to gender, involve increased discussion on the distribution of protection between other identity groups, such as ethnic groups, or when considering the situation for political groups that were not included in a peace agreement.

Second, when considering more gender-specific variations, analysts and practitioners need to further develop their understanding of what makes men and women more or less vulnerable from physical violence in general and how armed conflict plays into such a dynamic more specifically. Particularly regarding women's situation, the community concerned still has very limited systematic knowledge of how the level of violence against women in a society is affected by armed conflict. For example, domestic violence, the same as sexual violence, is predicted to increase during and after armed conflict. However, what are the variation and factors that can affect it? Working practically to improve women's protection, there are already several international conventions and documents which should guide international assistance and state behavior, such as the Convention on the Elimination of all Discrimination against Women and UN Security Council resolutions on Women, Peace and Security, just to mention a few.

Third, continuing to develop methods to collect gender disaggregated data on armed conflict is central for improved research on the different situations for men and women during armed conflict and conflict resolution. A positive development in recent years is the increase in systematic research focusing on understanding sexual violence in armed conflict.[16] With violence against women an indicator in the 2030 agenda's fifth goal of gender equality, there is hope of more data on other forms of violence becoming available. Improving the collaboration between researchers and women's organizations in the field could be another potential and practical way to increase the access to data.

Fourth, and finally, prevalence of high degrees of domestic violence or sexual violence after peace has officially been declared raises the important question of how much violence can be practiced in a society before it is considered as affecting quality peace? That there is no peace for women if their security is not considered important is a classical argument in feminist theory. With the slow but growing normative shift in how we perceive and acknowledge violence against women, there is hope for a more equal treatment of women and men in terms of access to protection. In so doing, it is, however, central to not lose track of the fact that security equality is a relational concept, not focused only on women but also giving us detailed understandings of men's security. Not over-simplifying their security situation is equally important. In quite a few scenarios, it can be important to label particularly young men as vulnerable. For all the above reasons, considering quality peace from a gender perspective is therefore central to keep up with international debates. The concept of quality peace has to encompass the notion of equal protection of men and women from the security threats that affect them respectively.

Notes

1. This chapter builds on, and develops, the ideas and text of Olsson's book *Gender equality and United Nations peace operations in Timor-Leste*, (Leiden and Boston: Brill 2009). The chapter is published with permission from Brill Publishers. The author wishes to thank Peter Wallensteen, John Darby, Madhav Joshi, Roxanna Sjöstedt, Monica Duffy Toft, Dara Cohen, and Mats Hammarström for valuable comments in the development of the chapter.
2. The concept of "security equality" was originally coined in Louise Olsson, *Equal peace. Gender power relations and United Nations peace operations in Timor Leste* (Uppsala: Dept. of Peace and Conflict Research, 2007) for the study of gender specific differences but can be used also in other areas (such as for analyzing differences in security relating to age, class, ethnicity etc.).
3. Rather than signifying only the lack of armed force being used by warring parties to obtain political goals.
4. SSR involves the strengthening of institutional structures and government control over security actors, such as, the military and police. See *The OECD DAC handbook on security system reform* (OECD 2008) for examples of practical implementation, and Fey et al. (2011) for broader discussions.
5. See *Human Development Index, 1995–2006*. Naturally, that does not say anything of dual relationships between individual women and individual men in a given state. On that analytical level, other factors, such as ethnicity and class, are important.
6. See Nordås 2011 for a description.
7. Michael W. Doyle and Nicholas Sambanis consider "peace" in two forms. One is more "lenient" (end of war violence and residual violence) and the other one is stricter (including the end of violence and increased political participation) (Doyle and Sambanis 2000). Naturally, this raises the question of if one risks including components in the measurement of peace that in effect are factors affecting peace sustainability. The same problematique can be identified in terms of equality that, as indicated in the initial quote from the UN Security Council, tend to be perceived of both in terms of factors affecting the sustainability of peace as well as being perceived of as a potential component of peace if the concept of peace is broadened.
8. In international organizations, such as the UN and more recently the EU and the North Atlantic Treaty Organization (NATO), there is an ongoing debate between two perspectives on the relevance of gender in international interventions and peace operations. The first relates directly to human rights and normative demands of considering the gender perspective. The second, which has become increasingly dominant, is the argument that neglecting to apply a gender perspective to the main part of an organization's work decreases the effectiveness. The reason is that the work then will fail to properly consider the substantive gender divisions of power, labor, and resource distribution in the host society. This can have long-term negative effects on peace. A failure to identify and adequately consider the difference in situation between men and women, i.e., the gender specificity, of the host population has also resulted in deteriorating gender power-relations, i.e., the relation becomes more unequal. For further discussion, see Olsson 2000 and 2005, and Olsson et al. 2009.
9. For example, this was a theme of the Global Summit to End Sexual Violence in Conflict which was held on June 10–13, 2014 in London.
10. This section builds on Olsson 2009. For references and more details on security equality, see that book.
11. In the last decade, the country has undergone considerable development.
12. See Olsson (2009: 51–139) for detailed descriptions of violence and protection.
13. This focuses on physical violence. With a different definition, for instance, on death through starvation and lack of health care, women and their dependents might have experienced more violence.

14. Policy work to implement gender in SSR has developed in later years. For example, see DCAF's *Gender and security sector reform: Examples from the ground* (DCAF 2011). For discussions on gender and DDR, see United Nations 2006 and Coulter 2015.
15. For further discussion, see Whitworth 2004, Alldén 2009, and Olsson 2009.
16. The Sexual Violence in Armed Conflict project at the Peace Research Institute Oslo (PRIO) is a case in point.

References

Alldén, Susanne. *How do international norms travel?: Women's political rights in Cambodia and Timor-Leste*. Umeå University, 2009.

Bjarnegård, Elin et al. "Gender, Peace and Armed Conflict," in *SIPRI yearbook 2015: Armaments, disarmament and international security*. SIPRI, 2015.

Caprioli, Mary. "Democracy and human rights versus women's security: A contradiction?" *Security Dialogue* 35, no. 4 (2004): 411–428.

Carpenter, Charli R. '"Women, children and other vulnerable groups': Gender, strategic frames and the protection of civilians as a transnational issue." *International Studies Quarterly* 49, no. 2 (2005): 295–334.

Cockburn, Cynthia. *The space between us: Negotiating gender and national identities in conflict*. Zed Books, 1998.

Coulter, Chris. *Bush wives and girl soldiers: Women's lives through war and peace in Sierra Leone*. Cornell University Press, 2015.

DCAF. *Gender and security sector reform: Examples from the ground*. DCAF, 2011.

Doyle, Michael W., and Nicholas Sambanis. "International peacebuilding: A theoretical and quantitative analysis." *American Political Science Review* 94, no. 4 (2000): 779–801.

Fey, Marco, Sabine Mannitz, and Niklas Schörnig. *Democracy, the armed forces and military deployment: The "second social contract" is on the line*. Peace Research Institute Frankfurt (PRIF), 2011.

Hudson, Heidi. "'Doing security as though humans matter: A feminist perspective on gender and the politics of human security." *Security Dialogue* 36, no. 2 (2005): 155–174.

Human Development Index, 1995–2006. New York: United Nations Development Programme (UNDP), 1995.

Höglund, Kristine, and Mimmi Söderberg Kovacs. "Beyond the absence of war: The diversity of peace in post-settlement societies." *Review of International Studies* 36, no. 2 (2010): 367–390.

Jacobs, Susie, Ruth Jacobson, and Jennifer Marchbank. *States of conflict: Gender, violence and resistance*. Palgrave Macmillan, 2000.

Kelly, Liz. "Wars Against Women: Sexual Violence, Sexual Politics and the Militarised State." In Susie Jacobs, Ruth Jacobson, and Jane Marchbank, Eds. *States of conflict: Gender, violence and resistance*. Zed Books, 2000.

Meintjes, Sheila, Meredeth Turshen, and Anu Pillay. *The aftermath: Women in post-conflict transformation*. Zed Books, 2001.

Nordås, Ragnhild. "Sexual violence in African conflicts." CSCW Policy Brief no. 1, 2011.

OECD, *The OECD DAC handbook on security system reform: Supporting security and justice*. Organisation for Economic Co-operation and Development, 2008.

Olsson, Louise. "Mainstreaming gender in multidimensional peacekeeping: A field perspective." *International Peacekeeping* 7, no. 3 (2000): 1–16.

Olsson, Louise. "The Namibian Peace Operation in a Gender Context." In Dyan Mazurana, Angela Raven-Roberts, and Jane Parpart, Eds. *Gender, conflict, and peacekeeping*. Rowman & Littlefield, 2005.

Olsson, Louise. *Gender equality and United Nations peace operations in Timor Leste.* Vol. 14. Brill, 2009.

Olsson, Louise and Johan Tejpar (Eds.). Operational Effectiveness and UN Resolution 1325: Practices and Lessons from Afghanistan. Defence Analysis, Swedish Defence Research Agency (FOI), 2009.

United Nations. *Disarmament, demobilization and reintegration standard.* United Nations, 2006.

United Nations Security Council. *Security council report: Cross-cutting report: Women, peace and security.* United Nations, 2012, No 1.

United Nations Security Council. *Preventing conflict, transforming justice, securing the peace. A global study on the implementation of United Nations Security Council resolution 1325.* United Nations Women, 2015.

Venis, Sarah, and Richard Horton. "Violence against women: A global burden." *The Lancet* 359, no. 9313 (2002): 1172–1172.

Watts, Charlotte, and Cathy Zimmerman. "Violence against women: Global scope and magnitude." *The Lancet* 359, no. 9313 (2002): 1232–1237.

Whitworth, Sandra. *Men, militarism, and UN peacekeeping: A gendered analysis.* Lynne Rienner, 2004.

PART II
Governance

4
GOVERNANCE AND NEGOTIATIONS
Whose quality standards?

Roger Mac Ginty

Introduction

In understanding peace processes and negotiations, this chapter makes three points. First, given the focus of this volume on the quality of peace, the chapter points to the prevalence of a success/failure benchmark for international peace-support interventions. It is argued that such a stark rubric is inconsistent with the messy nature of peace processes and peace accord implementation, and may be a poor guide to making assessments on the quality of peace. Second, the chapter advances the notion of hybridity as a way of understanding the dynamic nature of peace processes and implementation environments. Hybridity rests on the notion that no actor can unilaterally impose its will on others, and thus helps us transcend the success/failure rubric. Peace process environments are often an amalgam of top-down and bottom-up, as well as formal and informal, forces that conflict and coalesce to produce a hybridized context. Third, the chapter makes the point that the governance skills and environment surrounding peace process negotiations are often different from those surrounding peace accord implementation and acceptance. While peace negotiations may operate according to formalized rules of governance, the acceptance or rejection of a peace accord often relies on informal negotiation and governance that occurs at the individual, family, and community levels. This informal governance, or the internalization of a peace process or accord by individuals and communities, is under-studied yet seems crucial to the quality of peace.[1]

Absolutist notions of "success" and "failure" have become a feature of debate in politics, policymaking, and business. Illustrations from the business world are perhaps the starkest; corporations can be said to be in "trouble" or "failing" despite making multi-million profits. Over the past decade, for example, analysts questioned the long-term viability of Research in Motion, the Canadian company that makes BlackBerry smartphones. It has struggled as it faced competition from Apple and

Android devices. Yet, it is still profit-making and, in 2015, sat on a cash balance of US$3.27bn. The big problem for markets was that its economic performance did not meet the expectation of analysts (Dummett 2015). Similarly skewed perspectives can be found in the political and policymaking worlds in which deviation from the stated path can be ordained as "failure" and prompt calls for resignations and radical policy rethinks. Moreover, political and media actors may have unrealistic timeframes that fail to see peacebuilding as a long-term endeavor. This chapter recommends a more measured perspective on what constitutes success, failure, and quality with regards to governance and negotiations in peace processes, and thus in quality peace. It advances the notion of hybridity as a way of understanding peace processes and the implementation of peace accords, and as a way of transcending the blunt success/failure rubric.

Success and failure

Peace processes often involve constructive ambiguity, fudging, and the dissemination of different messages to different constituencies. Conflicts have messy legacies with a complex mix of awkward stories at the institutional, community, and personal levels. This is especially the case in deeply divided societies in which different communities continue to share the same space and must engage in creative conflict avoidance strategies that involve a good deal of looking the other way and pretending not to notice. This might especially be the case at the local level. Practical and ethical dilemmas abound concerning the rights of victims, the responsibilities of perpetrators, and who should be included in any negotiations or political process. Many of the dilemmas prove irresolvable, though sometimes they can be minimized through the passage of time and the human skills of constructive ambiguity.

In such circumstances, absolutist notions of success, failure, victory and loss seem unrealistic. Yet a series of oppositional binaries are often used to conceptualize peace and conflict. It is common for humans to perceptually order their world according to a series of dyadic categories. In conflict situations, these binaries may have an added pejorative dimension, with some categories associated with right and good, and others associated with wrong and evil. Thus, the perceptual and linguistic landscape of conflict and peacemaking is littered with a series of words and phrases that pigeonhole individuals, groups, and behaviors as legitimate or illegitimate: terrorist/freedom fighter, autocratic/democratic, irrational/rational, corrupt/accountable, evil/good, etc. Such binaries are attractive in reducing complex situations into understandable sound bites and can serve to reinforce the righteousness of the group that imposes the categorization while demonizing the other. Instructive in this regard is a side-by-side reading of the addresses by Israeli Prime Minister Benjamin Netanyahu and Palestinian leader Mahmoud Abbas to the 2011 United Nations General Assembly. Each depicts the other side as obstructionist and uninterested in peace, while emphasizing the patience and goodwill of their own side (Abbas 2011; Netanyahu 2011). While the speeches were made to an international audience, they were also addressed to home audiences who wanted a reaffirmation of the righteousness of their own cause and the iniquity of the other side.

In a conflict situation, the success/failure rubric maintained by antagonist groups is likely to depend on their ultimate goal, for example, secession, security, and mastery over an outgroup, or survival. Win/lose mentalities often help explain the perpetuation of conflicts and the failure of antagonists to investigate conflict transformation as opposed to more limited conflict resolution and conflict management outcomes (Lederach 1995). The "total victory" syndrome is often fueled by in-group rivalries in which ethnic entrepreneurs seek to depict their co-religionist or co-ethnic competitors as weak, naive or traitorous. "Ethnic outbidding" militates against peace processes and explicit compromises with opponents (DeVotta 2005: 141–142). In cases where there have been peace processes and accords, those involved are faced with a tricky decision on where to draw the line between a "mature and hard-won compromise" and defending the interests of the in-group. This is a difficult path to follow, as illustrated—at various times—by the fortunes of the United National Party in Sri Lanka, the Ulster Unionist Party in Northern Ireland, and the Labor Party in Israel, all of which were derided for being "weak" in pursuing peace opportunities. In other cases, of course, combatants have been able to make breakthroughs and to sell peace accords as historic compromises involving give and take on both sides.

Given the interest of this volume in third parties, it is worth concentrating on the extent to which such interveners might use, and suffer from, an overly rigid adherence to a success/failure rubric. This raises questions about the meanings of success and failure in peace processes, and the extent to which these meanings are distorted by other factors that may not be immediately connected to the conflict zone.

International intervening powers, whether mediators in peace negotiations or supporters of reconciliation and reconstruction programs, often suffer from "process bias" (Sisk 1996: 94). Intervening parties may have tightly confined goals and deviation from these goals is deemed to be failure. Given that these goals are often publicly articulated, then deviations may attract the full glare of publicity. With regards to both Bosnia-Herzegovina and Kosovo, for example, external mediators and interveners displayed either partiality, a commitment to a preferred outcome, or both. In Bosnia, local opinions that did not match the "script" preferred by the Office of the High Representative were often ignored or devalued (Sahovic 2007). In some cases, it seemed that the implementation of the preferred process was more important than alternative outcomes that may have delivered different (and possibly better) results. Yet "process bias" is not always evident. Norwegian third parties in Sri Lanka's failed peace process in the mid-2000s, for example, were careful to offer a facilitator rather than power-mediator role. They saw their role as facilitating the construction of a peace process by the participants to the conflict rather than providing a peace process template and recommending that the participants follow it (Salter 2015).

Process bias is reinforced by a Western (though by no means exclusively Western) political and economic culture that regards failure as unacceptable. Few political or business leaders can be seen to be wrong, and to admit failure or a mistake often leads to resignation or sacking. George Stephanopoulos' memoir of his time in the Clinton White House is revealing of a political culture in which the media script of "success" has priority over reality (2005: 325–328). His account of the 1993 signing of the Declaration of Principles between the Palestinian Liberation Organization and Israel on the White House lawn shows the extent to which the American voter rather than the Middle East was the primary audience, and so a story of success had to be promoted.

Western-dominated approaches to peacemaking, such as those favored by leading states in the global North and their allied international financial institutions, are not alone in their intolerance toward alternative approaches to peacemaking. There is little to recommend the Chinese "peace" in Tibet and Xinjiang, the Russian "peace" in Chechnya or the Saudi Arabian "peace efforts" in Yemen or Bahrain. Yet leading states in the global North can mobilize considerable material and symbolic power that promotes its version of peace as superior and legitimate, and alternatives as somehow deficient. This projection of a preferred form of peacemaking stretches, in various formats and degrees of intensity, from Timor-Leste to the Balkans. The October 2011 mobilization of Western states and institutions against the Palestinian bid for statehood at the UN General Assembly is instructive of the ability of a cohort of leading states and international institutions to sideline proposals that do not "fit the script."[2] Proponents of liberal internationalism may also be dismissive of forms of peacemaking that draw on traditional or indigenous sources (Mac Ginty 2008). Indeed, alternative voices may even be labeled as "resistance" (Scott 2008).

One reason for the readiness of the proponents of internationally supported peacemaking to approach their task with a success/failure metric is the growing use of technocracy in peacebuilding (Donais 2009). Technocracy is often more visible in post-accord peacebuilding and statebuilding environments than during the negotiation phase of peace processes. The rise of technocracy in peacebuilding is connected to much wider trends in information management and business organization whereby increasing power is ceded to "experts" and to systems that were often developed for the needs of businesses (Box 1999). The result has been the "businessification" of peacebuilding, or the ascension of the bureaucratic imperative. The effects of this technocratic turn are profound yet rarely commented upon. It can be seen in the creation of a cadre of peace "professionals" and "experts," the identification of best practices, and the standardization of operating procedures. There is also the proliferation of consulting firms and contractors who engage in peacebuilding and related tasks such as monitoring and evaluation. None of these initiatives are in themselves wrong. However, potential problems can arise because the technocratic turn risks reinforcing certain approaches to peace, and the positions of particular peacemakers. Consequently, alternative non-technocratic approaches to peacebuilding may be overlooked, at least by actors close to formal peacebuilding programs. For example, forms of peacebuilding that draw on customary or traditional practices and social networks may not be considered viable forms of peacebuilding. Technocrats tend to recommend technocratic approaches to conflict, and this, in part, explains how many activities that are described as "peacebuilding" are more precisely a technocratic remodeling in the form of statebuilding, institutional reform, and good governance interventions.

It is worth stressing that technocracy *per se* is not problematic. Yet, the emphasis on technocracy in contemporary approaches to peacemaking has two significant consequences. First, technocracy, or the bureaucratic imperative, tends to exclude creativity, innovation, and alternatives. It has a built-in dependency that emphasizes routine and systemic approaches to problems. As a result, alternative approaches to peace that stray beyond technocratic or prescribed guidelines may be undervalued. Second, technocratic approaches to peace are skewed toward a reliance on the success/failure rubric. For complex institutional reasons, many of them reasonable and entirely understandable, projects and programs are likely to have a series of metrics upon which success or failure can be judged: is the project on time; is it on budget; does it meet its aim as set down in the terms of reference; does it target the constituencies it is meant to target? These questions can be answered with a clear "yes" or "no," or often in measurable ways that point toward success or failure.

US policy in Afghanistan is revealing in the extent to which a series of metrics have been assembled by the Department of Defense and others to give Congress and the presidency indications of "success" or "failure." About 50 measurements combine to make up the government's metric, including the number of Afghan troops trained and the timely delivery of US resources (DeYoung 2009; Cordesman 2011). The metrics tend to be quantitative and observable, and to some extent, are creations of the political and economic dynamics of Washington rather than the exigencies of Afghanistan. The timeline for reporting, and judging success or failure, is set by the US electoral cycle rather than the local situation in Afghanistan. Such metrics risk creating an absurd political economy whereby, for example, US military commanders are judged on their "burn rate" (the rate at which they distribute cash to clients) or the number of *shuras* (local councils) they hold (Chandrasekaran 2010).

Aside from the stark example of Afghanistan, many peacebuilding programs are measured according to skewed metrics that emphasize quantity of delivery rather than quality. Perhaps the main bias is the focus on the intervention (project, program, or initiative) rather than on the wider post-peace accord environment. This is well illustrated by the EU's PEACE III Programme, a peacebuilding effort to support the Northern Ireland peace process. The Programme's aim was to "reinforce progress towards a peaceful and stable society and to progress reconciliation." The Programme was broken into a series of targets, many of them projects that were suspiciously close to recurrent expenditure by local and national government. Progress on meeting targets was measured by how much of the budget was spent, how many meetings were held, the numbers of people enrolled in conflict resolution training projects, and the number of road building and adjustment schemes underway (ASM Horwath 2010). It requires a leap of imagination to equate these targets with "reinforc[ing] progress towards a peaceful and stable society," yet they were taken as metrics of peacebuilding.

Monitoring and evaluation plays a central role in formal peacebuilding, with donors often expecting particular metrics (Kawano-Chiu 2011). Yet a difficulty with many metrics is that questions of quality may be overlooked in the quest to measure quantity. Moreover, many metrics are prone to measuring the success or failure of the intervention (program or project etc.) rather than the extent to which peace prevails or is becoming more embedded.

The key point of this section is to underline how a simplistic success versus failure rubric is often applied to peacemaking by third parties. This is not to say that local actors do not maintain similarly stark rubrics. Yet international actors often wield immense power in constructing the dynamics of peacemaking and so it is worth paying attention to the ways in which they adjudicate over the quality of an outcome.[3] Moreover, international actors may be predisposed to seeing a conflict and peacemaking effort in particular ways (Heathershaw 2008; Denskus 2012). They may be prone to a series of biases that encourage them to focus on peacemaking efforts that are formal, elite-level, focused on reaching a peace deal, and sponsored or approved by the international community. Such peace efforts may be important and have enormous potential, but to focus only on such peace efforts may overlook other initiatives, particularly those that may operate at the community and local levels. Such "initiatives" may take the form of everyday diplomacy by individuals and families as they navigate their way through the complexities of a deeply divided society (Mac Ginty 2014).[4] They may include travel to an area dominated by the outgroup, or economic activity with outgroup members. Much of this activity is likely to be highly localized, and to occur outside the knowledge of international actors. It can take the form of everyday conversations between Nepalese citizens, some of whom may have sympathized with the Maoists and others who were loyal to the monarchy.

While peacemaking at all levels can be prone to being judged against a success/failure rubric, formal and elite peacemaking may be more prone to being judged according to this scale. For example, a formal peace process may have a series of definitive "judgment points" in the form of ceasefires to be observed, deadlines to be met, documents to be agreed upon, or peace deals to be voted upon in a Parliament or more generally through a referendum. Local and community peace initiatives and reconciliation processes are also likely to have judgment points, but these may be informal and the repercussions of "failure" may be localized and contained.

Hybridity

Having cautioned against a blunt success/failure rubric for the measurement of peace processes and peace accord implementation, this section recommends the lens offered by the concepts of hybridity and hybridization as a way of capturing complexity. The hybridity lens encourages us to see the totality of a peacemaking situation over time, rather than compressing it into an elite-level and time-limited process.

Hybridity is not taken as the simple grafting together of two discrete units to make up a third unit. Instead, it is conceived as a longer-term process involving the interchange and negotiation between actors, ideas and practices to form a composite (Mac Ginty 2010, 2011). All societies are hybrids, but societies undergoing peace-support interventions are often prone to considerable hybridizing pressures as a series of international and local actors and norms engage in dizzying processes of conflict and cooperation. The interstices between international and local actors are the scene of hybridization and pattern the peace outcomes as an international-local mix (Richmond 2009).

Hybridization is visible in a post-accord statebuilding program, as internationally mandated standards meet with local customs. The extent of hybridity will differ from context to context. It can be seen, for example, in the adoption of customary practices alongside Western-style judicial processes in Timor-Leste (Gusmão 2003; Kent 2004). Countless subtle hybridizations abound as the local and the international mingle, often promoted by globalization and the influx of new ideas and actors.

This chapter visualizes hybridity in terms of a four-part model whereby various actors in a peace or conflict situation are in constant contact with each other, by accident or design. The parts of the model are in constant movement, and the actors in the model need not necessarily act with any degree of consistency. The four parts of the model are:

- the ability of international actors, structures, and networks to impose their will on local actors;
- the ability of international actors, structures, and networks to incentivize local actors to perform in certain ways;
- the ability of local actors, structures, and networks to adapt, resist, subvert, exploit, delay, ignore, and avoid international pressures;
- the ability of local actors, structures, and networks to construct alternatives to international actors and their version of peace.

The lens offered by hybridity has implications for how we might view peace processes and peace accord implementation. In short, they introduce us to a world in which no actor is able to steer a unilateral course; local actors must take account of international actors and pressures and vice versa so that peacemaking is not simply a case of top-down imposition. Local actors may have considerable agency in terms of delaying, exploiting, ignoring, complicating, and reinterpreting a peace process, and related peacebuilding and reconstruction initiatives. International powers can mobilize considerable resources, but they are also likely to experience blowback and mimicry as their ideas and practices meet with local ideas and practices. In almost every recent conflict zone, local actors have been able to frustrate the exhortations of external actors. At the same time, local actors, however geographically remote, cannot exist in isolation.

The notion of hybridity encourages us to look for fluidity both within and between categories, and to widen our gaze to include local and informal actors as well as the formally organized elites who dominate the study of peace processes. The picture that emerges through the lenses provided by hybridity is a blur of dynamics at once competing and coalescing. This is in keeping with the messy world of societies undergoing conflict and peace processes, in which irresolvable dilemmas and seemingly incompatible entities must somehow find space within the peace process and peace accord implementation program.

Governance, negotiations, and implementation

The concept of hybridity encourages us to examine, in a full way, the processes of negotiation that we find in peace processes. These are not just the formal peace negotiations across a conference table that may result in a peace accord. They also include a series of other informal and everyday negotiations whereby individuals and groups navigate their way through the social world. All individuals and groups, at all levels of society, engage in constant processes of social negotiation to understand their environment, position themselves within it, and to achieve goals (such as those related to livelihood or status). These processes of everyday negotiation may become more fraught in conflict or peace processes where individuals and groups are confronted with new experiences and choices. For example, a white, apartheid-supporting South African in the 1990s would have been confronted with a series of changes that challenged their known universe. Coming to terms with these changes, many of them antithetical to the foundational mores of the society in which they grew up, may require considerable mental and social dexterity. For some individuals, there may be a process of new civic and social engagements, and an acceptance of the existence and grievances of "the other side." For other individuals, there may be a sense of alienation within the new dispensation and a rejection of the notions of reconciliation and a fresh start that may be connected to the peace accord. The presence of a disaffected population may not herald the imminent collapse of a peace accord. Low electoral turnouts in many post-accord Balkan and Central American contexts indicate a resignation that the political classes, and their international backers, have a secure grip on power. Yet a politically disengaged population suggests poor quality peace.

Different forms of governance and negotiation attend different types or phases of negotiation, and this might have a bearing on the quality of peace and how it may be designated as a "success" or "failure." While it is too blunt to have a simple division between formal and informal sets of governance, it is possible to see loose categories around these headings. Formal governance rules are likely to have definitive indicators of whether the rules have been observed or not, or whether targets have been met. The language of "success" and "failure" can be more readily applied in formal governance contexts. For example, it should be possible to gauge if a justice ministry has met benchmarks (such as the training of personnel, or the rebranding of a police force) on a reform program. The picture is less clear with regards to informal governance rules, which will largely apply to the public negotiation, implementation and interpretation of a peace accord.

The formal inter-party negotiations in a peace process are likely to have explicit, often written, rules, perhaps agreed upon through "talks about talks" or in a framework agreement. These rules might cover the location, duration, agenda and participation list of talks (Du Toit 2003). While peace process negotiations have involved guerrillas with little negotiation experience meeting with government officials, in many cases those at the negotiating table have participated in politics before. The desired outcome of many peace negotiations is often a formal written peace accord, or a revised constitution. As a result, it has been common for negotiation teams to include lawyers in their delegations, or to seek negotiation training. Indeed, the Lord's Resistance Army recruited lawyers to its delegation prior to its 2007 negotiations with the Ugandan government (Mukasa 2007). Other forms of expertise have also been represented at the negotiation table, including those skilled at advising on resource sharing and technical economic matters. Formality and rules can play a crucial role in peace negotiations in terms of giving participants confidence in the negotiation process even if they do not have trust in each other. The development of, and respect for, common negotiation rules can act as confidence-building measures.

Just as formal governance rules and clear success/failure indicators are often visible in peace negotiations, they are also visible in many elements of the peace implementation phase of a peace process. This particularly applies to the statebuilding, good governance, DDR and SSR aspects, many of which may be facilitated by international actors and subject to international monitoring and evaluation. Programs and projects in these areas are likely to have metrics according to which donors can monitor progress and declare "success" or "failure."

Beyond the technocratic aspects of peace accord implementation, there is a range of local-level social negotiations less easily measured against the success/failure rubric. This refers to the interpretation and public consumption of the new peace accord and the more general environment in which it attempts to take root. This internalization of an accord is likely to vary according to the context, as well as the individual, group, and region within a post-conflict area. Depending on the context, the peace accord may make a substantive impact on how people lead their lives. For example, it might offer protections that were not previously in place enabling people to take up educational or economic opportunities that were previously unavailable. Some aspects of life may be unchanged, and others may change as an indirect result of peace. For example, the peace accord may result in economic change (good or bad) that has an impact on how life is lived. Many of the aspects of a peace process and accord are subject to informal governance, or a range of shifting societal norms and understandings that fall outside of the ambit of the formal peace process implementation rules. Individuals may speak and act differently in the private sphere—or in-group contexts—than they might in public spheres subject to scrutiny.

Imagine governance as a circle, with formal governance measures at the center. Many of these formal governance measures will be legally enshrined, and national or international actors may be ready to enforce their observance. These measures are likely to cover the core elements of a peace accord (constitutional changes, security provisions) and the statebuilding measures involved in peace accord implementation. Spreading outwards from the center of the circle are levels of governance with weaker formality. These rely on public acceptance and an individual's navigation through a new political landscape. This navigation is unlikely to be uniform across a territory and population, and is likely to take time to change. The success/failure rubric is more likely to pertain and be measureable at the center of the circle than toward its perimeter.

The internalization of a peace accord among individuals and collectives, or the acceptance that a conflict is over and that new modes of life are possible and permissible, may often depend on lived experience. At the local level, this may be a slow process, dependent on word of mouth and observed evidence. While individuals and communities are likely to have their own informal indicators of success or failure, these are unlikely to be measurable in a way that would meet strict bureaucratic or academic standards. The sources of governance (or the rules by which people organize their lives, and possibly their observance of the peace accord) may be extremely varied and draw from a hybrid of state-based legal authority and local norms and practices. Family or religious leaders may play a key role in granting or withholding legitimacy from a peace accord or new dispensation by encouraging subordinates to act in certain ways.

While a peace accord might recommend certain behaviors, there may be extreme variance in the observance of these behaviors. Legal prescriptions and proscriptions can only go so far. Instead, much of the fate of a peace process is likely to lie in the realm of everyday norm-setting and local interpretation. The tiny Gorani minority in Kosovo, for example, has the same formal rights and protections as other citizens, yet they have suffered attacks and discrimination from the Albanian majority because of the perception that they were collaborators with the Serbs (Bell 2008; Brown et al. 2010). The persistence, among some Albanians, of a political culture in which direct and indirect violence is permissible in the political sphere, stands in contradiction with the territory's internationally endorsed legal code.

What we see in many post-conflict societies is the development of hybrid political and legal orders in which the international and the local interact with one another (Bell 2008; Brown 2011; Mac Ginty 2011; Lunn 2013). This meeting of the de jure and de facto sees the merging of customary approaches to law, security, economics, and societal organization with more modern and legalistic forms that are endorsed in a peace accord or new constitution. The result is nondescript, and will not be pleasing to purists who might favor either traditional or modern-rational forms of governance. Herein lies a problem for those that approach peacemaking and peacebuilding from perspectives that draw on Western notions of legitimacy and legalism. Many proponents of such forms of peacemaking see the development of hybrid forms of politics as a deviation from the preferred model or as policy failure. Despite talk of partnership, local participation, and local ownership, many peacebuilding initiatives associated with liberal internationalism betray an intolerance toward deviation from the original policy objective. Under the success/failure rubric, hybrid forms of peace and politics are seen as "failures." Yet, in some cases, a more generous assessment is deserved. What Western donors and policymakers may see as failure may tell a more complex story of meaningful local engagement with policies. Formal methods of monitoring and evaluation that focus solely on a particular project or program, or on the strict observance of a peace accord, may fail to see the complex ways in which local communities may interact with a peace initiative or aspects of a peace accord.

It is important to not romanticize the local. Hybridity can act as a mask for exclusion, discrimination, or violence. Peace initiatives and accords can be diminished by local practices and interpretations that perpetuate conflict and the subordination of one group by another. Yet, in certain circumstances, hybridity can be regarded as a local engagement with aspects of a peace accord and the transformation of a formal document into a living accord. This might involve local and variable interpretations of aspects of a peace accord, and a deviation from its literal interpretation. According to a success/failure rubric, such hybridity would be failure. Yet such a view seems unrealistic given the on-the-ground experience of peace accords and peace accord implementation projects. It seems more sensible to regard peace as open to various interpretations. Rather than the complete implementation of a peace accord, most societies experience a partial implementation or a variable implementation. It seems prudent to aim for "enough implementation." Of course, the immediate questions are: How much is enough? And what elements of a peace accord are to be left unimplemented or partially implemented?

Perhaps such questions are best answered by way of an example. Consider the case of Nepal where a Comprehensive Peace Accord was reached in 2006. The peace accord, reinforced by a revised constitution, is a detailed document envisioning a socio-economic transformation as well as steps toward a political accommodation that would end the insurgency. The latter has ended (although final agreement on DDR did not occur until late 2011) and considerable political and security sector restructuring has taken place. Yet, many of the more ambitious socio-economic and cultural aims have only been addressed partially, or not at all. Moreover, the April 2015 earthquake added to the already daunting development and reconstruction problems. The peace accord seeks to "end discriminations based on class, ethnicity, language, gender, culture, religion and region and to address the problems of women, Dalit, indigenous people, ethnic minorities (Janajatis), Terai communities (Madheshis), oppressed, neglected and minority communities and the backward areas".[5] The resolution of such discrimination will involve long-term processes operating at all levels of society and involving multiple internal and external institutions. A literal evaluation of the peace accord may be tempted to declare progress in these areas as "failures" (just as an examination of discrimination in societies in the global North is likely to reveal some unpalatable truths). In some cases, however, a mix of formal (new legislation) and informal (conversations among families, observed experiences) governance may mean that there are some advances with regards to tackling discrimination. Such hybrid forms of governance would not meet the standards of Western liberalism, but they may be the modus vivendi required for the post-peace accord society to move on.

Conclusion

The key question stemming from this chapter is to consider whose quality standards are the best to judge peace? When discussing top-down and bottom-up approaches to peace, it is tempting to demonize all things international and external, and romanticize all things local and indigenous. In truth, both sets of actors and the values that they bring with them are likely to have merits and drawbacks. Moreover, both sets of actors and their values are likely to contain much diversity.

It seems that a balance must be struck in our analysis of peace. There has been a strong trend, driven by technocratic pressures, toward ways of measuring peace that tend to overlook the everyday and locally-lived experience of war-to-peace transitions. Many of these measures focus on the quantity of peace rather than on its quality. At the same time, those interested in the quality of peace cannot be expected to undertake a permanent ethnography that provides a micro-analysis of each community or individual during a war-to-peace transition. What is needed though, is an epistemology that is mature enough to appreciate both quantitative and qualitative approaches to peace, and has a humility that does not prioritize Western social science above all other possible ways of capturing peace. At the moment, many approaches to gauging the quality of peace seem overly focused on post-accord statebuilding milestones, and on the cessation of direct violence. These aspects of peace are important, but they cannot be considered sufficient measures of the quality of peace.

One of the noticeable aspects of many post-Cold War peace accord societies is that they have been able to chug along after the initial peace accord euphoria with low levels of popular legitimacy and often-poor social and economic inclusion. As long as the society does not slip back into all out civil war, and as long as it does not upset the international order, then it is regarded as "at peace." Yet, these are more accurately described as "no war, no peace" situations and can be found in Mozambique, Bosnia-Herzegovina, El Salvador and many other locations. Popular disaffection has not led to a reversion to civil war, but at the same time the absence of a new civil war should not be taken as an indicator of a quality peace.

Notes

1. This theme is also discussed in the contribution by Brounéus and Guthrey in Chapter 9 of this volume.

2. The move nevertheless resulted in Palestine being awarded the status of "non-member observer state" in the General Assembly in 2012, and having its flag with other states outside the building since 2015.
3. In the contribution by Guardado et al. in Chapter 5 of this volume, a different application of such measures is pursued.
4. See also the Everyday Peace Indicators project that attempts to crowd-source vernacular indicators of peace and change at local level in conflict-affected societies: everydaypeace indicators.org.
5. See https://peaceaccords.nd.edu/accord/comprehensive-peace-agreement.

References

Abbas, Mahmoud. "Full transcript of Abbas speech at UN Assembly." *Haaretz*, September 23, 2011. Accessed September 29, 2017 at www.haaretz.com/israel-news/full-transcript-of-abbas-speech-at-un-general-assembly-1.386385.

ASM Horwath. *Special EU programmes body, review of the implementation of PEACE III, theme 1.1, Building positive relations at the local level, final report*. October 21, 2010. Accessed September 29, 2017 at www.pobal.ie/Publications/Documents/PEACE%20III_ASM%20Howarth%20Theme%201.1%20final%20report%20-%20Oct%202010.pdf.

Bell, Christine. *On the law of peace: Peace agreements and the Lex Pacificatoria*. Oxford: Oxford University Press, 2008.

Box, Richard C. "Running government like a business implications for public administration theory and practice." *The American Review of Public Administration* 29, no. 1 (1999): 19–43.

Brown, Anne, Volker Boege, Kevin Clements, and Anna Nolan. "Challenging Statebuilding as Peacebuilding—Working with Hybrid Political Orders to Build Peace." in Oliver P. Richmond, Ed. *Palgrave advances in peacebuilding: Critical developments and approaches*. Palgrave, 2010: 99–116.

Chandrasekaran, Rajiv. "In Afghan region, US spreads cash to fight Taliban." *Washington Post*, May 31, 2010.

Cordesman, Anthony H. *Afghanistan and the uncertain metrics of progress*. Center for Strategic and International Studies, 2011.

Denskus, Tobias. "Challenging the international peacebuilding evaluation discourse with qualitative methodologies." *Evaluation and Program Planning* 35, no. 1 (2012): 148–153.

DeVotta, Neil. "From ethnic outbidding to ethnic conflict: the institutional bases for Sri Lanka's separatist war." *Nations and Nationalism* 11, no. 1 (2005): 141–159.

DeYoung, Karen. "US assembles metrics to weigh progress in Afghanistan and Pakistan." *Washington Post*, August 20, 2009.

Donais, Timothy. "Empowerment or imposition? Dilemmas of local ownership in post-conflict peacebuilding processes." *Peace & Change* 34, no. 1 (2009): 3–26.

Dummett, Ben. "BlackBerry posts surprise quarterly profit." *Wall Street Journal*, March 27, 2015.

Du Toit, Pierre. "Rules and Procedures for Negotiated Peacemaking." In John Darby and Roger Mac Ginty, Eds. *Contemporary peacemaking: Conflict, violence, and peace processes*. Palgrave Macmillan, 2003: 65–76.

Gusmão, Kay Rala Xanana. 2003. "Challenges for peace and stability." *The Vice Chancellor's Human Right's Lecture by His Excellency President Gusmão*. University of Melbourne, April 7, 2003.

Heathershaw, John. "Seeing like the international community: how peacebuilding failed (and survived) in Tajikistan." *Journal of intervention and statebuilding* 2, no. 3 (2008): 329–351.

Kawano-Chiu, Melanie. "Starting on the same page: A lessons report from the Peacebuilding Evaluation Project." Alliance for Peacebuilding, 2011.

Kent, Lia. "Unfulfilled expectations: Community views on CAVR's community reconciliation process." *Dili: Judicial System Monitoring Program* (2004).

Lederach, John Paul. *Preparing for peace: Conflict transformation across cultures*. Syracuse University Press, 1995.

Lunn, John. "Nepal's endless peace process, 2006–2012." *House of Commons Research Briefing, SN04229*, October 11, 2013.

Mac Ginty, Roger. "Indigenous peace-making versus the liberal peace." *Cooperation and Conflict* 43, no. 2 (2008): 139–163.

Mac Ginty, Roger. "Hybrid peace: The interaction between top-down and bottom-up peace." *Security Dialogue* 41, no. 4 (2010): 391–412.

Mac Ginty, Roger. *International peacebuilding and local resistance: Hybrid forms of peace*. Springer, 2011.

Mac Ginty, Roger. "Everyday peace: Bottom-up and local agency in conflict-affected societies." *Security Dialogue* 45, no. 6 (2014): 548–564.

Mukasa, Henry. "Lawyers in Juba to boost peace talks." *Africa News Service*, June 22, 2007.

Netanyahu, Benjamin. "Full transcript of Netanyahu speech at UN General Assembly." *Haaretz*, September 24, 2011.

Richmond, Oliver P. "Becoming liberal, unbecoming liberalism: Liberal-local hybridity via the everyday as a response to the paradoxes of liberal peacebuilding." *Journal of Intervention and Statebuilding* 3, no. 3 (2009): 324–344.

Sahovic, Dzenan. *Socio-cultural viability of international intervention in war-torn societies: A case study of Bosnia Herzegovina*. Umeå University, 2007.

Salter, Mark. *To end a civil war: Norway's peace engagement in Sri Lanka*. Oxford University Press, 2015.

Scott, James C. *Weapons of the weak: Everyday forms of peasant resistance*. Yale University Press, 2008.

Sisk, Timothy D. *Power sharing and international mediation in ethnic conflicts*. United States Institute of Peace Press, 1996.

Stephanopoulos, George. *All too human: A political education*. Back Bay Books, 2008.

5

QUALITY PEACE IN POST-CIVIL WAR SETTINGS

The role of local institutions

Jenny Guardado, Leonard Wantchekon, and Sarah Weltman

Introduction—The "peace" dilemma

How to achieve *quality* peace in post-civil war settings? In this chapter, we argue that the promotion of local-level institutions can significantly improve the success rate of peace agreements[1] in countries previously ravaged by civil war. By engaging actors at the local level, it is possible to reduce violence in the short term (*sustainable* peace) but also achieve the more substantive goal of giving local actors a stake in the construction of peace. Reducing violence *via* the promotion of local-level institutions channeling political conflict is what we call *quality* peace. Quality peace is a crucial goal considering the large number of countries that have experienced internal armed conflict in the post-World War II era.

However, while the bulk of the empirical literature has mostly focused on the *causes* of war, we follow a different trend (embodied in this volume) and examine conflict termination instead. Specifically, we look at the prospects for quality peace to emerge from negotiated settlements (or peace agreements) in contexts where civil war used to be the norm. That is, conditional on entering a peace agreement, can the inclusion of individuals and communities improve the success rates and quality of peace? Can the emphasis on individuals and communities better predict success rates than approaches focused on elites and security concerns? We look at *negotiated* conflict terminations because it provides a clear opportunity for Non-Governmental Organizations (NGOs), local communities, and grassroots actors to get involved in the implementation process, which is not always possible under other conflict termination situations.[2] Moreover, this topic is relevant considering how civil wars ending with negotiated settlements have been found prone to collapse and violence to reoccur (DeRouen and Bercovith 2008). In fact, peace agreements are arguably more prone to failure than peace reached by military victory by one of the warring sides (Licklider 1995; Fortna 2004a; Mason et al. 2005; Toft 2006).

For example, the UCDP Peace Agreement Dataset, which by definition looks at negotiated peace arrangements, shows how by the fifth year after the arrangement, 42 percent of peace agreements see violence resume among the same parties (Harbom et al. 2006). Still, trying to achieve peace via negotiations appears to be the preferred method of conflict resolution in the post-Cold War world (Hartzell and Hoddie 2007). Given the prevalence of armed conflict in the world, small policy changes that can be adopted to prevent war recurrence must be seriously considered.

Peace from "above" or peace from "below"?

Extant literature on post-conflict peacebuilding broadly fits one of two categories that can be called "top-down" measures in contrast to "bottom-up" approaches.[3] By "top-down" measures we refer to policies seeking peace through changes at the national level, involving national actors and institutions, so called "macro" changes. For example, measures promoting peace through disarmament among warring elites, often under close external supervision and intervention; views championing economic and social reforms at the national level as a guarantor of peace; and prescriptions for power-sharing among warring elites generally at the national level. The expectation is that once these measures are in place, peace will then "trickle down" from these macro changes to the micro level.

Yet, the lack of effects observed at the micro-level after "top-down" measures have been implemented calls into question the mechanism through which these effects might occur (Mvukiyehe and Samii 2010). Moreover, while the "top-down" approach was until recently the dominant explanation for sustainable peace, the recurrence of armed conflict in settings implementing this approach prompts the creation of additional policies focused at the local level to improve its rates of success. For instance, evidence on the role of external actors (a "top-down" measure) on lasting peace has provided mixed results at best. On the one hand, Doyle and Sambanis (2000) highlight the positive role of external actors by showing how the presence of UN peacekeepers serves as an enforcement mechanism in the absence of state capacity. Similarly, Fortna (2004a) establishes that peacekeeping operations help stabilize post-civil war countries by contributing to a lasting peace even once peacekeepers have departed. On the other hand, Gilligan and Sergenti (2008) find that while UN peacekeeping missions are successful in settings where civil wars are over, this is not the case for ongoing conflicts. Moreover, it is not clear whether UN peacekeeping operations can lead to a shorter duration of conflict or if the effects depend on which faction they side with (DeRouen and Sobek 2004). For instance, it appears that outside military intervention to support rebel groups does lead to a shorter duration of war (Collier et al. 2008). However, to indiscriminately support rebel factions to shorten war might not be a sound policy prescription. Part of these non-conclusive patterns are due to underlying coding issues, methodological hurdles, and the inclusion or omission of certain control variables. Hence, future research on specific mechanisms through which military intervention can shorten conflict must be explored.

The second key feature of "top-down" approaches is the inclusion of power-sharing agreements among the national elite as well as institutional reforms conducted at the national level. Glassmyer and Sambanis (2008) discuss power-sharing provisions and specifically highlight the benefits of military-based power-sharing to solve issues of credible disarmament. Military integration would in theory provide guarantees for rebel groups to enter peace agreements; yet, the authors do not find empirical support for its effect on sustainable peace. In the case of government integration, Joshi and Mason (2011) do provide evidence that negotiated arrangements enlarging the size of the governing coalition are key to lasting peace. Another example is given by Hartzell and Hoddie (2003a; 2003b; 2007), who argue that peace agreements including provisions for power-sharing in economic, territorial, government, and military areas result in longer periods of peace. The empirical evidence appears to support their claim, that a more "horizontal" division of power is conducive to peace thus highlighting the importance of the distribution of political power among different actors.[4] Power-sharing marks an important first step in the establishment of peace and political order following a civil war by attempting to create a fairer division of power. However, the policy prescription of centering on national institutions is misplaced considering these measures often fail to include small, yet powerful, local leadership structures that are quite frequent in highly decentralized countries. Thus, our argument runs parallel to that of power-sharing agreements (horizontal distribution), yet is expanded to include local-level institutions and actors (vertical integration).

The last main feature of "top-down" arrangements are those calling for some type of economic and/or institutional reforms, which some authors have highlighted as important for sustainable peace. For instance, Doyle and Sambanis (2000) have established how external peacekeepers may serve as a short-term substitute when local institutional capacity is lacking. Similar conclusions are reached by Collier et al. (2008) who note that peace agreements are more successful at higher levels of economic development. In response to such concerns, peacekeeping missions have now adopted a "multidimensional" approach by directing peacekeeping efforts to economic and social realms, beyond the mere provision of security. Still, it is not particularly clear that these efforts have been widely successful, or if they have, why this is the case (Mvukiyehe and Samii 2010).

In contrast to "top-down" measures, "bottom-up" approaches emphasize the importance of community engagement, inclusiveness of local actors and the importance of building peace from a micro-level (Mac Ginty 2008, 2010). Although a growing body of work has looked at the inter-connectedness of both approaches for sustainable peace (Donais 2012) and their potential limitations (Millar et. al. 2013), such "bottom-up" approaches remain both under-theorized and empirically under-tested, thus making the findings hard to generalize from. One exception to such trends is the foreign aid literature, which has coined the term "Community-Driven Reconstruction" (CDR) to refer to this "bottom-up" approach when referring to post-civil war settings or "Community-Driven Development" (CDD) to refer more broadly to development projects (Fearon et. al. 2009, 2015; Casey et. al. 2012; Avdeenko and Gilligan 2015; among others). The logic of CDR is similar to ours, by granting to the most affected individuals from conflict a stake in their own recovery as the path for sustainable peace and economic development. However, the CDR emphasis on individual participation has only cursorily looked at issues of local distribution of power, which coupled with governance sharing at the local level can give peace better prospects to last.[5] An important example of bottom-up approaches is that of Fearon et al. who find that enhanced social cohesion is an outcome that can be achieved through short-term foreign aid interventions (2009). Despite the belief that patterns of social interaction are a slow-changing variable, the authors do find that their short-term intervention significantly improved social cohesion while those communities in which it was absent fared worse.[6] We broaden this prescription by adding that beyond social cohesion, the culture of peacefully addressing political conflict must be built bottom-up starting at the community level and putting individuals in charge of their own fates and creating institutions able to address political conflict.[7]

In this chapter, we add to current studies of "bottom-up" approaches to peace in two ways. First, we emphasize the importance of provisions at the local level in peace agreements. While the inclusion of national elites and grand disarmament plans are crucial, sustaining long periods of peace may be better served by acknowledging the preferences of local actors often excluded from negotiation tables, hence avoiding excessive elite-centrism. Second, a focus on local-level provisions will give individuals, organizations, and communities a stake in the enforcement of the agreement, which will greatly enhance the prospects for peace in such places. These organizations may include labor unions, farmer groups, women's organizations, commerce associations, and student groups. By giving civilians a stake via local power-sharing in the enforcement and implementation of the peace agreement, these groups can constitute an essential component of the post-civil war equation. For instance, these groups can be useful to overcome the lack of credible commitment by various actors; a failure to observe the peace agreement will have additional costs (e.g., electoral and popularity) if the agreement involves a larger number of actors at every level of government (not only at the national one). Existing studies suggest this is the case (Nilsson 2012; Paffenholz 2014). In the next section, we look at whether the inclusion of such local provisions in the negotiation phase of peace agreements, as a proxy of local-level involvement, is an important variable that contributes to our understanding of quality peace.

Post-conflict peace and local institutions—the missing link

In this chapter, we rely on two datasets that provide information on conflict termination (UCDP Conflict Termination Dataset) and peace agreements (UCDP Peace Agreement Dataset). The idea is to provide two pieces of evidence that would help both clarify and support the idea of sustainable peace "from below" (or quality peace) at different levels of government. First, we show that the likelihood of an armed conflict between 1946 and 2009 ending in a peace agreement is actually slim for civil wars (Kreutz 2010). Second, conditional on negotiating a peace agreement, we look at the specific content of negotiated settlements signed between 1989 and 2005. As stated earlier, the content of peace agreements can greatly change the costs of reinitiating the conflict (Fortna 2004b). Therefore, if local provisions are associated with a lower recurrence of violence, it could be the starting point to adopt at the negotiating stage of the conflict.

In terms of the two datasets we use, both (conflict termination and peace agreements) are country-level or macro-level ones. Our first dataset, on conflict termination, contains information on the number of conflicts that ended and on the characteristics of how the conflict ended (Kreutz 2010). In its version v.2010–1, it covers conflict activity and means of termination for episodes between 1946 and 2009. We only focus on intrastate armed conflicts. This dataset helps us establish the likelihood of a conflict ending in a peace agreement or a military victory and gives us a sense of how often third parties can influence outcomes. In the second dataset, we use the peace agreement data (UCDP Peace Agreement Dataset) that covers all peace agreements among warring parties signed between 1989 and 2005 (first version). Although this dataset is comprehensive, the time span it covers does not entirely match the one covered in the conflict termination dataset, making it difficult to merge without losing a large number of instances of conflict. We will nonetheless conduct a separate analysis of such peace agreements. The idea of analyzing peace agreements is to assess to what extent peace processes are dominated by "top-down" approaches and how the incorporation of local provisions or "bottom-up" measures correlate with a reduction in future violence.

Conflict termination and peace agreements

First, how frequently do intrastate conflicts end in a peace agreement? To assess the likelihood of intrastate conflicts ending in peace agreements in the post-World War II era, we use the UCDP Conflict Termination Dataset. The dataset contains 265 intrastate conflict episodes out of 367 total conflict episodes. Of these, only 42 episodes (11.4 percent) ended in a peace agreement. By peace agreement, it is meant an agreement (or the first in a series of them) designed to solve the causes of the conflict. Similarly, agreements to ceasefire or regulate the conflict comprise around 39, or 10.3 percent, of all cases, which in addition to peace agreements, account for 21.8 percent of all conflict episodes. An alternative to a signed agreement is that of a military victory (*victory*) being the cause of violence termination. In this category, we find 102 observations of military victory, or 27.8 percent of the total. Finally, as stated by Kreutz (2010), a great majority of conflict terminations, around 40 percent, fall under the category of "low activity" and "other" thus challenging the common perception that either peace agreements or military victory are the relevant outcomes. Figure 5.1 exhibits the distribution of termination causes between 1946 and 2009 for each category.

80 J. Guardado et al.

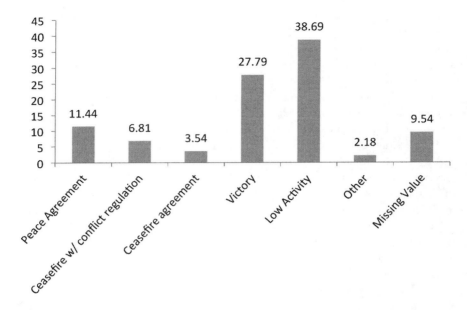

FIGURE 5.1 Distribution of *intrastate* conflict termination by type: 1946–2009
Source: Kreutz, Joakim. "How and when armed conflicts end: Introducing the UCDP Conflict Termination dataset." *Journal of Peace Research* 47, no. 2 (2010): 243–250.

Incorporating a time dimension, we find patterns consistent with previous results in the literature, in particular, the idea that negotiated peace has become the most prevalent method of conflict resolution after the 1990s (Hartzell and Hoddie 2007). Yet, which provisions in a negotiated accord can bring about sustainable peace? Below we analyze the data looking at the potential role of local-level provisions on sustainable peace.

Peace agreements: national or local power sharing?

Research on peace agreements as a determinant of sustainable peace has not received enough scholarly attention, excepting studies from Hartzell and Hoddie (2003a, 2003b, 2007) that examine power-sharing terms in the negotiated settlement. The content of peace settlements is crucial in designing institutions that would promote an enduring peace. For instance, Hartzell and Hoddie (2007) look at what can be called "horizontal" power-sharing institutions establishing the distribution of political, military, economic or territorial dividends. Instead, we look at "vertical" divisions of power that would grant more power to lower levels of government thus moving away from purely national elites. Both approaches should be seen as complementary to each other; as we move to lower levels of government (or "vertically" integrating), more horizontal power-sharing arrangements can be implemented. As suggested earlier, we believe this is a crucial feature in the agreement that would give voice to local actors (many of them with quite substantial local influence) and a stake in the duration of peace. Moreover, giving a voice to local actors organized in distinct groups would better enhance peaceful conflict resolution. Our expectation is that peace agreements introducing these local-level measures have an effect by not only being more specific, but also by including local actors.

Using the UCDP Peace Agreement Dataset from Harbom et al. (2006), we find a strong relationship between provisions for local-level measures (specifically, local governance) and lasting peace.[8] The dataset includes 148 peace agreements signed between warring parties during the period 1989–2005 for "territorial or governmental incompatibility" conflicts. Unlike Hartzell and Hoddie (2003a, 2003b), we look at a different time frame and dimensions of power-sharing by incorporating the local-level dimension. Our measures of local-level involvement are whether provisions for the warring factions to share power at the local level (*shaloc*) were included. Specifically, it refers to whether "the agreement granted the disputed region power-sharing in the local government." The second variable captures whether provisions for local governance "short of autonomy" were included in the peace agreement (*locgov*). In particular, the variable captures those "arrangements for local self-government short of autonomy or the exercise of power through municipal arrangements." Finally, the inclusion of cultural freedoms (*cul*) can also influence community interactions especially places with ethnic or religious minorities. We do not deem this variable as specifically "local" so we will analyze it separately.

As a measure of macro or "top-down" measures to peace we include three concepts. First, whether the peace agreement included power-sharing provisions such as the integration of rebel members into the army (*intarmy*), power-sharing in the government (*intgov*), or power-sharing in the civil service (*pp*). Such variables have been greatly emphasized by Hartzell and Hoddie (2003a, 2003b). Second, because a crucial concern of the "top-down" approach is whether security concerns are addressed, we create a variable indicating whether there is disarmament of warring parts (*ddr*) and/or the deployment of peacekeeping operations (*pko*). The idea is to look at whether the presence of external parties enhances peace durability. Our third way to measure "top-down" approaches focuses on political reforms, or whether peace agreements included elections (*elections*) as part of the settlement. Often, elections are a good way to solve incompatibility problems in the political arena (Harbom et. al. 2006).

Yet how frequently are "bottom-up" and "top-down" measures implemented? Table 5.1 shows the distribution of local provisions in the peace agreements studied. As shown, the vast majority of negotiated peace settlements include *no* provisions for local power-sharing, cultural freedoms, or local governance. Only 27 out of 148 peace agreements (18.24 percent) during the period included provisions for local governance; six agreements (4 percent) include local power-sharing provisions, and 14 cases (9.5 percent) include cultural freedoms in the agreement to end hostilities.

The evidence provided so far says nothing about their effect on sustainable peace, yet, it is still important to show the relative infrequency of "local" provisions in

TABLE 5.1 Peace agreements with local provisions: 1989–2005

Variable	Freq.	Percent
No local power-sharing	142	95.95
Local power-sharing	6	4.05
No cultural freedoms	134	90.54
Cultural freedoms	14	9.46
No local governance	121	81.76
Local governance	27	18.24

Source: Harbom, Lotta, Stina Högbladh, and Peter Wallensteen. "Armed conflict and peace agreements." *Journal of Peace Research* 43, no. 5 (2006): 617–631.

the peace negotiations. A possible reason is that these peace agreements are settled among the elites of warring parts that may then focus entirely on macro- or national-level reforms. In addition, one might think that provisions for local governance or for local power-sharing are exclusively concerned with *territorial* conflicts which might seek regional autonomy. Once we look at the proportions, we find some evidence to believe that the latter might be the case, yet, for our main variable of interest (local governance), the difference is small.

As shown in Table 5.2, local governance provisions are included in 36.3 percent of territorial conflicts, although only in 10.5 percent of government conflicts. In other words, local governance provisions are particularly absent from government conflicts and are effectively more prevalent in territorial conflicts. The same pattern is true for provisions that establish local government sharing. This pattern would be problematic if territorial conflicts had a higher likelihood of *not* relapsing into violence within the next 5 years. In such case, any positive effect of "local provisions" in sustaining peace would be only reflecting the type of conflict and *not* an independent effect of including these provisions. Therefore, in all our specifications we will include a control for the type of conflict.

TABLE 5.2 Local and cultural provisions by type of conflict

	Territory	Government	Total
No local governance	28	93	121
%	63.64	89.42	81.76
Local governance	16	11	27
%	36.36	10.58	18.24
No sharing local governance	39	103	142
%	88.64	99.04	95.95
Sharing local governance	5	1	6
%	11.36	0.96	4.05

Source: Harbom, Lotta, Stina Högbladh, and Peter Wallensteen. "Armed conflict and peace agreements." *Journal of Peace Research* 43, no. 5 (2006): 617–631.

In contrast to local-level or "bottom-up" provisions, Table 5.3 shows the proportion of agreements including "power-sharing" arrangements among the negotiating parties. By "power-sharing" we determine whether the peace agreement included military, government or civil service provisions to divide power among actors. If the peace agreement contained all three, the variable was coded as "3"; if it only included two then it was coded as a "2," and so on. As shown, most peace agreements do *not* include a power-sharing provision, with very few establishing all three types of power-sharing in the military, government and civil service (10.14 percent). This fact has motivated some authors to promote more comprehensive power-sharing agreements, yet, we argue that such divisions have to include more vertical integration among all levels of government and not only at the national level (or horizontal ones). Moreover, below we show that these power-sharing agreements have a smaller explanatory power with regards to sustainable peace than the inclusion of local governance ones.

The final concern is that of sustainable peace being mainly influenced by the implementation of disarmament and peacekeeping operations (*security*). Yet, interestingly enough, peace agreements with either disarmament or peacekeeping operations only comprise around 50 percent of the agreements (74 cases), yet, there is a significant number in which both are included (22 cases). Electoral provisions are not always included in peace agreements, since only 37.8 percent of the cases include elections as a measure of political reform at the national level. As expected, elections occur more frequently in cases of government incompatibility, than of territorial claims. In sum, while more prevalent, there is significant variation in the extent to which "top-down" and "bottom-up" measures are included in peace agreements. Yet, are "top-down" or "bottom-up" better able to predict the success rate of the peace agreement?

Table 5.4 presents results from a *probit* regression comparing violence outbreak within 5 years of the negotiated peace settlement with a "bottom-up" measure to those without it. As shown in Columns (1), (2) and (3), the "bottom-up" approach exhibits a larger and more robust *negative* effect on the likelihood of violence outbreak, at least within the following next 5 years after the peace agreement was signed. In Column (2) we included regional fixed effects (that controls for

TABLE 5.3 Peace agreements with power-sharing provisions: 1989–2005

Variable	Freq.	Percent
No power-sharing	83	56.08
One provision	31	20.95
Two provisions	19	12.84
All three provisions	15	10.14
Total	148	100

Source: Harbom, Lotta, Stina Högbladh, and Peter Wallensteen. "Armed conflict and peace agreements." *Journal of Peace Research* 43, no. 5 (2006): 617–631.

region-specific characteristics of the conflicts located in Europe, Middle East, Asia, Africa, and the Americas)[9] to control for any region-specific features that might influence how prone it is to resume violence. Since the omitted category is Europe, all other regions would naturally have a higher likelihood of violence outbreak starting with the Middle East, followed by Asia, Africa, and the Americas. The second main control is the type of "incompatibility" between the warring factions (territorial or governmental).[10] Although a crude measure, it might alleviate concerns that local provisions reflect a specific type of underlying conflict which in turn is less likely to relapse into violence. After controlling for these factors, a "bottom-up" approach still appears to have a strong positive effect on lasting peace. Other controls include year effects, which accounts for temporal shocks that might affect all agreements (e.g., end of the Cold War) in a given year and are included in all specifications. Finally, we control for the extent to which the agreement is comprehensive or not.

TABLE 5.4 *Probit* analysis of the effect of local provisions on violence outbreak

Variables	Violence—within 5 years				
	(1)	(2)	(3)	(4)	(5)
Local provisions	−1.279***	−	−	−	−1.351***
	(0.454)	−	−	−	(0.460)
Power-sharing	−	−0.776**	−	−	−0.796**
	−	(0.354)	−	−	(0.382)
Security	−	−	−0.254	−	0.0143
	−	−	(0.285)	−	(0.318)
Political (elections)	−	−	−	−0.465	−0.537
				(0.327)	(0.343)
Type of conflict	0.412	1.093**	0.694	0.919**	1.041*
	(0.478)	(0.513)	(0.428)	(0.442)	(0.595)
Comprehensive PA	0.645*	0.428	0.714**	0.794**	0.577*
	(0.332)	(0.316)	(0.316)	(0.309)	(0.340)
Middle East	6.891***	6.352***	6.300***	6.560***	6.878***
	(0.696)	(0.820)	(0.833)	(0.876)	(0.814)
Asia	6.591***	6.365***	6.223***	6.271***	6.763***
	(0.708)	(0.767)	(0.763)	(0.836)	(0.806)
Africa	6.029***	5.899***	5.701***	5.754***	6.197***
	(0.700)	(0.770)	(0.768)	(0.841)	(0.797)
Americas	5.437***	4.998***	5.079***	5.067***	5.000***
	(0.651)	(0.788)	(0.762)	(0.807)	(0.788)
Constant	−2.209***	−3.167***	−2.559***	−3.142***	−3.566***
	(0.836)	(1.049)	(0.921)	(1.083)	(1.116)
Observations	124	124	124	124	124

Robust standard errors in parentheses. *** $p<0.01$, ** $p<0.05$, * $p<0.1$

As shown in Column (1) the effect of local provisions has a negative and statistically significant effect on the likelihood of an outbreak of violence. Even after controlling for regionally-fixed effects and the type of conflict, the coefficient on the variable of power-sharing provisions appears to be even larger as shown in Column (2). Also, consistent with previous statements, *government* conflicts seem to have a higher likelihood of violent outbreaks than *territorial* incompatibilities. When we look at Column (3) we see that there is some evidence that "power-sharing" effectively reduces the likelihood of violent outbreaks, thus consistent with previous findings on the matter (Hartzell and Hoddie 2003a, 2003b). Yet we also notice that the coefficient is smaller in magnitude than the local provision variable, although statistically significant. Thus, there is some logic and support for the idea of negotiating among elites, although it is shown to have a lower explanatory power. Other concepts commonly considered as "top-down" such as security provisions (disarmament and peacekeeping operations) are not associated in any significant way with the likelihood of an outbreak of violence. A mere focus on security issues appears to not be the complete solution to the problem of lasting peace as shown in Column (4). In contrast, elections seem to have a negative and statistically significant effect, even larger than the coefficient of the "power-sharing" variable. However, this result is not robust with the inclusion of year-fixed effects; therefore, we will limit our discussion to the results from *power-sharing* and *local provisions* agreements.

One potential critique is that there is an overlap in what *local provisions* capture and the idea of *power-sharing*. However, the pair-wise correlation table (in the Appendix) shows how the correlation among power-sharing and local provisions is low and not statistically significant. In fact, we find a higher correlation between *power-sharing*, *security*, and *electoral* variables than with local provision. This result is not surprising considering they all reflect the "top-down" approach to peace negotiations. Therefore, local provisions seem to capture a specific type of peace agreement content and not just the same characteristics as those included in "top-down" approaches.

Finally, in Column (5) we include all the relevant variables and show how the sign and magnitude of the coefficient on the variable on local provisions is even greater than in previous specifications. Moreover, the coefficient on the variables of a "top-down" approach is still small compared to "local provisions." Although this analysis does not state a causal effect of "bottom-up" provisions on violence reduction, it does say that the inclusion of such measures is correlated with a lower likelihood of violence. However, different "local provisions" may have a different effect on violence reduction. Therefore, in Table 5.5 we separate the "local provisions" variables into its two components: local governance and local power-sharing. When comparing both variables we find that local governance is the variable driving the results with a large and negative effect on the likelihood of experiencing subsequent violence which remains significant even after controlling for all other provisions and different regions.

Similar to Table 5.4, the coefficients on power sharing are negative and statistically significant, yet of a smaller magnitude than local governance as shown in

Column (5). Even after including year effects, the larger effect of local governance remains. Finally, it is noteworthy that the effect of security provisions on preventing violence onset is not statistically different from zero.

One of the difficulties with this analysis is that durable peace settlements may be particularly likely to include local power-sharing agreements, thus confounding the otherwise positive impact these provisions could have (*selection bias*). Moreover, it is also possible that some unobserved variable is driving both the inclusion of local provisions and the likelihood that violence does not break out within the next 5 years (*omitted variable bias*). For instance, state capacity may play an intervening role (De Rouen et. al. 2010; McBride et. al. 2011). We do not have a specific way to tackle such problems, except for being cautious in the interpretation of the coefficients by stating only a correlation among them. Still, we find it insightful to look at the explanatory power of otherwise unexplored aspects of peace agreements, such as *local governance*. Finally, we also acknowledge that the dataset includes only certain types of conflicts (those that ended in a peace agreement) while we know that a large number of conflicts are settled with a military victory or not settled at all. Future research to systematically address peace agreements and their subsequent effect on violence outbreaks would be fruitful.

In sum, although the estimation of causal effects is beyond the scope of this chapter, there is a clear statistical association between the inclusion of local governance provisions and the lower recurrence of violence. It is also possible that peace agreements including local governance provisions tend to be more specific, which apparently increases the likelihood of the agreement to be enforced and peace to last (Fortna 2003). Even if this is so, the inclusion of local provisions is a policy associated with enhanced prospects of quality peace. For instance, at the negotiation stage of peace agreements, participants of the peace negotiations can be encouraged to think about local provisions at the community level in the form of village councils and neighborhood organizations which can be formalized (and implemented) to promote civilian participation and interaction. Engaging a large number of parties in local governance could in theory discourage defection and prevent violence from reoccurring.

Conclusion

This chapter has examined how local governance provisions affect the durability of peace agreements in post-civil war settings. Although peace agreements were not a common phenomenon until recently, we believe it is an area in which NGOs, foreign governments, and international organizations can greatly influence the terms in which peace is organized to reduce future violence. We present evidence showing that peace agreements with local governance provisions have had a positive effect on the reduction of violence even larger than those traditionally associated with peace durability. That is, the inclusion of local governance provisions in the peace agreement is correlated with a reduction in the likelihood of violence and its effect is larger than the inclusion of security, power-sharing agreements, or general

TABLE 5.5 Basic *probit* analysis of the effect of local governance on recurrence of violence within 5 years

Variables	(1)	(2)	(3)	(4)	(5)	(6)	(7)
Local governance	−1.502***	—	—	—	—	—	−1.549***
	(0.505)						(0.500)
Sharing local government	—	−0.461	—	—	—	—	−0.405
		(0.907)					(1.138)
Cultural freedoms	—	—	−0.172	—	—	—	0.133
			(0.714)				(0.859)
Power-sharing	—	—	—	−0.776**	—	—	−0.779**
				(0.354)			(0.389)
Security	—	—	—	—	−0.254	—	0.0231
					(0.285)		(0.324)
Political (elections)	—	—	—	—	—	−0.465	−0.547
						(0.327)	(0.344)
Type of conflict	0.440	0.694	0.688	1.093**	0.694	0.919**	1.069*
	(0.478)	(0.435)	(0.446)	(0.513)	(0.428)	(0.442)	(0.643)
Comprehensive PA	0.678**	0.662**	0.665**	0.428	0.714**	0.794**	0.611*
	(0.338)	(0.312)	(0.317)	(0.316)	(0.316)	(0.309)	(0.347)
Middle East	7.043***	6.482***	6.504***	6.352***	6.300***	6.560***	7.022***
	(0.676)	(0.843)	(0.845)	(0.820)	(0.833)	(0.876)	(0.783)
Asia	6.544***	6.330***	6.273***	6.365***	6.223***	6.271***	6.769***
	(0.675)	(0.802)	(0.802)	(0.767)	(0.763)	(0.836)	(0.785)
Africa	6.059***	5.753***	5.752***	5.899***	5.701***	5.754***	6.234***
	(0.673)	(0.805)	(0.807)	(0.770)	(0.768)	(0.841)	(0.741)
Americas	5.431***	5.265***	5.250***	4.998***	5.079***	5.067***	5.024***
	(0.615)	(0.796)	(0.796)	(0.788)	(0.762)	(0.807)	(0.744)
Constant	−2.328***	−2.505***	−2.496***	−3.167***	−2.559***	−3.142***	−3.693***
	(0.815)	(0.971)	(1.001)	(1.049)	(0.921)	(1.083)	(1.232)
Year effects	Yes	Yes	Yes	Yes	Yes	Yes	Yes
Observations	124	124	124	124	124	124	124

Robust standard errors in parentheses. *** $p<0.01$, ** $p<0.05$, * $p<0.1$

elections. These results are robust to region and year-fixed effects and are clearly distinguished from the dimensions measured by "top-down" approaches. We interpret this evidence as showing how moving toward the realm of local governance has a positive effect on peace duration. Local provisions may also provide an incentive for a vibrant civil society to emerge both to prevent elite capture and to provide citizens with a stake in the peace process. Although we do not specifically test our claim about the role of CSOs, we hypothesize that "going local" will encourage the formation of civil society thus mediating the relationship between local provisions and peace. Such a relationship is an important avenue for future study. In sum, a clear policy implication emerges from this analysis: including a local dimension in a peace agreement can play an important role in reducing the recurrence of violence. In this chapter, we have focused on the critical role of local governance in lowering the likelihood of future violence outbreak and achieving *quality* peace.

Notes

1. By success rate we refer to the non-outbreak of violence after an agreement is signed.
2. For example, conflicts ending with a clear military victor are more likely to set the terms of peace, which may or may not, promote *quality* peace. Similarly, cases of low violent activity generally prioritize achieving security in the short-term overlooking long-term solutions.
3. For a more detailed discussion see Richmond 2006 and Mac Ginty 2010.
4. However, DeRouen et al. (2009) find that such a result is not robust for partition agreements, a subset of all agreements.
5. One important exception is that of Beath et al. (2017), which explore the effects of different selection procedures of development projects.
6. In contrast to these findings, Avdeenko and Gilligan (2015) find no such patterns in South Sudan.
7. Cilliers et. al. (2016) explore in more detail the social and psychological underpinnings of the reconciliation process in post-conflict settings.
8. By local governance it is meant: "Local self-government includes arrangements for local self-government short of autonomy, or the exercise of power through municipal arrangements."
9. The omitted category is Europe. There is not enough power in the dataset to include country fixed effects considering the majority of countries have only one peace agreement over time.
10. Territorial = 1, Governmental = 2.

References

Avdeenko, Alexandra, and Michael J. Gilligan. "International interventions to build social capital: Evidence from a field experiment in Sudan." *American Political Science Review* 109, no. 3 (2015): 427–449.

Beath, Andrew, Fotini Christia, and Ruben Enikolopov. "Direct democracy and resource allocation: Experimental evidence from Afghanistan." *Journal of Development Economics* 124 (2017): 199–213.

Casey, Katherine, Rachel Glennerster, and Edward Miguel. "Reshaping institutions: Evidence on aid impacts using a pre-analysis plan." *The Quarterly Journal of Economics* 127, no. 4 (2012): 1755–1812.

Cilliers, Jacobus, Oeindrila Dube, and Bilal Siddiqi. "Reconciling after civil conflict increases social capital but decreases individual well-being." *Science* 352, no. 6287 (2016): 787–794.

Collier, Paul, Anke Hoeffler, and Måns Söderbom. "Post-conflict risks." *Journal of Peace Research* 45, no. 4 (2008): 461–478.

DeRouen, Karl R., and Jacob Bercovitch. "Enduring internal rivalries: A new framework for the study of civil war." *Journal of Peace Research* 45, no. 1 (2008): 55–74.

DeRouen, Karl, Mark J. Ferguson, Samuel Norton, Young Hwan Park, Jenna Lea, and Ashley Streat-Bartlett. "Civil war peace agreement implementation and state capacity." *Journal of Peace Research* 47, no. 3 (2010): 333–346.

DeRouen Jr, Karl, Jenna Lea, and Peter Wallensteen. "The duration of civil war peace agreements." *Conflict Management and Peace Science* 26, no. 4 (2009): 367–387.

DeRouen, Karl R., and David Sobek. "The dynamics of civil war duration and outcome." *Journal of Peace Research* 41, no. 3 (2004): 303–320.

Donais, Timothy. *Peacebuilding and local ownership: Post-conflict consensus-building*. Routledge, 2012.

Doyle, Michael W., and Nicholas Sambanis. "International peacebuilding: A theoretical and quantitative analysis." *American Political Science Review* 94, no. 4 (2000): 779–801.

Fearon, James D., Macartan Humphreys, and Jeremy M. Weinstein. "Can development aid contribute to social cohesion after civil war? Evidence from a field experiment in post-conflict Liberia." *The American Economic Review* 99, no. 2 (2009): 287–291.

Fearon, James D., Macartan Humphreys, and Jeremy M. Weinstein. "How does development assistance affect collective action capacity? Results from a field experiment in post-conflict Liberia." *American Political Science Review* 109, no. 3 (2015): 450–469.

Fortna, Virginia Page. "Inside and out: Peacekeeping and the duration of peace after civil and interstate wars." *International Studies Review* 5, no. 4 (2003): 97–114.

Fortna, Virginia Page. *Peace time: Cease-fire agreements and the durability of peace*. Princeton University Press, 2004a.

Fortna, Virginia Page. "Does peacekeeping keep peace? International intervention and the duration of peace after civil war." *International Studies Quarterly* 48, no. 2 (2004b): 269–292.

Gilligan, Michael J., and Ernest J. Sergenti. "Do UN interventions cause peace? Using matching to improve causal inference." *Quarterly Journal of Political Science* 3, no. 2 (2008): 89–122.

Glassmyer, Katherine, and Nicholas Sambanis. "Rebel—military integration and civil war termination." *Journal of Peace Research* 45, no. 3 (2008): 365–384.

Harbom, Lotta, Stina Högbladh, and Peter Wallensteen. "Armed conflict and peace agreements." *Journal of Peace Research* 43, no. 5 (2006): 617–631.

Hartzell, Caroline A., and Matthew Hoddie. "Institutionalizing peace: Power sharing and post-civil war conflict management." *American Journal of Political Science* 47, no. 2 (2003a): 318–332.

Hartzell, Caroline A., and Matthew Hoddie. "Civil war settlements and the implementation of military power-sharing arrangements." *Journal of Peace Research* 40, no. 3 (2003b): 303–320.

Hartzell, Caroline A., and Matthew Hoddie. *Crafting peace: Power-sharing institutions and the negotiated settlement of civil wars*. Penn State Press, 2007.

Joshi, Madhav, and T. David Mason. "Civil war settlements, size of governing coalition, and durability of peace in post-civil war states." *International Interactions* 37, no. 4 (2011): 388–413.

Kreutz, Joakim. "How and when armed conflicts end: Introducing the UCDP Conflict Termination dataset." *Journal of Peace Research* 47, no. 2 (2010): 243–250.

Licklider, Roy. "The consequences of negotiated settlements in civil wars, 1945–1993." *American Political Science Review* 89, no. 3 (1995): 681–690.

Mac Ginty, Roger. "Indigenous peace-making versus the liberal peace." *Cooperation and Conflict* 43, no. 2 (2008): 139–163.

Mac Ginty, Roger. "Hybrid peace: The interaction between top-down and bottom-up peace." *Security Dialogue* 41, no. 4 (2010): 391–412.

Mason, T. David, Mehmet Gurses, and Patrick Brandt. "Durable peace after civil wars? Civil war outcomes and the duration of peace." *Paper presented at the Annual Meeting of the American Political Science Association.* Washington, DC, August 31–September 3, 2005.

McBride, Michael, Gary Milante, and Stergios Skaperdas. "Peace and war with endogenous state capacity." *Journal of Conflict Resolution* 55, no. 3 (2011): 446–468.

Millar, Gearoid, Jair Van Der Lijn, and Willemijn Verkoren. "Peacebuilding plans and local reconfigurations: Frictions between imported processes and indigenous practices." *International Peacekeeping* 20, no. 2 (2013): 137–143.

Mvukiyehe, Eric N., and Cyrus Samii. "The subtle micro-effects of peacekeeping: Evidence from Liberia." In *APSA 2010 Annual Meeting Paper.* 2010.

Nilsson, Desirée. "Anchoring the peace: Civil society actors in peace accords and durable peace." *International Interactions* 38, no. 2 (2012): 243–266.

Paffenholz, Thania. "Civil society and peace negotiations: Beyond the inclusion–exclusion dichotomy." *Negotiation Journal* 30, no. 1 (2014): 69–91.

Richmond, Oliver P. "The problem of peace: Understanding the 'liberal peace'." *Conflict, Security & Development* 6, no. 3 (2006): 291–314.

Toft, Monica Duffy. "Peace through security: Making negotiated settlements work." *Paper presented at 47th Annual Meeting of International Studies Association.* San Diego, CA, March 22–25, 2006. Accessed at http://64.112.226.77/one/isa/isa06/.

Appendix

TABLE 5.6 Governance and violence

	Violence 5 years	Local provisions	Power-sharing	Security	Elections	Incompatibility
Violence 5 years	1	–	–	–	–	–
Local provisions	−0.2678★	1	–	–	–	–
Power-sharing	−0.1418	−0.039	1	–	–	–
Security	−0.0076	−0.019	0.3019★	1	–	–
Elections	−0.0714	−0.1043	0.2165★	0.3590★	1	–
Incompatibility	0.2409★	−0.3493★	0.2736★	0.0722	0.3246★	1

PART III
Economic reconstruction

6

BUSINESS ON THE FRONTLINES

Viva Ona Bartkus

Civil war, rebellion, and invasion ravage not the wealthy, but the poorest of the poor. The poorest billion face ongoing conflict. The citizens who gained independence from colonial powers in the 1960s now face the tragedy that after 50 years, their grandchildren's lives are worse off than theirs were. Many of these societies will fall back into war without accelerated economic growth in the near future. The World Bank, International Monetary Fund (IMF), UN, and many NGOs and international aid programs have dedicated billions of dollars to achieve two elusive goals—peace and prosperity. Yet the result resembles the toils of Sisyphus.

Beyond contributing to the discussion on quality peace, as introduced in Chapter 1 of this volume, the objectives of this chapter are threefold: first, to introduce a set of insights on the impact of business in post-conflict societies; second, to lay out a series of case studies on that impact utilizing a well-regarded economic framework; and finally, to conclude with reflections on what might be the possibilities in harnessing the energy of business toward quality peace.

Through a unique partnership among the faculty and students from across the University of Notre Dame and the international staff of humanitarian organizations and multinational corporations, Business on the Frontlines explores the impact of business in rebuilding war-torn societies; from therein arose the research for this chapter. As a university course, Business on the Frontlines creates opportunities for future business leaders to learn firsthand the impact that business can have in war-torn areas. As a unique collaboration between the University of Notre Dame, humanitarian organizations, and multinational corporations, Business on the Frontlines enables work on projects that build some measure of peace and prosperity within target conflict societies. The Business on the Frontlines research initiative seeks new insights regarding the role of business before, during, and after conflict. Successfully run for 8 years, this program has partnered graduate business, law, and peace studies students and faculty with local partners in nearly 20 countries: Bosnia, Lebanon, Kenya, Uganda, Egypt, Rwanda, Sierra Leone, Ghana, Senegal, Guatemala, Honduras, Nicaragua, Cambodia, Philippines, East Timor, Sri Lanka, and Indonesia. One example of the types of projects initiated includes teams who worked in Sarajevo, Mostrar, and Srebrenica to design a system of small business incubators across Bosnia. Other teams fostered new markets for ground nuts and soybeans in Kenya and Uganda, respectively, by creatively shortening the distance between producers and consumers. Still others developed an economic simulation tool and training program for the Lebanese private electricity market to show sectarian leaders how collaboration across distinct communities could improve the lives of all Lebanese. They worked to enhance the business acumen of small farmers within the context of some international development organizations' already successful agriculture programs in Rwanda and Mindanao, thereby fostering cooperation across tribal, religious, and socio-economic divides. In all, the insights for this chapter are drawn from nearly 30 Business on the Frontlines business and peace-related projects over the last 8 years.

Why business?

The argument for the importance of business for a quality peace is, at its core, a basic one. Under normal conditions, proprietors of businesses hire employees and pay them wages. They serve customers with products and services that they need. Proprietors of businesses take risks, and then use their rewards in terms of profit, if fortunate, to care for their families and to reinvest in their ongoing ventures. In post-conflict situations, businesses could play an important role in laying the foundation for community members to have a stake in the peace, however flawed. Under conditions of post-war reconstruction, businesses once again hire employees, some of whom are naturally former combatants. Through employment, businesses could provide a path for their reintegration into the community, not to mention providing ex-combatants with something productive to do with their days. For those ex-combatants with entrepreneurial talent, business activities also provide opportunities to launch new ventures that utilize their skills, tools, and post-conflict allowances; thereby beginning to rebuild their lives.

However, over the years, business in post-conflict societies has earned a rather mixed reputation. Consequently, one could legitimately ask the question as to why it should be a part of the equation for quality peace, particularly since experience on the ground of post-conflict situations falls so woefully short of the basic argument outlined above. After much reflection, this important question requires two types of answer: a look at the existing alternatives and an examination of the benefits of business while limiting its negative impact.

From the perspective of the entire society, economics revolves around the allocation of scarce resources in an attempt to satisfy unlimited wants. Because of limited resources, societies must allocate them as efficiently as possible to generate maximum production. At the level of an individual business, its objective is the production of goods and services that customers will pay for based on core competencies that drive a sustainable competitive advantage. Business can mean a local venture, a national company, or an international corporation—each allocates resources based on its own objectives and market signals. Individuals choose to consume or invest based on their own self-interest with as much information as possible. Different institutions allocate resources in different ways: bureaucracies allocate resources based on hierarchy, clans based on family priorities, and businesses based on price and market mechanisms. The principles of a well-functioning market and well-functioning state are known widely. Markets need flows of information, competition, and protection of property as ownership provides incentives to use or sell assets as productively as possible. Economic activity also requires a basic level of trust; even well-written contracts cannot account for all future contingencies. Well-functioning states have numerous responsibilities, including providing public goods at scale such as enforcing laws, establishing a basis for sound money, building infrastructure, providing education and healthcare, limiting the worst externalities such as environmental degradation caused by business, and helping those most vulnerable within the society.

No matter how well known these principles of economics and governance have become, their application in post-conflict societies has been extremely challenging. Many countries have witnessed a procession of worthy advisors from the World Bank and IMF, international NGOs, foundations, and governments of the developed world. These actors have invested countless billions from public funds and private funds over the last 50 years into developing post-conflict societies. Yet allocation of scarce resources—either from the societies' own enterprise or outside donors—either by government bureaucracy or according to clan priorities (as is frequently the case as a legacy of war) is fundamentally less efficient for the creation of economic wealth than through market mechanisms. And thus, the effect has been heartbreakingly negligible. According to World Bank statistics,[1] the economies of the poorest billion people, many of whom face persistent violence, grew by 0.5 percent in the 1970s, and shrank by −0.4 percent in the 1980s and −0.5 percent in the 1990s, reaching 0.5 percent growth in the early 2000s. Compare this with the rest of the world with growth at 2.5 percent in the 1970s, 4.0 percent in the 1980s, and 4.5 percent in the 1990s before the financial and economic melt-down and slow recovery of the early 2000s. As a consequence, the poorest not only suffer from an enormous development gap compared to the developed world, but have also become significantly worse off over the last 50 years by absolute measures.

Research by Anke Hoeffler and Paul Collier indicates that the risks of war are directly tied to initial levels of income, growth and primary commodity dependence (Collier and Hoeffler 1998, 2004). Indeed, halving the starting income of the society doubles the risk of civil war. With a typical low-income country facing the risk of civil war of approximately 14 percent in any given 5-year period, each 1 percent decrease in growth increases the risk of civil war by 1 percent. The experience of civil war itself roughly doubles the risk of another conflict. Further, the costs of war are borne by the society and its neighbors through migration, disease, and criminality. Civil war decreases economic growth by 2.3 percent, so the typical 7-year conflict leaves a country's economy and people 15 percent worse off in economic terms (Collier 2008, Collier et. al 2009).

To prevent the costly resurgence of repeating cycles of conflict, meaningful economic activity is necessary to provide both the poorest and richest members of society with a stake in peace. Although it presents many acknowledged challenges, nonetheless, business possesses the skills, resources, dynamism, and energy to foster economic activity in even the most war-torn areas. Massive poverty makes the poor extremely risk-averse, since the consequences of risking (and possibly losing) their assets can often lead to death. However, without risk there can be no reward. The basic operations of business rest on the careful weighing of risk and reward to make strategic investments to create greater production and wealth. Business rests on process discipline, accountability, and use of metrics to judge success, which further encourages the efficient and effective deployment of resources.

Consequently, without harnessing the energy, creativity, and dynamism of business, these societies will not lift themselves out of poverty and conflict. Many NGOs have a proven track record of helping provide basic food, shelter, clothing, and healthcare. Yet wealth creation remains the key to breaking the cycle of conflict, and business remains the key to wealth creation.

How business impacts post-conflict societies?

Building a business requires vision, capabilities, funding, and scale. Some aspects entrepreneurs bring themselves, such as the vision to serve an unmet customer need and their own capabilities. The state must ensure the conditions such as some degree of stability to generate investment financing of a venture. The business proprietor must save sufficient funds to invest in the venture or else society must save enough and provide the mechanisms to funnel those savings into productive investments either through formal banks or informal saving and lending institutions. Should you ask any founder of a new business venture, they will tell you that building a business is hard even on the best of days.

If business should be a part of the equation of quality peace, what is its role? And why has it not taken a bigger, more helpful role historically? What might be its benefits to a post-conflict society? And what problems might it present? The following section outlines both the benefits and pitfalls presented by business that post-conflict societies must navigate and the challenges that post-conflict societies present for building viable businesses.

The benefits in the short term are that, after the conflict, vibrant businesses create opportunities for meaningful work for those returning from war. Meaningful work, with a living wage, then creates incentives against destabilizing the fragile peace. In the medium and longer term, sustainable businesses provide the most efficient mechanism to allocate a society's resources—its labor, its savings, and its innovative flair—toward the most productive ends, thereby increasing economic activity and wealth. With reasonable distribution of opportunity, not necessarily income, the increase in wealth can help all members of the society adjust to the new circumstances presented by peace.

Yet business, by its very nature, represents private activity for private gain. To function appropriately, business requires that a set of rules—the rule of law, property rights, currency—be enforced to provide equal access to market opportunities. Without appropriate governance structures, private activity may become abusive or discriminatory to potential employees, customers, and society at large. Under such circumstances, rent-seeking behavior on the part of businesses results. The impact of corruption as individuals, firms, and even government agencies seek private benefit by manipulating the economic and legal environment has been well-researched elsewhere.

Furthermore, post-conflict societies bring along an additional set of challenges to launch businesses. To address these unique challenges to building businesses and enhancing their impact in post-conflict societies, Robert Solow's seminal work on the drivers of growth and wealth creation, known as the exogenous growth model or as the neo-classical growth model, will be illustrated through a series of case studies (Solow 1956, 1957). The chapter will close with a few thoughts regarding how post-conflict societies must also navigate around the pitfalls presented by business.

In any particular year, the entire growth of production of an economy (the Gross Domestic Product or GDP) depends on the level and growth of labor, capital, and another factor x, which Solow described as productivity growth or innovation. Businesses, with their owners and employees, with their investors and creditors, provide the mechanism to transform the raw components of economic activity such as the labor force and savings into productive activities that make the society as whole better off. Case studies from three diverse types of conflict, notably Mindanao, Rwanda, and Uganda illustrate the ways in which post-conflict societies present unique challenges for each variable critical to wealth creation through business. These are contrasted with two additional cases drawn from Lebanon and Bosnia, further illustrating the limits provided by the lack of trust in post-war society.

Labor in Mindanao: unique balancing act between risk and personal autonomy

Harnessing the productive efforts of the labor force is critical to raising society's standard of living and helping to prevent further conflict. Yet war-torn communities struggle to do so. An examination of the Catholic, Moro, and *lumad* (indigenous) coffee farmers in Mindanao illustrates an example of the unique balancing act that is required.

By some estimates, the conflict in Mindanao has lasted five centuries and continues today (Ongsotto and Ongsotto 2002). The Muslim population of a group of islands in Southern Philippines argue that they never fully succumbed to Spanish colonial rule and that the dominant Filipino Catholic national identity leaves no room for the unique expression of their religion and traditions. With less than one-tenth of the income per person of the rest of the Philippines, Mindanao's massive socio-economic disparities reinforce its religious and ethnic cleavages.

Yet Mindanao also possesses unique business opportunities that may present ways to increase cooperation and build social capital among these rival communities that live side by side on the island. Capturing those opportunities—based on making labor as productive as possible—requires a unique balance of priorities and values under uncertain conditions.

Mindanao's climate, soil, and high elevation combine to create conditions ideal for high quality Arabica coffee cultivation. Indeed, more than a century ago, the Philippines were the fourth-largest exporter of coffee in the world. However, due to the coffee rust disease epidemic in 1889, the coffee oversupply in the 1960s with its subsequent price collapse, followed by volatile international commodities markets in the 1980s and 1990s, current coffee production meets barely half of Filipino coffee drinkers' needs. One could argue that some of the basic blocks to building viable coffee businesses already exist; certainly, the vision to help the Philippines re-emerge as a major coffee exporter exists. Generations of Filipinos have possessed the capabilities required for excellent coffee cultivation. Recent ceasefire agreements among the combatants provide some semblance of the stability required for investment financing to follow this vision. Nevertheless, given the current limited level of coffee production, this path to greater prosperity, based on sound comparative advantage, has not yet been taken. For the coffee business in Philippines, the challenges are scale and labor.

The value chain of coffee cultivation requires scale. Although an individual farmer can plant, fertilize, prune, and pick coffee cherries, traders or other middlemen take the remaining steps including pulping, hulling, drying, and transporting the beans with larger equipment and then selling the green coffee beans to marketers who roast them and sell the finished coffee to consumers. Through the supply chain, the different steps add incrementally more economic value. The question becomes how to organize farmers to gain the scale that they need to take on more steps in the value chain, thereby creating and capturing more wealth for themselves. Although they represent the largest proportion of the population, even Catholic farmers in the various provinces of Mindanao cannot produce sufficient quantities of coffee to create viable coffee collectives—primarily due to the mountainous geography and limited transportation infrastructure. Neither can the Muslim Moros nor the *lumads* get the required scale on their own. The twin forces of geography and demography result in these communities living side by side on proximate mountainsides and valleys. As a result, successful coffee cultivation—here defined as subsistence farmers earning sufficient income to care for their families—requires collaboration among communities of Catholics, Moros and *lumads* to gain the scale needed for efficient production. Further, such collaboration to harness labor also requires a rather unique balancing of risks and personal values between two very different business alternatives.

An internationally award-winning coffee roaster, Rocky Mountain Coffee, presents one business alternative based on full control of the value chain. This well-capitalized Canadian company with a long track record of coffee success has already established ten coffee plantations and three processing facilities and still cannot meet growing customer demand for Mindanao's excellent coffee. Its CEO believes in a completely closed system to minimize coffee quality variation. Given the limitations on electricity, education, and transportation, farmers only deliver beans in cherry form to the central processing plant. Rocky Mountain Coffee requires farmers to organize into cooperatives and sign a 10-year exclusive contract for which they are paid a guaranteed but rather low price for as much coffee as they can grow. The farmers within Rocky Mountain Coffee's cooperatives have successfully organized themselves across religious and tribal lines in Mindanao. Farmers are trained on fertilization techniques and harvesting. Farmers can then focus on increasing their yield, which can vary from farm to farm up to tenfold. As one of the very few investors on the island, Rocky Mountain Coffee is already taking significant risks in building its business in war-torn Mindanao, and expects to be compensated with adequate returns.

An alternative business approach gaining ground in Mindanao rests on new equipment developed by Bote Central, which is an all-in-one huller, dryer, and roaster of coffee. Although the substitution of dry processing for wet processing somewhat reduces the quality of the coffee, the finished product is high-value roasted coffee that farmers could sell locally in Mindanao, further afield in the Philippines, or abroad. The possible economic value creation and capture for farmers is much greater selling directly into such markets rather than bringing coffee beans in cherry form to Rocky Mountain's processing plant, yet the risks rise commensurately. Knowledge of and relationships within coffee markets require years of diligence and may still lie outside the scope of most Mindanao farmers. The price of this equipment remains outside the collective resources of many communities, although those communities that have been able to purchase the equipment have been using it successfully.

The struggle becomes how to balance these competing business ventures from the perspective of the individual laborer. How should risk for the poorest be minimized while still providing them with the greatest opportunities to grow and prosper. One could make an argument that coffee farmers should take the Rocky Mountain deal, as it guarantees purchase of all their coffee production. Yet such a contract in the early years may look one way given market conditions, yet may change in outlying years. One could also make the argument that farmers should invest in education and Bote Central's equipment, as that path provides the opportunity to create and capture the most wealth for themselves. Yet the risks associated with this option are commensurately greater. As Mindanao's coffee farmers face the choice between signing up to more paternalistic systems versus more aggressive equipment investments, they must make delicate tradeoff between risks and their own sense of personal autonomy and dignity.

From the perspective of a durable peace in Mindanao, the Rocky Mountain Coffee cooperatives provide several notable benefits. This business program enables, encourages, and perhaps even forces farmers from three formerly actively fighting communities to interact—based on their own self-interest—due to the desire to sell produce at fixed prices, thereby limiting their downside risk and helping them provide for their families better. Repeated interaction among members of the three communities through cooperative initiatives, such as training programs, enables members to meet and build relationships with those from outside their community, increasing the social capital among them over time. Raising living standards and increasing interactions across deep ethnic and religious cleavages helps provide the foundation for quality peace.

In early 2014, the main parties to the conflict—the Moro Islamic Liberation Front and the Filipino government—negotiated an agreement that would provide Muslims with greater autonomy and was designed to end the long-standing conflict in Mindanao. These political developments significantly enhanced stability across Mindanao, creating the business conditions necessary for increased outside investment into the region, particularly in sectors such as agriculture and coffee, given the comparative advantages described earlier. However, many years of war have seemed to have built a deep-rooted risk aversion among Mindanao farmers leading them to opt for opportunities such as the Rocky Mountain deal, as it reduces their downside risks. Nevertheless, given the years needed to develop and solidify the conditions for quality peace, not to mention the years required to earn a return on many business investments, only directional observations on labor can be made at this time.

Capital in Rwanda: unique challenges of trust in business after violence

At its most basic level, wisely invested capital improves the productivity of labor, leaving the proprietor, employees, customers, and the society at large better off. The productivity of labor in many post-conflict and developing countries has been abysmally low. There can be a number of explanations for this observation. For many years, economists argued that developing economies were limited by their lack of capital, leading to many World Bank and IMF initiatives. The rise of microfinance and micro-saving institutions has disproved the common wisdom that the poorest of the poor were not capable of saving and investing. Many international corporations are now building businesses to capture the opportunities represented by the consumption and savings of those at the bottom of the pyramid.[2]

If actual savings were not the problem, perhaps it was the lack of a mechanism to channel savings into productive investment. However, the blossoming of microlending institutions, local banks, and regional private sector banks has stepped into this vacuum and now these financial institutions frequently provide the mechanism to turn savings into investments. Indeed, it is neither the savings rate nor the financial institution or lack thereof that prevents the effective deployment of capital in post-conflict societies. A loan, like any contract, depends on trust, as all future contingencies could never be written into a contract. The person taking the loan must trust that the lender has the ability, the integrity and the benevolence to uphold his end of the bargain, without abuse or discrimination. A case study of a Rwandan fruit juice producer illustrated just how difficult that is to accomplish in post-conflict societies. In 1994, Rwanda witnessed the most devastating genocide in the past 25 years, with over a million people killed by their fellow Rwandans in only 100 days. Since then, a minority-based regime has run the country. The regime has emphasized economic growth as a way to rebuild society. Nevertheless, one can imagine how the experiences of the last two decades have severely affected the level of trust in society.

The *Cooperative de Valorisation des Fruites de Gakenke* (COVAFGA) produces sweet-smelling and refreshing maracuja (passion fruit) juice that tastes far better than the alternatives and is shipped to customers in Rwanda and Burundi. Indeed, COVAFGA's fruit juice sells out early, leaving customers always asking for more. The cooperative started in 2007 with the savings of three members and has since grown to 21 members. It employs 11 orphans from the Rwandan genocide to cut the passion fruit with machetes, spoon the flesh from the rinds, and then use two machines to press the fruit juice into plastic 1-liter containers. Without its own transportation, COVAFGA ships boxes of 12 1-liter containers to Kigali by expensive taxi buses.

COVAFGA faces a rather unique business environment. Closer examination of its expenses—fruit, labor, electricity, plastic bottles, distribution—compared to its pricing per bottle and revenues reveals a healthy and profitable business. COVAFGA clearly creates value for its customers and captures some of that economic value for itself. Customers are requesting more of its juice than it can produce. It faces no constraints on labor, as many more orphans would like to work within its doors. Customers consistently sing its praises over alternative juices, implying that COVAFGA could certainly sell more juice should it be able to produce it, and perhaps charge a higher price. The Rwandan economy has a well-developed micro-finance sector with private banks and NGOs making loans to small ventures. The Rwandan government is actively pushing micro-finance lenders to extend more loans and has launched a Savings and Credit Cooperative Organization to finance medium-sized loans, for which COVAFGA may qualify. Based on simple calculations, an investment in an additional processing machine or pick-up truck for distribution could payback within 6 months, leaving more profits for the members and employees of the cooperative thereafter.

However, even though he fully understands the rapid payback for expansionary investment, the General Manager is adamant that the cooperative will take no more loans. The impact of the genocide and civil war has inflicted deep scars on Rwandans, even those with sharp business acumen. Even without knowing the general manager's ethnic background, one can imagine the extreme hesitation he may feel toward leaving himself vulnerable to a lender he may not know, may not understand, and may be from a different ethnic group.

A thoughtful reviewer of this chapter posed the question of whether something more could have been done during the post-conflict reconciliation process to better bridge the gulf among COVAFGA's management and lenders. Charting the road between vengeance and forgiveness, between reconciliation and forgetting, is certainly the work of wise and brave men and women. Overcoming the scars left by the genocide is unimaginably difficult. Indeed, to this external observer of Rwandan society, the fact that any business activity or civic society persists is a testament to the heroic resilience of the Rwandan people. One of the many legacies of the genocide has been extreme mistrust. Capital exists within Rwandan society to invest in their collective future, lending institutions are in place to deploy savings to investments, and the vision for possible investments such as COVAFGA exists, yet the basic underlying necessary trust remains out of reach.

Recent work in Rwanda indicates that the Rwandan government has stepped into this vacuum of insufficient private capital with its own public sector lending approaches. The Rwandan government-sponsored Savings and Credit Co-operative initiative has been designed to move beyond micro-finance to mezzanine loans, such that COVAFGA would qualify for its expansion. The Rwandan government, alongside these finance initiatives, has invested in educational programs designed to improve the management of money in small enterprises and extend proper investment practices. These initiatives have gone a long way to bridge the gap—and bring some investment capital to economic sectors such as agriculture. That being said, government-directed investment of capital may be a short-term solution for Rwanda; it does not represent a long-term sustainable solution for the challenges of capital.

Productivity—innovation in Uganda: new collaborations among unlikely partners

Business opportunities in post-conflict situations face limitations due to challenging circumstances for labor and capital. Yet years of economic stagnation or even destruction associated with war leaves tremendous opportunity for productivity improvements, with even modest innovations yielding significant returns both to the business and its employees and customers. In addition to the demographic expansion of labor and savings turned into productive capital investment, Solow argued that the growth of a country's GDP or wealth was powered by what he called the x factor, or innovation. Although what first comes to mind with innovation focuses around technology advances, innovation can stretch to products, services, even business processes and models. A case from Uganda involving water illustrates how sometimes innovation in post-conflict societies involves bringing together unlikely partners.

Water represents one of the basic needs to sustain life; however, over 800 million people lack access to a safe water supply with a further 3.5 million dying annually from water-related diseases. In Northern Uganda, the situation is dire; state governance has nearly collapsed after 20 years of fighting with the Lord's Resistance Army. Thousands of Internally Displaced Persons (IDPs) have slowly returned to their home villages to find little in the way of water and sanitation. If their village had a well, it is most likely broken and beyond repair.

Part of the challenge is that the existing technology is ill-equipped to handle the conditions and demands of Northern Uganda's villages. The standard pump, the Indian Mark II, uses cast iron riser mains to carry water from the bottom of the borehole to the surface, yet these rust within 2 years of placement, rendering the pump useless. The pump cylinder rests at the bottom of the borehole and needs periodic replacement. Yet to remove the cylinder, the riser main needs to be lifted out of the borehole—no easy task without equipment and training. Better functioning pumps exist, yet the Ugandan government places exorbitant import duties on such pumps. Indeed, the quiet consensus among NGOs is that government officials and their families profit handsomely from the ongoing use of the Indian Mark II water pump.

Possible technology solutions include utilizing materials other than iron, such as polyvinyl chloride (PVC), for the riser mains, as they may be less expensive and could last up to 15 years. Larger PVC riser mains could allow for the pump cylinder to be removed without lifting the riser mains out of the borehole. At present, a large multinational corporation is in discussions with a well-respected humanitarian NGO regarding this opportunity. The international company brings the depth of its research and development expertise from its infrastructure business unit to the venture to capture this clear unmet need, while the NGO brings its understanding of underlying market needs to help solve a humanitarian problem.

Such unconventional partnerships face their own unique challenges to success, which at their root may arise from vastly different conceptualizations of their world views and can lead to miscommunication without a common language. In this case, for example, the multinational company categorized Uganda as an "emerging market," while for the NGO it was a "developing country." The executives of the multinational company talked of the potential water pump innovation as addressing "an unmet market opportunity," while for the NGO "a humanitarian need." Both are speaking about the same place (Uganda) and about the same project (water pump technology). Perhaps the combination of goodwill and patience along with a healthy dose of overlapping self-interest for both parties will help this partnership blossom into the development of a well-adopted new pump.

Nevertheless, such technology innovation still appears further off, and thus, the innovation to address the acute water shortages at the village level may depend on bringing disciplined business practices into the management of a public good. Ultimately, some of the most successful ventures in Northern Uganda have built a sense of ownership of the water asset among those who use it and benefit from it the most. The formation of Water Committees, with widespread participation among village women who collect the water enables simple innovations. These include the collection of modest dues put aside as an insurance policy should the well require repair or new parts. The Water Committees also assign responsibility for maintenance. Overall, they build cohesion among the stakeholders of the well. These innovations in business processes free up significant productive labor, as the women who had been walking up to 4 hours round trip to collect water can take on additional responsibilities.

Innovation in post-conflict societies may include bringing together partners that may have never thought of working together, such as big multinational corporations and banks on the one hand, with humanitarian agencies on the other. Basic productivity increases may also mean arbitraging experiences and expertise from business to solve problems in new ways in the public sector. Perhaps the most significant barrier to such innovation and partnerships may be the lack of a common language and common perspectives.

Recent work in Uganda shows how innovations in civil society, and in particular the emergence of institutions, can reduce the tragedy of the commons. The development of local water committees, administered mostly by women, has served to extend the life of existing wells through proactive maintenance and other initiatives. Nevertheless, the emerging partnerships in Northern Uganda around water technology show that persistence in trying to address unmet needs—businesses' opportunities—may foster innovation even in the most unlikely arenas.

Business: an end in itself vs. a means to other ends

In each of these case studies, the business, whether a local cooperative, a national company, or a multinational corporation, makes decisions of what goods and services to produce based both on customers' demands and core competencies that drive its own sustainable competitive advantage. In meeting the needs of its customers, the business creates value for their customers and, through the prices charged for its goods and services, captures some of those for itself as profit. Each consumer and each business makes decisions on consumption and investment based on their own self-interest with as much information as possible at the time. Through their individual decisions, resources were allocated across the entire economy productively. Each case illustrated the unique challenges faced by business leaders to launch and expand a successful venture in post-conflict societies in terms of labor, capital, and innovation. Yet what if these businesses were not run as ends in themselves? Two cases from Bosnia and Lebanon illustrate the potential for detrimental impact if businesses are run as means toward other ends.

From an external perspective, the Aluminij Mostrar aluminum smelter is a model of post-war Bosnian enterprise. It employs more than 3,000 workers. It earns much of Bosnia's foreign currency through its exports. It produces nearly 130,000 tons of aluminum annually, exporting most of it to the construction and automotive industries in the EU. Its policies of hiring decommissioned soldiers from the Balkan Wars feel generous, with handicapped access in its plant that is unprecedented across Eastern Europe for workers with injuries. Bosnia's government has blocked recent possible plans to sell the aluminum smelter to European investors, ostensibly due to disagreements on electricity costs.

Yet when asked about the company's large-scale operations, the general director revealed that his business hires only Croats. When asked for further clarification, given that much might be lost in conversation and translation, the general director candidly explained that this business hires only Catholics. Although no negative intent was even inferred, one can only wonder what power or influence a disproportionately large, exclusively Croat Catholic business venture, with hundreds of millions of dollars in sales, with thousands of ex-combatant employees, may have on the fragile post-war Bosnian society. This company may be a business as an end in itself—the supply of high-quality aluminum to customers for profit—or it could be a means toward other ends yet undisclosed.

The 2006 Israel-Hezbollah border war wrecked immense damage on Lebanon's infrastructure and economy. Israeli bombing combined with intense fighting on the ground left Lebanon's roads, ports, airport, and even the electricity grid in tatters. When the high-powered business leaders of the banking, construction, retail, and consumer goods industries met at the Lebanese-American Chamber of Commerce in Beirut, the discussion quickly turned to rebuilding the electricity grid. The primary debate centered around how much redundancy to rebuild into the grid. Building some redundancy into the electricity grid makes business sense, as it would enable for expansion in consumption from a growing population and increased usage from rising industrial production. Yet building too many redundancies defeats the purpose of allocating scarce resources and assets toward their most productive use in the creation of wealth, as these assets would be underutilized. Whether capital or labor, these limited resources could be more efficiently and effectively used elsewhere in the economy. Since these were truly captains of industry and even three self-made billionaires, they understood well the concepts of risks and returns on investment, and thus, there were other ends in their reasoning behind excessive investment in the electricity grid.

Upon probing further, an implicit assumption or mindset of the Lebanese business leaders revealed itself. To a business leader, these Lebanese men and women simply assumed war was inevitable. Although they were not certain whether future war would be against its neighbors (like the Israeli-Hezbollah conflict), or among its neighbors (since Lebanon sits in a conflict-ridden neighborhood), or even among the Lebanese themselves as the wounds left within this sectarian society from the painful civil war still run deep, they planned accordingly. They would build excess capacity into the electrical grid, so that when the inevitable next war came, some economic activity could continue. Now in hindsight, as the Syrian civil war continues to rage across the border and with Lebanon providing refuge to over a million Syrian refugees, the Lebanese business leaders built and then lost much of the redundant electricity in the grid. The tragedy of this business mindset was that this investment in additional infrastructure capacity in effect reduced the cost of future war to the Lebanese.

What might be the possibilities of business in post-conflict societies?

Each society must chart its own journey after conflict between vengeance and forgiveness, retribution and forgetting the crimes of the past. This chapter does not seek to underemphasize the importance of peacebuilding initiatives and associated research conducted on macro-policies to improve governance and economic conditions in post-conflict societies. Corruption must be fought and transparency in government should be fostered to hold rulers accountable to the ruled. More must be done to strengthen local institutions and foster civic engagement. Humanitarian relief is still needed by many to meet their basic needs of food, water, shelter, and clothing.

Yet research has also shown that with increasing prosperity, both the poorest and the wealthiest members of a society have an increasing stake in peace. Growing wealth, reasonably distributed evenly throughout a society, reduces the chances of a society returning to civil war and open hostilities. No other allocation mechanism for scarce resources—neither a bureaucracy nor a clan—can match the productive creativity and wealth creation of business. Business builds economic wealth. The challenge is how to build more businesses, while limiting their potential negative influence, in post-conflict societies.

This chapter has outlined some of the unique challenges in bringing together labor, capital, and innovation in a post-war society. First and foremost, labor must be productively deployed—even when the options facing individual laborers may require a painful balancing act between managing risk and gaining personal autonomy. In many post-conflict societies, capital exists, but the legacy of the years of war means the basic ingredient to its deployment—trust—is nowhere to be found. Productivity increases through innovation are needed to pull together labor and capital, but innovation in post-conflict societies may take many new, unexpected, and creative forms, in processes, alliances, and partnerships—many of which are still unchartered. Society must keep business focused on its own needs, customers, employees, and other stakeholders, lest their investments or even mindsets be used for other purposes beyond its narrow interests. Furthermore, as illustrated in this chapter, business contributes best to trust in post-conflict societies by focusing on business development, rather than using business for other ends, notably ethnic solidarity or investing so as to make future wars less costly.

Never underestimate the dignity of a good day's work and providing for one's family. Viable business with employees, customers, economic activity, products and services, provide incentives for individual members of post-conflict societies to press for peace. Business, and the opportunities it creates, helps lay the foundation for quality peace from below. Returning to meaningful, productive work after years of war makes it that much more difficult to return to destructive conflict. As written in Genesis 2:15, "The Lord God took the man and put him in the Garden of Eden to work it and take care of it." This dignity of work is even more needed following the ravages of war.

Notes

1. See http://data.worldbank.org for the World Bank's economic growth rates by country over time.
2. For research into the business opportunities presented by the poorest of the poor, see Prahalad 2006.

References

Collier, Paul. *The bottom billion: Why the poorest countries are failing and what can be done about it.* Oxford University Press, 2008.

Collier, Paul, Lisa Chauvet, and Haavard Hegre. *The security challenges in conflict prone countries.* Paris Dauphine University, 2009.

Collier, Paul, and Anke Hoeffler. "On economic causes of civil war." *Oxford Economic Papers* 50, no. 4 (1998): 563–573.

Collier, Paul, and Anke Hoeffler. "Greed and grievance in civil war." *Oxford Economic Papers* 56, no. 4 (2004): 563–595.

Ongsotto, Rebecca Ramilo, and Reena R. Ongsotto. *Philippine history: Module-based learning.* Rex Printing Company, 2002.

Prahalad, Coimbatore Krishna. *The fortune at the bottom of the pyramid.* Pearson Education India, 2006.

Solow, Robert M. "A contribution to the theory of economic growth." *The Quarterly Journal of Economics* 70, no. 1 (1956): 65–94.

Solow, Robert M. "Technical change and the aggregate production function." *The Review of Economics and Statistics* 39, no. 3 (1957): 312–320.

7

PEACE PROCESSES, ECONOMIC RECOVERY, AND DEVELOPMENT AGENCIES

Achim Wennmann

Introduction

For many bilateral and multilateral development agencies, conflict situations are often perceived to be outside their mandate. As a result, some withdraw in the face of rising levels of armed violence in order to keep staff and resources away from risk, while others make development engagements dependent on the formal ending of hostilities through a peace agreement. Such attitudes toward peace processes and conflict situations are often justified with reference to the bounds of institutional mandates, the rejection of politicizing aid, and the difficulty of cooperating with rebel groups. In a national context, the topics of war and peace often fall more directly into the domain of other ministries—such as Defense or Foreign Affairs.

The role of development agencies during armed conflict and in peacemaking has become increasingly overtaken by the realities on the ground as well as the evolution of development policy. The link between peace processes and development actors is central in this chapter's analysis as it seeks to grapple with the role of economic recovery within quality peace. The importance of economic factors in quality peace is highlighted by work on the Structures of Peace—a statistical assessment of peace-enhancing structures based on 300 cross-country datasets. The Structures of Peace is a taxonomy of peacefulness and three out of eight elements of this taxonomy underline the critical role of economic factors. These economic factors in Structures of Peace include a sound business environment, the equitable distribution of resources, and low levels of corruption.[1]

In light of the importance of economic factors, this chapter explores how peace negotiations can initiate a process that strengthens prospects for post-conflict economic recovery and investigates the potential implications for development agencies in helping achieve quality peace. The chapter makes the following points:

- Peace processes are a development concern because they often set out future political and economic orders that frame post-conflict economic recovery and long-term economic development.
- Development agencies can be strategic actors in peace processes, especially as peace processes near their conclusions and the parties craft new economic futures. Development agencies are also important actors during the implementation phase and can positively influence how ex-combatants and local populations experience life after armed conflict.
- Development agencies have occupied various roles in past peace processes. In some contexts, they have facilitated dialogue between various parties to the conflict, managed expectations in the economy, and mobilized funding for post-conflict economic recovery.
- The development community can play an important role in strengthening quality peace by transforming the practice of peace mediation from an ad hoc response to a crisis to the creation of long-term national peace architectures.

The chapter first sets out the relevance of peace processes for economic recovery, before investigating the economic component in forward-looking peace process negotiations. The chapter also discusses the role of development agencies in peace processes and makes a series of propositions about how they can strengthen economic recovery during peace processes.

Peace processes and their relevance for economic recovery

Peace processes are "measures deployed to resolve differences, and settle disputes or conflicts, through diplomacy or other methods of peaceful settlement rather than violence" (Ramcharan 2009: 228). They usually address two critical elements: the resolution of an existing armed conflict and the creation of an order that manages future conflicts such that they do not become new armed conflicts. While the diversity and complexity of peace processes makes categorization difficult, a peace process may be said to exist if the protagonists are willing to negotiate in good faith, the key actors are included in the process, negotiations address one or multiple of the central issues in dispute, and the negotiators do not use force to achieve their objectives and are committed to a sustained process (Darby and Mac Ginty 2009: 7–8). Development actors and agencies play a pivotal role in this process and contribute to the post-conflict economic recovery.

For development agencies to be relevant for peace processes, they must relate to both the backward- and forward-looking dimensions of peace processes. The former relates to past violence and injustices and the latter to visions for the future and paths toward new political, economic, and societal orders. These two dimensions are intricately linked because without an understanding of, or credible guarantees for, these new orders, continuing armed violence may be perceived by the parties as their best option to secure a better life (Zartman 2005: 295).

Development agencies can have a special interest in a peace process if armed violence is motivated by economic issues such as horizontal inequalities or social exclusion, and if these issues are a structural catalyst for continued armed violence. Development agencies can even become strategic partners if the parties agree to negotiate a new vision of the economy and society that requires donor expertise in development planning. Credible commitments of development assistance can support momentum toward peace at a mature stage of negotiations and help shift the parties' attitudes from short-term gains to a long-term economic vision (Ball 1996: 69–70).

Charting new futures during the peace process

With the multiplication of donor activities in post-conflict and fragile contexts, there has been a growing interest in strengthening post-conflict transitions, making aid more effective, and preventing the recurrence of armed conflict (Ohiorhenuan and Stewart 2008). In this context, both formal and informal post-conflict economies are important because they absorb ex-combatants and provide populations with new livelihood opportunities (ILO 2009). The economy creates peace dividends that define how former fighters and the population in general experience the post-conflict period. If this experience is negative, chances are high that disillusionment feeds into the dynamics of conflict recurrence.

Economic recovery is also associated with the implementation of peace accords (Stedman 2002). Peace processes are a series of overlapping phases between the engagement of the parties and the transformation of the conflict. They involve pre-negotiations, confidence building, ceasefire talks, peace agreement negotiations, and implementation (Guelke 2002: 56). Economic recovery in the implementation phase is often complicated because it inherits flaws from previous phases that were necessary to ensure a ceasefire or peace agreement. The question therefore arises whether moving "upstream" into the peace process consolidates post-conflict transitions, and if and how the type, content, and quality of a peace agreement and the process that drives it can facilitate these transitions.

Peace negotiations can lay an initial foundation for post-conflict political and economic transitions and craft an economic vision that becomes the foundation for a new society. Even if addressing economic issues can be sensitive, taking this risk mitigates against violence and serves to craft a more credible reality at a time when the parties are considering a negotiated exit out of a conflict. In this way, development agencies facilitate the implementation of peace agreements, as well as DDR programs.

Addressing economic futures in peace processes has a significant political value for peace negotiations. From the perspective of the parties, having a solid agreement on economic issues can bridge the period between the signing of a peace agreement and the manifestation of peace dividends. When the parties agree to a peace agreement, they face immediate demands to lay down their arms. But in return, they usually only receive a vague promise of a better future in the long term. In this context, development assistance can be a significant financial incentive. The lag time involved, and each party's assessment of the likelihood of future economic benefits, affects their political commitment to a peace process. This commitment can be strengthened by placing post-conflict futures on the table and exploring ways to construct a new vision of the future and a credible prospect of success.

While the strategic utility of economic issues in peace processes has been recognized, the current practice of peacemaking appears biased toward military and political issues. A comparative analysis of 27 peace agreements suggests that most peace agreements focus on security and political power while economic provisions are marginal (Suhrke et al. 2007: 23). Economic provisions have been included where a conflict ended with a comprehensive settlement of the conflict, such as in Guatemala and El Salvador. The North-South peace agreement in Sudan included an income-sharing agreement and a range of institutional innovations to increase the predictability of economic transactions between parties that did not trust each other (De Vries et al. 2009; Wennmann 2009b). However, due to the recent trend toward step-by-step processes, many peace accords only mention economic principles and the specifics are delegated to a political process in the post-conflict period as in Nepal.

Negotiating economic futures remains a difficult challenge because ensuring a positive long-term effect of economic provisions depends on many uncontrollable factors. In Sudan, a difficult post-conflict implementation environment prevented the accrual of short-term benefits from a landmark wealth-sharing deal. In Nepal, economic issues became part of the post-conflict politics between the government and the opposition. In early 2009, the opposition sought to prevent any successes of the government in the field of economic development in order to expose the government's incapacity to deliver on promises and thereby delegitimize it (Wennmann 2009a: 18). In contrast, and despite obvious challenges, in Aceh the post-conflict economy recovered relatively quickly because the tsunami attracted unprecedented humanitarian and development attention, and the province had a much better economic base compared to Southern Sudan (Wennmann and Krause 2009: 18).

While recent trends suggest that the parties to the peace agreement include provisions on natural resource management, allocation, and sharing, as well as other key socio-economic issues in peace agreements, addressing economic modality in peace negotiations remains a sensitive endeavor in some instances (Blundell and Harwell 2016). In the 2002 peace talks in the Democratic Republic of Congo, economic issues were only addressed vaguely because none of the belligerents or complicit third parties wanted to openly acknowledge their economic agendas (Nest 2006: 55). In Nepal, the issue of "capitalist" development was sensitive because it sparked debates between ideological hardliners and political pragmatists among the Maoists (Wennmann 2009a: 15).

In sum, economics can influence the peace process in two different ways. First, by including economic provisions into an agreement, such as land reform, health care, education, rebuilding infrastructure, and access to credit; and second by calling upon donor agencies to support the peace process at the stage when parties move closer to signing an agreement and start considering its implementation.

The role of development agencies in peace processes

To overcome the challenge of creating new futures in the post-conflict period, there is a need to forge innovative strategic alliances. Peace negotiations and post-conflict economic recovery are often perceived as two distinct operations that are conducted in different contexts and by different institutions. However, making economic futures tangible necessitates transforming our understanding of peace-making as a two-stage process: before and after a peace agreement. Peacemaking must be understood as an ongoing process in which the resolution of a past conflict and the preparation for future political and economic orders go together. This trend has been broadly recognized by the Advisory Groups of Experts on the Review of the Peacebuilding Architecture that underlies the notion of "sustaining peace" as a shared responsibility across the UN system uniting the UN's work in the fields of peace and security, human rights, and development (United Nations 2015). For peace processes, such an integrated and system approach means that the know-how of development actors is important for mediators during a peace process in order to determine realistic economic futures; and the know-how of mediators is important for development actors in the post-conflict phase in order to prevent the relapse of conflict and maintain transitional pacts.

The investigation of the role of development agencies in peace processes occurs amid an evolving development doctrine. Development assistance has long been perceived as a merely technical and apolitical market solution to development problems. More recently, however, perspectives are shifting and development assistance is increasingly portrayed as a political process that involves state-building as well as governance reform. The United Kingdom's (UK) White Paper on Development, for example, argues,

> the best way to stem the rise of violence and create a platform for sustained growth is to build a state that is capable of delivering basic services effectively and fairly, and is accountable and responsive to its citizens. It also requires working more politically. Conflict and fragility are inherently political . . . [and] their solutions must be rooted in politics.
>
> (Maxwell 2009)

This changing development discourse opens new opportunities for development agencies to politically engage, such as in peace processes. What facilitates such engagement is that development agencies often maintain operations in countries that slide into armed conflict as well as in non-conflict countries with high levels of criminal violence. There has also been an ever-increasing awareness of the nexus between development and security that many development agencies embrace.[2] To a certain extent, one may claim that development agencies may even wish to attempt to recapture "their" development space after nearly a decade of war in Iraq and Afghanistan has seen a greater involvement of military actors in classic development tasks, especially in early recovery operations that initiate post-conflict development transitions.

These policy contexts in which development agencies operate do not cloak the fact that development agencies have been involved in various capacities in peace processes. They have a special relationship to peace processes if armed violence has been motivated by horizontal inequalities or social exclusion and if a peace process has attempted to deal with poverty or development programming. Development agencies can:

- ensure economic issues are placed on the agenda in a realistic way;
- develop mechanisms that lead to sustainable revenue management;
- foster realistic expectations among the parties on the amount and nature of development assistance after a peace agreement; and
- provide the financing necessary to implement a peace accord (Ball 1996: 67–68).

In this context, development agencies are crucial to launch Post-Conflict Needs Assessments (PCNAs) that in some contexts occur in parallel to peace negotiations. PCNAs are multi-stakeholder initiatives that conceptualize, negotiate, and finance a shared strategy for recovery and development of war-to-peace transitions. They are crucial for the creation of a vision for the future that is accepted by the parties, and consistent with economic realities. If PCNAs are conducted when a peace agreement is imminent they can provide an important momentum for peace talks (United Nations and World Bank 2007: 4, 8).

What is more, development assistance can be an important—and in the absence of private sector investment often the only—economic incentive for conflict-affected countries. They are usually applied in conjunction with political and military incentives such as the provision of legitimacy, recognition, or security guarantees. As with all incentives, their effectiveness depends on their perceived value, the credibility and mode of their delivery, and the timing and circumstances in which they are offered (Cortright 1997: 272–277). Development assistance is particularly effective as an economic incentive if it can provide a credible counterweight to political aspirations or war economies, support pro-peace constituencies, and influence the social and economic environment underlying a conflict (Uvin 1999: 4; Griffiths and Barnes 2008: 12). The use of aid as an incentive is, however, controversial within the development community. Particularly if aid is perceived as "neutral" and "needs-based" assistance, incentivizing aid is held to run the danger of becoming politicized or a "payoff" to belligerents.

If assistance is used wisely, therefore, development agencies can stimulate a tremendous optimism for peace if they can provide credible promises for development investments in the aftermath of war (Ball et al. 1997: 261). Donor conferences in support of post-conflict economic recovery have become a recurring feature as evidenced in Bosnia, Sudan, Iraq, and Afghanistan. However, if pledges remain unfulfilled, they can also foster frustrations and disappointment in the international community (Väyrynen 1997: 167–168). The credibility of the commitment of development assistance is, therefore, essential to support momentum during peace negotiations and help shift the parties' attitudes from short term gains to long-term economic planning (Ball 1996: 69–70).

Despite these potentially positive roles, development agencies have both internal and external constraints on their role in peace processes:

- Most development agencies are risk-averse and consider peace processes as "political" issues that are outside their direct mandate. Operations during "conflict" and "post-conflict" phases are institutionally divided between institutions that focus on their military, political, humanitarian, peacebuilding or development roles. This division limits the contribution of development agencies to peacemaking.
- The role of development aid can become contentious if it is perceived to assist non-state armed groups, especially those involved in human rights abuses. In this context, development agencies become easy targets for criticism in their own country, as well as others.
- There are divides within the development community as to the politicization of aid. Within the context of a peace process, development aid is often portrayed as an economic incentive for the parties. Such uses are rejected as being outside the real purpose of aid, which is poverty reduction and needs-based development.
- Member states of multilateral agencies are often unable to find a political consensus on how to engage in peace processes, which can therefore make the start of operations conditional on the existence of a peace agreement. Furthermore, the insecurity and instability in many post-conflict scenarios means that the conditions for the deployment of civilian personnel or the long-term commitment of development funding are not deemed appropriate (O'Donnell and Boyce 2007: 2).

Despite these constraints, there is a growing recognition in development agencies that engaging in peace processes can enhance development effectiveness in conflicted and fragile states (OECD 2001: 51–52). From the perspectives of development agencies, strategic engagement in peace processes prepares post-conflict aid delivery. Through such engagement, development agencies can place post-conflict economic recovery on the table and thereby use peace negotiations to set the parameters for early recovery operations. These include the legal and political framework for aid interventions, and the identification of local leaders and organizations as partners for future operations. A lesson from Liberia highlights that "the greatest scope for intervention in a sovereign state is immediately after the conclusion of conflict, in the elaboration of an internally-brokered peace process" (Dwan and Bailey 2006: 23).

The challenge for those supporting war-to-peace transitions is to steer these various interests toward constructive engagement and greater levels of commitment by the parties to a peace process. There is no one actor who can take on this challenge, but it is critical that the multitude of actors involved in and around peace negotiations better coordinate their involvement. If development assistance is an incentive, the main responsibility of the development agencies is to remain committed to their promises, and coordinate among themselves so that development funding is perceived by local populations as a credible peace dividend. It is also necessary to extend mediation support activities from the conflict to the post-conflict period in order to nurture the transitional pacts that are necessary for the implementation of peace agreements and economic recovery.

Strengthening economic recovery in peace processes

This section makes several propositions toward an action framework for development agencies to strengthen economic recovery during peace processes. The first proposition is that a peace process and post-conflict economic recovery are part of a continuum and not two separate phases. Actors commonly associated with the post-conflict phase—such as development agencies—can be a strategic partner in peace processes and support backward- and forward-looking peacemaking. Development agencies have a proven track record of engaging in peace processes and have provided important momentum at mature stages of negotiations when parties start crafting new visions for the future. In recent years, discussions on "fragility" or "fragile states" have made it easier for development agencies to program activities outside traditional conflict framings and to make constructive contributions to peace processes and political transitions (World Bank 2011; OECD 2015).

Second, development aid is inherently political, even if perceived as a needs-based, technical intervention. In a conflict context, aid becomes part of the conflict, and the recognition of aid as an incentive for peace can have important positive impacts on peace process negotiations. However, promised aid must be delivered to prevent disappointment, and its relative importance as an incentive depends on the magnitude and sub-national distribution of other financial incentives deriving from private sector investments or conflict economies.

Third, rapid post-conflict economic recovery requires the involvement of development agencies during the peace negotiations. Development agencies are strategic partners for peacemaking because they shape the frameworks, institutions, and alliances necessary to prepare post-conflict economic recovery. This engagement is important because a speedy economic revival is a crucial factor in fostering a successful peace accord implementation (Woodward 2002: 2).

Fourth, development agencies can assist in the formulation and implementation of peace agreements. While lessons are highly dependent on context, development agencies have placed economic issues on the agenda of peace talks in a realistic way, prevented the politicization of development concerns, provided incentives for peace through development aid, fostered realistic expectations in future economic development, offered development expertise for the creation of new economic orders and institutions, and provided the financing for the implementation of a peace agreement. A better understanding of the role of specific aid instruments (e.g., development projects, multi-donor trust funds, budget support, technical cooperation) in war-to-peace transitions would provide important guidance for aid effectiveness in post-conflict settings.

Finally, more attention and investments are needed to ensure mediation support in the aftermath of conflict. Armed conflicts do not end with the signature of a peace agreement but with its implementation. Post-conflict transitions can be highly conflictual and professional mediation support can facilitate managing disputes between political, military, or economic elites, and at the local and provincial level between communities. Development agencies can support national peace architectures through financial assistance and the provision of expertise as shown by the secondment of Peace and Development Advisors by the United Nations Development Program (UNDP) and the UN's Department of Political Affairs. They thereby strengthen the transitional pacts between local stakeholders that are necessary to implement a peace agreement and enable economic recovery.

Conclusion

Highlighting the economic dimensions of peace processes is an attempt to safeguard substantial investments in the resolution of conflicts while also seeking to create visions for a new society in which armed actors are convinced it is worthwhile to stop fighting. One of the first steps in forging a new vision is recognizing that armed conflicts, peace processes, and peacebuilding all have economic dimensions that must be managed to secure the quality of post-conflict peace.

The experience of many negotiated settlements suggests that peace processes do not end when the belligerent parties agree on a peace settlement. A negotiated exit out of armed conflict requires a strong transitional pact that must be nurtured and supported as the parties implement the agreement that ends their conflict and prepares whatever is next. These war-to-peace transitions require a constant human effort to succeed, as well as ongoing support mechanisms that facilitate progress toward a sustainable peace. While the mediation support infrastructure is growing at the bilateral, multilateral, and civil society levels, it tends to focus solely on ending violent conflict. However, without offering credible new futures and alternative livelihoods to those who were involved in the violent conflict, some groups and individuals might wish to continue their armed struggle or criminal activities. In other words, unless the economic pillars that address underlying conflict factors such as youth unemployment, socio-economic inequalities, or property rights are strengthened, it will be difficult for a quality peace to take hold sustainably.

Defining a role for development agencies as strategic partners for peacemaking is an important element to managing the transition from war to peace, and placing a conflict setting into a process toward quality peace. The engagement of development agencies during a peace processes can help strengthen a new vision of the economy and society that convinces parties that it is worthwhile to stop fighting. It can also encourage mediators to broker a short-term peace deal, while leaving long-term issues until later. Development assistance also represents important financial flows into conflict countries that could be used to strengthen the recovery in the immediate aftermath of conflict.

Yet to truly take on their role, development actors must also be introspective. They need to address their tendency to be risk-averse, to review engagement patterns that so far are related to the existence of a signed peace agreement, and find innovative ways to protect their staff stationed in conflict situations.

Notes

1. The other factors are well-functioning government, acceptance of the rights of others, good relations with neighbors, free flow of information, and high levels of education. See Institute for Economics and Peace (2011).
2. For the World Bank, see Zoellick (2008: 74–75); for Department for International Development, see DFID 2009. Over 100 countries have acknowledged the security and development nexus though support of the Geneva Declaration on Armed Violence and Development. See www.genevadeclaration.org.

References

Ball, Nicole. *Making peace work: The role of the international development community*. Vol. 18. Overseas Development Council, 1996.

Ball, Nicole, Jordana D. Friedman, and Caleb S. Rossiter. "The Role of International Financial Institutions in Preventing and Resolving Conflict." In David Cortright, Ed. *The price of peace: Incentives and international conflict prevention*. Rowman and Littlefield, 1997: 234–264.

Blundell, Arthur G., and Emily E. Harwell. *How do peace agreements treat natural resources?* Forest Trends, 2016.

Cortright, David. "Incentives Strategies for Preventing Conflict." In David Cortright, Ed. *The price of peace: Incentives and international conflict prevention*. Rowman and Littlefield, 1997: 267–301.

Darby, John. P., and Roger Mac Ginty. "Introduction: Comparing Peace Processes." in John P. Darby and Roger Mac Ginty, Eds. *The management of peace processes*. Macmillan Palgrave, 2009: 1–15.

Department for International Development (DFID). Emerging Policy Paper: *Building the State and Securing the Peace*. DFID, 2009.

De Vries, Hugo, Paul Lange, and Leontine Specker. "Economic Provisions in Peace Agreements." *CRU Occasional Paper*. The Hague: Netherlands Institute of International Relations, Clingendael (2009).

Dwan, Renata, and Laura Bailey. "Liberia's Governance and Economic Management Assistance Programme (GEMAP)." New York and Washington, DC: United Nations, Department of Peacekeeping Operations, Peacekeeping Best Practices Section, and World Bank, Fragile States Group, 2006.

Griffiths, Aaron, and Catherine Barnes. "Incentives and Sanctions in Peace Processes." In Aaron Griffiths and Catherine Barnes, Eds. *Powers of persuasion: Incentives, sanctions and conditionality in peacemaking. Accord* 19 (2008): 9–13.

Guelke, Adrian. "Negotiations and Peace Processes." In John Darby and Roger Mac Ginty, Eds. *Contemporary peacemaking*. Palgrave Macmillan, 2002: 53–65.

Institute for Economics and Peace. *Structures of Peace: Identifying what leads to peaceful societies.* Institute for Economics and Peace, 2011.

International Labour Organisation (ILO). *Post-Conflict Employment Creation, Income Generation and Reintegration.* Operational Guidance Note, Version 4. Geneva: ILO, November 4, 2009.

Maxwell, Simon. "Eliminating world poverty: Building our common future." *Development Policy Review* 27, no. 6 (2009): 767–770.

Nest, Michael Wallace. "The Political Economy of the Congo War." In Nest, Michael Wallace, Francois Grignon, and Emizet F. Kisangani, Eds. *The Democratic Republic of Congo: Economic dimensions of war and peace.* Lynne Rienner, (2006): 31–62.

O'Donnell, Madalene, and James K. Boyce. "Peace and Public Purse: An Introduction." In James K. Boyce and Madalene O'Donnell, Eds. *Peace and the public purse: Economic policies for postwar statebuilding.* Lynne Rienner, (2007): 1–4.

Ohiorhenuan, John F. E., and Frances Stewart. *Post-conflict economic recovery: Enabling local ingenuity.* United Nations Development, 2008.

Organisation for Economic Co-operation and Development (OECD)/Development Assistance Committee (DAC). *Helping prevent violence conflict.* Paris (DAC Guidelines and Reference Series) 2011.

Organisation for Economic Co-operation and Development (OECD). *States of fragility 2015: Meeting post-2015 ambitions.* OECD, March 26, 2015.

Ramcharan, Bertrand G. "Peace Processes." In Vincent Chetail, Ed. *Post-conflict peacebuilding: A lexicon.* Oxford University Press, 2009: 228–244.

Suhrke, Astri, Torunn Wimpelmann, and Marcia Dawes. *Peace processes and statebuilding: Economic and institutional provisions of peace agreements.* Bergen, Norway: Chr. Michelsen Institute, 2007.

Stedman, Stephen John. *Ending civil wars: The implementation of peace agreements.* Lynne Rienner, 2002.

United Nations. *Challenges of sustaining peace: Report of the Advisory Group of Experts on the review of the peacebuilding architecture.* United Nations, 2015.

United Nations and World Bank. "In support of peacebuilding: Strengthening the post conflict needs assessment." *PCNA Review Report,* January 2007.

Uvin, Peter. *The influence of aid in situations of violent conflict.* OECD, 1999.

Väyrynen, Raimo. "Economic Incentives and the Bosnian Peace Process." In David Cortright, Ed. *The price of peace: Incentives and international conflict prevention.* Rowman and Littlefield, 1997: 155–180.

Wennmann, Achim. *Economic issues in peace processes: Socio-economic inequalities and peace in Nepal.* CCDP, 2009a.

Wennmann, Achim. "Economic provisions in peace agreements and sustainable peacebuilding." *Négociations* 1, no. 11 (2009b): 43–61.

Wennmann, Achim, and Jana Krause. *Managing the economic dimensions of peace processes: Resource wealth, autonomy, and peace in Aceh.* Centre on Conflict, Development and Peacebuilding (CCDP), Graduate Institute of International and Development Studies, 2009.

Woodward, Susan L. *Economic priorities for peace implementation.* International Peace Academy, 2002.

World Bank. *World development report 2011: Conflict, security, and development.* World Bank, 2011.

Zartman, I. William. "Looking Forward and Looking Backward on Negotiation Theory." In William I. Zartman and Viktor Aleksandrovich Kremeniuk. *Peace versus justice: Negotiating forward- and backward-looking outcomes.* Rowman and Littlefield, 2005: 287–301.

Zoellick, Robert B. "Fragile states: Securing development." *Survival* 50, no. 6 (2008): 67–84.

PART IV
Reconciliation and transitional justice

8
FACTORING TRANSITIONAL JUSTICE INTO THE QUALITY PEACE EQUATION

David Backer

Introduction

In settings afflicted by conflict, a natural ambition is to exit these conditions and eliminate the ongoing threat of upheaval and violence. The desire for such relief does not mean, however, that everyone merely wants to end conflict and put what happened behind them. Instead, past transgressions and harms are rarely forgotten, especially by those victimized, and inevitably cast a shadow over efforts to fashion a better future.

The frequent circumstance of facing legacies of conflict has prompted the emergence of the field of transitional justice. Its contributors offer numerous inputs about what can and should be done, and why. A core dimension is the relationship between transitional justice and peace. The focus is not solely conflict termination; rather, the attributes of the resulting peace matter, as outcomes and an enabling environment. What is done about the causes and consequences of conflict can be linked to the progress of a peace process, the location of different actors in a post-conflict dispensation, and the subsequent evolution of lives and society.

Transitional justice in brief

Ruti Teitel coined the term "transitional justice" in 1991 (Teitel 2008). Her inspiration was the seismic shifts accompanying the fall of communism across Eastern Europe and the former Soviet Union, plus the reinstallation of civilian governments in many Latin American countries. The phenomenon of transitional justice is hardly unique to the late-twentieth century. Earlier examples date back, at least, to Athens circa 400 BC (Elster 2004). Moreover, every shift from an oppressive regime, a state of war, civil discord, or aggression between social groups could qualify as a transitional justice moment. What Teitel and her contemporaries astutely observed was that these sets of cases (like others), though dispersed and exhibiting distinct contexts, share histories of violence and abuses that present hard questions: should the situation be addressed and if so, how and to what end (Teitel 2000)?

As Teitel later described, the two decades since her innovation have witnessed the establishment of transitional justice as a field, building on a foundation that coalesced after World War II (2003). The field's definition and evolution was influenced by several factors: (1) waves of democratization—one commencing in the mid-1940s, the other in the mid-1970s and broader in scope, (2) the rash of internal conflicts during the 1990s and 2000s, (3) genocides in Europe, Asia and Africa, and (4) the emergence of the international human rights regime (Huntington 1993). In the process, transitional justice drew attention for its presumed relevance to conflict resolution and post-conflict peacebuilding.[1]

The practice has become pervasive, with increasing variety (Backer 2009a). Whereas punitive measures imposed by victors against antagonists predominated historically, the recent decades reveal a menu of transitional justice options, including:

- criminal prosecution by domestic, foreign, international, and hybrid courts;
- administrative sanctions, such as lustration (i.e., vetting of individuals to determine eligibility to hold official and state-subsidized positions), purges, and bans;
- investigations conducted by authorities, quasi-independent truth commissions, and independent inquiries;
- reconciliation initiatives by truth commissions, other national and traditional bodies, and via informal arrangements (e.g., victim-offender mediation);
- financial, material, and symbolic reparations that benefit individuals and communities;
- institutional changes like security sector reforms, the creation of human rights oversight, and constitutional development; and
- immunity through amnesties, pardons, and limits on accountability and punishment.

The different forms are utilized selectively and strategically over time in response to conditions, based on constraints, incentives, and expectations, and to achieve a range of objectives. A key in understanding the choice, implementation, and effects of these measures—and their relationship to peace—is to discern their respective features, appreciating when and why they are employed and tracing hypothesized relationships to outcomes. In addition, the most illuminating studies seek to gauge how people are involved in and affected by these processes.

Transitional justice and quality peace

Calculations about whether and how to address past transgressions regularly factor into efforts to terminate conflicts and the durability of post-conflict peace. Certain transitional justice measures can promote impunity and contribute to persistent violence. Meanwhile, trajectories of peacebuilding tend to exert a reciprocal influence on the pursuit of transitional justice. Measures can also enrich the characteristics of peace in other consequential ways. An exacting indicator of the quality of peace is the degree to which a transitional justice process responds to the needs and interests of victims. On occasion, however, measures are manipulated for purposes that have little to do with peace—or justice.

Transitional justice and conflict termination

Deliberations and decisions—whether unilateral or negotiated—to end wars and civil conflicts and to proceed with democratization often hinge on stipulations about transitional justice, which have a bearing on the orientations and behavior of actors who are implicated in abuses and could hold a veto or intervene as spoilers. When vulnerable to repercussions, they are prone to resist a transition, oppose the adoption of an agreement, resist the introduction or enforcement of provisions that envision the pursuit of wrongdoers, and even respond with force. If insulated from accountability, their willingness to accept a transition should increase.

Among the first to describe these scenarios was Huntington (1993), who argued that the risk of backlash cautions against pursuit of accountability at all costs. His controversial "guidelines to democratizers" advocates a pragmatic tradeoff: if the balance of power remains skewed toward those implicated in abuses, concede accountability. He placed a premium on not derailing transitions, reasoning that otherwise conflict resolution and subsequent gains are lost. His advice drew from a study of 31 cases between 1974 and 1990. Two illustrative examples are Argentina and Uruguay, both of which faced the threat of a military coup soon after reinstituting civilian rule during the 1980s. In response, Argentina curtailed and eventually backtracked on accountability efforts, establishing a deadline for criminal indictments, foregoing prosecution of lower-level military personnel, and eventually pardoning five imprisoned junta members. Meanwhile, voters in Uruguay narrowly accepted an amnesty in a national referendum.

The prospect of violence is quite real, as demonstrated by events in other countries, including several prominent assassinations linked to transitional justice measures:

- Guatemala (1998): Bishop Gerardi, head of the Recuperación de la Memoria Histórica (Recovery of Historical Memory) project, 2 days after this independent inquiry released its report.
- Serbia (2003): Prime Minister Zoran Đinđić, who handed over Slobodan Milosevic to the International Criminal Tribunal for the Former Yugoslavia (ICTY).
- Rwanda (2001–present): at least dozens and perhaps hundreds of witnesses from the *gacaca* proceedings, an application of a traditional system of community justice to dispose of cases of tens of thousands of individuals implicated in the 1994 genocide.

Also, Bass (2001) contends that the creation of the ICTY not only failed to serve as a brake on the Milosevic regime and end the civil war in the Balkans, as may have been hoped, but actually made the situation worse, prolonging the conflict and intensifying the violence. The explanation is that leaders were labeled as pariahs and faced with the likelihood of imprisonment or death, rather than continued power or freedom in exile, so they might as well go down fighting (Bass 2001).

The demand for amnesty and related protections continues to be commonplace, strong, and effective. In most countries, laws, decrees, peace accords, pacts, and constitutional provisions afford degrees of immunity from legal liability for some or all conflict-related transgressions (Mallinder 2008). Certain regimes adopt "self-amnesties," which can remain in force following a transition, even for decades. In addition, liability is restricted in other ways, such as lenient prosecutorial policies, statutes of limitation, pardons, and reduced sentences.

Nonetheless, the viability of relying on such measures has been weakened by an ongoing shift toward a global norm of accountability, at least for war crimes, crimes against humanity, and genocide (Sikkink 2011). Of note, the last 20 years have witnessed the creation of ad hoc tribunals for the former Yugoslavia and Rwanda, "hybrid" courts in Sierra Leone, Timor-Leste, and Cambodia, and the International Criminal Court (ICC), as well as trials in many countries under principles of universal jurisdiction. Concerns about undermining transitions to peace feature in debates about these undertakings, but rarely prevail. Some prosecutions are for acts committed long ago, with conflict termination moot. Even where violence is recent or ongoing, the risks of conflict tend to affect logistical matters (e.g., location) more so than the basic decision about whether to engage in accountability. Recently, the ICC indicted the sitting heads of state of Sudan and Libya during active conflicts, and was listed as a recourse, if needed (as ultimately transpired), in the accord negotiated following the 2007–2008 post-election violence in Kenya.

Transitional justice and conflict avoidance

Other measures that have come to the fore occupy the middle ground and temper what was historically depicted as a stark choice between accountability and amnesty (Pion-Berlin 1994). In principle, options like reintegration programs and truth commissions avoid the perils of either allowing perpetrators to remain unchecked, or pressing for punitive responses that could be upsetting. Instead, these measures aim to diminish the capacity for violence and the drivers of conflict.

Truth commissions are abundant, emerging as a standard step in conflict settings, especially in the wake of the South African TRC. Whereas the early truth commissions from the 1970s and 1980s were devised after transitions occurred, the TRC had been contemplated before the African National Congress (ANC) entered into final negotiations with the apartheid-era state and was then enabled by the terms of the Interim Constitution that led to democratization in 1994. The TRC differed from many of its predecessors in other respects, including the adoption of a more public and victim-centered approach and exposing the identities and actions of numerous perpetrators. Most subsequent commissions mirror the TRC model, particularly its emphasis on seeking reconciliation among conflicting parties within society. One aspect that has yet to be replicated is the TRC's conditional amnesty process, whereby individual perpetrators had to apply and meet several criteria, including identification of and full disclosure about specific offenses, committed for a political cause.

Transitional justice and the durability of peace

While conflict termination is desirable, the ensuing peace can be provisional, fragile, and fleeting. The legacy of upheaval indicates an inherent vulnerability and stimulates grievances, engendering a high risk of renewed conflict (Suhrke and Samset 2007). Durable peace, though difficult to achieve, is preferable to reversion to conflict and presumably essential to the realization of quality peace. What impact does transitional justice have in this regard?

A standard logic generalizes the aforementioned argument: the best recipe for durable peace is to placate potential spoilers, namely those who were responsible for past violence and/or possess the capacity to disrupt order (Humphreys and Weinstein 2008). Even if weakened or stripped of authority, they may possess sufficient means and motivation to resort to conflict. When faced with dangerous actors who signal their intent to intervene forcefully when under duress, accountability and investigative measures that would expose misdeeds can appear impractical and counterproductive.

The empirical literature supplies conflicting evidence on this count. A study of the 32 cases of civil war terminations from 1989–2003 concluded that amnesties substantially reduced the risk of recurrence, whereas the opposite is true of trials, while truth commissions are largely immaterial (Snyder and Vinjamuri 2003). Another study of 200 post-conflict societies from 1946–2003 found that (1) amnesty shortens the duration of peace; (2) exile lengthens the duration of peace; (3) non-retributive measures (i.e., reparations, truth commissions) lengthen the duration of peace only in democratic societies; and (4) some forms of accountability (e.g., criminal prosecutions, purges) may lengthen the duration of peace (Gates et al. 2007). Thus, the studies disagree about the validity of the pragmatic rationale for amnesty, as conducive to the durability of peace. Equally important, the second study provides credence to an alternative theory that retributive and reparatory forms of transitional justice are the most advantageous in sustaining peace.

Transitional justice and peace with impunity

Excessive attention may be paid to conflict termination and the durability of peace, thereby discounting other meaningful indicators of the quality of outcomes. An essential issue is whether transitional justice choices, especially at early stages, have offsetting deleterious effects.

Consider the decision to provide immunity for past transgressions, in order to mitigate the risk of backlash. A downside is that failing to hold perpetrators responsible for violent acts might be interpreted as implying that such behavior is not outside the bounds of acceptable behavior, despite representations that the transgressions are unconscionable. The lack of sanctions and implicit permissiveness in relation to these abuses can be viewed as tantamount to relaxing fundamental principles. Doing so on utilitarian grounds—to enable a transition—also accords precedence to a different value system, ahead of upholding human rights as sacrosanct. Thus, a salient question is whether amnesty weakens the moral fabric of a post-conflict society and diminishes the legitimacy and authority of the state.

One gauge is the assorted types of violence (criminal, sexual, domestic, etc.) that individuals experience in day-to-day life. The incidence of violence in post-conflict societies can resemble levels observed during conflict, and sometimes spike in the aftermath, for several reasons.[2] Individuals and communities may be habituated to pervasive violence. Under these conditions, restoring norms will inevitably take time. In addition, ex-combatants are accustomed to force as the dominant mode that allowed them to impose their will, a mindset that is hard to shed. Also, being shunned socially and facing economic hardships could stoke anger and induce illegality (Theidon et al. 2011). Measures like amnesty arguably fuel such violence because they foster a sense of impunity by demonstrating the state's inability to police limits on egregious behavior. No firm connections have been established, however, since empirical research on whether transitional justice measures contribute to tackling ordinary and structural violence remains uncommon.

No (quality) peace without justice

Another stance is to dismiss peace as a hollow illusion absent a sincere and vigorous agenda of confronting the past. A common refrain is "no peace without justice," a rallying cry especially for numerous human rights practitioners and advocacy organizations. Their concept of "justice" excludes measures that reinforce impunity. Beyond this, the proponents differ in terms of whether they focus exclusively on prosecutions, or are open to embracing a range of transitional justice options like truth commissions and reparations programs.

Should the refrain be taken literally, or as merely a rhetorical device for effect? The answer is somewhere in between. The proponents are generally principled purists who equate justice with entrenching universal human rights and the rule of law, which require the enforcement of standards that include protection from the serious transgressions of conflict. Therefore, accountability for the offenders of these standards is essential as a moral obligation and to uphold the norms of civilized society, which are also recognized in various international conventions. Other transitional justice measures, excluding amnesty, can contribute to institutionalizing these norms. Yet the proponents are surely savvy about practical constraints on what can be undertaken amid a transition. This awareness does not necessarily blunt the sense of what is right, but may inform strategies. The intent can be to urge everyone not to be satisfied with compromises and thus lose sight of the idea that peace alone, without true justice, is inadequate—and may not even be peace. In this volume, Knox provides ample evidence from Northern Ireland in this respect. The Good Friday Agreement eschewed both amnesty and prosecutions, but established the Northern Ireland Victims Commission and promoted various reparations mechanisms, including funding to meet the needs of victims (Peace Accords Matrix 2015).

Does quality peace require prompt transitional justice?

A different critique, which opposes postponing measures, is that justice delayed is justice denied. This view invokes British politician and jurist William Gladstone's reference to the inefficiencies that undermine the standards of due process, including the right to a speedy disposition of a case.

Victims have cause to demand expedited action, not least after the absence of protections in the past. When left on hold, pending trials or other measures, victims can feel ignored, which may be perceived as a further injustice. Resulting disaffection is often directed at the government, even if it is new, has no responsibility for what transpired previously, and would ordinarily receive victims' support. In practical terms, lengthy lags complicate the pursuit of justice, in so far as evidence evaporates and the will to undertake the necessary efforts fades (Backer 2010).

Those implicated in atrocities prefer to avoid measures that bring attention to their past activities, but also do not want to be in limbo or to cope with a turn of events.[3] Without an amnesty, they face uncertainty about whether prosecutions are forthcoming. Eliminating an amnesty and/or commencing trials after many years would upset settled expectations. While such circumstances might not elicit empathy for perpetrators, they can feel mistreated, which presents a danger if the emotions are channeled into violence.

From society's perspective, proceeding with transitional justice measures apace should help to forestall the possibility that residual issues from the past remain unresolved and fester. Putting things off may worsen the foundations of peace, by kindling unhappiness and creating a situation where post-conflict recovery is more difficult than if steps had been taken before. A risk exists of missing the window of opportunity to successfully implement measures.

Yet these valid concerns need not dissuade initiating measures well after conflicts conclude. Compelling arguments exist for understanding and addressing transgressions from long ago (Kaufman 2008). One prominent rationale is to learn the lessons of history—better late than never—in line with the notion that "those who cannot remember the past are condemned to repeat it" (Santayana 1905).

The proof that delayed justice is believed to be worthwhile includes the accumulating examples from recent years where measures were employed in relation to now-distant conflicts. Over the last two decades, Estonia, Latvia, Lithuania, Poland, and Romania conducted inquiries that went back to the Nazi occupations around

World War II, in addition to examining the intervening Soviet/Communist era. The two periods were seen as similar, intertwined, and in need of being studied together (Grodsky 2009).[4] Meanwhile, various Latin American countries have followed up on what was done during the initial stages of military-to-civilian transitions, among other things conducting new or more expansive investigations, organizing reparations schemes, and finally undoing amnesty provisions and conducting trials (Collins 2010). Analogous instances of "revisiting" after a lag, going further in truth-seeking, redress, and accountability, are observed elsewhere (e.g., Spain).

These cases endorse the argument that it is never too late to undertake transitional justice. Victims of conflict, and their advocates, rarely give up the cause. The recent activities fill in gaps left by silences and limited efforts at earlier points. Official recognition, plus corresponding steps to confront and remedy harms, may provide some solace, if only to victims' descendants.

(Quality) peace, then (transitional) justice

Peace, especially when enduring, can also facilitate transitional justice measures that had seemed impractical. With sufficient stability and distance from conflict, the tensions present at transition fade and claims that conditions are too sensitive to permit inquiries and accountability tend to lose weight. Taking these steps becomes less risky and more realistic.

In addition, measures might be implemented more appropriately and effectively than before (Quinn 2009). The passage of time reduces the chance of reflexively punitive processes that seek retribution and enact a biased "victor's justice" (Fletcher et al. 2009). Lasting peace is often accompanied by greater openness and improvements in infrastructure and resources, which together with a new generation of leaders can enable a stronger commitment to transitional justice. Elongating the time frame of implementation—perhaps separated into stages—might therefore be optimal to cement the incipient peace. Additional measures could demonstrate progress since the conflict ended and strengthen institutions and norms that ensure public order and protect human rights.

Transitional justice and the development of quality peace

The most optimistic visions see potential for transitional justice processes to contribute to consequential political, social, and economic development (Minow 1998; de Greiff and Duthie 2009). While certain claims are arguably unrealistic, they shed light on conceptions about the dimensions and correlates of quality peace. Empirical studies have begun to evaluate the associations between transitional justice measures and progress toward broader developmental outcomes.

The first outcome is a set of phenomena that could be grouped under the category of social harmony: reduced grievances and increased reconciliation, trust, and tolerance, both among people and groups and between people/groups and the state. All of these phenomena translate into diminished conflict and enhance the prospects of peace. They also facilitate collaboration and unity, plus free up resources for other productive activities, further improving the quality of peace. In theory, certain transitional justice measures boost the extent of social harmony. Suggestive evidence exists in support: for example, results from general population surveys in South Africa were interpreted as showing that the TRC contributed to inter-racial reconciliation and tolerance, by increasing the extent to which people shared understandings of the apartheid past (Verdoolaege and Gibson 2005).

A second set of outcomes is comprised of democracy, the rule of law, and the protection of human rights. Here, the favorable effects of transitional justice would derive from building necessary capacity and promoting complementary values, institutions, and processes. Some measures can also serve as test beds, with the potential for salutary demonstration effects. A recent study of 161 countries from 1970–2007 found that a combination of truth commissions, trials, and amnesties was associated with a greater degree of democracy and human rights, whereas the individual measures by themselves exhibited negative relationships (Olsen et al. 2010).

In addition, a meta-analysis of studies of the impact of transitional justice concluded that undertaking measures generally yields improvements and does not tend to make things worse (Thoms 2010).

Victim-sensitive transitional justice as an indicator of the quality of peace

When examining transitional justice, confining attention to macro-level dimensions overlooks the experiences of individuals, families, and communities. Victims of past violence are noteworthy, given what they suffered and how they are ordinarily positioned in post-conflict societies. Transitions to peace will fall short if victims are shortchanged or ignored (Backer 2004).

Yet other constituencies often receive preference in decisions about transitional justice measures. To reiterate, the overlapping groups of potential veto holders, spoilers, and various elites are typically taken seriously. Even the amorphous public can receive priority, with appeals to the common good and national interest, plus caveats about limits on the collective capacity to respond to the demands of post-conflict recovery.

Despite typical rhetoric of respecting the needs and interests of victims, they are not necessarily consulted. Even when involved, their role may be limited to supplying inputs within defined spaces created for them, after which their direct agency is attenuated. More can be done to improve participation, as well as responsiveness to expectations and contributions. What then are their preferences?

Surveys of victims of conflict in Ghana, Liberia, Nigeria, South Africa, and Sierra Leone have found that majorities approve of amnesty. These views do not imply a rejection of accountability—quite the contrary. Instead, most respondents accept amnesty as a precondition for peace, but feel the bargain is unfair. At the same time, their reservations about this compromise can be mitigated considerably by attaching conditions such as acknowledgement, truth, apology, and remorse (Backer 2009b). Longitudinal research in South Africa revealed declining support for amnesty, acceptance of its necessity, and belief in its fairness over the 5 years after the conclusion of the TRC process (Backer 2010). Together, these results suggest a desire for limiting the scope of amnesty to permit certain forms of accountability to be pursued, while also requiring those complicit in past abuses to engage in restorative and reparatory actions in exchange for protections from legal accountability, such as might be deemed prudent to facilitate a transition from conflict.

Transitional justice as a weapon

To caution, transitional justice measures are not always deployed in ways that are judicious, genuine, and progressive—or at worst benign. The measures are tools that can be manipulated for nefarious purposes. Recent history supplies instances where transitional justice is exploited for personal, partisan, and tactical reasons that have little to do with promoting peace.

For example, certain parties, factions, leaders, and candidates in the Czech Republic, Hungary, and Poland turned lustration laws and the release of police files of alleged collaborators into political ammunition. The purpose was to advance interests during election campaigns and wrangling for control of the government and the legislative agenda. Many records were inaccurate, with the involvement of citizens in the network of informants embellished or even fabricated. Consequently, relying on this information for lustration rulings—or to expose people publicly—could be devious, opportunistic, and divisive (Nalepa 2010).

Similar evidence is available from Serbia, Croatia, and Uzbekistan. The last case is conspicuous because independence from Soviet rule did not amount to much of a transition; instead, the Communist leadership maintained power. The country's truth commission, conducted in 1999, was a device for consolidating autocracy, by constructing a history flattering to the regime and supplying a basis for sidelining out-of-favor officials (Grodsky 2010).

Zimbabwe presents another instance where transitional justice measures are used to paper over transgressions while entrenching the authority of an incumbent regime. During Gukurahundi, a period of brutal suppression between 1980 and 1987, the army was sent in to quell a suspected revolt by the main opposition—concentrated in the Matabeleland region—to the governing party of then Prime Minister Robert Mugabe. Following the Unity Accord that ended the conflict, the dissidents demobilized and were granted amnesty, as were the soldiers, who committed atrocities on a massive scale. A truth commission was conducted in 1985, but the government never released its report. Mugabe acquired the position of president, with greater executive powers, that was created as part of the accord. He did not face significant political opposition for another 20 years, and kept power until 2017.

Meanwhile, ongoing events in Rwanda raise concerns about ethnic bias in transitional justice (Tiemessen 2004). Accountability for past violence—across the international tribunal, the national courts, and *gacaca*—is confined to the members of the Hutu majority who acted in concert with the former Hutu-controlled regime and allied paramilitaries. Meanwhile, atrocities committed by the Tutsi-affiliated Rwandan Patriotic Front, during the response to the onset of the genocide and the surrounding civil war, remain out of bounds to prosecute.

These cases deviate from the classic script where navigating transitional justice revolves around avoiding antagonism. Here, the approaches are provocative because they foster advantage by selectively directing the burden of accountability onto specific actors, while exempting others. The goal may not be to stir up controversy and enmity, but the tactics hardly shy away from destabilizing confrontations.

Alternatively, a regime may be compromised by a poor human rights record and bow to pressure by undertaking transitional justice measures, but simply to deflect scrutiny. Uganda under Idi Amin is illustrative. In 1974–1975, at the urging of the international community and domestic public, the government organized an investigation into alleged abuses since 1971. Public hearings were conducted, but the commission's report was not available until years later. Amin continued his despotic rein until an incursion by Tanzania's military forced him out of power and into exile in 1979.[5]

This discussion highlights the importance of transitional justice being undertaken sincerely: are the causes and effects of past conflict an honest source of concern, with measures designed to address, repair, and deter aggression and abuses? Otherwise, transitional justice is corrupted into another tool of authority and does not serve the interests of peacebuilding.

Conclusion

This chapter situates transitional justice amid efforts to achieve quality peace in the aftermath of conflict. Neither concept is reducible to just one simple quantity. Transitional justice encompasses an array of options for dealing with legacies of violence and associated transgressions. This breadth is well articulated by Mac Ginty in this volume, describing the hybridity of forms of governance and process. Quality peace is best understood as a state of affairs in which conflict is dormant and unlikely, while everyone enjoys an existence that represents clear progress relative to what was previously experienced. Both involve long-term processes.

The relationship between transitional justice and peace is complex. Observed patterns indicate that a vital synergy can exist, with each helping to advance the other. Studies suggest that the entire repertoire of transitional justice is conducive to peace, of a sort, when employed in hospitable settings, initiated at the right moments, and taking a suitable form. Measures can play a role in terminating conflicts and establishing a peace that is durable and offers other benefits. Yet the same measures can also coincide with diametrically opposite effects, again depending on where, when, and how they are implemented. Transitional justice is susceptible to magnifying the risks of continued and renewed conflict, contributing to a marginal peace marred by impunity, violence, and unresolved grievances, failing to promote advancement, and being exploited.

Further careful study is warranted to validate notable findings and reconcile conflicting results from the existing literature, in order to clarify the interactions between transitional justice and achieving, sustaining, and deepening peace. The research must overcome the challenges of theorizing, measurement, and analysis, among other things, by appropriately considering the choice of measures and evaluating their objectives, design, context, and timing.

The context and dynamics of transitional justice offer insight into the definition and prerequisites of quality peace. In particular, the endogenous relationship emphasizes the significance of societies afflicted by conflict halting aggression, ensuring stability and security, and affording citizens respectable lives. Moreover, the treatment and responses of victims during transitions from conflict stand out as crucial indicators of progress.

Notes

1. See, in particular, United Nations Security Council. 2004. Report of the Secretary General: The Rule of Law and Transitional Justice in Conflict and Post-Conflict Societies (Document S/2004/616); and United States Department of State, Post-Conflict Reconstruction: Essential Tasks. 2005. Washington, DC: Office of the Coordinator for Reconstruction and Stabilization.
2. See, for example, the Geneva Declaration.
3. See, for example, the discussion of the lengthy detention of suspected genocidaires in Rwanda by Kerr and Mobekk (2007).
4. Other countries in the former Communist bloc conducted inquiries: Uzbekistan, of the Russian, Soviet, post-Soviet eras; unified Germany and Hungary, solely of the Soviet era; and Serbia and Croatia, of the post-Communist nationalist era and the civil war.
5. This investigation is commonly characterized as the first truth commission, after appearing as the earliest entry on the lists compiled by Hayner (1994). Yet similar investigations were observed before. For example, British Consul Roger Casement conducted a 1903–1904 inquiry into reported abuses in the Congo Free State, a territorial possession of King Leopold II of Belgium, who established a commission of inquiry in 1905, which confirmed Casement's findings. Furthermore, Amin created the commission absent significant political change, so the inquiry does not qualify as a *transitional* justice measure.

References

Backer, David A. *The human face of justice: Victims' responses to South Africa's Truth and Reconciliation Commission Process*. University of Michigan, 2004.

Backer, David. "Cross-national comparative analysis." In Hugo van der Merwe, Victoria Baxter, and Audrey Chapman, Eds. *Assessing the impact of transitional justice: Challenges for empirical research*. United States Institute of Peace (2009a): 23–90.

Backer, David. "The layers of amnesty: Evidence from surveys of victims in five African countries." *Global Studies Review* 5, no. 2 (2009b).

Backer, David. "Watching a bargain unravel? A panel study of victims' attitudes about transitional justice in Cape Town, South Africa." *International Journal of Transitional Justice* 42, no. 2 (2010): 443–456.

Bass, Gary Jonathan. *Stay the hand of vengeance: The politics of war crimes tribunals*. Princeton University Press, 2001.

Collins, Cath. *Post-transitional justice: Human rights trials in Chile and El Salvador*. Penn State Press, 2010.

de Greiff, Pablo, and Roger Duthie, Eds. *Transitional justice and development: Making connections*. Social Sciences Research Council, 2009.

Elster, Jon. *Closing the books: Transitional justice in historical perspective*. Cambridge University Press, 2004.

Fletcher, Laurel E., Harvey M. Weinstein, and Jamie Rowen. "Context, timing and the dynamics of transitional justice: A historical perspective." *Human Rights Quarterly* 31, no. 1 (2009): 163–220.

Gates, Scott, Helga Malmin Binningsbo, and Tove Grete Lie. "Post-conflict justice and sustainable peace." *World Bank Policy Research Working Paper* 4191 (2007).

Grodsky, Brian. "Beyond lustration truth-seeking efforts in the post-communist space." *Taiwan Journal of Democracy* 5, no. 2 (2009): 21–44.

Grodsky, Brian. *The costs of justice: Understanding how new leaders choose to respond to previous rights abuses*. University of Notre Dame Press, 2010.

Hayner, Priscilla B. "Fifteen truth commissions-1974 to 1994: A comparative study." *Human Rights Quarterly* 16 (1994): 597.

Humphreys, Macartan, and Jeremy M. Weinstein. "Who fights? The determinants of participation in civil war." *American Journal of Political Science* 52, no. 2 (2008): 436–455.

Huntington, Samuel P. *The third wave: Democratization in the late twentieth century*. Vol. 4. University of Oklahoma Press, 1993.

Kaufman, Zachary D. "Transitional justice delayed is not transitional justice denied: Contemporary confrontation of Japanese human experimentation during World War II through a people's tribunal." *Yale Law & Policy Review* 26, no. 2 (2008): 645–659.

Kerr, Rachel, and Erin Mobekk. *Peace and justice: Seeking accountability after war*. Polity (2007).

Mallinder, Louise. *Amnesty, human rights and political transitions: Bridging the peace and justice divide*. Bloomsbury Publishing, 2008.

Minow, Martha. *Between vengeance and forgiveness: Facing history after genocide and mass violence*. Beacon Press, 1998.

Nalepa, Monika. *Skeletons in the closet: Transitional justice in post-communist Europe*. Cambridge University Press, 2010.

Olsen, Tricia D., Leigh A. Payne, and Andrew G. Reiter. *Transitional justice in balance: Comparing processes, weighing efficacy*. United States Institute of Peace Press, 2010.

Peace Accords Matrix. Northern Ireland Good Friday Agreement. April 10, 1998. Accessed September 30, 2017 at http://peaceaccords.nd.edu/accord/northern-ireland-good-friday-agreement.

Pion-Berlin, David. "To prosecute or to pardon? Human rights decisions in the Latin American Southern Cone." *Human Rights Quarterly* 16, no. 1 (1994): 105–130.

Quinn, Joanna R. "Chicken and egg? Sequencing in transitional justice: The case of Uganda." *International Journal of Peace Studies* 14, no. 2 (2009): 35–53.

Santayana, George. *The life of reason: The phases of human progress*. Charles Scribner's Sons, 1905.

Sikkink, Kathryn. *The justice cascade: How human rights prosecutions are changing world politics* (The Norton Series in World Politics). WW Norton & Company, 2011.

Snyder, Jack, and Leslie Vinjamuri. "Trials and errors: Principles and pragmatism in strategies of international justice." *International Security* 28, no. 3 (2003): 5–44.

Suhrke, Astri, and Ingrid Samset. "What's in a figure? Estimating recurrence of civil war." *International Peacekeeping* 14, no. 2 (2007): 195–203.

Teitel, Ruti G. *Transitional justice*. Oxford University Press, 2000.

Teitel, Ruti G. "Transitional justice genealogy." *Harvard Human Rights Journal* 16 (2003): 69–94.

Teitel, Ruti G. "Editorial note – transitional justice globalized." *International Journal of Transitional Justice* 2, no. 1 (2008): 1–4.

Theidon, Kimberly, and Kelly Phenicie with Elizabeth Murray. "Gender, conflict, and peacebuilding: State of the field and lessons learned from USIP grantmaking." USIP Peaceworks, 2011.

Thoms, Oskar N. T., James Ron, and Roland Paris. "State-level effects of transitional justice: What do we know?" *International Journal of Transitional Justice* 4, no. 3 (2010): 329–354.

Tiemessen, Alana Erin. "After Arusha: Gacaca justice in post-genocide Rwanda." *African Studies Quarterly* 8, no. 1 (2004): 57–76.

Verdoolaege, Annelies, and James L. Gibson. "Overcoming apartheid: Can truth reconcile a divided nation?" *African Affairs* 104, no. 414 (2005): 158–160.

9
THE CHALLENGES OF RECONCILING TRADITION WITH TRUTH AND RECONCILIATION COMMISSION PROCESSES

The case of Solomon Islands

Karen Brounéus and Holly L. Guthrey

Introduction

In the quest to build peaceful and sustainable societies after internal armed conflict, Truth and Reconciliation Commissions (TRCs) have come to play a pivotal role in many peacebuilding efforts around the world. These institutions have most commonly aimed to uncover truths about the past in the attempt to prevent the recurrence of conflict and facilitate reconciliation; increasingly, one focus has also been on promoting victim healing (Hayner 2010; Guthrey 2015). But do truth commissions contribute to a higher quality peace—and if so, how? In Chapter 1 of this volume, reconciliation was posited as a likely and important element in post-war reconstruction and the building of quality peace. Consequently, it is raised in several other chapters. Empirical research on the impact of truth commissions is relatively new, and has to date commonly focused on issues such as the effect of truth commissions and amnesty on durable peace at the global, transnational level (Snyder 2006; Gates et al. 2007), and country level (Čorkalo et al. 2004; Stover and Vinjamuri 2004; Meernik 2005). Research has also focused on victims and victim healing (Backer 2007; Hamber 2009; Brounéus 2010; Rimé et al. 2011; Guthrey 2015) as well as on human rights and democracy (Olsen et al. 2010; Wiebelhaus-Brahm 2010). While some studies suggest hope for these mechanisms, others identify severe risks with these complex processes.

Finding pathways that contribute to quality peace is fundamental: if peace can hold through the fragile post–conflict phase when the risk of relapse into war is at its peak, the hopes for peace gradually improve (Collier et al. 2003). So, apart from asking whether truth commissions contribute to quality peace, we must question the extent to which truth commissions function generically or are inextricably linked to their specific contexts, and also whether all peace processes benefit from having a truth commission or if there are circumstances when it would be advisable to take another path.

In this chapter, we will contribute to the discussion on reconciliation in post-conflict societies with an analysis of a truth commission that has received little public or scholarly attention in the West: The Solomon Islands civil war—often referred to as "the Tensions"—and the subsequent TRC. This TRC was the first to be established in a micro-state in the South Pacific. It concluded its work on February 28, 2012, when the TRC final report was officially handed over to the Prime Minister of Solomon Islands. Although the report was leaked by its editor in April 2013, it has not yet been officially released to the public at the time of writing. However, the TRC final report was in fact quietly tabled without a motion in Parliament by former Prime Minister Gordon Lilo in the last days of the 2014 Parliamentary session. Due to concerns among politicians that the report would lead to unrest and political embarrassment (several former militants are MPs), this was a politically smart move, however it has also meant the final report has remained hidden from the public eye. However, Lilo was soon defeated as a Member of Parliament and the new Prime Minister, Manasseh Sogavare, in early 2016 began a formal process of evaluating and implementing the TRC final report's recommendations. Yet, transcripts from a June 2017 Parliamentary session refers to the "TRC's report which Parliament is yet to look at". Hence, the implementation of recommendations outlined in the TRC Final Report has yet to be realized.

The Solomon Islands TRC has fomented some progress in peacebuilding after the Tensions despite great challenges with, for example, external and internal clashes of bureaucracy and funding. We will argue that a primary difficulty during this process has been to achieve cultural legitimacy of the TRC itself, and to find ways of weaving the foreign-based idea of public truth-telling with traditional reconciliation or community-based conflict resolution practices that flourish at the grassroots level. In addition, this legitimacy challenge can likely create a disjuncture between victims' expectations and the actual work of the TRC. This difficulty of cultural legitimacy is even more complex because of the context in which it occurs: Solomon Islands is an ethnically fragmented country where there is little sense of nationhood, minimal trust in government, and where a sense of belonging, identity and accountability lies at the micro-level of the *wantok*.[1]

Bringing in examples from other TRCs around the world, we suggest that while it is yet uncertain if short-term problems may lead to long-term gains, the "cookie-cutter" approach to TRCs is not the most beneficial pathway (Guthrey 2016). Without fundamentally grounding the TRC in culturally appropriate—and gender sensitive—ways of dealing with conflict and trauma and weaving it with customary reconciliation, the TRC risks being hollowed out from within. Apart from being a costly undertaking during dire post-conflict hardship, the frustration and disillusionment that can result from a poorly executed process may lead to more pitfalls than promises for peace.

The Tensions and the TRC

The armed conflict in Solomon Islands broke out in 1998, when young Guadalcanal militants terrorized, raped, and forced thousands of Malaitans from their Guadalcanal homes. In response, young Malaitan militants took up arms (Bennett 2002; Kabutaulaka 2002; Dinnen 2002, 2009). Five years of low-intensity civil war began, characterized by severe violence and killings, the displacement of over 20,000 people, and a *coup d'état*. The violence formally ended with an invited external intervention led by Australia in 2003, the Regional Assistance Mission to Solomon Islands (RAMSI) (Moore 2004; Fry and Kabutaulaka 2008). The conflict had a profound impact on the small island nation with a population of around 500,000, not least on its women (Leslie 2000; Leslie and Boso 2003; Corrin 2008). Gender-based violence against women and girls was rampant on both sides during the conflict (Amnesty International 2004; Moore 2004; Corrin 2008); rape was one of the most common forms of violence and was committed as a form of retaliation by rival militias (Leslie and Boso 2003).

Influenced by the South African model, the Solomon Islands Christian Association (SICA) initiated the idea of a TRC soon after the conflict ended amid high political turmoil. In April 2009, this vision was realized when Archbishop Desmond Tutu inaugurated the Solomon Islands TRC, the aim of which was to promote national unity and reconciliation (National Parliament of Solomon Islands 2008). According to its mandate, the TRC would investigate human rights abuses that took place during the civil strife of 1998–2003. The TRC began taking statements in 2010, conducting a series of 11 public hearings and collecting roughly 4,000 statements, until its last hearing in September 2011. During its last year of work, the TRC also instituted an exhumation program intended to recover bodies of those killed during the Tensions with the aim to facilitate closure for relatives of the deceased and contribute to the national narrative of the conflict. The TRC submitted its final report including further recommendations on February 28, 2012.

To understand the underlying complexities and challenges facing this TRC, we must go back in time. The particular dynamics of this small country where *kastom*[2] and social relations, status and big men, orbit around the fundamental concepts of *wantok* and kinship—"the cement of each society, binding the individual to the group" (Bennett 2002)—make the Solomon Islands TRC an interesting case study. The case sheds light on questions of how to weave customary procedures with "new," or more aptly imported, peacebuilding mechanisms, and whether every peace process benefits from a TRC. By looking more deeply into one TRC conducted in a small, ethnically fragmented and developing country, we attempt to highlight issues and questions that lie at the heart of every existing or proposed TRC process in the world—to lesser and higher degrees.

The roots of the conflict in Solomon Islands lie both in immediate precipitating political and regional causes, and in deep-lying historical, social, and postcolonial legacies (Bennett 2002; Kabutaulaka 2002; Moore 2004; Hameiri 2009). The 900 islands and atolls that constitute Solomon Islands in the Southwest Pacific were "discovered" and named by Spanish explorer Álvaro de Mendaña in the sixteenth century, who soon realized—then as now—the numerous societies, cultures, and languages that make up this archipelago (Bennett 2002). In 1893, Solomon Islands became a British protectorate. Nearly half a century later, Solomon Islands was the scene of the World War II Battle of Guadalcanal in which Allied forces fought the Japanese intention of expanding their hold on the Southwest Pacific. The fighting was intense and bloody, strongly affecting indigenous communities that relocated inland to escape the conflict (Fraenkel 2004; Moore 2004).

After World War II, the capital of the country was moved from Tulagi to Honiara on the island of Guadalcanal with an influx of people from the neighboring island of Malaita, which was agriculturally overpopulated, looking for better economic opportunities (Liloqula 2000; Braithwaite et al. 2010). The migration of many Malaitans to Guadalcanal, and to the new economic center of Honiara, was the beginning of strained relations between Malaitans and Guales.

Independence from Great Britain was gained in 1978 and the new Constitution provided for the "freedom of movement of all peoples" (Liloqula 2000: 41), a factor that was used to justify the migration of Malaitans to the capital in Guadalcanal. As the population in and around Honiara grew, so too did the tensions between Malaitans and Guales. Intermarriages between Guales and Malaitans led to complexities in land acquisition: Guale land acquisition is matrilineal while Malaitan acquisition is patrilineal, thus giving Malaitan men marrying Guale women the right to land in both Malaita and Guadalcanal while Guale men are left with fewer women and less land (Braithwaite et al. 2010). This factor contributed to the discontentment of many people of Guadalcanal, who were forced to give up claims to land they believed to be theirs.

Strained relations continued to intensify after 1988, when a petition was submitted to the government from the "indigenous people of Guadalcanal," calling for "the government to find 'ways and means to repatriate all nonindigenous unemployed illegal squatters' [i.e., Malaitans] . . ." (Fraenkel 2004: 47) until a Guale uprising—the Isatabu insurgency—began in 1998. This movement was aimed at forcing Malaitan settlers off the island of Guadalcanal. It was a low-intensity civil war, fought by a "bark cloth-clad . . . insurgent group armed mainly with home-made guns . . . against the considerably superior armed forces of the state . . ." (Fraenkel 2004: 7). In late 1999, the rival Malaitan Eagle Forces (MEF) emerged, to which many of the paramilitary wing of the police were loyal. In a "joint operation," the MEF and paramilitary overthrew the government in June 2000 (Fraenkel 2004: 87).

Shortly thereafter, peace talks were initiated between the conflicting parties in October in Townsville, Australia, which resulted in the signing of the Townsville Peace Agreement (TPA) on October 15, 2000. The TPA was seen as "a deeply flawed document, a militants' charter . . ." and the subsequent agreed disarmament of the warring factions was "fatally limited" (Fraenkel 2004: 101). After a brief period of celebrating the TPA, there was a "criminalisation of the conflict" (Braithwaite et al. 2010: 45): militants who had gone home to collect repatriation payments began regrouping, violence erupted anew, and it soon became clear that the coup was "less about *capturing* state power and more about *ransacking* the state" (Fraenkel 2004: 106). A period of exploitation of government funds, organized crime, and weapons and drug trading began.

In 2003—after having declined several previous requests—Australia accepted an invitation from the Solomon Islands government to intervene. In July 2003, RAMSI arrived in Honiara, quickly reinstating law and order. Following this lauded initial intervention, RAMSI became increasingly criticized for not having a clear exit strategy, and for having taken over much of the state bureaucracy and security sector instead of building local capacity in such fundamental sectors of society. Many feared this would backfire as it did after independence from British colonialism, when Solomon Islanders were left to run a foreign-built state system without any training—and which, combined with the traditional system of *wantokism* and big men, became an implosive cocktail. After 10 years however, RAMSI withdrew its military contingent in 2013; it continued as a policing mission until June 2017 at which point it ended its entire mission.

The reconciliation process

Following the Tensions, several reconciliation initiatives were undertaken at both a government/church[3] level and at a grassroots level to address the conflict's severe consequences on the people of Solomon Islands. The Ministry of National Unity, Peace and Reconciliation was created in 2001 to promote reconciliation between the people of Guadalcanal and Malaita. Perhaps its most notable work toward reconciliation was the proposal of the Truth and Reconciliation Commission Act in 2008. In addition to being involved in the creation of the TRC, churches also had a role in other reconciliation efforts in Solomon Islands. The Melanesian Brotherhood has endeavored to promote reconciliation between Guales and Malaitans, using their high status in Solomon Islands society to influence the process and pave the way for peace. The Anglican Church of Melanesia has a Peace and Reconciliation program with reconciliation events at the local level, for example on the Weather Coast of Guadalcanal. The Sycamore Tree Project, an ecumenical group that helps to facilitate reconciliation between prisoners serving time for criminal acts conducted during the Tensions and victims, began working in the Solomon Islands in 2008. The Sycamore Tree Project brings prisoners together with victims and encourages forgiveness from the victim, apologies from the offender, and reconciliation between the parties. Ex-militants especially have been able to identify with the program, which also hosts local reconciliation events.[4]

Important reconciliation initiatives of a different nature also began at the local level after the Tensions. In Solomon Islands, the concept of reconciliation is strongly tied to *compensation*—an "ancient element of Melanesian culture" (Bennett 2002). Compensation—in which payments are made in the form of, for example, shell money, pigs, betel nut, or modern cash currency—maintains social harmony and positive relationships between people and is used "as a mechanism to restore social equilibrium after a dispute or wrong action" (Moore 2004: 125). Disputes between tribes, between the government and tribes, or between people, are all addressed through the provision of compensation to restore dignity, status, and relationships. Fraenkel states that payment of compensation is a cornerstone of the justice system in Melanesia, where justice focuses on "rebuilding *relationships* between people as members of communities, rather than as individuals" (2004: 108). The community, rather than individuals, is the foundation for building social harmony. Importantly, a fundamental component of compensation is that, after a dispute has been settled through traditional reconciliation, often culminating in a feast between conflicting parties, the issue should not be spoken of publicly again. This aspect of leaving the past behind after settlement, and the significance of silence, is similar to other traditional reconciliation practices in the world[5] and is critical to consider in the discussion of truth commissions. Aiming for the same goal of reconciliation and healing, truth commissions revisit the past in the search of establishing a narrative of the truth, inevitably opening old wounds in what may become a clash of traditions.

Rift between traditional and Western reconciliation

Hence, while the TRC has provided many victims with an opportunity to tell their story and participate in the creation of a national narrative of the conflict, the process has some inconsistencies with local socio-cultural norms (Guthrey 2016). Solomon Islands culture, not least its traditional reconciliation practices, revolves around the idea that after a wrong is addressed both victim and perpetrator leave the incident in the past and move forward.[6] This process of reconciling and moving on is traditionally undertaken between victim, perpetrator, and the clan/tribe of each party, and does not involve the greater public or media. Similarly, burial is considered a sacred ritual that should take place in a private setting. One woman from Guthrey's (2015) study commented,

> I think, I feel that they are re-opening old wounds, I think it should be buried, forgotten and we should forget about everything rather than go and re-open them [the wounds] again like the graves [where] we dig up the bones. I don't think it's a good thing.

To this end, the practice of bringing up past crimes and exhuming bodies in a public context has been viewed by some as being inappropriate and not culturally sensitive to the Solomon Islands context.

Another aspect of the work of the Solomon Islands TRC that illustrates this disconnection is the creation of a pre-hearing counseling program intended to prepare victims for giving testimony. As found in interviews conducted by Guthrey

(2015), one victim who testified in a TRC public hearing remarked that the counseling helped her to feel better and reduce her fears when she testified. Another interviewee, however, mentioned that the concept of counseling fails to take into account the socio-cultural norm of moving on and not dwelling in the past, saying,

> You see, what happened is beyond counselling. It's beyond counselling. I don't know about white people, but us Melanesians from Solomon Islands, we don't do it this way . . . the level of trauma that people went through, counselling is not the solution . . . it's nowhere near the experience that we went through.
>
> (Guthrey 2015: 145)

The positive benefits that some victims experienced from the counseling process (which is arguably an improvement from other commissions which have not employed such a program) should not be discounted; it is, however, important to identify how healing and recovery are achieved within specific contexts to ensure the appropriateness and efficacy of TRC programs.

Looking at this issue from an Asia Pacific regional perspective, merging Western-style justice norms with traditional practices also created some areas of incongruence in the Commission for Reception, Truth and Reconciliation in Timor-Leste (known by the Portuguese acronym CAVR). In an effort to incorporate a degree of traditional practices in the post-conflict process, United Nations Transitional Administration in East Timor Regulation 2001/10[7] integrated Community Reconciliation Processes (CRPs) into the work of the Commission. CRPs were designed to help integrate perpetrators of less serious crimes into their former communities by relying on traditional norms, based on *lisan*.[8] These processes utilized the practice of *nahe biti* (literally: "stretching out the mat," in Tetum), which has been used to restore social harmony in communities after crimes have been committed (Babo-Soares 2004). The term "reconciliation" has been described as somewhat of a new word to many East Timorese. However, the notion of community-based meetings to address social imbalances resulting from crimes has been a cornerstone of East Timorese culture throughout time, long before the inclusion of CRPs in the CAVR process (Babo-Soares 2004). This discrepancy between language and practice is an issue that should be taken into account when creating and publicizing the work of a truth commission in a transitioning society.

Although the CRPs were largely considered to be successful for undertaking a larger than expected number of cases and facilitating the reintegration of many perpetrators into their communities, they were limited by several factors. First, because of the intended mandate of these processes to address only lesser crimes (excluding crimes such as murder or sexual violence, which reflects traditional uses of *nahe biti*), they were not always able to secure a sense of justice that some victims may have expected after the experience of such intense trauma during the Indonesian occupation and the violent aftermath of the 1999 referendum for independence. Sometimes it was only discovered after a process had already begun that the perpetrator had committed crimes that fell out of the purview of the CRP, thus halting the process and necessitating that it be tried through the judicial system (Larke 2009). Victims would then need to wait for the court system to dole out justice in a more drawn-out timeline. The agreements that resulted from CRPs illustrated a divergence from reconciliation practices based on *lisan*, as "CRAs [Community Reconciliation Agreements] did not require the consent of the victim" (Senier 2008). In fact, the wording of UNTAET Regulation 2001/10 avoided focusing on victims as a central aspect of these processes, a deviation from traditional *lisan* (Senier 2008). In light of the achievements and shortcomings surrounding the inclusion of traditional justice mechanisms in the work of truth commissions, a further look into how traditional justice and reconciliation measures can be best integrated into Western techniques is necessary.

When truth commissions are not advisable

Truth commissions can be an important step in securing some sense of post-conflict justice and promoting reconciliation and healing. However, when created without proper consideration of culture and conflict context, these processes may risk inciting frustration and disheartening the people they are aiming to help.

Since 1974 when the first truth commission was created in Uganda, over 40 commissions have been implemented in states transitioning from conflict or authoritarianism (Hayner 2010). As a response to conflict or an authoritarian regime in a country, commissions' motivations and aims have differed. One complication of initiating a truth commission to promote post-conflict justice is that commissions are sometimes created in a situation that is lacking the political will to ensure their success. When the state is not truly supportive of a truth commission process, their work can suffer, whether through dissolution of the commission before the completion of their work (e.g., Bolivia, Former Yugoslavia) or the inability to encourage widespread participation of victims and perpetrators (e.g., Democratic Republic of the Congo). Furthermore, when a process is designed without careful consideration of the context of the conflict, cultural norms, and the needs of victims, the process is likely to leave many feeling disenchanted, if not retraumatized.

The implementation of post-conflict processes that emphasize the individual over the community may also be problematic, particularly in approaching healing. Solomon Islands, like many other transitional settings, places a high value on the group instead of individuals. Contemporary truth commissions tend to encourage victims to publicly disclose their personal experiences of abuse and how it affected them as individuals; however, in many settings it is more common and appropriate to describe the effects of transgressions on the community. The approach of some contemporary truth commissions hence conflicts with traditional notions of story-telling and healing by placing less emphasis on the collective impacts of mass violence.

Without the capacity and/or motivation to follow-up on recommendations provided in a truth commission final report, the process can also suffer. Individuals who participated, particularly those who may have shared traumatic stories about themselves or family members, may develop feelings of hopelessness or that their effort was for naught if they do not feel their participation has contributed to change or positive developments. This can be seen in both Solomon Islands and Timor-Leste, where little has been done to implement the report recommendations since the culmination of these Commissions' work in 2012 and 2005, respectively. In Guthrey's interviews with victims who testified in the CAVR national public hearings in Timor-Leste, several individuals expressed disappointment and sadness that they had received no benefit from their participation in the CAVR process (2015). Most interviewees remarked that telling their story was good in that it contributed to the historical data about the country's past experiences during the Indonesian occupation. However they expressed curiosity about what will come next, as that has yet to be sufficiently answered by the CAVR or the government (Guthrey 2015).

The situation in the Solomon Islands continues to unfold as we write (November 2017) and will be interesting to follow. After 5 years of being comfortably hidden from the public eye, the TRC final report is now a focus, and plans are being made for how to implement its recommendations. This has great potential for the peace-building process. Recent interviews suggest there has been widespread dissatisfaction with the withholding of the report.[9] Interviews with victims suggest disappointment concerning the lack of tangible benefits resulting from their participation in the TRC (Guthrey 2015). Some victims remarked on their sense that the TRC had done little more with their testimony than compile it into a larger report, which has not contributed in providing support for the loss of property, life, and injury during the conflict. This incongruence between victim expectations and reality is important to consider (2016). In some interviews, it seemed clear that there was not a full understanding on the part of victims as to how the TRC was going to benefit them or contribute to post-conflict peace and reconciliation.[10] Thus, truth commissions must make an effort to fully publicize the aims of their work and the intended outcomes in a straightforward manner. Understanding of a TRC's work could allay frustrations that arise from lack of clarity on how, for example, victim testimony will be used. Similarly, the disconnection between the traditional and the new should be investigated—a complexity indicative of a larger issue in truth commission implementation worldwide, as these organizations are often created without sufficient cultural and contextual adaptation (Shaw and Waldorf 2010). The Solomon Islands TRC completed its work in early 2012; the Solomon Islands government has finally—in early 2016—began discussing its recommendations. The government now has the opportunity to show ways to learn from the traditional and incorporate it into the new—and thereby perhaps reconcile the rift between traditional and Western practices.

How truth commissions may contribute to quality peace

Truth commissions indeed take place in imperfect circumstances, after a period of violence and turmoil within a country. However, these institutions have significant potential to address the needs of a nation and the victims who suffered during conflict and thereby contribute to helping society move toward quality peace. In order to accomplish a truth commission's potential, certain characteristics are vital. First, it is critical that a truth commission is adapted to fit the cultural context of location. As truth commissions are being increasingly created in transitional nations, but with relatively sparse evaluation of their ability to carry out the aims they strive for, they have often been placed into a context based on examples set by previous Commissions, with little change. Although the intent is positive, a truth commission must consider how best to address the needs of the nation in which it is created. For instance, many Commissions endeavor to promote reconciliation, but a majority have not incorporated traditional reconciliation practices into their processes. In Solomon Islands, several individuals interviewed about their experience in the TRC expressed the sentiment that traditional reconciliation was the proper path toward moving on from the past conflict (Guthrey 2015). Reconciliation, based on traditional practices, is a cornerstone of Solomon Islands culture and way of life, thus the lack of inclusion of this concept in the TRC has left some people confused about how their participation in the process, or the process itself, will resolve conflict (Vella 2014; Guthrey 2015). Traditional or indigenous and more Western-based conceptions of reconciliation are not necessarily incompatible, but it is important to consider the ways that people of a particular setting resolve conflict and move past problems in order to make the reconciliation process suitable for their needs.

Second, the experience of trauma during conflict is also an issue that needs to be addressed to encourage long-lasting and sustainable peace. Recently, some truth commissions, such as the Solomon Islands TRC, have begun thinking about addressing victim needs through counseling. For some, this appears to be beneficial, while others feel that Western-style counseling is not appropriate for their culture. To ask victims to participate in psychological counseling that has not been part of the way their society deals with past trauma can be a concept that is foreign and confusing, detracting from the intended aim of such a program. Thus, a critical eye must be cast on how healing and recovery is encouraged in a particular context to ensure that the work of a TRC is not incongruent with traditional practices of moving on after conflict and trauma.

Third, in the majority of cases, a truth commission is created in an attempt to do *something* to promote post-conflict justice, particularly if the prospect of securing punitive justice against former perpetrators does not look promising. The problem is that many commissions are not actually able to achieve grand results because of lack of time, resources, and restrictions in the mandate. As the transition from conflict often leaves the political structure of a country in a fragile and fragmented state, it can be difficult to secure political will to implement recommendations that are provided in truth commission reports. In these instances, the work of the truth commission is often perceived by people, particularly those who testified, as just sitting on the shelf collecting dust. Hence, clarity of TRC aims at the onset creation as well as high level of assurance that every measure will be taken to implement the recommendations of the final report should be considered to ensure that the work of a Commission can contribute to quality peace. In a situation with restricted mandate and resources, it could be argued that it is better for a process to endeavor to achieve a few concrete aims that can actually be realized than to reach for abstract goals that leave feasible actions as a distant dream. Furthermore, adapting truth commissions into culturally-viable and appropriate institutions can not only encourage the participation of society, but also the potential for the resulting work and recommendations to be accepted by a greater number of victims and perpetrators alike. When a highly participatory process such as a truth commission is understood and recognized by the members of a society affected by conflict, while also respecting their cultural needs and values, the likelihood that it will contribute to a more sustainable peace is greatly increased.

Recommendations

1. Ensure cultural appropriateness by adapting commissions to the specific context and relying on traditional norms and language.
2. Assess political will and capability to carry out the commission's resulting recommendations to limit public discontent. If none is present, stakeholders should consider a delay in creating a commission.
3. Develop clear, specific, and concrete aims of the TRC and publicize those aims to participants and the greater society, in order to avoid overly high hopes and expectations.
4. Ensure the recommendations of the TRC final report are concrete and manageable; if the final report is overwhelming there is an imminent risk it will be regarded as impossible to implement and as such disregarded.

Notes

1. Literally, "one talk," i.e., people who speak the same language; fundamental concept in Solomon Islands meaning kinship bonds or "one's people with whom one shares a set of social obligations," (Braithwaite et al. 2010).
2. The customs or procedures for how things are done in Melanesia and Solomon Islands concerning everything from meetings and consultations to customary law.
3. When speaking of the "Church" in Solomon Islands, this most often refers to one of the five main Christian churches included in SICA: the Anglican Church of Melanesia, the Roman Catholic Church, the South Seas Evangelical Church, the Seventh-day Adventist Church and the United Church.
4. Private communication with Bishop Terry Brown, Honiara, April 14, 2012.
5. Babo-Soares discusses this issue in regard to Timor-Leste in Babo-Soares 2004.
6. Personal communication with Solomon Islands anthropologist David Akin and Bishop Terry Brown.
7. This regulation established the mandate of the CAVR and outlined its creation.
8. *Lisan* can be described as a "system [that] resolves criminal and civil disputes through a process of elder-facilitated public consultation between parties" (Senier 2008).
9. Brounéus, interviews 2015.
10. Brounéus, focus groups Solomon Islands, October 2011; Guthrey 2015.

References

Amnesty International. *Solomon Islands: Women confronting violence*. London: Amnesty International Research, ASA 43/001/2004, 2004.

Babo-Soares, Dionisio. "Nahe Biti: The philosophy and process of grassroots reconciliation (and justice) in East Timor." *The Asia Pacific Journal of Anthropology* 5, no. 1 (2004): 15–33.

Backer, David. "Victims' Responses to Truth Commissions: Evidence from South Africa." In Muna Ndulo, Ed. *Security, reconstruction, and reconciliation: When the wars end*. Boca Raton, FL: CRC Press, 2007.

Bennett, Judith. "Roots of conflict in Solomon Islands-though much is taken, much abides: Legacies of tradition and colonialism." Canberra: *Australian National University Working Paper*, 2002.

Braithwaite, Valerie, Sinclair Dinnen, Matthew Allen, John Braithwaite, and Hilary Charlesworth. *Pillars and shadows: Statebuilding as peacebuilding in Solomon Islands*. Australian National University Press, 2010.

Brounéus, Karen. "The trauma of truth telling: Effects of witnessing in the Rwandan Gacaca courts on psychological health." *Journal of Conflict Resolution* 54, no. 3 (2010): 408–437.

Collier, Paul, Lani Elliott, Anke Hoeffler, Marta Reynal-Querol, and Nicholas Sambanis. *Breaking the conflict trap: Civil war and development policy*. Washington, DC: The World Bank (2003).

Čorkalo, Dinka, Dean Ajduković, Harvey Weinstein, Eric Stover, Dino Đipa, and Miklos Biro. "Neighbors again? Inter-community relations after ethnic violence." In *My neighbor, my enemy: Justice and community in the aftermath of mass atrocity*. Cambridge: Cambridge University Press, 2004.

Corrin, Jennifer. "Ples Bilong Mere*: Law, gender and peace-building in Solomon Islands." *Feminist Legal Studies* 16, no. 2 (2008): 169–194.

Dinnen, Sinclair. "Winners and losers: Politics and disorder in the Solomon Islands 2000–2002." *Journal of Pacific History* 37, no. 3 (2002): 285–298.

Dinnen, Sinclair. "The crisis of state in Solomon Islands." *Peace Review* 21, no. 1 (2009): 70–78.

Fraenkel, Jon. *The manipulation of custom: From uprising to intervention in the Solomon Islands*. Wellington: Victoria University Press, 2004.

Fry, Greg, and Tarcisius Tara Kabutaulaka, Eds. *Intervention and state-building in the Pacific: The legitimacy of cooperative intervention*. Manchester: Manchester University Press, 2008.

Gates, Scott, Helga Malmin Binningsbo, and Tove Grete Lie. "Post-conflict justice and sustainable peace." *World Bank Policy Research Working Paper* 4191 (2007).

Guthrey, Holly L. "Making Sense of the Findings from Timor-Leste and Solomon Islands." In *Victim healing and truth commissions*. New York City: Springer International Publishing, 2015: 153–177.

Guthrey, Holly L. "Local norms and truth telling: Examining experienced incompatibilities within truth commissions of Solomon Islands and Timor-Leste." *The Contemporary Pacific* 28, no. 1 (2016): 1–29.

Guthrey, Holly L. "Expectations and promises in the quest for truth: Examining victims' perceptions of truth commission participation in Solomon Islands and Timor-Leste." *Peace and Conflict: Journal of Peace Psychology* 22, no. 4 (2016): 306–317.

Hamber, Brandon. *Transforming societies after political violence: Truth, reconciliation, and mental health*. Berlin: Springer Science & Business Media, 2009.

Hameiri, Shahar. "State building or crisis management? A critical analysis of the social and political implications of the Regional Assistance Mission to Solomon Islands." *Third World Quarterly* 30, no. 1 (2009): 35–52.

Hayner, Priscilla B. *Unspeakable truths: Transitional justice and the challenge of truth commissions.* London: Routledge, 2010.

Kabutaulaka, Tarcisius Tara. *A weak sate and the Solomon Islands peace process.* Honolulu, Hawaii: East-West Center: Center for Pacific Islands Studies, University of Hawai'i at Manoa, 2002.

Larke, Ben. "'. . . And the truth shall set you free': Confessional trade-offs and community reconciliation in East Timor." *Asian Journal of Social Science* 37, no. 4 (2009): 646–676.

Leslie, Helen. "Conceptualising and addressing the mental health impacts of gender roles in conflict and peace making." *Development Bulletin* 53 (2000): 65–69.

Leslie, Helen, and Selina Boso. "Gender-related violence in the Solomon Islands: The work of local women's organisations." *Asia Pacific Viewpoint* 44, no. 3 (2003): 325–333.

Liloqula, Ruth. "Understanding the conflict in Solomon Islands as a practical means to peacemaking." *Development Bulletin* 53 (2000): 40–43.

Meernik, James. "Justice and peace? How the International Criminal Tribunal affects societal peace in Bosnia." *Journal of Peace Research* 42, no. 3 (2005): 271–289.

Moore, Clive. *Happy isles in crisis: The historical causes for a failing state in the Solomon Islands, 1998–2004.* Canberra: Asia Pacific Press, 2004.

National Parliament of Solomon Islands. *Truth and Reconciliation Commission Act.* August 28, 2008.

Olsen, Tricia D., Leigh A. Payne, and Andrew G. Reiter. *Transitional justice in balance: Comparing processes, weighing efficacy.* Washington DC: United States Institute for Peace (2010).

Rimé, Bernard, Patrick Kanyangara, Vincent Yzerbyt, and Dario Paez. "The impact of Gacaca tribunals in Rwanda: Psychosocial effects of participation in a truth and reconciliation process after a genocide." *European Journal of Social Psychology* 41, no. 6 (2011): 695–706.

Senier, Amy. "Traditional justice as transitional justice: A comparative case study of Rwanda and East Timor." *PRAXIS The Fletcher Journal of Human Security* 23 (2008): 67–88.

Shaw, Rosalind and Lars Waldorf. "Introduction: Localizing Transnational Justice." In Rosalind Shaw, Lars Waldorf, and Pierre Hazan, Eds. *Localizing transitional justice: Interventions and priorities after mass violence.* Redwood City, CA: Stanford University Press, (2010): 3–26.

Snyder, Jack, and Leslie Vinjamuri. "Trials and errors: Principle and pragmatism in strategies of international justice." *International Security* 28, no. 3 Winter (2006): 5–44.

Stover, Eric, and Harvey M. Weinstein. *My neighbor, my enemy: Justice and community in the aftermath of mass atrocity.* Cambridge: Cambridge University Press, 2004.

Vella, Louise. "What will you do with our stories? Truth and reconciliation in the Solomon Islands." *International Journal of Conflict and Violence* 8, no 1(2014): 91–103.

Wiebelhaus-Brahm, Eric. *Truth commissions and transitional societies: The impact on human rights and democracy.* London: Routledge, 2010.

10

RECONCILIATION AND QUALITY PEACE

Alexander Dukalskis, Laura K. Taylor, and John Darby

It is unfortunate that the term reconciliation has become embedded in discussion about social reconstruction. It is the wrong word. It implies a prior state of conciliation, just waiting to be reinstated were it not for the inconvenient intervention of violence. It panders to a nostalgia myth, common in violently divided societies, that the conflicting groups had enjoyed at worst an uneasy peace and at best some golden age of harmony and fairness before the violence, a condition that only exists in the imaginations of the mythmakers (Darby 1986). The danger in this view is that it suggests that the violence itself, rather than the underlying disputes that led to it, is the main problem. Whatever new relationships might emerge from a peace agreement, there is one certainty: they will be different from how relationships operated in the past.[1]

The central question is how relationships can be changed in the aftermath of violence not only to forestall a return to outright physical force, but also to contribute to a quality peace. The reluctance to address sufficiently the issue of reconciliation during peace negotiations is driven by the perception among negotiators that their energy should be concentrated on more immediate and important tasks. The strongest argument cutting against this view is the demonstrable reality that lack of reconciliation has the potential to derail or overturn a peace agreement. The view that peace agreements are the products of negotiations between political leaders is an accurate but incomplete view because negotiations are related to long-term processes of reconciliation or acrimony that themselves underlie relations between conflicting groups.

This chapter will point to the various roles that reconciliation can play in the aftermath of political violence by, in the following order, discussing definitional issues, considering reconciliation at the international, state, and intergroup levels, mapping reconciliation's place in this volume's conception of quality peace, and concluding with remarks about the ways in which reconciliation may be built into indicators of quality peace as well as lines of potential research and practice.

Defining reconciliation

In 2006, David Bloomfield pointed to a parallel growth in both interest in reconciliation and confusion about what it actually means. The growth is easily demonstrated; at the turn of the century reconciliation projects ranked third in value of all peacebuilding initiatives receiving support from donors, after political development and socio-economic assistance (Smith 2004). Yet confusion still abounds about the meaning of the term.

> Is it an individual, psychological, even "theological" process? Is it a process at all, or does it describe a state of relationships at the end of a process? . . . For many people, especially since the South African Truth and Reconciliation Commission, 1995–2003—certainly not the first of its kind, but definitely the most high-profile of all—the term is closely related to "truth" and "forgiveness," even if those also both remain disputed terms in themselves.
> (Bloomfield 2006)

If "reconciliation" is a problematic term for its ambiguities and for the connotations that its prefix evokes, its root—"conciliate"—calls forth associations that reveal what is unique about reconciliation as an approach to understanding conflict. One way to think about conciliation is a means to make disputing parties compatible in some way that they were not previously. Despite the various definitions that writers on the subject have proffered, it is the *relational* character of reconciliation that remains its most distinctive contribution to thinking about quality peace. On this account, violence stems from contentious relationships that are embedded in structures that cannot effectively manage the conflict that occurs in a given society. Often juxtaposed with approaches that emphasize criminal responsibility and/or liberal democratic conceptions of individual rights (Philpott 2006), reconciliation is seen as a way to recognize that political violence is relational and that to overcome violence, some change or transformation in previous relationships is necessary.

Such conceptual breadth allows those concerned with reconciliation to draw on an array of sources to develop their understandings of the term and, consequently, helps foster the definitional confusion that Bloomfield identifies. Thus, Philpott roots his notion of "restoration of right relationship" firmly in religious tradition (2006), while Bloomfield and his co-authors take a more secular approach and emphasize that reconciliation "is a process through which a society moves from a divided past to a shared future" (2003). Lederach draws on his personal peacebuilding experiences to conceive of reconciliation as both an analytical tool and as a social space where the ambiguities and contradictions of truth, justice, peace, and mercy encounter one another (1997).

An approach emphasizing reconciliation in the aftermath of violence begs the question of which relationships ought to be the concern of reconciliation processes. The short, but obviously unsatisfactory answer, is all relationships. Violent conflict impacts the most specific dyads of combatant-combatant, mother-child, and aggressor-victim, up through to the more ambiguous relations between social groups or even between states. To avoid the danger of reconciliation becoming a shapeless, all-inclusive term, we propose focusing on the ways that a relational approach to conflict can contribute to quality peace at three roughly divided, but overlapping levels: international, state-citizen relations, and intergroup (Jackson 1945).[2]

International reconciliation

With the recent emergence of ad hoc international or hybrid tribunals for Yugoslavia, Rwanda, Sierra Leone, and Cambodia, as well as the growing influence of the ICC, it is perhaps easy to think of international actors as new arrivals to discourses of transitional justice and reconciliation. In many ways, however, modern approaches to post-atrocity justice and reconciliation are based on the experiences of Germany and Japan after World War II. The International Military Tribunals at Nuremberg and for the Far East established individual criminal accountability as a norm of international justice and moved away from collective responsibility imposed on militarily defeated states. In taking a firm stand on many difficult moral and ethical dilemmas of collective guilt, head prosecutor at Nuremberg Robert Jackson (1945) argued in his opening speech that he had "no purpose to incriminate the whole German people" and that the crimes committed were so great that responsibility "may not be shifted to that fictional being, 'the State,' which can not be produced for trial, can not testify, and can not be sentenced."[3]

As the ICC becomes more established, the norm of individual accountability must coexist with the emerging norm of reconciliation, often institutionalized, particularly after the aforementioned South African TRC, in the form of truth commissions. Early literature on transitional justice tended to see a dichotomy between "peace" and "justice" and found ways in which trials upset efforts at reconciliation. Yet more recent formulations have begun to map potential synergies.[4] International accountability may aid reconciliation by, for example, extracting those who may frustrate reconciliation efforts from positions of influence or by establishing clear and detailed evidence about the crimes that took place. These actions can hedge against denial and provide an intelligible foundation for reconciliation initiatives. Combining the two emerging international norms of individual accountability and social reconciliation in the form of a truth commission provides both opportunities and constraints (Dukalskis 2011). More generally, too much of a focus on either human rights legalism or restorative justice may miss out on the "gray zone" between victim and perpetrator in the aftermath of mass violence (Leebaw 2011).

These international norms also make themselves felt in relations between states. Often using case studies from Germany, Japan, and their World War II adversaries, scholars have opened new lines of research on interstate reconciliation.[5] If Germany has made considerable progress reconciling with its erstwhile enemies, animosity persists in Northeast Asia between Japan and its un-reconciled neighbors: China, South Korea, and North Korea. From their perspective, Japan's lack of acknowledgement, half-hearted or defensive apologies for abuses like those committed against the Korean "comfort women," and glorification of war criminals through ministerial visits to the controversial Yaskuni Shrine, where Japan's war dead are honored, stokes the sense that Japanese officials do not think the state did anything wrong in the 1930s and 1940s. From Japan's perspective, it has apologized enough, offered reparations, and endured an international victor's justice trial, while its former colonies have brushed indigenous collaboration with the empire aside.[6] Inflammatory rhetoric by staunch nationalists on all sides exacerbates tensions. For example, as of this writing, the December 2015 agreement between Japan and South Korea to definitively settle the legacy of the "comfort women" issue is facing implementation difficulties as some Japanese officials continue to deny the Japanese state's wartime involvement in sexual slavery.[7] Efforts at reconciliation, such as jointly-authored history textbooks, aim to overcome these animosities and move the region from a tense peace to a quality one.

State-citizen reconciliation

If reconciliation is important in international conflicts, communal wars are a different species. When a violent internal conflict comes to an end, the combatants continue to occupy the same contested arena. Their daily lives are often intermeshed with those of their enemies. Withdrawal behind a recognized frontier is not an option, although opponents may continue to operate within increasingly segregated communities. If the fighting is not to resume in the future, the disputes that caused it in the first place must be tackled. Communities need arrangements to deal with disagreements, which are likely to recur on a regular basis—over jobs and resources, culture, religion, status—and the arrangements must be negotiated between groups who distrust and fear each other. Reconciliation is a fundamental requirement for long-term stability.

In practice, as the two paradigmatic cases of South Africa and Northern Ireland illustrate, reconciliation is often sidelined to prioritize more immediate goals. In South Africa, the management of the negotiations dominated the peace process until the agreement was signed in 1994, and the TRC only started its work in 1996, delivering its final report in 2001. During this time, it investigated 14,000 cases of political killings and granted 127 applications for amnesty. The state is paying around 22,000 one-off payments of about $4,600, although implementation has been a problem. Whatever reconciliation resulted was greatly assisted by a series of magnanimous acts by Nelson Mandela and the ANC, and by the successful adoption by followers of all groups of a new South African anthem, an agreed national flag and other symbols representing an agreement between all major parties to advance as a united country. South Africa as a state has been accepted and even welcomed by the conflicting parties, but it is less reconciled on matters of socioeconomic transformation (Gibson 2004). The underlying social inequalities remain and may become a greater threat to post-war reconstruction unless addressed more radically. Nevertheless, any objective audit would still support Timothy Sisk's assessment that "the TRC has mostly succeeded in putting the past to rest, as least in terms of transitional justice" (2009).

In Northern Ireland, the delay between the agreement and reconciliation was even greater. The refusal by Protestant Unionists to redress the systematic economic and social disadvantages facing Catholic Nationalists fueled minority discontent in the 1960s and provided the stimulus for the resurgence of the IRA and the 25 years of violence known as the Troubles. The 1998 Good Friday Agreement established a power-sharing executive led by the Democratic Unionist Party (DUP) and Sinn Féin, traditionally the two most intransigent parties, and has attracted international praise. However, the issue of reconciliation, which had been so openly confronted in South Africa, has hardly been tackled at all in Northern Ireland. No truth and reconciliation commission has been established, and the only major attempt to tackle the problem of reconciliation—a government-sponsored consultation exercise on community relations called *A Shared Future* that indicated a wide concern about the levels of division in the community and expressed wide support for stronger measures to encourage reconciliation—has been allowed to wither away (Darby and Knox 2004). In fact, demographic segregation between Catholics and Protestants had grown significantly along with the number of "peace walls" between neighboring Catholic/Protestant areas since the Troubles. In 2002, 62 percent of the population believed that community relations had worsened in the 8 years since the 1994 ceasefires (Brown 2002). A heavily segregated society remained heavily segregated. There has been little appetite for tackling this issue, and less invention. A companion chapter in this volume by Colin Knox assesses Northern Ireland on various measures of quality peace, including reconciliation processes.

Both the South African and Northern Irish peace processes can point to considerable successes, but in different aspects of post-war reconciliation. In general terms, South Africa managed to forge a sense of common purpose among white and black South Africans—at least during the critical phase of political transition—but the continuing and growing economic disparities breed disaffection, especially from the poorest elements in society. In Northern Ireland, the balance of success and failure lies in the opposite direction. Northern Ireland's civil rights campaign was fueled by the institutional bias against Catholics, but there is no longer a strong perception of such bias (Mac Ginty and Du Toit 2007); indeed, some Protestants argue, rather unconvincingly, that the balance has swung in the opposite direction. The point is that the inequalities that dominated debates in the 1970s and 1980s are no longer a matter of political dispute. On the other hand, there is a growing perception that, despite the amelioration of these equity issues and the evident success of the top-level peace process, relationships between Catholics and Protestants remain tense, and have not been sufficiently addressed during, or in the decade following, the Good Friday Agreement.

Intergroup processes

Reconciliation can be understood as the quality of intergroup relations, attitudes, and behaviors.[8] Salient group identity can be defined not only as ethnic or racial division, but also as between warring factions. The key concepts presented in this section may also be more broadly applied to post-accord societies where adversarial relations are not defined by ethnicity.

Social Identity Theory (SIT) and contact theory offer two related approaches to improve intergroup relations in the wake of mass violence. SIT describes how individuals derive meaning and self-esteem from associations with an in-group and comparisons with relevant outgroups (Tajfel 1982). SIT outlines the motivational sequences of intergroup conflict and behavior, with particular attention to group status, permeability of group boundaries, and uniformity within the group. When conflict occurs between groups with differing status (e.g., government vs. rebel forces, perpetrator vs. victim, etc.), reconciliation processes should create mechanisms for lower status groups to gain rights, recognition, and access to resources, while providing security measures and safeguards to protect higher status groups from extreme backlash or loss in the restructuring of the social order (Tajfel 1982). Allport's original hypothesis was that contact between conflicting groups decreases prejudice and discrimination (1954). However, the optimal conditions for contact— equal status, common goals, intergroup cooperation, and authority support—are rarely met in post-accord contexts. For example, cross-ethnic friendships are not immune to polarization by political opportunists and have proven insufficient to stop mass violence (Čorkalo et al. 2004). These two theoretical approaches also help move beyond decreasing prejudice and toward building positive group relations (Tropp and Mallett 2011).

Positive intergroup relationships can be examined on several dimensions; perhaps those most relevant for linking reconciliation to a quality of peace are mutually respectful identities, trust, empathy, forgiveness, positive-future orientation, and generational approaches. The idea of *mutually respectful identities* emerges from the limitations of a common in-group identity model (Dovidio et al. 2009). Rather than a focus on harmony between groups or formation of a superordinate identity, this approach focuses on social justice and considers conflict a natural part of intergroup relationships and a necessary component of collective action (Kriesberg 2003). Respect for diversity between groups and protecting low-status groups from discrimination are key elements of this multiple identity model informed by SIT.

Trust is at the foundation of good relations, and yet it is one of the first casualties of conflict; if distrust among adversaries persists, the likelihood of reconciliation decreases. Past research has found that outgroup trust—or the positive expectation about the outgroup's intentions, motives, and behaviors—mediates the impact of intergroup contact on outgroup behaviors (Tam et al. 2009). Although an important construct for reconciliation, there may be limits to the role of third parties in promoting trust between conflict parties in a dispute (Shnabel et al. 2014). Outgroup trust is also a necessary condition for intergroup *empathy* to promote positive intergroup attitudes (Nadler and Liviatan 2006). Empathy—or the ability to take on another's point of view and the capacity to respond to emotional reactions of others—mediates the positive association between cross-group friendships and positive outgroup attitudes (Swart et al. 2011). On the other hand, when an outgroup member who is *not* trusted expresses empathy, it is perceived as manipulative and can worsen negative intergroup attitudes (Nadler and Liviatan 2006).

Trust and empathy may be the foundation for *forgiveness*. Morton Deutsch has described forgiveness as "giving up the rage, the desire for vengeance, and a grudge toward those who have inflicted grievous harm on your, your loved ones, of the groups with whom you identify" (2008: 478). Although forgiveness can be embedded in justice procedures and other mechanisms that aim to restore victim perpetrator relationships, or have religious connotations or motivations (Tutu 1999), forgiveness often assumes a collective dimension in intergroup conflict. Forgiveness in these settings may be rooted in social psychological processes, such as mutual security, respect, and humanization of the other (Deutsch 2008; Tam et al. 2007). To balance forgiveness, which tends to be focused on the past, an optimistic view of future group relations is also needed for reconciliation (Lederach 1997; Tutu 1999).

Positive future orientation has both personal and collective dimensions. That is, an individual's future orientation can be directed to his/her own life course as well as to his/her social group (Seginer 2008). Youth's individual expectations about educational, employment, and social life outcomes are related to their willingness to work for peace or engage in violence (Solomon and Lavi 2005). For example, the future orientation of child soldiers should be incorporated into demobilization programs to enhance reconciliation (Blattman and Anan 2010). Yet, youth's attitudes and beliefs are also shaped by parental beliefs and community values (Bronfenbrenner 1979). Collective expectations about the future inform intergroup attitudes and actions; conflict is exacerbated by zero-sum political outcomes, or when "each group's best hope for the future is the other's worst fear" (Leach and Williams 1999). For reconciliation to take root and positive peace to grow, policies must balance the fears and hopes of conflicting groups through governing or territorial strategies that provide an alternative to a winner-take-all approach.

Finally, reconciliation of intergroup relationships requires "decades thinking" (Lederach 2005), or *generational approaches* to build a shared future. With this long-term perspective, the role of youth becomes particularly important (Cairns 1996; McEvoy-Levy 2006; Barber 2008). For example, children born after the formal end of war may have more negative outgroup attitudes and be more likely to discriminate compared to their parents (Ajduković and Čorkalo Biruski 2008). Whether as former fighters, victims, bystanders, or those born after peace agreements, youth are key "to the construction of a new, more humane era after accords" (McEvoy-Levy 2006: 21), and should be included in post-accord planning.

Synthesis: contributions of reconciliation toward a quality peace

In highlighting three overlapping levels of relationships at which reconciliation can be analyzed, the previous sections have oversimplified or bypassed a number of dilemmas. Important ethical-political debates such as those that surround the appropriateness of the state constructing national-level reconciliation narratives (Mamdani 2000; Wilson 2001; Moon 2009), the desirability of governments deploying a discourse of therapy in conflict situations (Humphrey 2005), and the role of deliberation processes vis-à-vis restorative justice in reconciliation efforts (Gutmann and Thompson 2000) have all been side-stepped for want of space. Nevertheless, relational approaches to the study of violent conflict can potentially contribute to quality peace by speaking to some of these difficult dilemmas on four levels.

First, there are ethical and practical reasons to emphasize democratic participation in attempts to reconcile societies after periods of violence or repression. In commenting on the lessons learned from German unification, philosopher Jürgen Habermas argued that more public discussion would have allowed East Germans to come to their own terms with the legacy of their regime rather than West Germany's (Habermas 1996). Empirically, greater attention to public participation in truth commission processes bodes well for the consolidation of democratic institutions years down the road when compared to truth commissions that were less public (Taylor and Dukalskis 2012). Repoliticizing transitional justice and reconciliation through democratic participation has the potential to unmask power relations that may remain hidden in de-politicized contexts like tribunals or parliamentary commissions that do not seek participation.[9] The opportunity for inclusive participation allows individuals affected by violence to come to their own understanding of reconciliation and to opt out if they so choose. On state-citizen and intergroup levels, broad participation has the potential to foster narratives about violent periods that reflect the experience of the participants who lived through them and to undercut the possibility of power-brokers to highjack the process for their own ends. Of course democratic politics can be noisy and cumbersome for reconciliation, as difficulties in the Japanese-South Korean relationship demonstrate, but stifling democratic impulses in pursuit of quality peace seems both empirically and ethically dubious.

Second, a relational approach calls for attention not only to material concerns, but also to symbolic ones. For a country coming out of war, it is especially important to encourage common loyalties to counter the divisions of the past. Flags and anthems are often difficult to negotiate, but sports suggest interesting symbolic possibilities. Nelson Mandela's public embrace of the majority white Springbok rugby team was a brilliant and symbolic recognition of the need to set a new tone for the new South Africa. The subsequent attraction of black and colored players and supporters to South Africa's rugby and cricket teams encouraged a national compact. The 2010 soccer World cup, which was hosted by South Africa, was consciously exploited to encourage national integration and international approval. In Northern Ireland, allegiance to a common soccer team has actually diminished in strength since the agreement, although other sports including rugby and golf have attracted more general support. In 2011, the Sinn Féin minister attended a Northern Ireland soccer international game for the first time, and in 2012, the DUP First Minister attended his first Gaelic football game. The banality of both gestures did not diminish their significance, and may suggest the possibility that carefully chosen symbolic cross-sectarian gestures should be regarded as the first phase of a reconciliation policy, paving the way to more pragmatic concessions later. In some cases, they may be parallel tracks.

Third, considering reconciliation from a psychosocial perspective highlights important intergroup dynamics that may undermine or enhance reconciliation efforts. Powerful motivational factors, such as intergroup fear and anxiety, while often overlooked by policymakers (Kaufman 2006; Shapiro 2010), may help to explain the efficacy of reconciliation initiatives. In deeply divided societies, positive intergroup relations may be fostered through mutually respectful identities, trust, empathy, forgiveness, positive-future orientation, and generational approaches. Efforts to foster reconciliation and improve the quality of peace should consider power and status differences among groups, caution against the appeal to superordinate identities, move beyond prejudice reduction and toward positive intergroup relations, and include youth and their families in program planning.

Finally, reconciliation calls attention to the inter-generational dynamics of violent conflict. Conflicts that have evolved over decades and that have been reproduced over generations cannot be quickly resolved (Lederach 2005). As Verdeja notes, "political violence does not end with the last death" (2009: 2). The fact that the vast majorities of people in present-day Northeast Asia were not alive during World War II, let alone directly involved in the conflict, demonstrates that careful attention should be paid to the lingering effects of political violence on intergroup, state-citizen, and international relations. In Northern Ireland, the international community has invested millions to address post-accord intergroup conflict (Niens and Cairns 2005), yet segregation has deepened since the Belfast Agreement and permeates many aspects of social life (Shirlow and Murtagh 2006; Hughes et al. 2007). By not incorporating generational approaches into reconciliation policies, societies will be ill-equipped to prevent the reoccurrence of hostility and tension (e.g., marching season), much less to propose programs that can contribute toward a "shared future" and a deeper quality of peace (Darby and Knox 2004).

Conclusion

If reconciliation can contribute to quality peace, it must address the underlying relationships formed during a period of political violence. This chapter identified three levels—international, state-citizen, intergroup—that could serve as a useful heuristic to compare dynamic reconciliation processes that are situated in, and must be responsive to, particular social contexts. There is considerable potential for reconciliation to constrain or contribute to quality peace and this chapter has broadly mapped some potentially useful conceptual and empirical contours. We highlighted key priorities at each level of analyses that should be considered by peace negotiators, policymakers, and civil society actors concerned with creating a lasting peace.

The question remains, and future research should focus on, ways in which to measure reconciliation. Gibson has gotten political science scholars off to an impressive start with his work in South Africa on inter-racial reconciliation, but efforts by other scholars to develop and extend his formulations for use in other contexts have been slow. Psychological literature on intergroup relations may have much offer to the interdisciplinary study of reconciliation, including theory and instruments to measure the quality of intergroup relations, attitudes, and behaviors. Developing indicators that can capture these dynamic and interactive processes that change over time should be a priority for reconciliation researchers interested in promoting positive peace. A companion volume to this book by Christian Davenport, Erik Melander, and Patrick M. Regan has usefully begun to do so. The authors draw on indicators such as physical integrity rights, women's rights, social capital, and intergroup relations to explore the extent to which they can provide new insights on reconciliation at the state and group levels.

Notes

1. For further discussion on these issues, see Darby 2010.
2. For an excellent and systematic discussion of reconciliation at four levels—political society, institutional/legal, civil society and interpersonal—see Verdeja 2009.
3. On individual and collective guilt in the German context, see Jaspers 1961.
4. See, for example, Johansen 2010 and Akhavan 2009.
5. For a recent review, see Tang 2011.
6. On Japanese attitudes to the Military Tribunal for the Far East, see Futamura 2008; for a focus on the Sino-Japanese relationship, see He 2009.
7. See Tatsumi 2015 and McCurry 2016. Also, see for instance www.cnn.com/2017/05/11/asia/south-korea-japan-comfort-women/index.html (accessed September 29, 2017).
8. Interpersonal reconciliation may also be a priority in post-accord societies; however, it falls outside the scope of the current chapter. For some relevant readings, see *Peace and Conflict: Journal of Peace Psychology* 13 no. 1, 2007; Backer 2010; and Brounéus 2008, 2010.
9. On the pitfalls of de-politicizing public memory, see Leebaw 2011.

References

Ajduković, Dean, and Dinka Čorkalo Biruski. "Caught between the ethnic sides: Children growing up in a divided post-war community." *International Journal of Behavioral Development* 32, no. 4 (2008): 337–347.

Akhavan, Payam. "Are international criminal tribunals a disincentive to peace?: Reconciling judicial romanticism with political realism." *Human Rights Quarterly* 31, no. 3 (2009): 624–654.

Allport, Gordon W. *The nature of prejudice*. Addison-Wesley, 1954.

Backer, David. "Watching a bargain unravel? A panel study of victims' attitudes about transitional justice in Cape Town, South Africa." *International Journal of Transitional Justice* 4, no. 3 (2010): 443–456.

Barber, Brian K. *Adolescents and war: How youth deal with political violence: How youth deal with political violence*. Oxford University Press, 2008.

Blattman, Christopher J., and Jeannie Anan. "The consequences of child soldiering." *The Review of Economics and Statistics* 92, no. 4 (2010): 882–898.

Bloomfield, David. *On good terms: Clarifying reconciliation*. Vol. 14. Berlin: Berghof Research Center for Constructive Conflict Management, 2006.

Bloomfield, David, Terri Barnes, and Lucien Huyse, Eds. *Reconciliation after violent conflict: A handbook*. International IDEA, 2003.

Bronfenbrenner, Urie. *The ecology of human development: Experiments by design and nature*. Harvard University Press, 1979.

Brounéus, Karen. "Truth-telling as talking cure? Insecurity and retraumatization in the Rwandan Gacaca courts." *Security Dialogue* 39, no. 1 (2008): 55–76.

Brounéus, Karen. "The trauma of truth telling: Effects of witnessing in the Rwandan Gacaca courts on psychological health." *Journal of Conflict Resolution* 54, no. 3 (2010): 408–437.

Brown, Paul. "Peace but no love as Northern Ireland divide grows ever wider." *The Guardian*, January 4, 2002.

Cairns, Ed. *Children and political violence*. Blackwell Publishing, 1996.

Čorkalo, Dinka, Dean Ajduković, Harvey Weinstein, Eric Stover, Dino Đipa, and Miklos Biro. "Neighbors Again? Inter-community Relations after Ethnic Violence." In Eric Stover and Harvey Weinstein, Eds. *My neighbor, my enemy: Justice and community in the aftermath of mass atrocity*. Cambridge University Press, (2004): 143–182.

Darby, John P. *Intimidation and the control of conflict in Northern Ireland*. Syracuse University Press, 1986.

Darby, John. "Reconciliation (Reflections from Northern Ireland and South Africa)." In Oliver Richmond. *Palgrave Advances in Peacebuilding*. Palgrave Macmillan UK, (2010): 294–360.

Darby, John, and Colin Knox. "'A shared future': A consultation paper on improving relations in Northern Ireland: Final report." Paper commissioned by the Office of the First Minister and Deputy First Minister (OFMDFM). Northern Ireland, Belfast: OFMDFM, January 21, 2004.

Deutsch, Morton. "Reconciliation After Destructive Intergroup Conflict." In Arie Nadler, Thomas E. Malloy, and Jeffrey D. Fisher, Eds. *The social psychology of intergroup reconciliation*. Oxford University Press, (2008): 471–485.

Dovidio, John F., Samuel L. Gaertner, and Tamar Saguy. "Commonality and the complexity of "we": Social attitudes and social change." *Personality and Social Psychology Review* 13, no. 1 (2009): 3–20.

Dukalskis, Alexander. "Interactions in transition: How truth commissions and trials complement or constrain each other." *International Studies Review* 13, no. 3 (2011): 432–451.

Futamura, Madoka. *War crimes tribunals and transitional justice: The Tokyo trial and the Nuremburg legacy*. Routledge, 2007.

Gibson, James L. "Overcoming apartheid: Can truth reconcile a divided nation?" *Politikon* 31, no. 2 (2004): 129–155.

Gutmann, Amy and Dennis Thompson. "The Moral Foundations of Truth Commissions." In Robert I. Rotberg and Dennis Thompson, Eds. *Truth v. justice: The morality of truth commissions*. Princeton University Press, (2000): 22–44.

Habermas, Jürgen. "National unification and popular sovereignty." *New Left Review* 219 (1996): 3.

He, Yinan. *The search for reconciliation: Sino-Japanese and German-Polish relations since World War II*. Cambridge University Press, 2009.

Hughes, Joanne, Andreas Campbell, Miles Hewstone, and Ed Cairns. "Segregation in Northern Ireland: Implications for community relations policy." *Policy Studies* 28, no. 1 (2007): 35–53.

Humphrey, Michael. "Reconciliation and the therapeutic State." *Journal of Intercultural Studies* 26, no. 3 (2005): 203–220.

Jackson, Robert H. "Opening statement before the International Military Tribunal." Robert H. Jackson Center, 1945. Accessed September 29, 2017 at www.roberthjackson.org/the-man/speeches-articles/speeches/speeches-by-robert-hjackson/opening-statement-before-the-international-military-tribunal.

Jaspers, Karl. *The question of German guilt*. Capricorn Books, 1961.

Johansen, Robert C. "Peace and Justice? The Contribution of International Judicial Processes to Peacebuilding." In Dan Philpott and Gerard F. Powers, Eds. *Strategies of peace: Transforming conflict in a violent world*. Oxford University Press, (2010): 189–230.

Kaufman, Stuart J. "Escaping the symbolic politics trap: Reconciliation initiatives and conflict resolution in ethnic wars." *Journal of Peace Research* 43, no. 2 (2006): 201–218.

Kriesberg, Louis. *Constructive conflicts: From escalation to resolution*. Rowman & Littlefield, 2003.

Leach, Colin Wayne, and Wendy R. Williams. "Group identity and conflicting expectations of the future in Northern Ireland." *Political Psychology* 20, no. 4 (1999): 875–896.

Lederach, John Paul. "Building peace: Sustainable reconciliation in divided societies." United States Institute of Peace, 1997.

Lederach, John Paul. *The moral imagination: The art and soul of building peace*. Vol. 3. Oxford University Press, 2005.

Leebaw, Bronwyn. *Judging state-sponsored violence, imagining political change*. Cambridge University Press, 2011.

Mac Ginty, Roger, and Pierre Du Toit. "A disparity of esteem: Relative group status in Northern Ireland after the Belfast Agreement." *Political Psychology* 28, no. 1 (2007): 13–31.

Mamdani, Mahmood. "The Truth According to the TRC." In Ifi Amadiume and Abdullahi An-Aa'im, Eds. *The politics of memory: Truth, healing, and social justice*. Zed Books, (2000): 176–183.

McCurry, Justin. "Former sex slaves reject Japan and South Korea's 'comfort women' accord." *The Guardian*, January 26, 2016.

McEvoy-Levy, Siobhan. *Troublemakers or peacemakers?: Youth and post-accord peace building*. University of Notre Dame Press, 2006.

Moon, Claire. *Narrating political reconciliation: South Africa's Truth and Reconciliation Commission*. Lexington Books, 2009.

Nadler, Arie, and Ido Liviatan. "Intergroup reconciliation: Effects of adversary's expressions of empathy, responsibility, and recipients' trust." *Personality and Social Psychology Bulletin* 32, no. 4 (2006): 459–470.

Niens, Ulrike, and Ed Cairns. "Conflict, contact, and education in Northern Ireland." *Theory into Practice* 44, no. 4 (2005): 337–344.

Philpott, Daniel. "Beyond Politics as Usual: Is Reconciliation Compatible with Liberalism?" In Daniel Philpott, Ed. *The politics of past evil: Religion, reconciliation, and the dilemmas of transitional justice*. University of Notre Dame Press, (2006): 11–44.

Seginer, Rachel. "Future orientation in times of threat and challenge: How resilient adolescents construct their future." *International Journal of Behavioral Development* 32, no. 4 (2008): 272–282.

Shapiro, Daniel L. "Relational identity theory: A systematic approach for transforming the emotional dimension of conflict." *American Psychologist* 65, no. 7 (2010): 634.

Shirlow, Peter, and Brendan Murtagh. *Belfast: Segregation, violence and the city*. Pluto Press, 2006.

Shnabel, Nurit, Arie Nadler, and John F. Dovidio. "Beyond need satisfaction: Empowering and accepting messages from third parties ineffectively restore trust and consequent reconciliation." *European Journal of Social Psychology* 44, no. 2 (2014): 126–140.

Sisk, Timothy D. *International mediation in civil wars: Bargaining with bullets.* Routledge, 2009.

Smith, Dan. *Towards a strategic framework for peacebuilding: Getting their act together.* Royal Norwegian Ministry of Foreign Affairs, 2004.

Solomon, Zahava, and Tamar Lavi. "Israeli youth in the second Intifada: PTSD and future orientation." *Journal of the American Academy of Child & Adolescent Psychiatry* 44, no. 11 (2005): 1167–1175.

Swart, Hermann, Miles Hewstone, Oliver Christ, and Alberto Voci. "Affective mediators of intergroup contact: A three-wave longitudinal study in South Africa." *Journal of Personality and Social Psychology* 101, no. 6 (2011): 1221–1238.

Tajfel, Henri. "Social psychology of intergroup relations." *Annual Review of Psychology* 33, no. 1 (1982): 1–39.

Tam, Tania, Miles Hewstone, Ed Cairns, Nicole Tausch, Greg Maio, and Jared Kenworthy. "The impact of intergroup emotions on forgiveness in Northern Ireland." *Group Processes & Intergroup Relations* 10, no. 1 (2007): 119–136.

Tam, Tania, Miles Hewstone, Jared Kenworthy, and Ed Cairns. "Intergroup trust in Northern Ireland." *Personality and Social Psychology Bulletin* 35, no. 1 (2009): 45–59.

Tang, Shiping. "Reconciliation and the remaking of anarchy." *World Politics* 63, no. 4 (2011): 711–749.

Tatsumi, Yuki. "Japan, South Korea reach agreement on 'comfort women'." *The Diplomat*, December 28, 2015. Accessed September 30, 2017 at http://thediplomat.com/2015/12/japan-south-korea-reach-agreement-on-comfort-women/.

Taylor, Laura K., and Alexander Dukalskis. "Old truths and new politics Does truth commission 'publicness' impact democratization?" *Journal of Peace Research* 49, no. 5 (2012): 671–684.

Tropp, Linda R., and Robyn K. Mallett, Eds. *Moving beyond prejudice reduction: Pathways to positive intergroup relations.* American Psychological Association, 2011.

Tutu, Desmond. *No future without forgiveness.* Random House, 1999.

Verdeja, Ernesto. *Unchopping a tree: Reconciliation in the aftermath of political violence.* Temple University Press, 2009.

Wilson, Richard. *The politics of truth and reconciliation in South Africa: Legitimizing the post-apartheid state.* Cambridge University Press, 2001.

PART V
Civil society

11

IS CIVIL SOCIETY NEEDED FOR QUALITY PEACE?

Thania Paffenholz

Introduction

Civil society gives voice to the unheard (Pearce 1998; Fetherston 2000; Richmond 2005; Paffenholz 2010a), and makes important contributions to political change (Kasfir 1998: 143; Ikelegbe 2001: 20). This has been demonstrated in various regions such as the Middle East and North Africa in 2010 or the Eastern European Revolutions of the late 1980s. Moreover, some researchers have found a positive correlation between civil society involvement in peace negotiations and the sustainability of the agreements (Wanis-St. John and Kew 2008). The UN Secretary General in his report on mediation also highlights the importance of involving broad-based and widely respected civil society groups into mediation processes (Moon 2009). The objective of this chapter is to critically assess if, how, and under which conditions the involvement of civil society in a peace process contributes to the quality of peace.

Civil society is not a homogenous actor. It can be "civil" or "uncivil" depending on the divided or hierarchical nature of society at large. Inclusive, civic, bridging and pro-peace organizations can be found alongside exclusivist and sectarian ones—occasionally even xenophobic and militant groups (Belloni 2001; Ikelegbe 2001; Orjuela 2003). In cases such as Sri Lanka or Cyprus, civil society has demonstrated how to act against a peace agreement (Çuhadar and Kotelis 2010; Orjuela 2010). Civil society is not automatically the "good society" that supports the peace process and thus the subsequent quality of peace that must be taken into account when assessing civil society's contribution (Edwards 2004: 37). This requires making distinctions regarding civil society's role and functions.

The task of isolating civil society as a factor in promoting quality peace is complex. The challenges linked to this endeavor are similar to the challenges the entire project on quality peace is facing conceptually, methodologically, and normatively: how to assess whether civil society is a necessary factor for quality peace without an agreed framework; what kind of methodology to apply for assessing under which conditions civil society's contribution to quality peace is low, medium or high; and who has the power to determine this?

With this chapter I will suggest one possible approach for how to address these challenges in the case of civil society. This requires an understanding of what constitutes civil society's contribution to quality peace. This volume conceptualizes quality peace as significant social, political, and economic changes in the context of sustainable peace following armed conflict. The absence of violence is the most important issue for the immediate quality of people's lives. Additionally, a peace agreement must be also sustainable in order to create suitable conditions for a society to flourish. Finally, the breaking down of social polarization, and the strengthening of institutions to deal with conflicts constructively, helps to ensure peace in the long term. I argue that civil society is successful in supporting the development of quality peace if it contributes to: (1) reducing violence, (2) facilitating an agreement, (3) helping to ensure medium- to long-term sustainability of the peace agreement, and (4) establishing conditions to address the causes of conflict constructively within society at large.[1]

Civil society can play a direct and significant role in influencing this process. In the remaining parts of the chapter I will first give an explanation of the concept of civil society. Second, I will briefly explain the approach to addressing the aforementioned conceptual, methodological, and normative challenges for the case of civil society. I will assess how effectively civil society contributes to the quality of peace in these different roles. I then consider the relevance of different civil society roles in various phases of peace processes to allow for a better understanding of their implication for success. This analysis will also allow for a more distinctive approach to understanding success. It will also give practitioners and scholars more detailed success factors for civil society involvement. Also included are the results of a gender analysis. In the concluding remarks, I will sum up and draw lessons for the overall research question.

The evidence presented in this chapter is based on comparative research conducted from 2006–2009 in 12 case studies under the project "Civil Society and Peacebuilding" (Paffenholz 2010a). A companion chapter by Jones in this volume highlights many examples of civil society's involvement in El Salvador.

Civil society during armed conflict

Generally, civil society is understood as the arena of voluntary, collective actions of an institutional nature around shared interests, purposes, and values that are distinct from those of the state, family, and market (Merkel and Lauth 1998). Civil society consists of a large and diverse set of organizations that are not purely driven by private or economic interests, are autonomously organized, show civic virtue, and interact in the public sphere. While civil society is independent from the state, it is oriented toward, and interacts closely with, the state (Spurk 2010: 6–9). According to Spurk (2010), the main actors who comprise civil society are:

professional associations and unions; faith-based organizations; NGOs (mainly focusing on advocacy, human rights, peacebuilding or service delivery); clubs and societies; special interest groups (e.g., youth, women, or minorities); traditional entities including elders and other community groups; or movements.[2] These groups play different roles depending on whether there is an active armed conflict or post-armed conflict context. As the context changes, these groups shift their focus depending on the context and phase of the conflict, as explained by Jones in his chapter in this volume.

During and following an armed conflict, civil society actors have to adapt to difficult environments and new power relations. In the context of active armed conflict, the state is weak and generally oppressive toward civil society actors. Insecurity and fear, induced by years of civil war, hinder people from participating in local community development (Pearce 1998). Moreover, many civil society actors go into exile in times of conflict, thereby weakening the capacity of the organizations that remain. When civil society actors are weak, the influence of uncivil, xenophobic, or mafia-like groups tends to become stronger (Belloni 2001, 2006: 8–9), limiting the potential influence of civil society groups working for cross-ethnic understanding. This creates incentives for civilians to revert to their "primary groupings" such as kinship, tribal, religious, and traditional political structures, as well as communities (Pouligny 2005: 498). While the use of these networks serves as a coping strategy for people in response to state weakness, it also creates the possibility that primary groupings will be used by political actors for political reasons. As a result, space for civil society to contribute to quality peace is likely to diminish in such a context (Orjuela 2004: 59; Pouligny 2005: 498; Goodhand 2006; Spurk 2010: 17–20).[3] Nevertheless, it is still interesting to explore what and how civil society can still contribute to the quality of peace in the context of armed conflict and peace processes. In the next section, I identify four context specific phases for the role of civil society actors and analyze meta-data from 13 case studies to explore the conditions under which civil society actors contribute to quality peace.

Context, analytical framework, and cases

I explain the contribution of civil society groups to quality peace by utilizing the analytical framework developed in Paffenholz and Spurk (2010a). This framework identifies different roles/functions of civil society based on an analysis of theory and case study research in the context of armed conflicts and peace processes (Paffenholz and Spurk 2006). The Paffenholz and Spurk framework is an improvement upon Merkel and Lauth's (1998) functional model for civil society in democracy (Paffenholz and Spurk 2006; Paffenholz and Spurk 2010b). This analytical framework describes seven distinct functions and roles for civil society groups as potential pathways for contributing to the quality of peace: protection, monitoring, advocacy, socialization, social cohesion, facilitation, and service delivery. From the literature on armed conflict, peace negotiation, and post-conflict violence, I identify three different context specific phases of armed conflict and the subsequent peace process. These phases are: (1) armed conflict; (2) windows of opportunity for peace negotiations; and (3) post-agreement violence.[4] The Civil Society and Peacebuilding project evaluated these functions and phases in 12 qualitative cases, selected on the basis of four criteria: context of armed conflict, involvement of a broad variety of civil society actors, availability of data, and geographical distributions. These cases are from Africa (Somalia, Nigeria, and Democratic Republic of the Congo), Latin America (Guatemala), Europe (Northern Ireland, Bosnia-Herzegovina, Cyprus, and the Kurdish conflict in Turkey), the Middle East (Israel/Palestine) and South and West Asia (Afghanistan, Nepal, and Sri Lanka).[5]

In each case, the framework was composed of the following elements: analysis of context; identification of civil society activities and attribution to functions; assessment of the relevance of function in each phase and the effectiveness of activities within each function; and conclusions for each case. The *context analysis* was comprised of: (1) countries' general background and main actors; (2) conflict causes and dynamics; (3) needs for quality peace; and (4) historical evolvement and composition of civil society. The *function analysis* was comprised of: (1) contextualization of each function; (2) identification of civil society activities within the functions; (3) assessment of the relevance of each function for quality peace (clustered into high, medium, low) against the needs in the respective context and phases of conflict;[6] (4) analysis of the activities implemented by others besides civil society actors within the functions; and (5) assessment of the contribution of civil society quality peace.[7]

Effective quality peace

This section presents the results of effective civil society contributions to quality peace. The Civil Society and Peacebuilding project found that the effectiveness of civil society activities depends on two sets of variables: context- and function-specific as presented below. Functions are more effective in certain combinations, and in certain phases, as explained below. In addition, context variables can enable or constrain civil society's contribution to quality peace.

Protection

Protection refers to the provision of security needs by civil society actors, either alone or in cooperation with other agencies. This is normally one of the core functions provided by the state; however, in cases of acute state fragility and conflict, the relationship between state and society can break down.

Initiatives have been more effective when they were systematically combined with monitoring activities and advocacy campaigns, including an integrated media strategy of outreach and cooperation with international networks. The example of refugees returning shortly before the end of the Guatemalan civil war illustrates an effective combination of monitoring, advocacy, and protection. The agreement signed between the government of Guatemala and the Permanent Commission of Guatemalan Refugees in Mexico on October 8, 1992 provided an official role for NGOs, international organizations and private individuals to accompany the return from Mexico and resettlement of Guatemalan refugees displaced by the conflict. NGOs, including Peace Brigades International and Foro Internacional, ran accompaniment programs that went beyond the immediate return of refugees to encompass long-term monitoring and advocacy. The sense of security provided by these programs enabled the return of over 2500 refugees before the end of the conflict (Levitt 1999).

Monitoring

International and local civil society groups monitor relevant issues such as the human rights situation or the implementation of agreements. They issue recommendations to decision makers and provide human rights and advocacy groups with information. Such monitoring can work to hold governments and armed groups accountable for abuses or substandard performance, and can also serve as an early warning system (e.g., the joint early warning initiative between the United Nations Office for the Coordination of Humanitarian Assistance (UN OCHA), the Economic Community of West African States (ECOWAS), and a regional NGO peace network to conduct early warning in West Africa). The effectiveness of monitoring has been higher when activities were designed to reinforce protection and advocacy initiatives. Outreach to national and international networking also fostered effectiveness.

Advocacy

Advocacy refers to agenda setting and the application of pressure by CSOs. Civil society actors can push for the commencement of negotiations, the implementation of negotiated agreements, or against the recurrence of warfare. Also important are global international advocacy campaigns that lobby, for example, against land mines, blood diamonds, or the abuse of children as soldiers.

These initiatives have increased their effectiveness when organizations had campaigning know-how and based their advocacy on results of monitoring initiatives in combination with targeted media strategies. International attention additionally enhanced effectiveness.

Socialization

Socialization refers to in-group bonding that supports democratic behavior and promotes tolerant and peaceful values within society. This is realized through the active participation of citizens in various associations, networks, or movements. Socialization takes place only within groups, not between former adversary groups (which is social cohesion, discussed below).

These initiatives have been more effective when there was a low level of violence and initiatives engaged in a longer process with influential and established organizations such as schools or associations that do have the power to socialize people. In-group socialization of marginalized groups has been more effective when the empowerment did not foster radicalization. The experience of civil society in Nepal between 2001 and 2006 illustrates the potential for in-group socialization to contribute to quality peace. Identity-based CSOs took steps to organize, network, and advocate on behalf of communities previously marginalized from the Nepali political process, including women, Madhesi from the Southern plains, and indigenous populations. After the 2005 royal coup, these groups were cohesive and organized enough to form a broad civil society coalition that was instrumental in the protest movement that led to the capitulation of King Gyanendra. This protest movement prepared the ground for the peace agreement in 2006 (Chalmers 2010: 277–280).

Social cohesion

Social capital between groups is invariably degraded or destroyed during war between those groups. Therefore, it is crucial to build "bridging ties" across adversarial groups as well as (peaceful) "bonding ties" within specific groups. The objective of social cohesion is to help these groups learn to live together in peaceful coexistence.

These initiatives have been more effective when there was a low level of violence or an absence of violence; when initiatives aimed at bringing people together for a common cause (concrete outcome-orientation instead of a reconciliation-only focus). Long-term systematic initiatives have been more effective than short-term scattered events, especially when they focused on a wide range of societal cleavages and bridged difficult groups. In 2005, Çuhadar and Dayton conducted a study on the Israeli-Palestinian Track 2 social cohesion initiatives and compiled a list of 80 initiatives undertaken between 1989 and 2004 (excluding those carried out inside Israel between Palestinian and Jewish citizens) (Çuhadar et al. 2008). They found that interventions that focus on bringing people together for a common task and are held with influential people of equal status were more useful than those that attempt to build relationships through dialogue alone (Çuhadar and Hanafi 2010).

Facilitation

Civil society can function as a facilitator to help bring parties together in a peace or transition process. Facilitation can take place both on the local and the national level. Local facilitation has been performed at all times, mostly without external support. This also holds true for national facilitation by eminent civil society groups. We lack data for this function to come to valid conclusions about comparative experiences. Nevertheless, in some cases we found that the effectiveness of existing initiatives has been enhanced when targeted—in place of general or broad—training was provided.

Service delivery

During armed conflict, state structures are either destroyed or weakened, and the population may be starved for essential services. Civil society actors (mainly NGOs, but sometimes associations as well) can and do step forward to provide aid and social services. These activities have only been effective for quality peace when they created entry points for other functions. During times of violence, protection could be supported. After large-scale violence ends or in phases with low levels of violence, aid projects have been very effective in creating platforms of cooperation and dialogue for adversary groups with a common purpose. In Afghanistan, the service delivery activities of NGOs between 2001 and 2009 illustrate some of the challenges inherent in this function. Service delivery is generously funded by donors, and less challenging and politically controversial than other peacebuilding activities. This leads to a neglect of other peacebuilding functions. Even where aid is intended as an entry point, this goal has often been overtaken by the requirements of delivering services (Borchgrevink and Harpviken 2010).

Relevance of civil society in different phases of a peace process

In this section, I will present the results for relevance of civil society activities in support of quality peace in the three phases of peace processes. Overall, results from qualitative analysis demonstrate that there is a significant disconnect between implemented civil society activities and their relevance for quality peace in each phase (Paffenholz 2010b). Even when a function was highly relevant or needed in a particular phase, it was not necessarily performed.

Phase 1: armed conflict

Civil society's space to act becomes drastically reduced during periods of armed conflict. The key activities that civil society can pursue in a relevant manner are human rights violations monitoring, advocacy for the protection of people, dialogue facilitation, and ultimately the protection of people from violence. In other words, civil society's functions of *protection, monitoring, advocacy,* and *facilitation* are of high relevance here. When used as an entry point for the other functions, *service delivery* can also be of high relevance. This means that aid projects can also use their presence in a conflict zone to protect people by performing monitoring as well as informing other organizations about the situation, or by engaging in direct protection activities. Initiatives to socialize people for peace values (e.g., peace education, reconciliation or dialogue initiatives), with their long-term goal of changing people's behavior, are of low relevance *during* war because people focus mostly on their immediate needs. This is exemplified in the El Salvador case study by Jones (Chapter 12) in this publication.

Analyzing the actual level of implementation of civil society activities according to their functions during the armed conflict phase, the cases studies demonstrate that the actual type of civil society activities implemented did not match their relevance. While *protection, monitoring,* and *service delivery* were of high relevance, they were underrepresented among civil society's activities during this phase. The situation was slightly better for *facilitation* and *advocacy*. Many *social cohesion* and *socialization* activities were conducted, despite their lower relevance during war and most armed conflict settings.

At first glance, these findings are surprising but it is necessary to evaluate the relevance of civil society functions in terms of what civil society can actually achieve in the context of ongoing armed conflict. Civil society actors seem less involved in critically relevant roles such as service delivery, protection, and monitoring. One of the reasons could be related to the fact that service delivery, protection, and monitoring activities require a lot of resources and mobilization of resources. For example, service delivery in a war zone is costly and dangerous, and often beyond the capacity of civil society actors. Similarly, without cooperation from warring sides and adequate resources, civil society cannot perform monitoring and protection functions during armed conflict. From the analysis of cases, therefore, it emerges that the most logical and effective functions that civil society actors can perform during an armed conflict phase are advocacy and facilitation. These functions are critical to initiate or reactivate the negotiations through which parties can explore ways to address underlying grievances and initiate a journey toward peace.

Phase 2: windows of opportunity for peace negotiations

The concept of windows of opportunity for peace is an answer to problems inherent in the idea of "ripeness" associated with the work of Zartman. Zartman and others argued that a peace intervention could only contribute to solving a conflict if that conflict was ripe for resolution (Stedman 1991; Zartman 1989). While the idea of ripeness is helpful, it is empirically very difficult to distinguish from the question of the success of outcomes, i.e., if the conflict was not ripe, there was no chance for a successful peace intervention; if a peace intervention succeeded, then the conflict must have been ripe (Kleiboer 1994)! The idea of windows of opportunity reflects the reality that the chances for intervention come and go and must be continually monitored and analyzed. For example, the Norwegian-mediated Oslo Process, made effective use of such a window of opportunity that was identified by a Norwegian NGO and then supported by the Norwegian Foreign Ministry (Paffenholz 2004).

During this phase, civil society can take up very important—and in some instances crucial—roles to create a favorable environment for opening the space for dialogue between armed actors, facilitate the actual negotiations when opportunities arise, or to advocate for including pertinent issues in a negotiated settlement. While the relevance of all other functions remains the same as for the armed conflict phase, the relevance of *advocacy* is higher in this phase. Two types of advocacy become especially relevant at this stage: mass mobilization for the peace agreement as seen in Nepal, Northern Ireland, or Cyprus, and agenda setting through targeted advocacy campaigns for the inclusion of relevant issues into the peace agreement as seen in Guatemala, Northern Ireland, the Democratic Republic of the Congo, and Israel/Palestine.

Comparing the actual level of implementation of civil society activities in this phase, the case study findings show mixed results. In a few cases, the high relevance of advocacy did match with the actual activity level (Nepal, Northern Ireland, Cyprus, and Sri Lanka). It is worth mentioning that in Sri Lanka, for example, the pro-negotiation peace groups were by far outnumbered by the pro-war civil society groups. Activities for social cohesion and socialization initiatives reached the highest activity level (an actual mushrooming of initiatives) during this phase as we found a high level of external attention and funding across cases. This occurred even more in highly mediatized conflicts like Israel/Palestine, Sri Lanka, Cyprus or Northern Ireland. This reinforces the role and contribution of civil society actors in finding sustainable peace by facilitating negotiations.

Phase 3: post large-scale violence

In this phase, the need for protection decreases, although this entirely depends on the patterns of violence specific to each context, as in some settings violence can continue, albeit in other forms (e.g., crime, household violence, ineffective disarmament and demobilization processes). In Guatemala, for example, more people died from homicides and crime in the years after the peace agreement than during the armed conflict and war phases. Monitoring still remains relevant in this phase, along with facilitation and service delivery. Once the large-scale violence is over, social cohesion and socialization become more relevant as people are able to focus on issues beyond immediate survival. This is the time to invest in initiatives that rebuild relationships, reconcile with ex-combatants who return to civilian lives, and address root causes of conflict by reforming social, political, and economic institutions as a means of preventing future conflict.

Comparing the actual activity level of initiatives with their relevance during Phase 3, the case studies found that most but not all relevant activities have increased. A successful social cohesion initiative from Bosnia after the war illustrates this. Local community mediators were trained to mediate between returning refugees and/or internally displaced people and exiting communities. Their targeted engagement greatly facilitated reconciliation between the different groups. Similarly, in Northern Ireland, civil society groups played an important role in reforming social, political, and economic institutions that contributed to good governance and economic development. In this volume, Colin Knox provides a closer look at the Northern Ireland case and the role of civil society in contributing to quality peace.

In sum, civil society plays distinct and important roles during different conflict phases. There is significant variation in the functional role and relevance of civil society actors in these different phases, which could greatly influence the quality of peace. The section below specifically examines how civil society contributes to quality peace.

Quality peace: civil society and relevance of context

While I highlighted seven different functions of civil society and analyzed three different contexts, the effectiveness of civil society and its contribution to quality peace depends on underlying contexts and its own relevance. The Civil Society and Peacebuilding project found that the main contextual variables that affect civil society's influence on quality peace are the level of violence, behavior of the state, performance of the media, behavior and composition of civil society itself (including Diaspora organizations), and the influence of external political actors and donors. These contextual variables are interrelated.

Violence

Violence is the main hindering factor for civil society to make greater contributions to quality peace. The higher the level of violence, the more reduced the space for civil society to act—and consequently to support quality peace.

The behavior of the state

The more repressive a state is toward civil society actors, the more it limits the space for action; the more democratic the form of governance, the greater the space for civil society to act. The problem with this finding is that most conflict or post-conflict countries have authoritarian or semi-democratic forms of governance. Hence, the space for civil society to act is often limited. Nevertheless, civil society is able to act even in authoritarian systems, as seen in different Middle Eastern and Northern African countries during the "Arab Spring." These cases also exemplify the dependency of civil society on the state's reaction toward civil upheavals. The state can limit and control civil society's space not only through violent responses as seen in Syria, but also through legal actions as seen in restrictive NGO laws in a number of countries.

Media performance

Mass media are among the key opinion leaders in society. Hence, they can tremendously strengthen or limit civil society's contributions to quality peace. Without unbiased media coverage, civil society initiatives can get significantly lower public attention. This is especially true for protection, monitoring, advocacy, and socialization. Unfortunately, the media can also play a destructive role due to their biased reporting. In response, donors often choose to support peace media, albeit with limited effect since such outlets usually do not enjoy a broad audience.

Composition of and relationships within civil society

The composition and characteristics of civil society also influence its effectiveness, i.e., the more civil society is polarized and radical, the more difficult it becomes for it to make substantial contributions to quality peace. This also includes Diaspora organizations that can be extremely influential. We found that men from dominant groups in society (ethnic, religious, castes, etc.) hold most of the leading positions in CSOs. When civil society actors come from different sectors and influence the peace process, quality peace can be assured. Diverse civil society groups participated in and facilitated the pro-democracy and peace movement in Nepal in 2006 in favor of negotiations with the Maoist rebels and in opposition to the direct rule of the monarchy. Civil society maintained their advocacy and facilitation during the peace process and contributed to securing increased representation of women in political positions, representation of minority groups, and broader political reforms in Nepal.

Influence of external political actors

Although there are many important external political actors that can influence war and peace, in our case studies we found that strong regional political actors have the power to create suitable conditions for civil society's contributions: they can influence the peace process itself. In other words, they have the power to create (or limit) the space for civil society to act.

Influence of external funding

Funding enhances many initiatives and contributes to professionalization. Yet, funding has often contributed to the "NGOization" of peace work, the transformation of social movements into NGOs, the reduction in voluntarism, and the shift of accountability from local and national constituencies to international NGOs and donors.

Effectiveness of specific civil society actors

Civil society is not only composed of NGOs. While NGOs can be effective in carrying out civil society functions such as protection and advocacy, I found that a wide spectrum of other civil society actors are also engaged in support of quality peace (explicitly and implicitly). This includes associations, community and religious-based organizations, mass movements, traditional elders, or religious leaders. Traditional community organizations have far greater potential to promote socialization and social cohesion—even though their performance was rather low or often even counterproductive during contentious periods of an armed conflict. Traditional and local entities (like elders or spiritual leaders) are effective in facilitation and protection, and eminent civil society leaders can be effective in preparing the ground for national facilitation and in helping parties break out of a stalemate in negotiations. Women's groups seem to perform well in support of women's and minority issues and can be effective in bridging existing divides. It is also clear that broader change requires the uniting of all available mass movements. Aid organizations, if they are aware of their potential contribution to quality peace and make systematic use of it, can support protection, monitoring, and social cohesion.

Gender roles

Women have traditionally been perceived as having their primary place in the domestic sphere (to a greater or lesser extent in all studied societies), leaving the public sphere—state, market, and civil society—as male-dominated. Hence, the possibilities to organize in civil society differ from men to women (as it differs between people from different classes or ethnic backgrounds). The lack of political representation and voice has resulted in a limited representation of women in peacemaking attempts and in the implementation of peace agreements. In cases where women do participate in peace processes, they were not necessarily able to influence them as seen in the Inter-Congolese Dialogue or the Afghanistan negotiations in 2001. CSOs that are formed by women usually focus on women or minority issues.

Conclusions

Civil society has the potential to contribute to quality peace through protecting civilians from violence and facilitating peace negotiations and agreements. Civil society can also help to ensure medium- to long-term sustainability of the peace agreement through monitoring the implementation process, advocating for the implementation of provisions, reducing polarization, and building relationships. However, the assessment presented in this chapter demonstrates the complexity of the issue and the need to be precise in our analysis. The results show first that civil society's contribution to quality peace depends on: (1) the relevance of a function performed in a specific phase of conflict; (2) the context in which initiatives take place; and (3) the way initiatives are planned and implemented.

Second, the results also demonstrate that a better understanding of what constitutes quality peace is needed as well as approaches to assess this quality. This finding has a number of implications for the overall research on the relationship between civil society and quality of peace:

1. The context is an essential variable that must be an integrated part of any quality of peace analysis, as different contextual variables can both support or hinder the quality of peace.

2. Peace is a long process. Hence, the quality of peace needs to be analyzed more distinctively along different phases of the peace process.
3. Analyzing specific actors beyond civil society is necessary. As diverse groups can take up various roles in different phases, a functional approach is recommended.
4. A distinction between relevant and effective contributions to quality peace is helpful. The assessment presented in this chapter demonstrates that functions that are relevant (e.g., human rights monitoring during times of war) are not necessarily implemented in a way that makes them effective.

Notes

1. For more information, please refer to section *Research Design and Methodology* later in this chapter, and to Paffenholz 2010a: 65–76.
2. See more details on definitions and understanding in different geographical contexts in Spurk 2010: 3–27.
3. Also see the contribution by Richard Jones in this publication, Chapter 12.
4. A distinction between war and low-intensity conflict is based on the UCDP definition of armed conflict. Furthermore, these phases are not mutually exclusive. For example, third phase overlaps with the first and second one, and a number of conflict/peace phases usually occur several times in a particular case study conflict/peace cycle.
5. Among 12 cases analyzed and coded, 11 case studies were published. The Democratic Republic of Congo case study was not published but used in the data analysis.
6. For methodological details see the peacebuilding relevance assessment methodology as developed by Paffenholz and Reychler (2005).
7. See more in Paffenholz 2010a: 65–76.

References

Belloni, Roberto. "Civil society and peacebuilding in Bosnia and Herzegovina." *Journal of Peace Research* 38, no. 2 (2001): 163–180.

Belloni, Roberto. "Civil Society in War-to-Democracy Transitions." In Anna K. Jarstad and Timothy D. Sisk (Eds.). *From war to democracy: Dilemmas of peacebuilding*. Cambridge University Press, (2006): 182–210.

Borchgrevink, Kaja, and Kristian Berg Harpviken. "Afghanistan: Civil Society Between Modernity and Tradition." In Thania Paffenholz, Ed. *Civil society and peacebuilding: A critical assessment*. Lynne Rienner, (2010): 235–257.

Chalmers, Rhoderick. "Nepal: From Conflict to Consolidation a Fragile Peace." In Thania Paffenholz, Ed. *Civil society and peacebuilding: A critical assessment*. Lynne Rienner, (2010): 259–296.

Çuhadar, Esra, Bruce Dayton, and Thania Paffenholz. "Evaluation in Conflict Resolution and Peacebuilding," in Dennis J. D. Sandole, Sean Byrne, Ingrid Sandole-Staroste, and Jessica Senehi, Eds. *Handbook of conflict analysis and resolution*. Routledge, (2008): 383–395.

Çuhadar, Esra, and Sari Hanafi. "Israel and Palestine: Civil Societies in Despair." In Thania Paffenholz, Ed. *Civil society and peacebuilding: A critical assessment*. Lynne Rienner, (2010): 207–234.

Çuhadar, Esra, and Andreas Kotelis. "Cyprus: A Divided Civil Society in Stalemate." In Thania Paffenholz, Ed. *Civil society and peacebuilding: A critical assessment*. Lynne Rienner, (2010): 181–206.

Edwards, Michael. *Civil society*. Cambridge, UK: Polity Press, 2004.
Fetherston, A. Betts. "Peacekeeping, conflict resolution and peacebuilding: a reconsideration of theoretical frameworks." *International Peacekeeping* 7, no. 1 (2000): 190–218.
Goodhand, Jonathan. *Aiding peace?: The role of NGOs in armed conflict*. Lynne Reimer, 2006.
Ikelegbe, Augustine. "The perverse manifestation of civil society: Evidence from Nigeria." *Journal of Modern African Studies* 39, no. 1 (2001): 1–24.
Kasfir, Nelson. "Civil society, the state and democracy in Africa." *Commonwealth & Comparative Politics* 36, no. 2 (1998): 123–149.
Kleiboer, Marieke. "Ripeness of conflict: A fruitful notion?" *Journal of Peace Research* 31, no. 1 (1994): 109–116.
Levitt, Barry. "Theorizing Accompaniment." In Lisa L. North and Alan B. Simmons. *Journeys of dear: Refugee return and national transformation in Guatemala*. McGill-Queen's Press, (1999): 237–254.
Merkel, Wolfgang, and Hans-Joachim Lauth. "Systemwechsel und Zivilgesellschaft: Welche Zivilgesellschaft braucht die Demokratie." *Aus Politik und Zeitgeschichte* 6, no. 7 (1998): 3–12.
Moon, Ban Ki. "Report of the Secretary General on enhancing mediation and its support activities." United Nations, S/2009/189: April 8, 2009.
Orjuela, Camilla. "Building peace in Sri Lanka: A role for civil society?" *Journal of Peace Research* 40, no. 2 (2003): 195–212.
Orjuela, Camilla. *Civil society in civil war. Peace work and identity politics in Sri Lanka*. Department of Peace and Development Studies, Göteborg University, 2004.
Orjuela, Camilla. "Sri Lanka: Peace Activists and Nationalists." In Thania Paffenholz, Ed. *Civil society and peacebuilding: A critical assessment*. Lynne Rienner, (2010): 297–320.
Paffenholz, Thania. "Designing Transformation and Intervention Processes." In Alex Austin, Martina Fischer, and Norbert Ropers, Eds. *Transforming ethnopolitical conflict: The Berghof handbook*. Spring VS, (2004): 151–169.
Paffenholz, Thania, Ed. *Civil society and peacebuilding: A critical assessment*. Lynne Rienner, 2010a.
Paffenholz, Thania. "Conclusion." In Thania Paffenholz, Ed. *Civil society and peacebuilding: A critical assessment*. Lynne Rienner, (2010b): 425–430.
Paffenholz, Thania, and Luc Reychler. *Aid for peace*. Nomos Verlagsgesellschaft, 2005.
Paffenholz, Thania, and Christoph Spurk. "Civil society, civic engagement, and peacebuilding." *Social Development Paper* 36, 2006.
Paffenholz, Thania, and Christoph Spurk. "A Comprehensive Analytical Framework." In Thania Paffenholz, Ed. *Civil society and peacebuilding: A critical assessment*. Lynne Rienner, (2010a): 65–78.
Paffenholz, Thania, and Christoph Spurk. "Sri Lanka: Peace Activists and Nationalists." In Thania Paffenholz, Ed. *Civil society and peacebuilding: A critical assessment*. Lynne Rienner, (2010b): 297–320.
Pearce, Jenny. "From civil war to 'civil society': Has the end of the Cold War brought peace to Central America?" *International Affairs* 74, no. 3 (1998): 587–615.
Pouligny, Béatrice. "Civil society and post-conflict peacebuilding: ambiguities of international programmes aimed at building 'new' societies." *Security Dialogue* 36, no. 4 (2005): 495–510.
Richmond, Oliver P. *The transformation of peace*. Palgrave Macmillan, 2005.
Spurk, Christoph. "Understanding Civil Society." In Thania Paffenholz, Ed. *Civil society and peacebuilding: A critical assessment*. Lynne Rienner, (2010): 2–28.
Stedman, Stephen John. *Peacemaking in civil war: International mediation in Zimbabwe, 1974–1980*. Lynn Rienner, 1991.

Wanis-St. John, Anthony, and Darren Kew. "Civil society and peace negotiations: Confronting exclusion." *International Negotiation* 13, no. 1 (2008): 11–36.

Zartman, I. William. *Ripe for resolution: Conflict and intervention in Africa.* Oxford University Press, 1989.

12

CIVIL SOCIETY AND QUALITY PEACE

What happened in El Salvador?

Richard Jones

Introduction

On the evening of January 16, 1992 a jubilant crowd gathered in the Plaza Cívica, the central square in San Salvador to celebrate the signing of the peace accords bringing an end to the 12-year civil war. Ines, a woman forced to flee her home 10 years before and mother of ex-combatants turned to me and said, "Finally we have arrived – the promised land."[1]

The phrase "promised land" encapsulates the hopes and aspirations of many Salvadorans and activists at the time: an end to a bloody 12-year civil war that tore apart families and polarized the country. The roots of the war lay in a military dictatorship and an unequal economic structure dominated by the coffee oligarchy while more than 70 percent of the population lived as landless peasants. When the Catholic Church, unions, students, and peasant farmers began organizing for human rights and democracy in the 1970s, military repression was swift and severe. The war left 75,000 dead and a legacy of torture and terror over the civilian population. Over a million people were displaced, creating over-crowded shanty towns in and around the capital city of San Salvador. The "promised land" signified societal transformation toward a new society based on peace, democracy, and social justice.

Initially the 1992 peace accords seemed to confirm that promise. The accords were hailed by many as a negotiated revolution, and held up around the world as a symbol of the peace dividend promised by the end of the Cold War. That dividend was expected to foster an improved standard of living, transformation of political culture, institutional change, better social relationships, and greater security for citizens. There were no serious violations of the ceasefire after the accords were signed (Vickers et al. 1992; Spence et al. 1994). Ex-combatants from the insurgency and military were demobilized, a new civilian police force was created, and the mandate of the military changed. Reconstruction in the areas most affected by the conflict began in earnest. The FMLN became a political party and democratic elections were held just 2 years later. All of these steps seemed to lead toward a successful peace process. Yet, 24 years later, El Salvador is one of the most violent countries in the world in terms of homicides per capita. Nearly 20 percent of the population has immigrated to the US in search of economic opportunity and 10 percent of the population controls 48 percent of the wealth. While the current violence is certainly distinct from that experienced during the 12-year civil war in terms of actors, and dynamics, the levels of violence, emigration, and inequality question the quality of the peace achieved to date. They beckon a deeper exploration of the relationship of post-war violence to the war and the peace process.

How and what kind of peace was created in the post-war process are important questions. The fact that the former insurgency has been democratically elected to run the executive branch of government for two consecutive periods (2008–2013, 2013–2018) is a sign that some transformation of the political culture has occurred. At the same time, the fact that in January 2016 a court in Spain ordered the capture of 17 Salvadoran military personal accused of crimes against humanity in the case of assassinated Jesuit priests, their housekeeper, and her daughter in 1989, is a sign that events from the war and peace accords are still unresolved and relevant. These events also signal that the current period is largely shaped by the war and the peace accords. The two main political parties in power today were either created during the war (Alianza Nacional Republicana (ARENA) in 1981) or as part of the peace accords (FMLN in 1992). The fact that an emblematic case is being brought internationally for crimes against humanity are signs that the quality of peace is still an open, relevant question despite the time that has passed.

This chapter will explore the direct and indirect links of the war and peace process to the current violence and look at the contributions of civil society to peace during the armed conflict through dialogue and negotiations. The chapter will also address the post-war present in order to see what civil society did, how effective they were, and to explore the legacies and limits of their actions. Finally, the chapter will explore how these issues contribute to our understanding of what might constitute quality peace.

In the case of El Salvador, peacebuilding efforts by civil society were shaped by two different currents within the country: the "popular movement" sector including labor, peasant farmers, student movements, and churches on one side; and "elite civil society" consisting of private foundations leading the other.[2] The popular movement re-emerged in the early 1980s after most of the historical organizations were decapitated or wiped out due to the severe military repression of the late 1970s. Churches and international solidarity movements supported human rights, humanitarian aid and created the space for new organizations, many which had ties to the FMLN. Meanwhile, in 1983, a few wealthy families and the United States Agency for International Development (USAID) created the Salvadoran Foundation for Economic Development (FUSADES) that spawned several other private sector foundations, all beholden to US foreign policy and financial support.[3] So while the insurgents and government battled for control over the country, local, and international groups battled over the space and direction of civil society (Foley 1996: 68–70).

This created a polarized civil society with each current having its political alignments that framed its vision, discourse, and approaches. If the biblical metaphor of the "promised land" defined the aspirations for churches and the popular movement, the metaphor of the "American dream," and free market opportunity captured the vision of elite civil society. Both visions led the two currents to engage in a political and programmatic battle over economic, political, and institutional reform issues. The polarization filtered issues related to peace accords through a political lens, which meant those issues considered to be politically benign were not given importance.[4] For example, the social/gang violence that was emerging in the mid-1990s was considered non-political, named common crime, and not given priority. Whether or not the war and peace accords did contribute to the conditions that fostered this violence (topics taken up later in this chapter), this violence has certainly undermined the quality of life and the quality of peace that Salvadorans experience. In this sense, although it is non-political, it must be at least considered a type of spoiler violence (Mac Ginty 2006).

If peacebuilding aims to end violence and create a situation of greater justice in which people can flourish, then it must address the root causes of conflict, and also transform the way people live, heal, and structure their relationships, including security and living standards. How well this is done affects the quality of peace. In the case of El Salvador, civil society made important contributions to ending the war, facilitating space for negotiations and addressing key structural issues like human rights, democracy, and the economic and political roots of the war. However, polarization created a narrow lens that frequently fails to see the connections of the current social violence to the war and the peace process[5] or the fact that the experience of the war was not structural but subjective. The war was an experience of fear, terror, and mistrust that required attention to victims, healing, reparation, and reconciliation. Some of the reasons why these latter issues never became part of the government or civil society's programmatic agenda for addressing the war and/or consolidating the peace is explored in the following sections.

Civil society actions during the conflict

The churches and the popular movement were active in defending human rights and providing humanitarian aid in El Salvador. They were effective at shaping international public opinion and creating an international network for advocacy. However, the principal efforts to influence public opinion and policy marginalized efforts to deal with social reconciliation and trauma, leaving society fragmented and traumatized at the time of the peace accords. This has serious implications for the quality of peace because time does not heal all wounds. Trauma can be passed from one generation to the next and contribute to a new cycle of violence.[6]

Human rights monitoring and advocacy

When civil society was silenced by the military repression at the end of the 1970s, one of the few remaining voices able to speak out publicly was Catholic Archbishop Oscar Romero. He was considered by supporters as "the voice of the voiceless," denouncing human rights violations in his weekly homilies, addressing social and political issues in his pastoral letters, and pleading with then US President Carter to stop US military aid to the Salvadoran government.[7] Romero's actions, leadership, and eventual assassination led him to become a symbol for human rights, calling faith-based communities to action. The assassination of Romero was emblematic of many priests and nuns who were killed in El Salvador. Progressive segments within the Catholic Church used theological ethics to tell a story of martyrdom of these priests and nuns, a compelling narrative of sacrifice and justice that gave meaning to repression and political assassination, and which mobilized political resistance, inspired human rights activists, and galvanized international solidarity (Peterson 1997: xxiv, 211). Romero was eventually beatified in 2015 by Pope Francis, and despite the fact that the Catholic hierarchy remains divided on multiple issues and does not have a shared program for building post-war peace, Romero remains an unrivaled symbol for justice, peace, and human rights in Salvadoran society.

The Archdiocesan Office for Human Rights, Tutela Legal, organized faith-based activism into effective protection of human rights. The volume of cases (Tutela documented over 15,000 human rights violations) and the international network they created is a testament to their efficacy. Tutela, along with other human rights organizations, sent weekly advisories to church networks, Amnesty International, Americas Watch, and other international solidarity groups who pressured the international community to act.[8] These links to the international community played a significant role in conditioning aid.

In the US, these efforts initially resulted in linking military aid to improvements in human rights. Subsequently, in 1989, the outcry of condemnation over the brutal assassination of six unarmed Jesuit priests, their housekeeper, and her daughter brought US military aid to a halt. This was a major achievement of the human rights organizations in conjunction with the international solidarity movement. It had a direct impact on pushing the Salvadoran military and government to the negotiating table by removing American financial support (Cortright 1997: 197). The other major achievement of international solidarity was getting the US government to grant asylum status for Salvadorans and Central Americans fleeing the war.[9]

It is important to understand that these international solidarity movements were supported by a network of Salvadoran immigrants, many who had ties to the FMLN. This meant that their agenda was essentially driven by the political and tactical decisions of the FMLN. The importance of FMLN-linked groups cannot be underestimated for giving international solidarity a sense of purpose and direction. When the war ended and many of these actors returned home, the FMLN discontinued support and ceased communications. Many Salvadoran organizations in the US like El Rescate, CARECEN, and Centro Presente that were extremely active in organizing the solidarity movement became more concerned with services to the Salvadoran Diaspora, more involved in US domestic and immigration policy, and less engaged with the peace process. Once the peace accords were signed, the international solidarity movements floundered for lack of a clear agenda and purpose. This not only limited the struggle for human rights but strategic peace-building more broadly in terms of building a wider movement for social justice while also empowering local communities (Lederach and Appleby 2010).

Humanitarian aid

A massive humanitarian crisis was created due to the military strategy of "draining the sea" designed to eliminate the civilian base of support of the FMLN in rural areas. The Salvadoran military burned villages and massacred civilians, displacing over a million people who fled to the capital city of San Salvador and to the neighboring countries of Honduras, Nicaragua, and Costa Rica. The churches and the popular movement responded to this crisis, negotiating access to the population in conflict-affected areas with both the FMLN and the government. Through these negotiations, they got an agreement to a ceasefire for one day a year to implement a vaccination campaign. In 1985, they negotiated the return of 187 civilians to their homes in war-torn Tenancingo in the middle of the country. According to Auxiliary Bishop Gregorio Rosa Chavez,

> This action was real and symbolic. The vaccinations were necessary to protect the lives of women and children. The return to Tenancingo meant that people had a right to live in their homes and have their lives respected. We felt that if we could negotiate one day of ceasefire then dialogue and negotiations were possible.[10]

The humanitarian aid actions and negotiations with the FMLN and military created the possibility for dialogue, as noted by Monsignor Rosa Chavez. The churches and the popular movement also used the access to victims to shape international public opinion. They collected testimony about what was happening on the ground, the impact of the military's strategy on displacement, the use of torture, and massacres of civilians. The testimonies told the story of a war that was about repression, torture, and the abuse of human rights. This provided a different view of the war than the one given by the US-backed military who presented the war as one to contain communism.

These testimonies were supported and enhanced by public opinion research carried out by the University Institute for Public Opinion (IUDOP). IUDOP began taking the pulse of public opinion regarding the war, elections, and national politics. IUDOP's internationally accepted polling practices and well-trained staff provided churches and civil society actors with credible research for informed public debate. The humanitarian service and personal testimonies mobilized international public opinion that shifted and shaped the debate toward a peace based on human rights.

In this way, humanitarian aid provided opportunities to meet peoples' needs but also to shape public opinion, advocate for rights and foster dialogue. The imperative of providing humanitarian aid to victims of war did not mean that civil society had to be neutral or limit their efforts to only providing aid, but that these efforts, if well-linked to a peace agenda, could strengthen human rights and influence public opinion.

While the popular movement's humanitarian response was effective in pushing a larger peace agenda, it was less effective in laying a foundation for reconciliation. Despite recognition of the negative impact of massive displacement, disappearance, torture, and massacres on individual and interpersonal relations, the actions and resources to address the these issues were generally limited, and practically non-existent among the IDPs crowding into slums in San Salvador.[11] The churches focused on human rights and shaping public opinion, and less on trauma healing and building social trust. The lack of attention to trauma and social cohesion led to greater levels of fragmentation and mistrust within communities and between communities and government. The churches never developed a compelling narrative or action for healing and reconciliation. Addressing these issues would be a necessary foundation for transforming conflicts constructively in the long term and overcoming trauma, exclusion, and the breakdown in the social fabric.

Civil society contributions to dialogue and negotiations

While the end of the Cold War and the efforts of multiple governments helped to push for negotiations outside the country, the church and civil society were instrumental in ensuring space for dialogue inside the country. They played a relevant and effective role in setting the stage for a ceasefire and negotiations. Three preconditions contributed to their effectiveness: (1) humanitarian aid efforts lent credibility and legitimacy for dialogue; (2) there was wide support among the Catholic bishops for the Archbishop to mediate;[12] and (3) Archbishop Rivera y Damas had personal connections to parties on both sides (Klaiber 1998: 184).[13] The mediation role created new spaces for civil society actors that came together in the National Debate for Peace (CPDN). However, the CPDN was unable to convince elite civil society to participate. This failure to come together would deepen the schism between the two currents and limit the impact of several specific peace accords.

Between 1984 and 1988, the Catholic Church played a key role in facilitating dialogue. The initial talks were moderated by the Catholic Bishops Conference of El Salvador which gave credibility to the dialogue. Archbishop Rivera y Damas' public communication about the efforts provided opportunities for civil society actors to express their support for dialogue without fearing repression and to legitimize their opinions both in El Salvador and internationally. The second dialogue, also facilitated by the church, included agreements to foster "freedom of movement" which allowed the labor movement to create the Foro Nacional (National Forum) in 1985 designed to contribute to dialogue and negotiation. However, the National Forum became polarized in favor of the FMLN and moved away from dialogue (Klaiber 1998: 184–185). In 1987, the Catholic Church provided the space and facilitation for dialogue at the Papal Nunciature in San Salvador. These talks were acknowledged by both the government and the FMLN as a landmark in the process of resolving the conflict.[14]

Shortly after the Nunciature meetings, the FMLN withdrew from the process over the assassination of Herbert Anaya Sanabria, coordinator of the non-governmental Human Rights Commission and a government critic. Despite this setback, in 1988 Rivera y Damas moved on to promote the CPDN, hoping to achieve a wider acceptance for negotiations and a political solution to end the civil war.

Riviera y Damas convened all sectors to participate in the CPDN. In addition to widening the space for civil society participation, the CPDN orchestrated a nationwide survey whose results included an overwhelming condemnation of the war, and a unanimous call for dialogue (Klaiber 1998: 188–192). The results were distributed nationally and internationally, adding pressure for negotiations. The creation of the CPDN signaled a turning point. Now there was a more active role for multiple groups including churches, labor, peasant farmers, and slum dwellers to advocate for a peaceful solution to the war. Once again, credible research allowed civil society to shape Salvadoran and international public opinion.

Although the contributions to dialogue and shaping international opinion were successful for moving toward a negotiated settlement, they ultimately had limited influence on the negotiations because elite civil society refused to participate, which reduced critical support. The lack of elite participation meant that that the deep schism between elite and popular movements remained and that the path toward peace would be one in which each side would constantly jockey for position and influence. It also left the peace accords to be determined by the belligerent parties (Salvadoran Army with wealthy elites, and the FMLN) and not by civil society (Foley 1996). In some ways the lack of more direct civil society participation in the peace accords or even the creation of a commission to monitor the peace process left the implementation of accords principally in the hands of political actors.

Elite civil society did influence the negotiations and was able to ensure that structural adjustment language was included in the peace accords by using its contacts in the government. This language would lay the groundwork for economic liberalization that would dominate the economic development debate for the next 20 years.[15] Economic liberalization favored export-led growth, strengthening financial institutions and privatization over local sustainable development and government intervention. This entrenched the divisions between the popular movement and elite civil society, set their battles primarily along ideological lines and weakened other accords designed to bridge the economic and social divide. The economic framework and divisions frustrated the Social and Economic Forum mandated by the peace accords. The Forum was supposed to bring together key economic actors from private sector to labor, but the Forum only met three times before the end of 1993 and never advanced. The government and private sector argued that the peace accords already outlined the economic liberalization path and there was nothing else to decide. The forum failed due to refusal by the Government and private sector to dialogue over economic liberalization (Foley 1996; CIDAI 2007).

This "liberal peace" unfortunately has been unable to deliver economic growth or improved livelihoods. For the past decade, economic growth has been less than 2 percent and today more than 73 percent of Salvadorans work in the informal sector as the formal economy remains unable to meet people's basic needs. This illustrates not only a failure of the liberal peace model pursued in El Salvador, but also the economic conditions of poverty and exclusion experienced by the post-war generation that has been an incubator for violence. While not all poor people engage in violence, organized criminal groups have thrived in the informal markets and gangs have flourished in the marginal neighborhoods created by massive internal displacement during the war.

Civil society actions and omissions in post-war period

The divisions, roles, and priorities of civil society that were shaped during the conflict and negotiations deepened during the post-war period. USAID favored elite civil society to the exclusion of the popular movement, the FMLN withdrew support for the Diaspora, and civil society focused on macro, structural issues like elections, human rights, and privatization at the expense of reconciliation, social cohesion and, initially, the social violence and crime that was emerging in the mid-1990s. This was particularly detrimental given the levels of emigration that continued to tear apart the social fabric, along with the growing gang phenomena, organized criminal groups, and drug trade that laid the foundation for social violence. The period can be divided into three parts: the first from 1992–1997, the second from 1998–2008, and finally from 2009-present.

1992–1997

In the years following the accords between 1992 and 1997, civil society responded to the agenda set by the peace accords for human rights, reintegration of ex-combatants, and reconstruction. According to the peace accords the national reconstruction process was supposed to focus on reconstruction, local development, and reconciliation through an inclusive process with the government, NGOs, and donors. In the end, USAID and government bureaucrats wrote the reconstruction plan, focused largely on infrastructure and channeled funds through the ARENA government-controlled municipalities, FUSADES and the National Commission for Restoration of Areas (CONARA), the national counterinsurgency agency that excluded the popular movement groups linked to the FMLN (Murray 1994: 16–20, 50).

The European donors took a different approach by supporting efforts at local development managed by FMLN-affiliated NGOs. The differences in donor approaches and the exclusion of FMLN-related groups to national reconstruction funds widened the divisions in civil society and heated the debate over economic liberalization versus local development. None of the programs explicitly addressed the needs for reconciliation or rebuilding the social fabric (Thompson 1997: 504–506).[16]

The fact that none of these programs targeted the internally displaced nor did they explicitly address trauma or reconciliation affected the ability of communities to work together for economic and social development (Ostrom and Walker 2003).[17] For example, after experiencing initial success in collectively marketing tomatoes, farmers in the war-torn department of Morazán abandoned the process. When asked why, several reported that they could not trust the other due to past affiliations with either the military or FMLN.[18] Despite common interests in selling tomatoes, personal mistrust inhibited progress. Morazán remains the poorest of the 14 departments, despite having received more aid than any other.

In addition to the bias in funding and focus for reconstruction, the General Amnesty Law passed by the government prejudiced the pursuit of human rights. The law exonerated those involved in the war from being tried for war crimes or human rights abuses, creating total impunity for perpetrators of human rights abuses. The Salvadoran court has used the law for nearly 22 years to reject human rights cases and curtail any judicial reform. Although the constitutional court has argued that the General Amnesty does not apply in cases of crimes against humanity, lower courts have failed to prosecute human rights cases. As a result, no one has ever been tried in El Salvador for any human rights violations. The judicial system was also shielded from serious changes. Despite minor changes to the criminal code in 1996 and the system for electing judges, the Salvadoran state remains ineffectual in providing access to justice or reparations to victims of the war or post-war violence (Betancur et al. 2001).

The General Amnesty also silenced the Truth Commission Report (TCR), an independent report mandated by the peace accords, to study what happened during the war, why it happened, who was responsible and what should be done to remedy it. The report did not become part of school curriculum nor even widely circulated, impeding civil society efforts to socialize people toward peace and resolve conflicts constructively. Today there is little consensus about what happened, or who was responsible, which allows the perceptions of the war to be formulated according to partisan needs and feeds political polarization that reinforces an "us-versus-them" mentality.

Rather than socializing this and the next generation to peace, the "us-versus-them" mentality simply reinforced the sense of exclusion and mistrust within communities (and between communities and government) and increased ignorance of the war and peace accords among the general population. This combination of mistrust, exclusion, trauma, and near total impunity was devastating for the internally displaced living in the major slums of San Salvador, fueling domestic and social violence (Savenije and Andrade-Eekhoff 2003: 127–132). The vast majority of homicides in El Salvador today take place in many of those marginalized urban slums populated by the massive internal displacement that occurred during the war. The gang phenomena spread throughout these neighborhoods in the mid- to late-1990s. By 2005, between 11,000 and 30,000 youth were involved in gangs, homicides, and violent crime (USAID 2006: 17). In many ways, the war and post-war conditions contributed to the rise of gangs and social violence. They thrived in the marginal communities of internally displaced people. They were the result of the Salvadoran Diaspora facing rival groups in Los Angeles and the failures of the economic liberalization that left young people in these neighborhoods with almost no alternatives for licit livelihoods. As important as the links of the current violence are to the war and peace process is the fact that this violence certainly undermines the quality of life and peace and points to the fact that whether war-related or not, post-war security and crime is an important issue affecting the quality of peace.

Security was high on the peace accord agenda. The new National Civilian Police (PNC) force was created as part of the accords and was intended to replace the existing National Police, Treasury Police, and National Guard that were an institutional part of the armed forces and notorious for perpetrating human rights abuses. The police initially were founded to be a professional security force based on the rule of law and to contribute to a culture of peace.[19] However, there is ample evidence that this noble mandate was undermined from the very beginning. In 1992 President Alfredo Cristiani, in breach of the peace accords, incorporated the intelligence units from the former National Police, Treasury and National Guard into the new PNC. From there, the intelligence units began to control and corrupt the PNC from within. Former PNC Directors have been implicated in using the institution to support the drug trade, protect organized criminal groups, obstruct justice, and guarantee impunity for those with enough money or influence. The first signs of problems were identified in 1993 by a joint research group created by the UN after several assassinations of political activists put the peace process at risk. The UN-sponsored joint group warned that the clandestine armed groups linked to the state continued to operate, and had begun transforming into structures of organized crime (Silva 2015). This period also saw the emergence of social cleansing groups called Sombra Negra, or Dark Shadow, which operated in San Miguel in 1994 and 1995. Among the 14 people arrested for participation in the group which threatened judges, harassed political activists, and assassinated young people were at least three police officers and one local Police Division leader (Valencia 2014). David Morales, a lawyer with Tutela Legal del Arzobispado, the Catholic Church's legal aid office in San Salvador, told Inter Press Service that even though the Joint Group "recommended that former president (Armando) Calderón (1994–1999) take measures to dismantle these groups, the recommendation was never heeded."[20]

1998–2008

When the UN declared the peace process completed, civil society did clamor that the peace process was incomplete, citing the General Amnesty and the failures of the economic forum and structural adjustment programs as signs of an unequal economic system that was failing to address the root causes of the war. By 1998, the popular movement's attention focused on electoral politics as the FMLN became the second strongest political party. The government, supported by elite civil society, focused on structural adjustment programs, privatizing state institutions from the banking system to social security. Civil society would galvanize against privatization issues in health and water, for example in 2002 over 200,000 people marched in San Salvador against the privatization of the health care system, and in 2005 thousands rallied against the privatization of water (Almeida 2011: 307–312).

During this time, the Catholic Church had turned its attention to other issues and remained ambivalent on economic globalization and electoral politics. The official end of the peace process, electoral politics, and economic globalization drew attention away from the peace accords, security issues, and reconciliation. The division between elites and the popular movement was also mirrored by a de facto split between the churches and the popular movement that no longer had a clear and common agenda.[21]

Even local development projects continued to be affected by mistrust. A USAID-sponsored project that linked remittances to education in 2005–2006 encountered difficulties in cultivating relationships between Diaspora Home Town Associations in the US and communities and schools in El Salvador. When the program manager suggested that Banco Agricola, the local, private sector partner, work with REDES, an organization that had expertise in working with Diaspora groups, Banco Agricola refused to work with them accusing them of being tied to the FMLN and later refused to work with the local program manager for suggesting it.[22]

The human rights organizations remained focused on the peace accords, pursuing court cases and carrying out symbolic actions and education. Yet no human rights cases were tried in El Salvador due to the Amnesty Law. As Roberto Burga, a lawyer for IDHUCA, explained, "It's a shame that we have to seek justice in the United States, or Costa Rica, what we want is that the Salvadoran judicial system works."[23]

IDHUCA began the "Festival Verdad" commemorating the *Truth Commission*, the pro-Monument Committee erected a public monument with the names of civilians killed or disappeared during the war as a tribute to their dignity and memory. Other efforts by ProBusqueda to heal the memories of the past remained marginal despite recognition that historical memory and trauma healing is a part of fostering social cohesion and contributing to the quality of peace.[24] Even if the latest sentence of the Inter-American Court is implemented, it may have little more than symbolic impact if it is not accompanied by measures for judicial reform and to address social fragmentation, fear, and mistrust.

Human rights did become part of the school curriculum and there was a boom in laws for women's and children's rights. However, education in human rights was not accompanied by building skills for resolving conflicts constructively, nor did schools incorporate it. The schools continued to favor punitive responses to discipline that suspended and expelled students for misbehaving. Families did not learn alternatives to physical punishment for solving problems. Punitive approaches, repression, and physical punishment continued to be the norm in families, schools and communities.

Government institutions responded in similar fashion. Punitive law enforcement approaches were implemented in 2004 that proved to be ineffective, as homicides increased by 22 percent in 2004 and 28 percent in 2005 (Aguilar 2010). The repressive tactics taken on by the police began to override the mandate for a professional security force dedicated to upholding the law and contributing to the culture of peace and increasingly gave way to the use of force as the modus operandi. To make matters worse, internal controls were weakened and the police began to be infiltrated by gangs and other criminal groups.

2009–present

The year 2009 marked a political transition from 20 years of governance by the right-wing ARENA party to the FMLN (the former insurgency) assuming the presidency. Early actions by the new government gave hope for the struggles of human rights, impunity, and social violence. In 2010, President Funes officially named the international airport "Oscar Arnulfo Romero Galdamez" after the martyred Archbishop. In 2010, the government accepted the role of the state in the massacre of El Mozote. In 2011, the government accepted the jurisdiction of the Inter-American Commission and Court for Human Rights. It also publicly assumed responsibility for disappearances of children during the civil war, made apologies and initiated reparations to the families.[25,26] Although a 2013 Executive Order created a reparations program for victims from the war, the program remains unfunded and is not applied, leaving victims to fend for themselves.[27] Despite initial attempts to begin to rid corruption from the police force and recognize the role of the state in human rights abuses, events soon began to overtake the new government.

Notwithstanding these advances to contest the amnesty provision and impunity, the FMLN governments have not been able to stem the spread of corruption. Initial attempts to purge the police of criminal elements and those accused of past human rights atrocities were halted in 2010, apparently due to negative political consequences. The FMLN began to use the military in conjunction with the police to address the rising levels of violence and has continued to do so for the past 6 years. Use of the military in police functions is only allowable in exceptional circumstances as mandated by the peace accords. This action is contributing to the militarization of security and the spiral of violence.

In 2012, the government led by the Minister of Justice, a former military general, negotiated a truce with gang leaders inside the prison system. While the truce did lead to a reduction of the homicide rate by half, the truce began to unravel more than a year after it was initiated. Lack of transparency as to what was negotiated, lack of participation of the justice and security institutions, combined with lack of a strategy for integration of gang members into licit activities, led to a loss of credibility. Perhaps the single most important factor that stopped the truce was the fact that the Minister of Justice, one of its principal architects, was forced from office because as stipulated in the peace accords, the Minister of Justice must be a civilian. The new Minister of Justice did not support the truce. Not only did it unravel, but the murder rate began to rise to point where in 2015, El Salvador was projected to be the most violent country in the world in terms of homicides per capita[28] and occupied eighth place in the Global Impunity Index. Today, only 5 out of every 100 homicides are prosecuted and result in sentences. This can be linked to the overall amnesty that contributed to the culture of impunity that has continued throughout the post-war period (Ruada Zablah 2015).

During the three periods, the quality of peace was eroded by social violence, weak police and judicial institutions, a return to government repression in the first decade of this century, ongoing polarization, the rupture of the social fabric, and the failure of economic liberalization to improve the standard of living for the majority of Salvadorans. The divisions within civil society continued to deepen, which created a mentality of "us versus them," which has only been reinforced by the current spiral of violence.

Conclusions

Civil society in El Salvador made great contributions to ending the violence and fostering dialogue particularly through their efforts to protect human rights and deliver humanitarian aid. Their effectiveness in pushing for dialogue and ending the violence was due to several factors: (1) the specialization of human rights; (2) local knowledge and expertise in the form of contact with victims and affected communities; (3) the international solidarity network that created effective channels for advocacy; (4) the public opinion polls that provided credibility and information and was a positive force in the media; (5) the ability of civil society to connect to leaders from both sides of the conflict; and (6) internal cohesion and a common agenda among the popular sector and churches. Although some of these attributes of effectiveness are related to actors outside the country, it is important to note that it is the actions inside the country that make them effective.

This effectiveness was hindered by divisions within civil society that created two camps focused on battling one another over ideological economic and political issues. Also internal divisions and lack of a clear and common agenda between the churches and the popular movement weakened the ability of both to sustain the peace process and build long-term capacity for resolving conflict constructively. Nor was the church able to create the same powerful narrative for reconciliation and collaboration as they had for mobilizing and catalyzing efforts around human rights and dialogue. This limited their effectiveness in the post-war period.

The divisions within civil society were deepened by decisions made by the government, FMLN, and international donors in the post-war period that contributed to the entrenched positions taken up by the two currents in civil society. Despite the fact that some civil society groups did recognize the need for trauma healing and rebuilding the social fabric, civil society actors allowed the structural issues and decisions by key political actors to dominate their agenda.

While the latter demonstrates the complexity of civil society and the often symbiotic relationship between civil society and key political actors, civil society does have a choice and can influence peace processes as is shown by their actions during the conflict in fostering dialogue. Part of their effectiveness is in leveraging symbiotic relationships toward peace as they did in shaping international opinion and facilitating dialogue in El Salvador. When they do not act to influence those relationships, issues remain unaddressed as is the case with reconciliation or rebuilding the social fabric, a fact that points to the relevance and influence of their actions.

In this way, civil society can be a key contributor to the quality of peace, although they do not control the whole process. In this case, they were successful in contributing to ending the war, negotiations, and structural issues like human rights, and democracy. However, they failed to assume roles and functions for social cohesion in the post-war period that allowed violence to grow and diminished the quality of peace.

In terms of peacebuilding, this case suggests that civil society efforts must address structural issues, institutional reform, trauma, and social cohesion in ways that are mutually reinforcing. The roles and functions for civil society are likely to be different at various stages of the conflict, but working on all four of these levels is critical over time to achieve a greater quality of peace. Additionally, as this case shows, civil society can also be polarized and contribute to increasing fragmentation rather than social cohesion. The need to understand the relationships between civil society and government, and among civil society, is important for the post-accord era. Fostering spaces and processes for reconciliation are essential in situations of protracted conflict if a greater quality of peace is to be achieved.

In terms of the quality of peace, the case of El Salvador shows that key areas must be taken into consideration: the impact of economic liberalization, liberal peace, and security issues (common crime or politically motivated) that have the capacity to undermine the quality of life and peace. Human rights remain critical issues, and in this case, although the amnesty allowed former enemies to integrate into political life, the long-term result has been to foster impunity. Finally, more needs to be explored in terms of attention to victims, reparations, and reconciliation, as this case shows, unattended trauma can contribute to ever-increasing levels of personal and social violence.

For the people living in El Salvador today, the quality of peace that was created and the pending agenda are life and death issues. Ines, the women quoted at the beginning of this chapter, now lives alone, as most of her children have immigrated to the US and she lives on the money they send home. She remains in a community of displaced people, now riddled with gangs, unemployment, and crime. Ultimately, it is here in the lives of women like Ines that the quality of peace must be defined and measured.

Notes

1. Navidad, Ines Carlota (January 16, 1992) Personal Interview. Author was together with Ines Carlota Navidad, at the Celebration of the Peace Accords in San Salvador.
2. The issue of civil society in El Salvador is also treated in the chapter by Dinorah Azpuru, Chapter 14, as part of an application of the five dimensions of quality peace. The purposes and perspectives are different in the two chapters.
3. For example, FUSDADES received over $150 million in USAID during the war. See Rosa 1993.
4. For a discussion on violence in postwar situations, see Steenkamp et al. 2011: 358.
5. Christina Steenkamp clearly argues that both the war and the peace process may contribute to postwar violence (2011: 357–60).
6. The *Little Book of Trauma Healing* demonstrates that unresolved trauma does not disappear, but rather can get expressed in new forms of violence (Yoder 2015).
7. Romero wrote four pastoral letters on the crisis, one largely dedicated to the right to association of popular organizations and the fourth, and last, called for non-violent social change and national dialogue. These pastoral letters were widely disseminated and discussed among the popular sectors, inspiring activists to organize. The letters were also used as an internal call to allow for freedom of association and dialogue.
8. Two other prominent human rights organizations include the Institute for Human Rights of the Central American University and the Non-Governmental Commission for Human Rights. Both used Tutela's legal investigations to follow up on cases and make denouncements.
9. Over 500 religious congregations openly defied US federal law by providing shelter to Central American refugees and asylum seekers. They eventually filed suit in American Baptist Churches vs. Thornburgh. Although the court ruled against the plaintiffs, the movement won public sympathy and the government eventually granted asylum status to many of the refugees involved in the trial. Furthermore, many Congressional Democrats took up the cause of the Central American refugees, due in large part to the lobbying and publicity efforts of Sanctuary members. In 1990, the House and Senate approved a bill granting temporary protected status to Central Americans in need of safety.
10. Interview with Monsignor Gregorio Rosa Chavez, August 2011.
11. Jesuit Psychologist Ignacio Martin-Barró wrote numerous articles on displacement, trauma, and understanding the impact of the war on social cohesion. The Association de Capacitacion e Investigacion para la Salud Mental and Sr. Patricia Farrell with CAPACITAR began work on trauma healing with refugees and communities that were returned and repopulated between 1986 and 1988. See also Gaborit 2006.
12. Previously the bishops were divided on how to approach the political crisis. For example, only one bishop, Rivera y Dámas attended Romero's funeral.
13. Rivera y Dámas was personal friends with Duarte and had personal contacts with several leaders of the FMLN.
14. Joint communiqué of the third meeting was published in *Estudios Centroamericanos* in 1998.
15. See Revista Proceso No. 1225. Centro de Información y Documentación y Apoyo a la Investigacion (CIDAI) January 17, 2007 and also the concertación por la paz evaluatión on 15 years after the peace accords called "Evaluación de 15 años después de la firma de los Acuerdos de Paz en El Salvador." Both of these discuss the breach between the peace accords and the economic plan and structural adjustment process created by the government.

16. See also Azpuru et al. 2007 and Cuellar 2007.
17. Ostrom makes the point that trust and reciprocity are essential to economics, and without them the system fails.
18. Personal interview with Farmers from the Association of Vegetable Growers of Corinto Morazán, a USAID sponsored project in June 2002.
19. Page 5 of the *Chapultepec Peace Accords 1991–1992* outlines the mandate of the PNC.
20. Interview with David Morales (now Human Rights Ombudsperson), December 2015.
21. While this is generally true, the exception that seems to prove the point is that the churches together with the popular movement worked together to stop Pacific Rim from starting open pit mining for gold between 2005 and the present.
22. Personal Interview with Katherine Andrade, project manager for USAID project in 2007.
23. Personal Interview with Roberto Burga, June 2009. In 2004, Salvadoran President Francisco Flores publicly rejected the recommendations of the InterAmerican Commission for Human Rights to accept responsibility for the disappearance of children.
24. Trauma healing by Pro Busqueda has been done primarily with families of the disappeared but not with communities or between people who were on different sides of the conflict.
25. Personal Interview with David Morales, representative of the Salvadoran Government to the InterAmerican Commission for Human Rights, June 2, 2011. See also "El Salvador Pide . . ."
26. Two other cases, the assassination of Archbishop Romero and the massacre of El Mozote were accepted by the InterAmerican Court in 2009 and 2011 respectively.
27. *Executive Decree 204* created the reparations program for victims of the armed conflict between 1980 and 1992.
28. El Salvador is presently considered the most violent country in the world, with a homicide rate of 95 per 100,000 inhabitants, according to the 2015 forecast (Valencia 2015). In addition to homicide, countless Salvadoran families suffer other criminal acts, such as robbery, theft, abduction, extortion, sexual abuse, rape, trafficking, and disappearance of persons. In terms of the latter crime, the General Attorney's Office reports 3,765 cases of disappeared persons between June 2014 and June 2015. It is assumed that the majority have been murdered.

References

Aguilar, Jeanette. "Las Cifras de La Criminalidad en El Salvador." *UCA Editores*, (2010): 2.
Almeida, Paul. "Olas de movilización popular: movimientos sociales en El Salvador, 1925–2010." *UCA Editores*, 2011.
Azpuru, Dinorah, Ligia Blanco, and Ricardo Córdova Macías. *Construyendo la democracia en sociedades posconflicto: Un enfoque comparado entre Guatemala y El Salvador*. International Development Research Centre, 2007.
Betancur, Belisario, Reinaldo Figuerdo Planchart, and Thomas Buergenthal. *From madness to hope: The 12-year war in El Salvador: Report of the Commission on the Truth for El Salvador*. Washington, DC: United States Institute for Peace, 2001.
Centro de Información y Documentación y Apoyo a la Investigacion (CIDAI) Revista Proceso No. 1225. Universidad Jose Simeon Cañas. San Salvador, January 17, 2007
Chapultepec Peace Accords 1991–1992. Uppsala Conflict Data Program (UCDP), 1992. Accessed September 30, 2017 at www.ucdp.uu.se/gpdatabase/peace/ElS%2019920116b.pdf.
Cortright, David, Ed. *The price of peace: Incentives and international conflict prevention*. Rowman & Littlefield, 1997.
Cuellar, Benjamin. *El Salvador, Quince Años Después: Otra Lectura*. IHDUCA, 2007.
"El Salvador Pide Perdón Ante Corte IDH Por Niños Desaparecidos." *La Prensa Grafica*, May 18, 2011.

Foley, Michael W. "Laying the groundwork: The struggle for civil society in El Salvador." *Journal of Interamerican Studies and World Affairs* 38, no. 1 (1996): 67–104.

Gaborit, Mauricio. "Memoria Histórica: Relato de las víctimas." *Pensamiento Psicológico* 2, no. 6 (2006): 7–20.

Klaiber, Jeffrey L. *The church, dictatorships, and democracy in Latin America*. Orbis Books, 1998.

Lederach, John Paul, and Scott Appleby. "Strategic Peacebuilding: An Overview." In Daniel Philpott and Gerard Powers, Eds. *Strategies of peace*. Oxford University Press, (2010): 19–44.

Mac Ginty, Roger "North Ireland: A Peace Process Thwarted by Accidental Spoiling." In Edward Newman and Oliver P. Richmond, Eds. *Challenges to peacebuilding: Managing spoilers during conflict resolution*. United Nations University Press, (2006): 153–172.

Murray, Kevin, and Ellen Coletti. *Rescuing reconstruction: The debate on post-war economic recovery in El Salvador*. Hemisphere Initiatives, 1994.

Ostrom, Elinor, and James Walker, Eds. *Trust and reciprocity: Interdisciplinary lessons for experimental research*. Russell Sage Foundation, 2003.

Personal Interview with David Morales, representative on the Salvadoran Government to the InterAmerican Commission for Human Rights, June 2, 2011.

Personal interview with Farmers from the Association of Vegetable Growers of Corinto Morazán, a USAID sponsored project in June 2002.

Personal Interview with Katherine Andrade, project manager for USAID project in 2007.

Personal Interview with Roberto Burga, June 2009.

Peterson, Anna Lisa. *Martyrdom and the politics of religion: Progressive Catholicism in El Salvador's civil war*. SUNY Press, 1997.

Rauda Zablah, Nelson. "El Salvador ocupa el puesto 8 en el Índice Global de Impunidad." *La Prensa Grafica*, May 3, 2015. Accessed September 30, 2017 at www.laprensagrafica.com/2015/05/03/el-salvador-ocupa-el-puesto-8-en-el-indice-global-de-impunidad.

Rosa, Hernan. "AID y las Transformaciones Globales en El Salvador." Managua, Nicaragua: Coordinadora Regional de Investigaciones Econmicas y Sociales (CRIES), 1993.

Savenije, Wim, and Katharine Andrade-Eekhoff. "Conviviendo en la orilla. Violencia y exclusión social en el Área Metropolitana de San Salvador."*FLACSO-Programa El Salvador* (2003): 65–193.

Silva, Héctor. "Infiltrados. Crónica de la corrupción en la PNC (1992–2013)." *UCA Editores*, 2015.

Spence, Jack, George Vickers, and Margaret Popkin. *A negotiated revolution?: A two year progress report on the Salvadoran peace accords*. Hemisphere Initiatives, 1994.

Steenkamp, Christina. "In the shadows of war and peace: making sense of violence after peace accords." *Conflict, Security & Development* 11, no. 3 (2011): 357–383.

Thompson, Martha. "Conflict, reconstruction and reconciliation: Reciprocal lessons for NGOs in Southern Africa and Central America." *Development in Practice* 7, no. 4 (1997): 505–509.

US Agency for International Development (USAID). *Central America and Mexico Gang Assessment*, 2006.

Valencia, Robert. "La Sombra Negra." *elfaro*. April 26, 2014. Accessed September 30, 2017 at www.salanegra.elfaro.net/es/201404/bitacora/15308/La-Sombra-Negra.htm.

Valencia, Robert. "La tasa de homicidios de El Salvador supera a la de Honduras." *elfaro*, August 19, 2015.

Vickers, George, Jack Spence, and David Holiday. *Endgame: A progress report on implementation of the Salvadoran peace accords, December 3, 1992*. Hemisphere Initiatives, 1992.

Yoder, Carolyn. *Little book of trauma healing: When violence strikes and community security is threatened*. Skyhorse Publishing, 2015.

PART VI
Case studies

13
QUALITY PEACE IN CAMBODIA
20 years after the Paris Peace Agreement

Kheang Un

Introduction

The invasion of Cambodia in 1979 by the Vietnamese Army in response to the government of Democratic Kampuchea's aggressive behavior toward Vietnam, and the subsequent decade of Vietnamese occupation of Cambodia through its installed government—the People's Republic of Kampuchea (PRK)—culminated in a Cambodian civil war that lasted until 1991. This period of civil war—which was marked by cycles of offensives by the resistance armies in the rainy seasons followed by counter-offensives by the Vietnamese and PRK forces in the dry seasons—ended in a stalemate. Given the international genesis of the Cambodian conflict, the transformation of global geopolitics orchestrated by the waning Cold War led outside powers to believe that the end of the Cambodian civil war was in their interests. The patrons of the Cambodian warring factions intended an inclusive solution, an intention that paved the way for the 1991 comprehensive political settlement to the conflict, known as the Paris Peace Agreement (PPA). The PPA aimed to achieve lasting peace, liberal democracy, and a free market economy in Cambodia. Over the next decade, a form of low-scale civil war and political conflict continued, but by the late 1990s, Cambodia achieved stable peace and sustained economic growth. Taking the quality of peace to mean the absence of war, economic growth, and deepening democracy, Cambodia's quality of peace across the two decades since the agreement has been mixed, advancing in some areas while receding in others. This chapter reflects on these conditions by examining five factors—post-agreement security, economic reconstruction, the role of civil society, transitional justice, and governance—to assess how they impede or promote Cambodia's quality of peace.

Post-agreement security

In order to achieve lasting peace and to construct a liberal democracy, the PPA's basic premise was to secure a ceasefire and subsequently a neutral political environment for a multiparty electoral contest free from threats of violence and intimidation.[1] To achieve these objectives, the United Nations Transitional Authority in Cambodia (UNTAC) needed to disarm and demobilize the factional armies and oversee Cambodia's critical administrative institutions that had the greatest potential influence over the electoral outcome, namely the ministries of finance, defense, interior, information, and foreign affairs. To maintain a neutral political environment, all parties to the conflict had to cooperate and to see the UN as a neutral broker. The State of Cambodia (SoC)[2] believed that, as the party that controlled most of the territory, they faced unfair treatment by receiving the most attention from the UNTAC forces. They thus designed plans to evade UNTAC's control. As a result of the SoC's limited cooperation, compounded by UNTAC personnel's lack of knowledge about Cambodian politics and society, and the slow deployment of troops and personnel, UNTAC could never really "control" SoC's existing administrative structure nor effectively implement its other mandates, particularly military demobilization (Doyle 1995). This allowed the SoC to use its security personnel and state resources for politically focused violence, intimidation, and propaganda. Convinced that they would win the election, the Cambodian People's Party (CPP) cooperated with UNTAC on elections logistics, including trucking in voters from outlying areas and deploying troops to protect the voting process on the election days (Heder and Ledgerwood 1995).

The Khmer Rouge used UNTAC's inability to control the SoC's existing administrative structure, and false claims of a continued presence of Vietnamese soldiers, as pretexts for its own non-cooperation with UNTAC. It accused UNTAC of favoring the SoC refusing to disarm its own forces or to allow UNTAC to establish presence in its controlled zones. The Khmer Rouge's strategy as intended spoilers was not so much the result of their perception of UNTAC, but rather the result of their estimation of the political loss they would incur by participating in the peace process. Despite its shortcomings, UNTAC achieved some limited influence over the SoC, without which the extent of the SoC's harassment and intimidation of its political opponents would have been greater, likely jeopardizing any prospects for a free and fair election. With only limited cantonment and disarmament as per the PPA, the SoC persisted in political intimidation and violence against opposition parties, particularly *Front uni national pour un Cambodge indépendant, neutre, pacifique et coopératif* (FUNCINPEC), and the Khmer Rouge threatened and attacked UNTAC personnel, SoC targets, and ethnic Vietnamese civilians. These developments blocked prospects for a neutral political environment. Rather than acquiescing to the Khmer Rouge's demands, UNTAC adopted a departing train strategy, leaving the Khmer Rouge in the jungle and shifting its mission from maintaining a neutral political environment to preparing acceptable conditions in which to hold a democratic election. FUNCINPEC, and the smaller Buddhist Liberal Democratic

Party (BLDP), had the most to gain from cooperating with UNTAC. They needed UN protection as their activists returned to the country from border camps and overseas. They did canton and demobilize their troops, and used UN media outlets and UN logistical support for their campaigning (Heder and Ledgerwood 1995).

UNTAC's successful campaign to encourage freedom of expression and to publicize and ensure secrecy of the ballot built a sense of electoral self-determination for the first time in Cambodian history. Voter turnout was approximately 90 percent of registered voters. Contrary to general expectations that the population was economically distressed, politically oppressed, and psychologically traumatized by years of economic hardship, civil war and autocratic rule, and would not cast protest votes against the well-armed ruling CPP, voters did just that. FUNCINPEC won with 45 percent of the vote; the CPP earned 38 percent and the BLDP about 10 percent, with the rest split between smaller parties.

Although the international community endorsed the UN-sponsored elections, the CPP initially refused to accept the election results. The CPP/SoC organized a cessation movement in the Eastern part of Cambodia to put pressure on UNTAC to conduct a re-vote in four provinces. UNTAC stood firm, rejecting allegations of fraud, maintaining that the election was free and fair and reflected the will of the Cambodian people. Facing UNTAC's firm stance, and with the former King Sihanouk's mediation, the parties that won seats in the new Constitutional Assembly settled their deadlock within the framework of the PPA, including the promulgation of a new Constitution and a new National Assembly. UNTAC proclaimed its mission a success and left the long-term goals of political and economic reconstruction in the hands of a new regime which was deeply divided but legitimized by UNTAC's intervention and continued international engagement.

However, the 1991 UN-brokered peace settlement and subsequent UN-sponsored elections failed to bring total peace or political stability to Cambodia for three reasons. First, following its boycott of the 1993 elections, the Khmer Rouge continued to pose a security challenge to the government until 1998, even as the elections and the groundwork laid by the PPA isolated the Khmer Rouge domestically and internationally. This isolation, compounded by the government's co-optation through the provision of amnesty and regional autonomy, eventually led to the Khmer Rouge's final collapse. Second, the CPP refused to play an opposition role, but rather shouldered its way back into state control, using its military strength and administrative domination. The CPP forced FUNCINPEC, the winner of the election, into a subordinate position in a coalition government with co-Prime Ministers. The coalition was an uneasy and compromised arrangement wherein the CPP had de facto control over the government. The situation worsened on account of mistrust among former enemies who lacked shared background or common goals. Third, the Khmer Rouge, which still possessed a sizeable number of soldiers, became a wild card that could tip the balance of power between FUNCINPEC and the CPP.

Facing unequal power relations, FUNCINPEC demanded more power from the CPP and planned to incorporate the Khmer Rouge forces into its camp. While also negotiating with the Khmer Rouge, the CPP responded preemptively to FUNCINPEC's moves through a coup d'état in June 1997 that resulted in the extra-judicial killing of dozens of FUNCINPEC's military and police officers. This forced the opposition parties' leaders into temporary exile. The 1997 coup produced temporary short-term political instability. However, in the long run, the CPP's hegemonic position gained through the coup created a lasting peace, moving Cambodia from a post-conflict society into a society undergoing extensive political and economic transformation, as discussed below.

Economic reconstruction

As part of its fundamental aim of ending the civil war and building long-term peace, the PPA addressed Cambodia's economic reconstruction.[3] The PPA committed the international community to the reconstruction of Cambodia with a special declaration on rehabilitation and reconstruction that aimed not only to address "immediate needs," but also "to lay groundwork for the preparation of medium- and long-term reconstruction plans," (Boutros-Ghali 1995: 109). At the outset of the UN's engagement, 33 countries and multilateral institutions pledged US $880 million for the reconstruction and rehabilitation of Cambodia. Over the past two decades, this international financial engagement has not only continued but also increased with the entry of emerging donors such as China and South Korea. Overseas Development Assistance (ODA) has, since the early 1990s, constituted about 50 percent of the Cambodian government budget. By 2011, the overall ODA disbursement reached over US $12 billion. ODA has funded infrastructure projects such as roads, electricity, bridges, and public services such as healthcare and education (Council for Development 2011). The construction of regional road networks and feeder roads linked to these networks has led to increased economic activities and new growth in many regions of Cambodia. Freedom to travel on improved infrastructure and with physical security are critical outcomes of the peace process for Cambodians. For instance, 82 percent of Cambodia's eligible voters in 2008, 79 percent in 2009, and 79 percent in 2010 believed that Cambodia was headed in the right direction. The overwhelming majority of these positive respondents (73 percent in 2008, 76 percent in 2009, and 78 percent in 2010) cited infrastructure improvement as the source of their confidence in the government (IRI 2009, 2010a, 2011).

By the early 2000s, Cambodia had moved beyond a post-conflict situation into an era of transformation evidenced by major political and economic indicators. Politically, Prime Minister Hun Sen has maintained firm control over his party and security forces, ending any rumor of factionalism within the ruling CPP. In the meantime, opposition parties' ability to mount any challenge to Prime Minister Hun Sen's rule, through either elections or mass protest, has diminished. These developments have brought about political stability. Cambodia has experienced political stability under the control of Prime Minister Hun Sen and the CPP. This stability has had positive spillover effects on the economy in a number of critical ways. In the 1990s, Cambodian elites behaved like roving bandits engaging in decentralized, unplanned, unregulated, and uncoordinated exploitation of natural resources (particularly timber) geared toward short-term gains. Yet in the early 2000s, elites adopted the mentality of stationary bandits, believing that they have a stake within the society and thus are more likely to engage in coordinating long-term investment plans and natural resource extraction linked to regional and global economies (Hughes and Un 2011).

Furthermore, political and macro-economic stability has made Cambodia attractive to foreign investment in sectors beyond natural resource extraction, including construction, manufacturing and agro-business investment. Fixed asset approval increased from US $282 million in 1994 to US $4.6 billion in 2011. The total capital invested from 2011 to 2015 was US $2.3 billion (Council for Development 2016). With these favorable economic conditions, Cambodia's economy has grown at a substantial rate since 1993, particularly between 1999 and 2008, during which the average annual economic growth was 9.4 percent (IRI 2010b). Whether such investment will be sustainable with inclusive benefits is another matter. Of course, the current patterns of natural resource extraction have generated insecurity for people. IRI's 2010 survey shows that 5 percent of the population have lost their land to land grabs. Income inequality has widened; the Gini-coefficient increased from 0.35 in 1994 to 0.40 in 2004 and appears to continue to rise. The global economic crisis hit the country, plunging the economic growth rate to 0.1 percent in 2009 but it bounced back to 6 percent in 2010 and continued to grow at a healthy rate of just over 7.3 percent between 2011 and 2014 (World Bank, Cambodia n.d.; World Development Indicators n.d.). The fruit of the peace dividend has been high. GDP per capita grew over 3.6 times between 1995 and 2015, rising from 280 to 1,020 (World Development Indicators). Rising income levels have translated into a significant decline in rates of poverty. The poverty headcount ratio at the national poverty line dropped from 47 percent in 1994 to 17.7 percent in 2012.[4] Other human development indices have also shown signs of improvement. For example, the infant mortality rate has fallen 57.5 percent between 1991 (the year of the signing of the PPA) and 2010—from 120.8 deaths in 1991 to 51 deaths in 2010 per 1000 births. Infant mortality rate further declined to 1 in 29 in 2014 (Cambodia Demographic Health Survey 2014). Life expectancy also saw signs of significant improvement climbing from 53 in 2002 to 68 in 2013 (World Bank 2006). In the meantime, the number of people who have access to "improved drinking water" increased from 34 percent in 1995 to 42 percent in 2000, and to 55 percent in 2008 (JMP for Water Supply and Sanitation n.d.), and further to 75 percent in 2016 (East & Southeast Asia: Cambodia 2016).

Retributive justice and national reconciliation

Driven by ultra-nationalist and utopian ideals, the Democratic Kampuchea regime (1975–1979), better known as the Khmer Rouge, undertook massive socio-economic engineering, depopulated urban centers, and enslaved the entire population, forcing them to engage in intense agricultural activities with heavy workloads and little food. Facing economic failure and paranoid of enemy infiltration, the Khmer Rouge searched for enemies, a drive that ran through the entire polity and finally cut deeply into the regime's governing structure. The insistence upon complete control, intertwined with an increasing sense of insecurity, lead to the deaths of over 2 million people from starvation, overwork, disease, and outright execution (Chandler 1991).

Because of the internationalized nature of the Cambodian conflict during the Cold War, the issue of justice and human rights was highly politicized. Therefore, since the defeat of the Khmer Rouge in 1979 and until 1997—with the exception of the 1979 People's Revolutionary Tribunal that condemned and sentenced top Khmer Rouge leaders in absentia—there was no concerted effort by the international community to bring former Khmer Rouge leaders to justice.[5]

To reach an inclusive political settlement, the framers of the PPA did not address the issue of grave human rights abuses committed by the Khmer Rouge regime. Nor did the agreement stipulate any mechanisms that would hold former Khmer Rouge leaders to account for their crimes. Instead, they inserted a clause that stressed that Cambodia must "take effective measures to ensure that the policies and practices of the past shall never be allowed to return" (Boutros-Ghali 1995: 108)

Many analysts and human rights activists share the belief that "[T]here will be no lasting peace and stable democracy in war-torn societies without truth, justice, and reconciliation" (Lambourne 2004: 20). These principles led the UN, after years of protracted and mistrustful negotiations with the Cambodian government, to create a hybrid body consisting of international and Cambodian judges and prosecutors wherein decisions had to be agreed by a supermajority. Theoretically the tribunal, if properly managed and free of political interference, will help to promote lasting peace via its potential impact on critical elements of the justice system. First, the tribunal, which contains a combination of international and national lawyers, allows the personnel of the Cambodian legal system to interact with Western legal codes and norms. Such interaction, Hirschl argues, helps lead to "judicialization"—the increasing role of the judiciary in shaping politics and government policy (2008).

Second, given global geopolitics and domestic upheaval, the truth of the Khmer Rouge crimes had never been revealed, preventing any possibility for closure and thus reconciliation. Third, it is hoped that Cambodian judges, prosecutors, and clerks will bring good practices including due process, impartiality, and legal reasoning to the Cambodian judiciary, which is characterized by injustice for the poor and the powerless and a widespread culture of impunity, upon the completion of their missions at the hybrid tribunal. Fostering judicial independence will strengthen democracy as a bedrock for social economic and political equity—ingredients for quality peace.

The hope is that the Extraordinary Chamber in the Court of Cambodia (ECCC) might have a positive spillover effect on Cambodia's justice system, as reconciliation is limited given Cambodia's cultural, political, and historical contexts.[6] The desire to maintain power and the belief in contextual particularity that rejects the belief in the universality of human rights and Western legal concepts is reflected in over two decades of struggle between the Cambodian government and the international community over the issue of judicial reform. For these reasons, as well as embedding of the Cambodian courts in the existing political system wherein rule of law is subject to patronage politics, the impact of the tribunal on the overall Cambodian judiciary will be minimal and is unlikely to bring any substantial change in the way the local courts operate (Un and Ledgerwood 2010). Contrary to the hope of ending impunity, the trends in legal development in Cambodia could well be the presence of rule by law rather than rule of law, meaning "for my friends, everything; for my enemies, the law" (O'Donnell 2004: 40). Even while the tribunal is underway, the Cambodian government has the confidence and power to use the legal system to prosecute government critics and opponents.

Furthermore, it is often argued that a fair tribunal would bring about national reconciliation. Such a trial, arguably, might not be relevant to national reconciliation given Cambodia's cultural and historical contexts. Culturally, due to an absence of satisfactory answers from either political or historical narratives, many Khmer Rouge survivors turned to religion as a means of reconciling with their past. As Buddhists, many of these survivors believe that the fate of the perpetrators will be determined by *Karmic* justice and thus no modern legal retributive justice is adequate or necessary. This belief in *Karmic* justice also helps to explain how so many Cambodians have lived peacefully for decades in local communities with low-level perpetrators.

Historically, many Cambodians favored incorporation of the former Khmer Rouge guerrilla movement into the government if that meant ending armed conflict. FUNCINPEC in the 1993 election campaign promised to end the bloody conflict through an inclusive political settlement, offering Khmer Rouge leaders a role in the future government despite their boycott of the UN-sponsored elections. In an effort to undermine FUNCINPEC, the CPP equated FUNCINPEC and BLDP with the Khmer Rouge. The 1993 CPP election campaign slogan states:

> Which party gives life to the people?
> The CPP
> Which party kills the people?
> The Khmer Rouge and Pol Pot.
> Which parties cooperate with Pol Pot? FUNCINPEC and Son Sann.
> (Frieson 1995)

Despite the CPP's efforts, the majority of Cambodian voters voted for FUNCINPEC based on its promise of national reconciliation.

Ultimately, peace was achieved in Cambodia, in part, through amnesty for Khmer Rouge perpetrators. As hideous as the Khmer Rouge crimes were, the PPA and the UN Mission did not bring peace to Cambodia, which continued to face ongoing civil war, economic deprivation, and political instability. Both political parties negotiated with the remnants of the Khmer Rouge in the 1990s. It was the ruling

CPP, through its amnesty program, that dismantled the Khmer Rouge as a guerrilla movement and brought total peace to Cambodia for the first time since 1970s. Cambodians themselves are divided on the need for a Khmer Rouge tribunal. No public protest arose inside Cambodia to oppose such amnesty. While some believe that the tribunal is necessary to learn the truth or to punish senior Khmer Rouge leaders, many share Prime Minister Hun Sen's assertion that, "if the wound does not hurt, don't poke it." Such a statement suggests that retributive justice is not a remedy for national reconciliation because it creates new social and political rifts. While it is unlikely that a tribunal would result in renewed conflict, many Cambodians feel the tribunal does not fit Khmer culture, which stresses resolution through non-confrontational negotiations. They would argue that Cambodia has already reconciled with former members of the Khmer Rouge military and their families who have integrated into mainstream society over the last 30 years.

In the end, the Tribunal became operational in 2009. The Cambodian government has allegedly interfered in the affairs of the Tribunal by limiting prosecution to only five senior Khmer Rouge leaders—Ieng Sary, Kieu Samphan, Noun Chea, Kaing Guek Eav (alias Duch), and Ieng Theary. While Ieng Sary died during his trial, Ieng Thearith was pronounced mentally unfit to stand trial by the court. Duch was found guilty on charges of crimes against humanity, enslavement, torture, sexual abuse, and war crimes and was sentenced to life imprisonment. Noun Chea and Khiev Samphan were found guilty on charges of crimes against humanity and were sentenced to life imprisonment. At the time of this writing, the two are on trial on charges of committing genocide. After several years of legal and political disagreement between the ECCC's Cambodian judges and prosecutors and their international counterparts, and between the ECCC and the Cambodian government, the Tribunal finally agreed to expand the universe of defendants to include three mid-level Khmer Rouge leaders—Meas Muth, Yim Tith, and Oa An—charging them with crimes against humanity and genocide (ECCCs). As far as the Tribunal is concerned, many observers have argued that it did not bring complete justice to victims of the Khmer Rouge regime. As this author argues elsewhere, the Tribunal is a "politically compromised search for justice" and therefore will not be just (Un 2013).

Civil society organizations

The PPA called for the involvement of NGOs in economic and political reconstruction. The agreement also required that UNTAC "be responsible during the transitional period for fostering an environment in which respect for human rights should be ensured ..." (Boutros-Ghali 1995: 99).[7] With financial assistance and political support from the international community, the number of CSOs grew dramatically, from essentially zero before the implementation of the PPA to over 3,000 by 2010. Cambodian NGOs generally fall into three groups: service delivery NGOs, advocacy organizations, and community-based organizations (CBOs). Their contribution to quality of peace has been positive though limited in important ways.

Economic growth accompanied by improved quality of life has accorded the current regime legitimacy, a foundation for political stability and lasting peace. Service delivery NGOs have contributed significantly to this growth, for which the government has taken credit. Given low government capacity, weak public financial management, and some donors' preference to work with Cambodia's CSOs, a large percentage of ODA have been allocated to specific projects implemented by NGOs (Chanboreth and Hach 2008). Because of its non-political nature, the government has not only granted service delivery NGOs freedom of operation, but also formed partnerships with these NGOs in the provision of healthcare, education, and other services. These activities have improved the lives of many Cambodians.

Other NGOs have worked to promote normative values of peace—democracy, human rights, and a culture of peace and gender equity. These NGOs have adopted and adapted global concepts and localized them through education and training campaigns that have had widespread impact in raising people's awareness of the concepts. These educational campaigns have instilled these new concepts, making them part of the normal political discourse. These NGOs, individually and as a network, have maintained extensive monitoring programs that identify and help victims of human rights violations and advocate for gender equality, institutional reform, and legal reform.

It should be noted that NGOs have faced limitations on their advocacy and monitoring activities due to internal and external constraints. Externally, NGOs dealt with politically sensitive issues such as judicial reform and civil and political liberties. This advocacy effort generally fell on deaf ears because of the deep-seated interests of those involved. Second, with access to the government blocked, these NGOs turned to donors for assistance in lobbying the government for institutional reform. Thus far, lobbying and advocating through donors have not yielded significant results due to donors' lack of consistency, unity, and forcefulness in pressuring the government for change (Un 2006). Another factor that hinders the work of NGOs is the government's views toward human rights and democracy NGOs. Although the post-agreement's constitution formally adopted the universal concept of human rights, the Cambodian government has not accepted liberal ideas emphasizing the significance of human rights, the rule of law, transparency, accountability, and liberal democracy. Viewing these ideas as unsuitable to Cambodia, the government has accused NGOs of being agents of foreign neo-liberals attempting to bring alien Western ideas to Cambodia. Consequently, the government often imposed restrictions on and sometimes-intimidated NGOs that attempted to establish links with local people.

Furthermore, NGOs face three internal constraints. First, NGOs did not emerge out of, to use Salamon's terms, "spontaneous grass-roots energies;" rather they were the product of international intervention and continued support (Salamon 1994). Under these circumstances, prominent NGOs, particularly democracy and human rights NGOs, are urban-based with little or no grassroots membership. As such, the voluntary aspect of traditional non-profit organizations remains nascent two decades following their births (Mansfield and MacLeod 2002). These NGOs also have relied on international financial assistance. The government underscores NGOs' lack of membership and financial dependence to delegitimize the organizations. However, over the past several years, urban-based NGOs have created links with some CBOs working to highlight issues critical to local communities such as access to forest resources and land grabbing, thereby forcing land concessionaires and the government to address their grievances. In some resource-rich areas, there have emerged new patterns of local community user groups that symbolize a genuine bottom-up social movement (Henker 2011; Sedara and Ojendal 2011). Although actions by CBOs, NGOs have won cases on behalf of the poor, they have not been successful in defending local interests when faced with powerful actors who are part of the ruling party's neopatrimonial system (Un and So 2011). Furthermore, the 2015 passage of a restrictive NGO Law, and the arrest of land rights activists show the state's efforts to limit civil society mobilization.

Governance and approaches to negotiations

The PPA objective, as discussed above, was to build lasting peace in Cambodia via the establishment of a democratic system based on the principles of rule of law and inter-institutional accountability. However, given the deep-rooted existence of patron-client networks, a state characterized by independent institutions has not yet taken root. Political compromise in the form of coalition governments, with concomitant mistrust within and across parties in the post-UNTAC period, and subsequent personalization of state institutions by Hun Sen and the CPP have further consolidated patron-client networks which are thoroughly embedded within and across state institutions.

Patronage politics and mistrust rendered the government inefficient and ineffective as political leaders had to accommodate their clients' requests, tolerate their behaviour, and protect their interests. Political infighting leading up to 1998 produced low levels of political stability and high rates of violence captured at −1.37 in 1996 and −1.15 in 1998 on the World Bank scale which ranges from −2.5 (highest political instability) to +2.5 (highest political instability) (Kaufman et al. 2008). During this period, individual security and social order were low as signified by the presence of large numbers of firearms and high rates of homicide (UN Office on Drug and Crime 2004). Between 1993 and 1998, the physical integrity of Cambodians was poor due to occurrences of extra-judicial killings, torture, and politically related killings. Political killings peaked in 1997, when alleged government security personnel attacked a peaceful demonstration led by opposition leader, Sam Rainsy; killing 16 people and wounding 100 more, followed by the political violence surrounding the 1997 coup orchestrated by Hun Sen to topple Prince Norodom Ranariddh, which killed more than 40 top FUNCINPEC military and political officers (Amnesty International 1997).

However, the quality of governance has improved after the consolidation of power by Prime Minister Hun Sen/CPP following the defeat of FUNCINPEC

Since then, Cambodia appears to be moving in the direction of centralized patrimonial-centric development that stresses economic development but not human rights and democracy. Cambodia under centralized neo-patrimonialism saw increased investment in rural areas in terms of infrastructure, agriculture, and education by both the government through the official budget and by leaders of the dominant CPP through political patronage funds. Using these slush funds, the CPP and its de facto leader—Hun Sen—invested an unknown (but generally believed to be substantial) amount of money in rural areas. Within centralized neo-patrimonialism, the state under Hun Sen/CPP is ensuring that government officials would not withhold all the proceeds from rent-seeking activities for themselves. A certain amount of the resources extracted are channeled back into local communities through these patronage networks.

In terms of the state administrative structure, the PPA addressed the issue of building democratic governance at the national level. Up until early 2002, the pre-settlement sub-national governance structure continued as before. This was a highly centralized system dominated by the CPP, devoid of local participation in decision-making processes, that prevented opposition parties from establishing a foothold in local politics. Consequently, throughout the 1990s and early 2000s, commune chiefs appointed during the People's Republic of Kampuchea in the 1980s continued to dominate local authorities, providing the CPP with a formidable base for nationwide accumulation and extension of power (Un and Ledgerwood 2003).

With its grip on power secure by the turn of the century and given pressure from the donor community, the CPP agreed to implement a devolution process that involved decentralization and de-concentration. Decentralization refers to "the delegation of political and administrative authority, from the central to the commune/*sangkat* level," while de-concentration entails "the delegation of administrative responsibilities, decision making and authority from central ministries to sub-national provincial departments and/or district offices," (World Bank 2004). The devolution process embarks on a dual goal to improve local democratic participation and to enhance participation in local economic planning and development.[8]

With a long monopoly over local government, well-organized networks, abundant financial and human resources, and political control, the CPP has been able to capture an overwhelming number of the local top offices. Despite the CPP's domination, these local elections open new possibilities for local politics, governance, and development. Decentralization has generated some positive outcomes in the further democratization of local politics. First, the local elections terminated the CPP's sole control over local politics and opened a new vista of competition for opposition parties that now could establish a presence in the hinterland. In areas where there are conflicts over resources, the opposition parties have made an imprint in local politics. Second, decentralization has produced "new attitudes and practices" at the local level (Ninh and Henke 2005: 33), mainly an increase in inter-party collaboration leading to a reduction in politically motivated violence (Rusten et al. 2004: 107). Decentralization has also increased collaboration between local government and NGOs resulting in improved service delivery and thereby generating further demands by people from their elected councilors, deviating from the previous era when people "never expected much from the commune," (Rusten et al. 2004: 170).

Conclusion

The international intervention via the PPA ended Cambodia's internationalized conflict restoring peace to the country. However, the quality of peace is mixed. The five factors explored in this chapter—post-agreement security, economic reconstruction, the role of civil society, transitional justice, and governance—did not work in parallel to enhance the quality of peace. While separately they work to enhance certain aspects of quality peace, they also hinder other factors that could potentially contribute to higher quality peace. Post-agreement security developments resulted in the presence of a dominant party system under the control of the CPP. Such domination has brought about political stability and stable macro-economic conditions that made possible sustained economic growth, accompanied by improved physical well-being. Such political domination and economic growth existed under the conditions of widespread corruption and patronage that prevented meaningful top-down, systemic governance reform. The absence of such reform prevented the positive development of other governance factors such as CSOs and judicial systems, limiting higher quality peace. However, the absence of success in top-down reform has been offset by developments at the local level that are characterized by the presence, however limited, of pluralistic socio-economic participation and accountability. The process might lead—if current trends persist—to bottom-up reform, and thus, enhanced quality peace.

However, political stability that exists under autocratic political conditions frustrates a higher quality peace in terms of development of normative quality peace such as human rights and democracy. On the one hand, since the implementation of the PPA, new discourses—on gender, human rights, democracy, rule of law—have evolved through education campaigns by NGOs assisted by their international linkages. On the other hand, the dominant party system limits NGOs' critical activities in advocacy efforts to promote human rights, democracy, and rule of law. Finally, the potential of transitional justice to promote a higher quality of peace has thus far proven limited due to Cambodia's historical, cultural, and political context. Cambodia established peace and reconciliation without any attempt at bringing former Khmer Rouge leaders to justice or seeking the truth behind the mass killing. The majority of Cambodians appear to be indifferent to this development. Retributive justice through mixed tribunals, with the objective of promoting rule of law and national reconciliation, appear to have little impact on Cambodia's lasting peace. The ruling party, whose objective is to strengthen rule by law rather than rule of law, has allowed the tribunal to function as an island of justice under the principle of victor's justice.

Notes

1. This issue is addressed by Terrence Lyons in Chapter 2 of this volume.
2. SoC, the successor to the People's Republic of Kampuchea, which ruled Cambodia with Vietnamese support from 1979–1992.
3. For more on economics after post-war, see chapter 5 by Guardado et al. in this volume.
4. For a discussion of the poverty rate in 1994, please see World Bank 2006.
5. The 1979 People's Revolutionary Tribunal was perceived as a political trial focusing on global geopolitics and lacking independent legal foundations.
6. For detailed discussion on this issue see Un 2013.
7. For more on civil society, please see the contribution to this volume by Richard Jones, Chapter 12.
8. Despite the following positive developments, there is reservation over the effectiveness of decentralization due principally to inadequate devolution of power and financial resources and secondarily to the lack of capacity among local councilors. First, decentralization's objective of alleviating poverty through local participatory development remains largely unrealized due to a lack of resources and the absence of autonomy. Currently, commune councils are mainly funded by (1) Commune/*Sangkat* Fund; (2) local contributions; and (3) income through service delivery such as civil registration and the issuance of marriage, birth, and death certificates. Communes/*Sangkat* have not been given the legal power to raise local revenues or to manage local resources such as forests and land.

References

Amnesty International. *Kingdom of Cambodia: Arrest and Executive of Political Opponents*. ASA 23/29/97. London, UK: Amnesty International, July 18, 1997.

Boutros-Ghali, Boutros. *The United Nations and Cambodia, 1991–1995*. United Nations Blue Books Series. United Nations Press, 1995.

Cambodia Demographic Health Survey 2014 (CDHS), The. The DHS Program, 2014.

Chanboreth, Ek, and Sok Hach. *Aid effectiveness in Cambodia*. Brookings Institution's Wolfensohn Center for Development, 2008.

Chandler, David P. *The tragedy of Cambodian history: Politics, war, and revolution since 1945*. Yale University Press, 1991.

Council for the Development of Cambodia, CDC. "Investment trend." 2016. Accessed February 28, 2016 at www.cambodiainvestment.gov.kh/investment-enviroment/investment-trend.html.

Council for Development of Cambodia Council Report. Royal Government of Cambodia, 2011.

Doyle, Michael W. *UN peacekeeping in Cambodia: UNTAC's civil mandate*. Lynne Rienner, 1995.

"East & Southeast Asia: Cambodia." *The world fact book*. Accessed February 28, 2016 at www.cia.gov/library/publications/the-world-factbook/geos/cb.html.

"Extraordinary Chambers in the Courts of Cambodia." Accessed October 1, 2017 at www.eccc.gov.kh/en.

Frieson, Kate. "The Politics of Getting the Votes in Cambodia." In Steve Heder and Judy Ledgerwood, Eds. *Propaganda, politics, and violence in Cambodia: Democratic transition under United Nations Peace-Keeping*. M.E. Sharpe, 1995.

Heder, Stephen R., and Judy Ledgerwood, Eds. *Propaganda, politics and violence in Cambodia: Democratic transition under United Nations Peace-keeping*. M.E. Sharpe, 1996.

Henker, Roger. "Accountability and Local Politics in Natural Resource Management." In Caroline Hughes and Kheang Un, Eds. *Cambodia's economic transformation*. Nordic Institute for Asian Studies, (2011): 288–309.

Hirschl, Ran. "The judicialization of mega-politics and the rise of political courts." *Annual Review of Political Science*. 11 (2008): 93–118.
Hughes, Caroline, and Kheang Un. "Cambodia's Economic Transformation: Historical and Theoretical Frameworks." In Caroline Hughes and Kheang Un, Eds. *Cambodia's economic transformation*. Nordic Institute for Asian Studies, (2011): 1–26.
International Republican Institute, The (IRI). "Survey of Cambodian opinion, October 22–November 25, 2008." Washington, DC: IRI, 2009. Accessed September 30, 2017 at www.iri.org/news-and-resource?type=1&country=670.
International Republican Institute, The (IRI). "Survey of Cambodian opinion, July 31–August 26, 2009." Washington, DC: IRI, 2010a. Accessed Accessed September 30, 2017 www.iri.org/resource/iri-releases-latest-survey-cambodian-public-opinion-0.
International Republican Institute (IRI), The. "Survey of Cambodian voters." Phnom Penh: IRI, 2010b. Accessed June 3, 2016 at www.iri.org/sites/default/files/2011%20January%2020%20Survey%20of%20Cambodian%20Public%20Opinion,%20July%2012-August%206,%202010%20-%20Khmer%20and%20English%20version.pdf (accessed June 3, 2016).
International Republican Institute (IRI), The. "Survey of Cambodian opinion, July 12–August 6, 2010." Washington, DC: IRI, 2011. Accessed September 30, 2017 www.iri.org/resource/iri-releases-latest-survey-cambodian-public-opinion.
Joint Monitoring Programme (JMP) for Water Supply and Sanitation. "Improve water source, rural (% of rural population with access)." World Bank, n.d. Accessed October 1, 2017 at http://data.worldbank.org/indicator/SH.H2O.SAFE.RU.ZS/countries/KH?display=graph.
Kaufmann, Daniel, Aart Kraay, and Massimo Mastruzzi. "Governance matters VII: Aggregate and individual governance indicators." *The World Bank, Policy Research Working Paper*, 2008.
Lambourne, Wendy. "Post-conflict peacebuilding: Meeting human needs for justice and reconciliation." *Peace, Conflict and Development* 4, April 2004.
Mansfield, Cristina, and Kurt MacLeod. "Advocacy in Cambodia: Increasing democratic space." *Pact Cambodia*, 2002.
Ninh, Kim, and Roger Henke. *Commune councils in Cambodia: A national survey on their functions and performance, with a special focus on conflict resolution*. The Asia Foundation, May 2005.
O'Donnell, Guillermo A. "Why the rule of law matters." *Journal of Democracy* 15, no. 4 (2004): 32–46.
Rusten, Caroline, Kim Sedara, Eng Netra, and Pak Kimchoeun. *The challenges of decentralisation design in Cambodia*. Phnom Penh: Cambodia Development Resource Institute, October 2004.
Salamon, Lester M. "The rise of the nonprofit sector." *Foreign Affairs* 73, (1994): 109–122.
Sedara, Kim, and Joakim Ojendal. "Accountability and Local Politics in Natural Resource Management." In Caroline Hughes and Kheang Un, Eds. *Cambodia's economic transformation*. Copenhagen: Nordic Institute for Asian Studies, (2011): 266–287.
Un, Kheang. "State, society and democratic consolidation: The case of Cambodia." *Pacific Affairs* 79, no. 2 (2006): 225–245.
Un, Kheang. "The Khmer rouge tribunal: A politically compromised search for justice." *The Journal of Asian Studies* 72, no. 4 (2013): 783–792.
Un, Kheang, and Judy Ledgerwood. "Cambodia in 2002: Decentralization and its effects on party politics." *Asian Survey* 43, no. 1 (2003): 113–119.
Un, Kheang, and Judy Ledgerwood. "Is the trial of 'Duch' a catalyst for change in Cambodia's courts?" *Asia Pacific* 95, (2010): 1–12.
Un, Kheang, and Sokbunthoeun So. "Land rights in Cambodia: How neopatrimonial politics restricts land policy reform." *Pacific Affairs* 84, no. 2 (2011): 289.

United Nations Office on Drug and Crime. "Intentional homicide, rate 100,000 population, 2004." *International Homicide Statistics (IHS)*, 2004.

World Bank. "Cambodia." The World Bank, n.d. Accessed January 10, 2012 at http://data.worldbank.org/country/cambodia.

World Bank. "Decentralization: Enhancing accountable service delivery for the poor," World Bank, *Cambodia at the crossroads: Strengthening accountability to reduce poverty*. Report No. 30636-KH, East Asia and the Pacific Region. Washington, DC: World Bank, (November 15, 2004): 50–67.

World Bank. *Cambodia – halving poverty by 2015 – poverty assessment 2006*. Washington, DC: World Bank, February 7, 2006. Accessed September 30, 2017 http://documents.worldbank.org/curated/en/2006/02/16489688/cambodia-halving-poverty-2015-poverty-assessment-2006.

World Development Indicators. "Data: GDP per capita (current US$)." The World Bank, n.d. Accessed January 10, 2012 at http://data.worldbank.org/indicator/NY.GDP.PCAP.CD/countries/KH?display=graph.

14

EL SALVADOR 20 YEARS LATER

Successful democratization but questionable peace

Dinorah Azpuru

Introduction

El Salvador is often seen as a successful case of peacebuilding and democratization. To be sure, the peace accords signed in January 1992 ended a bloody armed conflict which lasted 12 years and left a toll of over 75,000 casualties; they also brought about profound changes to the existing political system that resulted in the deepening of democratization, to the extent that the two warring factions became the strongest political parties in the country. However, 20 years later, violence and crime were rampant and many citizens were more worried than during the civil war about being murdered in the streets. The situation in El Salvador two decades after the signing of the peace accords can hardly be considered peaceful.

This chapter evaluates the quality of peace in El Salvador after the first 20 years of post-war experience, 1992–2012. It does so by examining five variables: governance and negotiations; post-accord security; economic reconstruction and development; civil society and reconciliation; and transitional justice. The choice of variables was made following the guidelines provided by the editors of this book. Although the Salvadoran peace accords were basically political in nature, all these variables are crucial for societies emerging from violent conflict. The assessment of the first three variables is made using a variety of quantitative indicators; when feasible the assessment focuses on cross-time changes in the past 20 years in El Salvador. The assessment of the last two variables is more qualitative, given the lack of data to assess longitudinal change.

Background of the conflict and the peace accords

The civil war in El Salvador lasted for 12 years (1980–1992). It was a Cold War ideologically based armed conflict between a guerrilla movement, united in the Frente Farabundo Martí para la Liberación Nacional (FMLN), and the Salvadoran government, particularly the armed forces. The FMLN contested the authoritarian military regime that prevailed in El Salvador for most of its independent history as well as the subsequent limited democracy that was established in that country beginning in 1984. During the initial years of the civil war, the primary goal of the FMLN was to overtake control of the government through a popular Marxist-inspired revolution similar to the one that had taken place in Nicaragua in 1979. In turn, the original goal of the Salvadoran government was to achieve a military victory. Serious negotiations began in 1990, only after the government realized that the conflict had reached a stalemate and international conditions changed, in particular the foreseeable end of the Cold War.

The origin of the Salvadoran civil war was primarily political: a closed political system that did not allow any space for leftist parties, progressive CSOs, or redistributive social policies, particularly if they threatened to change the status quo and the privileges of the economic elite. Nonetheless, as in the case of other armed conflicts in Central America, social and economic inequality have often been mentioned as root causes of the conflict (Arnson and Azpuru 2003). In view of the nature of the conflict, the agenda of the negotiations and subsequently the peace agreements themselves were predominantly political.

Governance and negotiations

This variable is particularly relevant in the case of El Salvador since this was the main focus of the negotiations and the subsequent peace accords. In order to fully understand the state of governance by 2012, it is important to remember that even though El Salvador underwent sweeping political changes as a result of the peace agreements in 1992, in reality the country had more long-term structural stability than many post-conflict societies. In 1838, El Salvador became an independent republic, with a unitary government, and adopted a presidential political system, all of which have remained ever since.[1]

Although those structural features of the Salvadoran political system remained stable since independence, there was no constitutional stability: the country had 15 different constitutions from independence until 1983, when a new constitution was drafted at the outset of the political transition to democracy. Even though the 1983 constitution underwent major reforms in 1991 as a pre-requisite to the signature of the final peace accord,[2] it is considered that one of the major political achievements has been the maintenance of the same constitutional framework for three decades.[3]

With regards to the type of political regime, El Salvador did not become a democracy after independence and authoritarian regimes were the rule rather than the exception throughout its history (Booth et al. 2009). There is no consensus on when the authoritarian regime in El Salvador changed to a democratic regime. Some scholars contend that the transition to democracy began with the drafting of the 1983 constitution and the subsequent 1984 election, when the first civilian president in 50 years was elected. Many argue that the influence of the military over the civilian government and the gross violations of human rights disqualify the pre-accords regime as a democracy,[4] contending that democracy really began in El Salvador after the signing of the peace accords, and more specifically with the 1994 elections when the left (represented by the FMLN) was finally able to participate. This discussion goes beyond the purpose of this chapter. What is undisputable is that democratization became *the* central issue in the negotiations and in the subsequent agreements that were signed.[5] For that very reason, it is essential to assess the fate of democracy in the post-conflict period. In order to do this, it is useful to examine indicators that reflect the level of democracy in El Salvador.

The indicator of democracy most commonly used among academics is the Freedom House Index, which is a composite measure of civil liberties and political rights used as a proxy for democracy. Another indicator commonly used by scholars is the Polity IV Index, which assesses institutional democracy by measuring how executive recruitment is conducted, what constraints on executive authority exist, and whether there is political competition. Table 14.1 shows the longitudinal results of both indicators, comparing the pre-accords situation (1990) with the situation in 2012, 20 years after the signature of the peace accords.

With regards to Freedom House, it is notable that El Salvador moved from the partly free category to the free category in 1997. The Polity IV score also improved. Figure 14.1 clearly shows the improvement in institutional democracy that has occurred in El Salvador since 1946. It is particularly relevant to look at the contrast between 1980 (when the civil war begun) and 2010. As noted earlier, the final peace accord signed in January 1992 was preceded by a process of political liberalization that began in 1983 with the drafting of a new constitution and other subsequent institutional reforms.

It is important to go beyond the indicators that provide an overall perspective of the level of democracy. It is often the case in post-conflict societies that there are certain groups that remain excluded from the decision-making process, even if those societies have a democratic regime; therefore, assessing the degree of political inclusiveness is highly relevant. El Salvador is a fairly homogenous society,[6] and

TABLE 14.1 Indicators of regime type in El Salvador, 1990 vs. 2012

Indicator	*1990*	*2012*
Freedom House★	3.5 (partly free)	2.5 (free)
Polity IV★★	6.0	8.0

★ Freedom House has a range of 1–7 points, in which 1 represents most free and 7 represents less free. There are three categories: free, partly free and not free. El Salvador falls in the free category in 2012.

★★ Polity IV has a range of −10 to +10 points, in which −10 represents extreme autocracy and +10 maximum democracy.

Source: Prepared by author with data from Freedom House and Polity IV.[1]

1. Freedom House: www.freedomhouse.org. Polity IV: www.systemicpeace.org/polity/polity4.htm.

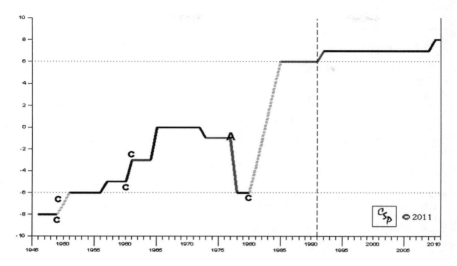

FIGURE 14.1 Authority trends in El Salvador: 1946–2010

Source: Polity IV website www.systemicpeace.org/polity/polity4.htm Reproduced with permission.

the war did not break out because of ethnic or religious reasons. The exclusion that led to the civil war was ideological: the right governed the country since independence, and for most of the country's history, the left was persecuted, particularly in the context of the Cold War. For that reason, the peace accords aimed at ending that exclusion by opening the political system via the political participation of the FMLN.

The FMLN participated as a political party for the first time in the 1994 elections, the first electoral process held after the signature of the final peace accord; at that time, the former guerrilla turned political party obtained 24.9 percent of the vote in the first round of the presidential election and 31.6 percent in the runoff election.[7] In the legislative election that year the FMLN obtained 21 out of 84 seats in the Legislative Assembly. From then on, it became the second strongest and largest party in the country, only surpassed by the conservative free market-oriented party, the Alianza Nacional Republicana (ARENA). Table 14.2 shows the results obtained by the FMLN in the presidential and the legislative elections between 1994 and 2012.

As can be observed, the number of seats obtained by the FMLN in the legislature increased steadily until the setback suffered in 2012. The most important accomplishment was that in 2009 the former guerilla party won the presidential election. Another major achievement (not shown in Table 14.2) was that FMLN won the mayoral race in the capital city, San Salvador, several years in a row since 1997, only losing narrowly in 2009.[8] There is widespread consensus that the incorporation of the former armed opposition to the political process in El Salvador has been largely successful.[9]

TABLE 14.2 Electoral results for the FMLN, 1994–2012

Presidential (percentage)				Legislative (seats)						
1994	1999	2004	2009★	1994	1997	2000	2003	2006	2009	2012
24.99	51.96	57.71	51.32	21	27	31	31	32	35★★	31★★★

★ For the first time won the presidential elections.

★★ For the first time obtained the larger number of seats, albeit not a majority. The Salvadoran Legislative Assembly has had 84 seats since 1994.

★★★ In the March 11, 2012 legislative elections the FMLN lost four seats.

Source: Prepared by author with data from the Political Database of the Americas,[1] Córdova, et. al.[2] and Tribunal Supremo Electoral de El Salvador.[3]

1. Georgetown University http:pdba.georgetown.edu.
2. See Azpuru.
3. Tribunal Supremo Electoral de El Salvador.

Another way to assess political inclusion is to examine the levels of citizens' political participation.[10] Turnout in the elections is a key measure. Table 14.3 shows the turnout in the Salvadoran presidential elections since 1984.[11] We can see that the levels of turnout were low for several years, particularly in the aftermath of the signing of the peace accords, but electoral participation increased in the 2004 and 2009 elections.

Another issue that should be highlighted as a positive indicator of political development in post-war El Salvador is the relative stability of the political party system. As mentioned earlier, the two main political parties since the post-war have been the same: the FMLN (the former guerilla organization) and a business-supported party, ARENA. Even though there has been ideological polarization in the country and some splits within the parties, they have both had electoral successes and continue to be strong.[12] There are other smaller parties that obtain some representation in the Legislative Assembly, but the fragmentation of the political party system is low. A frequently used measure to gauge party stability is electoral volatility—the changes in voting behavior between elections. Volatility has

TABLE 14.3 Turnout in presidential elections in El Salvador, 1984–2009

1984	1989	1994	1999	2004	2009
65.0%	54.70%	46.16%	38.57%	66.16%	61.91%

Source: Prepared by author with data from 1989–2009: International IDEA. 1984: Barnes (1998). This is an estimate by Barnes.[1]

1. International IDEA 2011; Barnes 1998.

diminished significantly in El Salvador since the first post-war elections in 2004, when the volatility index was 22.09. By 2003, it had diminished to 5.3 and has remained in that range since.

As a result of the peace accords, the other area that has experienced reforms in the past 20 years has been electoral legislation; a legislative commission proposed a new electoral code, which was enacted in 1993. More reforms related to the identity document were implemented in 2001 and comprehensive electoral reforms were approved in June 2011.

A good way to summarize the trends in different aspects of "governance" in El Salvador is to examine the governance indicators developed by the World Bank.[13] These indicators are available starting in 1996, 4 years after the signature of the peace accords, but can provide a good perspective on the longitudinal changes that occurred up to 2012. Table 14.4 shows the detailed results of all six indicators comparing the scores of 1996 with those of 2012. The governance scores range from −2.5 to +2.5, with higher values corresponding to better governance.[14] Over the years there has been some improvement in El Salvador, but all the indicators remained close to the midpoint (.00). The indicators in which the country showed more improvement are Regulatory Quality and Political Stability, both of which moved to the positive range. Next are those that measure Government Effectiveness, Voice and Accountability, and Control of Corruption that remained on the negative range, but showed improvement in the post-war period. It is important to highlight that corruption has been a serious issue at all levels of government; a new law to promote transparency and accountability was approved by the legislature in 2011. Corruption, however, is a widespread problem in most Latin American countries, not only post-conflict societies.

At the other extreme, the improvement in the governance indicator that assesses the Rule of Law was almost nil. Figure 14.2 compares the Political Stability indicator and the Rule of Law indicator over time. The indicators go in opposite directions: while Political Stability shows steady improvement in the post-conflict period, the Rule of Law shows a negative trend—although it had a slight improvement in the mid-2000s it deteriorated since 2006. The latter coincides with the increase in violence and insecurity in El Salvador, an issue that will be addressed in the following section.

TABLE 14.4 World Bank governance indicators for El Salvador, 1996 vs. 2012

	Regulatory Quality	Political Stability	Government Effectiveness	Voice and Accountability	Control of Corruption	Rule of Law
1996	−0.01	−0.30	−0.72	−0.15	−0.90	−0.93
2012	+0.32	+0.22	−0.14	−0.07	−0.38	−0.75

Source: Prepared by author with data from the World Bank.

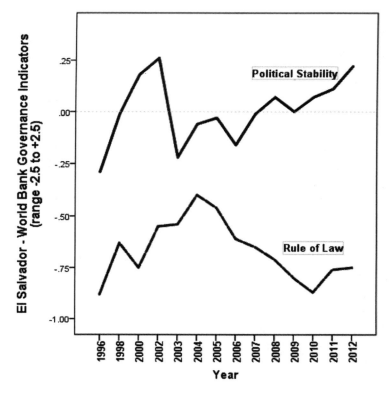

FIGURE 14.2 Selected governance indicators in El Salvador: 1996–2012
Source: Prepared by author with World Bank Governance Indicators data.

Post-accord security

Security is closely linked to the broader issue of the rule of law. Most countries in Central America are characterized by the lack of judicial efficacy. Impunity is widespread and conviction rates are extremely low.[15] The population often mistrusts the police and the government security forces are often insufficient and ill-equipped to fight against powerful mafias. Violence and insecurity have increased dramatically in El Salvador in recent years, particularly in urban areas, to the extent that it has become one of the most violent countries in the world. Insecurity has been considered the Achilles' heel of El Salvador in the post-conflict period. The high levels of violence called into question the quality of peace in the post-war period and have overshadowed the advancements made in democratization.[16] In the words of one citizen interviewed in 2011 (Newman 2011):

> Before everyone knew who was who. Now we live in permanent fear of getting robbed or killed at any time, day or night. The younger generation

doesn't fight for a cause, it is simply being swallowed up by the despair, inequality, corruption and lack of opportunities that caused the war in the first place. This country is still not at peace.

The most common indicator to assess the level of violence in a country is the homicide rate (the number of homicides × 100,000 inhabitants). Table 14.5 shows the progression of homicide rates in El Salvador since the early years of the post-war.

Although homicides decreased by half in the immediate post-accords years, the homicide rate for El Salvador remained high vis-à-vis other countries in the world, and increased dramatically after 2005. Twenty years after the peace accords, El Salvador had become one of the most violent countries in the world. The 2011 World Bank report "Crime and Violence in Central America: A Development Challenge" notes that El Salvador had the highest homicide rate in Latin America.[17] According to that report violence goes beyond homicides and includes burglary, robbery, assault, and extortion among other crimes. The World Bank contends that there are several sources of the current violence, some of them related to the past

TABLE 14.5 Post-accord homicides in El Salvador, 1993–2012

Year	Homicides per 100,000 population
1993★	141.3
1994★	164.6
1995	139.1
1996	117.3
1997	112.6
1998	95.0
1999	65.0
2000	39.3
2001	36.9
2002	37.0
2003	36.4
2004	45.8
2005	62.2
2006	64.4
2007	57.1
2008	51.7
2009	70.9
2010	64.1
2011	69.9
2012	41.2

★ UNDP data cited in Córdova et al. 2007.

Source: Prepared by author with data from UNODC, Global Homicide Report 2013.

civil wars in the region, which left two legacies: the availability of arms that were not confiscated or destroyed and a culture of violence among the population. In addition to the legacy of war, there are other conditions such as the dramatic increase in the presence and activities of narcotraffic in the region (which uses Central American countries as transit routes), as well as structural problems of poverty and social exclusion. The biggest trigger of violence since 2005 is, according to multiple sources, the exponential growth of violent youth gangs, which generate violence against the population in general, but particularly against each other. The gangs have also internationalized and become more ruthless and sanguinary, and as Farah reported, the situation is only growing worse (2016).[18] "The spreading wave of savagery—including beheadings, dismemberment, and systematic rape—is the result of the growing involvement of the Mara Salvatrucha (MS13) and Barrio 18 gangs in the global cocaine trade. The increasing revenues of these transnational gangs have pushed the groups toward greater sophistication and political awareness. The result is a lethal combination of political messaging that is part liberation theology and part Pablo Escobar—the outcome being that these gangs now boast vast territorial control, growing military power, and rapidly expanding criminal enterprises."

Beyond homicide rates, another way to gauge the impact of insecurity in post-war El Salvador is by examining the perception of its citizens. The Americas Barometer has gathered public opinion data regularly in the post-conflict period. One of the questions asked over the years is "which is the most important problem in the country." Table 14.6 shows the results.

As can be observed, an important percentage of the population in the post-conflict period considers common crime (and violence) one of the most important problems in the country, to the extent that in 2010 and 2012 it was considered the most important problem.

TABLE 14.6 Most important problem in El Salvador, 1991–2012 (in percentages)

Issue	1991*	1995	1999	2008	2010	2012
Armed conflict	42.1	–	–	–	–	–
Economic problems (inflation, unemployment, poverty, economic crisis)	42.2	53.6	36.8	61.2	35.3	46.1
Common crime, violence	0.8	37.8	52.3	32.8	60.6	49.0
Other problems	14.9	8.6	10.9	6.0	4.1	4.9
TOTAL	100 %	100 %	100 %	100 %	100 %	100%

* Urban sample only.

Source: Prepared by author using datasets from Americas Barometer surveys in El Salvador.[1]

1. The Americas Barometer by the Latin American Public Opinion Project (LAPOP), www.Lapop Surveys.org. The author thanks the Latin American Public Opinion Project (LAPOP) and its major supporters (the United States Agency for International Development, the United Nations Development Program, the Inter-American Development Bank, and Vanderbilt University) for making the data available.

Although insecurity in post-conflict societies is often associated with violence generated either by the government or by other actors that participated in the conflict (Lappin 2010), that is not the case in El Salvador; for the most part the current insecurity is related to common crime, gang activity, and drug-trafficking. The discussion of this issue goes beyond the scope of this chapter, but it is important to note that international factors are also associated with the increase in violence. On the one hand, the displacement of drug networks to Central America were the consequence of successful anti-drug programs in Colombia, particularly through the so-called Plan Colombia. On the other hand, the growth and constant increase in gang activity in the Northern Triangle in Central America is related to the deportation of thousands of young men from Guatemala, El Salvador, and Honduras from the US.[19]

The exhaustive reforms to the armed forces after the peace accords signing and the establishment of a new police force, formed in part by former members of the army and former combatants from the FMLN, eliminated large-scale state-sponsored human rights violations that were the main cause of fear and insecurity during the civil war (Negroponte 2011). The analysis of the reforms to the army and the police goes beyond the scope of this chapter, but there is widespread consensus that, albeit the tensions generated by the 1993 purge of the High Command, the process was overall successful.[20] In Negroponte's words: "The Chapultepec Accords of January 1992 destroyed the political power of the Salvadoran armed forces and reduced them to a size necessary to respond to natural disasters" (2011: 163–169). With regards to the police, Negroponte also asserts that by 2011 "The civilian character and professionalization of police personnel has progressed substantially" (2011: 163–169).

In spite of the fact that there is no longer a policy of state-sponsored human rights violations, cases of state agents involved in human rights violations still occur. In its 2010 Human Rights Report on El Salvador, the US Department of State asserted (Bureau of Democracy 2011):[21]

> There were no verified reports that the government or its agents committed politically motivated killings; however, there were reports that security forces were involved in unlawful killings. During the year, the Office of the Ombudsman for Human Rights (PDDH) received eight complaints of alleged unlawful killings by the National Civilian Police (PNC), three killings by the Prison Authority, and two killings by the armed forces. Although the PDDH defines all killings by government entities as "extrajudicial killings," there were no verifiable reports of deliberate unlawful killings carried out by order of the government or with its complicity.

In the same vein, a UN Working Group on Arbitrary Detention that visited El Salvador in February of 2012 "voiced concern about the right to security impinging on the right to be free from arbitrary detention in El Salvador, as well as extreme overcrowding in prisons and police facilities in the Central American nation" (United Nations 2012a, 2012b).

The high levels of crime and violence have brought along other types of problems that can have long-lasting effects on democratization, more specifically on the trust (legitimacy) in government institutions and the justice system. Table 14.7 shows the cross-time results of several individual-level variables related to the rule of law and institutional legitimacy.

The longitudinal analysis shows that there have not been major changes in the past two decades overall, and the average trust in the different institutions has remained in the range of 40 points. However, it is noteworthy that the average trust in the armed forces increased from 45.9 points in 1995 to 67.4 in 2012. It is evident that the armed forces have become the most trusted institution in El Salvador. If one recalls the flagrant human rights violations carried out by the armed forces during the civil war, it is surprising to see the high level of trust they generate among the population. Even in 1991, when the armed conflict was still ongoing, the army had relatively high levels of trust.

On the other hand, the trust in the National Civilian Police—created as a result of the peace accords—decreased in recent years. The National Police had higher levels of trust than the armed forces in 1995 and 1999, but as crime has continued rising, trust in the police has decreased and trust in the armed forces has increased. There is in fact a positive statistical correlation between the perception of security, and the trust in the armed forces. This situation contravenes the intent of the peace accords, which aimed at the detachment of the armed forces from internal security issues. The problem of crime has become so large and complex that the post-war

TABLE 14.7 Perceptions about the rule of law and legitimacy of institutions in El Salvador, 1991–2012

Averages in 0–100 scale

Variable	1991*	1995	1999	2004	2006	2008	2010	2012
Trust in the armed forces	48.6	45.9	58.9	68.6	60.4	56.5	67.7	67.4
Trust in the National Civil Police	n/a	59.9	59.1	64.6	52.3	48.6	49.3	53.9
Trust in the Legislative Assembly (Congress)	50.8	48.1	48.4	52.5	48.7	40.3	52.1	49.3
Belief that courts guarantee a fair trial	32.9	41.3	46.8	49.5	45.1	43.9	45.0	45.5
Belief that citizens' basic rights are protected by the political system	39.4	42.8	47.3	50.1	45.1	42.7	48.3	47.8
Respect for political institutions	67.8	68.2	72.0	68.3	70.2	68.3	71.3	69.6

* Urban sample only.

Scale 0–100 (results under 50 represent a negative score).

Source: Prepared by author using datasets from Americas Barometer surveys in El Salvador.

government administrations (both ARENA and the FMLN) have found it necessary to deploy the armed forces to fight crime alongside the National Police.

Economic reconstruction and development

Different scholars acknowledge that socio-economic issues were scantly addressed in the Salvadoran peace accords. Negroponte asserts that "the peace accords focused on security and political problems, relegating socio-economic issues to a secondary position" (Negroponte 2011: 46). Likewise, Córdova Macías and Ramos indicate that "as many scholars have noted, the peace accords did not seek to address the socioeconomic causes of the war" (Córdova Macías and Ramos 2012: 83). Wood also highlights that "the core of the peace agreement consisted of reforms intended to create a transition to a democratic political regime" (Wood 2005). The majority of provisions regarding socio-economic issues were aimed at the economic reintegration of former armed combatants from the army and the FMLN, including a land transfer program.[22]

The reconstruction of the infrastructure damaged by the civil war and the implementation of the peace accords, including land distribution to former combatants, required vast amounts of funding. Negroponte indicates that in February 1993 the Salvadoran government's planning department estimated the cost of implementing the accords at $435 million; of this $141 million was needed to establish the new civilian police alone. In the end, there were serious shortfalls for a variety of reasons. One of them was that although the international community pledged more than $800 million, in the end it did not deliver on all of the necessary and committed funds (Negroponte 2011: 150).

The economic reconstruction in El Salvador encountered another difficulty: the conservative ARENA party, which was in power when the peace agreements were signed and was elected three times in a row in the post-war period, adopted a neoliberal economic model. In the immediate post-accord period, the government embarked in a series of structural adjustment policies implemented under the umbrella of the so-called "Washington Consensus." Among other things, these policies mandated the reduction of the size of the state, tax breaks for businesses and investment venues, and the privatization of state enterprises.[23] These neoliberal policies contradicted the need for a strong state that could invest in things such as providing land to ex-combatants, reconstructing infrastructure, revamping existing institutions and creating the new ones mandated by the peace accords. Wade (2016) argues that the economic elites in El Salvador had disproportionate influence on the peacebuilding process and therefore captured its development, especially through their direct participation and control of ARENA.[24]

The goal of the structural adjustment measures was to achieve macro-economic stability. This was partially accomplished: by the end of the 1990s inflation rates had fallen and the external public debt and the fiscal deficit were drastically reduced; however, growth rates remained elusive. El Salvador grew at a slow rate in the post-war period, as can be seen in Figure 14.3. The global economic

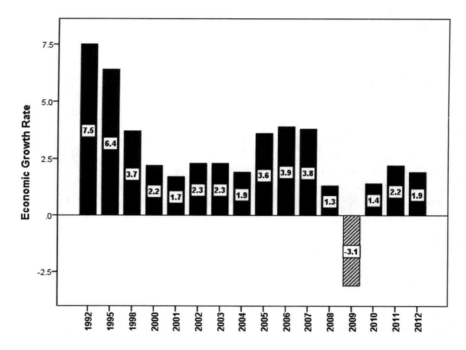

FIGURE 14.3 Economic growth rates in El Salvador: 2000–2010
Source: Prepared by author with data from CEPAL, www.eclac.org/estadisticas/default.asp?idioma=IN

downturn in 2008 had an important impact on the Salvadoran economy, particularly because of the high level of dependency on the US economy. During the civil war thousands of Salvadorans fled to the US and their remittances continue to be one the main sources of external revenue for El Salvador.[25]

Beyond macro-economic indicators, it is important to look at indicators that are more closely related to the quality of life for Salvadorans. In truth, the ARENA administrations made some efforts to promote social policies for two reasons: on the one hand organizations such as the World Bank began pressing for the inclusion of social reforms that went beyond mere neoliberal economic measures (Lehoucq 2012: 104). On the other hand, it was important for ARENA to have an electoral base among the population. Table 14.8 summarizes some socio-economic indicators, comparing the period that preceded the signature of the 1992 peace accords and the situation 20 years later, in 2012.[26]

The results of Table 14.8 show a relatively positive trend in socio-economic indicators in El Salvador over the span of 20 years following the signature of the peace accords in early 1992. Although the country is still a medium human development country, some progress has been made: the Gini Index that measures inequality decreased and the percentage of the urban population increased by 15 percent. The latter is seen as a positive trend given that rural areas in El Salvador (and other Latin American countries) are consistently poorer than urban areas.

TABLE 14.8 Cross-time selected socio-economic indicators for El Salvador

	Pre-Accords	Post-Accords
Level of human development (1)	Medium (1990)	Medium (2012)
Human Development Index (1) *Highest possible score: 1.000*	0.511 (1990)	0.659 (2012)
Urbanization (percentage of urban population) (2)	49% (1990)	65% (2012)
GDP per capita (in current US$) (2)	998.0 (1990)	3,921.7 (2012)
Income inequality (Gini Index) (3) *Perfect equality: 0.0*	0.507 (1995)	0.437 (2012)
Poverty (percentage of the population) (3)	58.7% (1992)	34.5% (2012)

Source: Prepared by author with data from

(1) United Nations Development Program, Human Development Report, 2014[1]

(2) World Bank indicators[2]

(3) BADEINSO/CEPAL[3]

1. United Nations Development Program, Human Development Report website http://hdr.undp.org/en/reports/.
2. World Bank website http://data.worldbank.org/indicator.
3. BADEINSO/CEPAL website www.eclac.cl/cgi-bin/getprod.asp?xml=/deype/noticias/BaseDatos/9/14869/P14869.xml&xsl=/deype/tpl/p13f.xsl&base=/deype/tpl/top-bottom.xsl.

Progress was also made in the Human Development Index, which increased by 0.15. The poverty rate decreased by 24 percent, but it was one of the lowest reductions in Latin America in the past two decades (Azpuru 2012).

These results do not imply that El Salvador has successfully addressed what some consider the root causes of the civil war. Poverty is still widespread, high income inequality persists, and Salvadorans in recent years have endured harsh economic conditions due to the dollarization of the economy and the world economic crisis. Although there have been changes, the basic economic structure has not been modified and economic exclusion remains rampant.

Civil society

Foley indicates that CSOs were one of the main victims of the war: "in El Salvador we are witness to the reconstruction of civil society in the wake of a terrible civil struggle, one which began with an attempt to eradicate the most vital elements of that society in the name of 'anticommunism'" (1996).

Two basic types of CSOs emerged in the post-war period: grassroots organizations and formal organizations without a mass constituency. In the aftermath of the war, grassroots organizations, such as women's organizations, grew largely because of available funding and support from external actors such as USAID and the European Union (EU), but also private funding from so-called solidarity groups around the world (Jamal 2012). The other type, the non-grassroots-based organizations, generally registered as formal legal entities (i.e., think-tanks and development NGOs) also grew with the support of the domestic and international organizations. Social and popular organizations (i.e., labor groups) also grew at a slower but consistent pace. In addition, according to Córdova Macías, Ramos, and Loya (Córdova Macías et al. 2007), certain social movements began articulating interests in the post-war period and grew into organizations that demanded specific measures or policies, such as the demobilized guerrillas and the former paramilitary groups.[27]

Overall, with regards to the role of civil society in the post-war period, Negroponte argues that it has not been substantial (2011: 169):

> Throughout the civil war, NGOs played a role in mustering support for the FMLN, raising awareness and money successfully. During the negotiations to end the war mediators on both sides expected a greater contribution from civil society, but this did not occur. . . . Organizations with close relationships to the business community continued their work, but others faded away for lack of funds and insufficient commitment to the role of a civil society.

Whether organized religious organizations such as the Catholic Church or the Evangelical Church should be considered "civil society" is debatable; they are devoted to the practice of spirituality, and not to promote particular policies. In any case, the Catholic Church did play a key role in the changes that took place in El Salvador; it provided shelter to victims of repression and promoted social justice. In general terms, it was detached from the implementation of the peace accords, but in the post-war period it has warned that the growing violence in society can undermine the future of the country (Negroponte 2011: 170). More specifically, in March 2012 it led the effort to mediate a truce among gangs that at least in the short run decreased the levels of violence (Córdova Macías and Ramos 2012: 208).

Overall, although the post-war period has presented the conditions for the emergence of civil society groups, their capacity to propose specific policies has been limited because they lack a comprehensive perspective and unity of criteria.[28]

The fact that El Salvador has a strong party system has meant that many of the demands from CSOs are channeled through the political parties, and particularly the FMLN. An exception worth noting are certain selected formal organizations that have acted as liaisons between civil society and the government through mechanisms that attempt to promote dialogue and build consensus about policies. An example was the so-called Consejo Económico y Social, CES (Economic and

Social Council), created in September of 2009 by FMLN President Funes. The goal of this council was to facilitate dialogue and consensus about public policies, related to the economic and social agenda of the country. The CES was inspired on the idea of the failed Foro de Concertación Económico y Social (Forum of Economic and Social Concertation) that was created from the peace accords. Four sectors of society were represented in the CES: the business sector, the social and popular movement, the labor movement, and the academic sector. The CES failed to reach its objectives and faded away. The business sector withdrew from the Council 18 months after it began, contending that the mechanism didn't have any influence on policy making. It finally died off with the second FMLN administration of President Sánchez Cerén in late 2014.[29] It has not been evaluated why these mechanisms failed, but it is possible that the level of political polarization in El Salvador explains, at least in part, their lack of success.

Reconciliation and transitional justice

The last variable discussed in this chapter is reconciliation. As in the case of civil society, this is an issue that is difficult to quantify because of its nature. Furthermore, little has happened in 20 years in El Salvador in terms of bringing the perpetrators of human rights violations to justice or compensating the victims of those violations.

Two commissions were created to investigate the human rights violations that occurred during the civil war. One of them, a United Nations Truth Commission formed and financed entirely by foreigners, was installed 7 months after the signature of the final peace accord in July of 1992.[30] The mandate of the commission was to investigate within 6 months of its formation "serious acts of violence that have occurred since 1980 and whose impact on society urgently demands that the public should know the truth" (Popkin 2004). The second one was called the "ad hoc" commission and unlike the Truth Commission, it was formed by Salvadorans and had to report directly to the President of El Salvador at the time, Alfredo Cristiani (Negroponte 2011: 138).

The ad hoc commission finished its inquiries first and produced a report in September of 1992. According to Popkin, the report focused on the higher echelons of the military hierarchy and recommended the transfer or discharge of 103 officers, including virtually the entire High Command. The report attributed the majority of violations of human rights to the Salvadoran state—more specifically the armed forces—but it also found that the FMLN had committed violations. When the incumbent conservative government of ARENA attempted to purge the High Command as a result of the report, the older generation of military officers resisted and threatened destabilization (Negroponte 2011: 140–142). In the end, the entire High Command was forced to retire, but it took strong international pressure and commitment from the US to allow some of the retired generals to move there.

The UN Truth Commission published its report in March 1993. The commission chose to investigate 32 cases of human rights violations, which produced the names of military officers responsible for the abuses. The passing of an Amnesty Law by the legislature relieved the perpetrators of human rights violations of judicial and civil responsibilities for crimes committed before the signature of the peace accords. In compliance with Truth Commission's recommendations

> and significant pressure from the United Nations, a new Criminal Procedure Code was passed in 1996, enhancing the procedural rights of defendants and of victims, which was one of the commission's recommendations. The structure for judicial appointments and review of performance was also reformed.
> (USIP 1992)

In the early postwar, the most prominent human rights trial was related to the assassination of six Spanish Jesuit priests which occurred in 1989. Colonel Guillermo Benavides and Lieutenant Yussi Mendoza were sentenced to 30 years in prison in 1992; after serving only 15 months they were released in April 1993, when the Salvadoran Congress passed an Amnesty Law. A major development occurred in 2011, when Spain's National Court indicted 20 former military for the murders and issued international arrest warrants. Benavides returned to jail after El Salvador Supreme Court struck down the Amnesty Law in 2016, clearing the way for prosecutions (Malkin and Palumbo, 2016). However, Benavides was released again in 2017, when El Salvador's Supreme Court quashed arrest warrants and denied the extradition of any of the accused military. Extradition to Spain is still likely for Salvadoran military living in the US, where a federal judge ruled in August 2017 that one of the accused, Orlando Montano, can be extradited (Drew, 2017). In addition, Salvadoran victims were plaintiffs in American courts against some of the Salvadoran generals who moved to the US; while criminal lawsuits were not successful, civil lawsuits have awarded the victims millions of dollars.

One of the few breakthroughs in the area of reconciliation took place in January of 2012 when President Mauricio Funes, on behalf of the Salvadoran state, apologized to the victims of state repression in the town of El Mozote in 1981. In that massacre, more than 1,000 villagers—including women and children—were killed by the armed forces.[31]

Assessing whether Salvadoran society is reconciled 20 years after the signature of the peace accords is difficult. Salvadorans are highly polarized in ideological terms; according to the Americas Barometer data as of 2012 around 22 percent of Salvadorans considered themselves on the extreme left of the political spectrum and around 35 percent on the extreme right. However, a high degree of political polarization does not imply a lack of reconciliation. If anything, political differences in El Salvador are now channeled through the ballot box. What is more revealing in a survey conducted by the Universidad Centroamericana of El Salvador in November of 2011, around 73 percent of Salvadorans agreed that the human rights violations that occurred during the war should be investigated, while only 27 percent disagreed (IUDOP 2011).

Conclusion

This chapter has discussed some of the crucial variables that should be addressed when assessing the situation in El Salvador 20 years after the peace accords were signed in 1992. On the whole, the picture that emerges is mixed. El Salvador has made great progress in aspects related to governance, which includes the democratization of the political system and the dismantling of the structures that violated human rights during the civil war. In a survey conducted on the eve of the twentieth anniversary of the signature of the peace accords, Salvadorans acknowledged that after the signature of the peace accords positive changes have occurred with regards to freedom of expression, the respect for human rights, and the emergence of a plural political party system. In contrast, they considered that insecurity, deficient justice, and poverty are still unresolved issues (IUDOP 2011). The viewpoints of Salvadorans coincide with outsiders' evaluations of the major challenges faced by El Salvador. In a statement commemorating the twentieth anniversary of El Salvador peace accords, United Nations Secretary General Ban Ki-moon summarized those challenges (United Nations 2012b):

> As we acknowledge the success of the peace process in El Salvador, we cannot forget that peace consolidation is a long process that requires addressing the root causes of the conflict . . . Tangible peace dividends must materialize in citizens' daily lives. Addressing socio-economic inequalities and advancing the reform of rule of law institutions in the face of citizen insecurity are among key challenges yet to be addressed at the national and regional level.

In sum, achieving quality peace in El Salvador 20 years after the peace accords were signed is still a work in progress. The majority of the current problems in El Salvador should not be considered directly as failures or shortcomings of the peace accords themselves. Overall the peace accords accomplished the major political goals they were originally designed to achieve. Instead, new circumstances have contributed to create the current challenges, such as the increase of international narcotrafficking activities in the country and the dramatic deterioration of gang violence (which have compromised the security situation), as well as the economic decline of recent years and the lingering structural socio-economic disparities (which contribute to the pervasive poverty). If anything, the peace accords are indirectly responsible for the current situation because of the issues that they did not address, particularly socio-economic reforms and the strengthening of state institutions. In the end, it is the weakness of the Salvadoran state that has permitted the penetration of narcotraffic and the expansion of gangs, and has hampered the implementation of economic and social policies that provide access to an adequate quality of life for most Salvadorans.

It is important to briefly reflect on why socio-economic issues were not addressed in the Salvadoran Peace Accords, but the explanations are not simple. On the one hand, the parties sitting at the negotiations table seemed more concerned with addressing the more immediate cause of the civil war, which was political in nature: the historical lack of space in the political system for parties to the left of the political spectrum. On the other hand, the parties and the UN moderators probably anticipated—and tried to avoid—discussing an issue that, because of its complexity, would have dragged on the negotiations for a longer period, when in reality the moment for signing the final peace accord seemed ripe.[32]

At the time of editing this chapter in late 2017, violence in El Salvador is even worse than it was on the twentieth anniversary of the signature of the peace accords in early 2012. This, together with the lack of economic opportunity for large segments of the population, is having profound social consequences, such as the flight of thousands of women and children to other countries, in particular the US.[33] The democratic political process continues to develop normally, but polarization is high and neither political party seems to have a clear answer to curtail violence or poverty, at least in the short run.

Notes

1. El Salvador became independent in 1821, but for several years was part of the Federation of Central American States.
2. The 1991 reforms aimed at the subordination of the army to the elected civilian governments, the separation of the army from internal security issues, and consequently, the separation of the police from the Ministry of Defense. They also included reforms for improvement of the judiciary and the creation of an Ombudsman office. The constitutional reforms also created the Supreme Electoral Tribunal, the institution in charge of overseeing electoral processes.
3. Only one new set of constitutional reforms was made in 2000, related to extradition and asylum.
4. See for instance Karl 1990.
5. Different authors have always coincided that democratization was the essence of the peace accords. See for instance Cañas and Dada 1999. More recently, see Córdova Macías and Ramos 2012.
6. The ethnic fractionalization index for El Salvador is 0.1978. Comparatively, neighboring Guatemala in which the population is clearly divided in indigenous and non-indigenous, the index is 0.5122. Another neighboring country, Nicaragua, also has a higher fractionalization index of 0.4844.
7. In the 1994 presidential election the FMLN participated in an alliance with two leftist parties that were not part of the armed opposition, Convergencia Democrática (CD) and the Movimiento Nacional Revolucionario (MNR).
8. In the March 2012 elections, the FMLN candidate lost by a significant margin to the incumbent Mayor from ARENA, Norman Quijano.
9. See for example Arnson 2012 and Colburn 2009.
10. It is important to consider that in many post-conflict societies women are often also subjects of exclusion. The Global Gender Gap Index can help assess the level of inclusion of women in society. The overall score for El Salvador in 2011 was 0.6567, which ranked the country as 94 out of 136 included in the study. As a parameter of comparison, the score for Iceland—the country ranked as #1—is 0.8530. The index is disaggregated into three different categories: educational attainment; economic participation and opportunity; and health, survival and political empowerment. In terms of political empowerment of women, the score obtained in 2011 ranks El Salvador as 72 out of 136 countries (Hausmann et al. 2011).

11. It should be remembered that electoral reforms, including issues such as new ID cards, may have influenced the results.
12. See Azpuru 2010.
13. According to the World Bank, governance consists of the traditions and institutions by which authority in a country is exercised. This includes the process by which governments are selected, monitored and replaced; the capacity of the government to effectively formulate and implement sound policies; and the respect of citizens and the state for the institutions that govern economic and social interactions, among them. For more information see http://info.worldbank.org/governance/wgi/index.aspx#home (accessed October 1, 2017).
14. Countries with a higher positive score are considered to be better in terms of governance than countries with negative scores. As an example, the Rule of Law score for the United States in 2010 was +1.58.
15. See Millet and Stiles 2008.
16. See Córdova Macías and Ramos 2012, and Moodie 2012.
17. El Salvador, Guatemala and Honduras, the so-called Northern Triangle in Central America, have particularly high levels of violence (Serrano-Berthet and Lopez 2011).
18. Farah also notes that the homicide rate in El Salvador decreased in 2012 as a result of the truce between the gangs brokered by the Organization of American States. However, the homicide rate has soared again in 2014 after the truce ended (Farah 2016).
19. It is estimated that 46,000 convicts were deported to Central America—mainly to Guatemala, El Salvador, and Honduras—between 1998 and 2005. Many of the deportees were members of US street gangs, particularly from Los Angeles. There are now between 70,000 and 100,000 gang members in the Northern Triangle and the deportations continue increasing (Azpuru 2014).
20. In Chapter 2 in this volume Terrence Lyons refers to the demilitarization process in El Salvador.
21. In addition, the report indicates that the Ombudsman office received 558 complaints alleging the use of excessive force or mistreatment of detainees, 228 complaints of arbitrary arrest or detention, and 143 complaints of illegal detentions during the year 2010 (Bureau of Democracy 2011).
22. Socio-economic issues were tabled to be discussed in the post-conflict period. A commission by the name of Foro de Concertación Económica y Social was created to discuss socio-economic issues, but it did not have significant achievements. See the section on civil society in this chapter.
23. According to Lehoucq (2012: 102), the ARENA administrations implemented the following neoliberal reforms: President Cristiani (1989–1994) liberalized interest rates, freed the prices of many regulated goods, abolished the state marketing board for coffee and sugar exports, re-privatized the banking industry, and established the autonomy of the Central Bank. President Calderón Sol (1995–1999) privatized the state communications and electric monopolies, established a new calendar for reducing tariffs, and increased the VAT from 10 to 13 percent. It also privatized social security. President Flores (1999–2004) fixed the national currency to the US dollar (Lehoucq 2012).
24. Wade argues that the private sector dictated the course of peacebuilding, especially through the control of the government under the post-war ARENA administrations (2016).
25. Lehoucq indicates that it is estimated that 15 percent of the Salvadoran population lives in the US. Their remittances now consist of the equivalent of more than half of exports (Lehoucq 2012: 113).
26. Exact information for the same years is not always available and in those cases the year that is closest to the target year is used in the table.
27. On the twentieth anniversary of the signature of the final peace accord, there are still lingering problems with regards to these groups; in 2012 President Mauricio Funes offered health care and pensions to 22,000 former FMLN combatants. Army soldiers who fought in the war already have pensions (Associated Press 2012).

28. Confirmed in author interview with Ricardo Córdova Macías in San Salvador, February 4, 2012.
29. There was no formal ending, but rather a gradual weakening of the Council, which the new president made no attempts to revive (Accessed at "Sánchez Cerén dejó morir el Consejo Económico inspirado en Acuerdo de Paz," August 14, 2015, www.elsalvador.com/articulo/nacional/sanchez-ceren-dejo-morir-consejo-economico-inspirado-acuerdo-paz-84590).
30. The Commission was formed by three members appointed by the United Nations: Belisario Betancur, former president of Colombia; Reinaldo Figueredo, former foreign minister of Venezuela; and Colombia and American Law Professor Thomas Buergenthal.
31. President Funes announced several measures to compensate the communities, including a census to identify the victims. As of March of 2012, nothing concrete had been implemented to this respect. Author interview with Ricardo Córdova Macías, San Salvador, February 4, 2012; "Funes apologizes to repression victims in El Salvador." *Prensa Latina News*, January 17, 2012. Accessed October 1, 2017 at http://cispes.org/uncategorized/el-salvador-apologizes-for-state-violence-on-20th-anniversary-of-peace-accords.
32. Azpuru et al. argue that the peace accords in El Salvador went in-depth into the reform of the political system, which contributed to the success of democratization in that country. In comparison, the peace accords in Guatemala covered a large number of issues, including socio-economic ones, but in a superficial way, which in turn has produced a less successful political system in Guatemala. In other words, the depth of the Salvadoran peace accords contrasts with the breadth of the Guatemalan peace accords.
33. See Farah 2016.

References

Arnson, Cynthia J., Ed. *In the wake of war: Democratization and internal armed conflict in Latin America*. Stanford University Press, 2012.

Arnson, Cynthia J. and Dinorah Azpuru. "From Peace to Democratization: Lessons from Central America," in John Darby and Roger Mac Ginty, Eds. *Contemporary peacemaking: Conflict, violence and peace processes*. Palgrave Macmillan, (2003): 197–211.

Associated Press. "El Salvador offers pensions, care to ex-rebels." *Boston.com*, January 13, 2012. Accessed October 1, 2017 at http://archive.boston.com/news/world/latinamerica/articles/2012/01/13/el_salvador_offers_pensions_care_to_ex_rebels/.

Azpuru, Dinorah. "The salience of ideology: Fifteen years of presidential elections in El Salvador." *Latin American Politics and Society* 52, no. 2 (2010): 103–138.

Azpuru, Dinorah. "Democracy and Governance in Conflict and Postwar Latin America: A Quanitative Assessment." In Cynthia J. Arnson, Ed. *In the wake of war: Democratization and internal armed conflict in Latin America*. Stanford University Press, 2012.

Azpuru, Dinorah. "The multiple causes of the border crisis." *Panoramas*, October 20, 2014.

Barnes, William A. "Incomplete democracy in Central America: Polarization and voter turnout in Nicaragua and El Salvador." *Journal of Interamerican Studies and World Affairs* 40, no. 3 (1998): 63–101.

Booth, John A., Christine J. Wade, and Thomas W. Walker. *Understanding Central America: Global forces, rebellion, and change*. Fifth Edition. Westview Press, 2009.

Bureau of Democracy, Human Rights, and Labor. *2010 country reports on human rights practices: El Salvador*. Washington, DC: US Department of State, April 8, 2011. Accessed October 1, 2017 at www.state.gov/j/drl/rls/hrrpt/2010/wha/154505.htm.

Cañas, Antonio, and Héctor Dada. "Political Transition and Institutionalization in El Salvador." in Cynthia J. Arnson, Ed. *Comparative peace processes in Latin America*. Stanford University Press, 1999.

Colburn, Forrest D. "The turnover in El Salvador." *Journal of Democracy* 20, no. 3 (2009): 143–152.
Constitutions and Comparative Constitutional Study. Political database of the Americas. Georgetown University. Accessed at http://pdba.georgetown.edu/Constitutions/con studies.html.
Córdova Macías, Ricardo, Nayelly Loya and Carlos Ramos. "La contribución de la paz a la construcción de la democracia en El Salvador (1992–2004)," in Dinorah Azpuru et al., *Construyendo la Democracia en Sociedades Posconflicto*. Ottowa and Guatemala: International Development Research Center and F&G Editores, 2007.
Córdova Macías, Ricardo, and Carlos Ramos. "The Peace Process and the Construction of Democracy in El Salvador: Progress, Deficiencies and Challenges." In Cynthia J. Arnson, Ed. *In the wake of war: Democratization and internal armed conflict in Latin America*. Stanford University Press, 2012.
Drew, Jonathan. "Top Trump lawyer urges extradition of ex-Salvadoran official." *Los Angeles Times*, November 10, 2017. Accessed November 10, 2017 at www.latimes.com/sns-bc-us--jesuit-massacre-20171108-story.html.
Farah, Douglas. "Central America's gangs are all grown up: And more dangerous than ever." *Foreign Policy*, January 19, 2016. Accessed at http://foreignpolicy.com/2016/01/19/central-americas-gangs-are-all-grown-up/.
Foley, Michael W. "Laying the groundwork: The struggle for civil society in El Salvador." *Journal of Interamerican Studies and World Affairs* 38, no. 1 (1996): 67–104.
Hausmann, Ricardo, Laura D. Tyson, and Saadia Zahidi. *The global gender gap report*. World Economic Forum, 2011.
Instituto Universitario de Opinión Pública (IUDOP). "Los salvadoreños y salvadoreñas evalúan el cumplimiento de los Acuerdos de Paz." *Boletín de Prensa Año* XXVI, no. 1, 2011.
International IDEA. "Voter turnout data for El Salvador." Stockholm, Sweden: International IDEA. Accessed October 1, 2017 at www.idea.int/vt/countryview.cfm?CountryCode=SV.
Jamal, Manal A. "Democracy promotion, civil society building, and the primacy of politics." *Comparative Political Studies* 45, no. 1 (2012): 3–31.
Karl, Terry Lynn. "Dilemmas of democratization in Latin America." *Comparative Politics* 23, no. 1 (1990): 1–21.
Lappin, Richard. "What we talk about when we talk about democracy assistance: The problem of definition in post-conflict approaches to democratisation." *Central European Journal of International and Security Studies* 4, no. 1 (2010): 183–98.
Lehoucq, Fabrice. *The politics of modern Central America: Civil war, democratization, and underdevelopment*. Cambridge University Press, 2012.
Malkin, Elisabeth, and Gene Palumbo. "Salvadoran Court Overturns Wartime Amnesty, Paving Way for Prosecutions." *New York Times*, July 14, 2016. Accessed November 10, 2017 at www.nytimes.com/2016/07/15/world/americas/salvadoran-court-overturns-wartime-amnesty-paving-way-for-prosecutions.html?ref=nyt-es&mcid=nyt-es&subid=article.
Millett, Richard, and Thomas Shannon Stiles. "Peace without security: Central America in the 21st century." *Whitehead Journal of Diplomacy and International Relations*, 9 (Winter/Spring 2008): 31–41.
Moodie, Ellen. *El Salvador in the aftermath of peace: Crime, uncertainty, and the transition to democracy*. University of Pennsylvania Press, 2012.
Negroponte, Diana Villiers. *Seeking peace in El Salvador: The struggle to reconstruct a nation at the end of the Cold War*. Palgrave Macmillan, 2011.
Newman, Lucia. "Fear and loathing in El Salvador." *Al Jazeera*, August 14, 2011.

Popkin, Margaret. "The Salvadoran Truth Commission and the search for justice." *Criminal Law Forum*, 15, no. 1 (2004) 105–124.

Serrano-Berthet, Rodrigo and Humberto Lopez. *Crime and violence in Central America: A development challenge*. World Bank, 2011.

Supreme Electoral Tribunal. Accessed October 1, 2017 at www.tse.gob.sv.

United Nations. "El Salvador must address social inequality to consolidate its peace process." *United Nations News Centre*, January 16, 2012a. Accessed at www.un.org/apps/news/story.asp?NewsID=40955&Cr=latin+america&Cr1#.VzrDOJMrLok.

United Nations. "El Salvador: UN panel voices concern at arbitrary detention, prison overcrowding." *UN News Centre*, February 2, 2012b. Accessed October 1, 2017 at www.un.org/apps/news/story.asp?NewsID=41122#.Vzq0A5MrLok.

United States Institute for Peace (USIP). "Truth Commission: El Salvador." United States Institute of Peace, July 1, 1992. Accessed October 1, 2017 at www.usip.org/publications/1992/07/truth-commission-el-salvador.

Wade, Christine J. *Captured peace: Elites and peacebuilding in El Salvador*. Ohio University Press, 2016.

Wood, Elisabeth Jean. "Challenges in Political Democracy in El Salvador." in Frances Hagopian and Scott P. Mainwarring, Eds. *The third wave of democratization in Latin America: Advances and setbacks*. Cambridge University Press, (2005): 179–201.

15
QUALITY PEACE
A Northern Ireland case study

Colin Knox

Introduction

The international community considers Northern Ireland to have reached a degree of political stability, with the five main political parties working as a power-sharing coalition in a devolved government at Stormont since May 2007. The existing arrangements are rooted in the Belfast (Good Friday) Agreement of 1998 that provided for, *inter alia*, a devolved Assembly with full executive and legislative authority for all matters that are the responsibility of Northern Ireland government departments. Despite substantial public endorsements of the Agreement via referenda in both Northern Ireland and the Republic of Ireland, devolution faltered largely over the decommissioning of paramilitary weapons. From the inception of devolution in December 1999 until October 2002, the Assembly was suspended four times with intermittent flurries of public administration and legislative business conducted. The British Secretary of State dissolved the Assembly in April 2003 and local political parties engaged in a review of the Belfast Agreement with the aim of restoring devolution. A political breakthrough came in the form of the St. Andrews Agreement in October 2006, which set out a timetable to reinstate devolution and fixed the date for the third elections to the Northern Ireland Assembly. Following the elections, devolved power was restored to the Assembly on May 8, 2007 with a power-sharing executive headed by Ian Paisley as the DUP First Minister (now replaced by Arlene Foster) and Sinn Féin's Martin McGuinness as Deputy First Minister. Although Northern Ireland has witnessed many "historic breakthroughs," a public meeting between Ian Paisley (then DUP leader) and Sinn Féin leader, Gerry Adams, carried huge symbolic significance as a turning point that copper-fastened the peace process.

Concomitant with this working system of local governance (since 2007), described by the (then) First Minister, Peter Robinson, as the "most settled period of devolution for over forty years" (2009), there has been a significant reduction in violence. An uninterrupted period of devolution from May 2007 until January 2017, the transfer of policing and justice powers to the Northern Ireland Assembly (the so-called final piece of the "devolution jigsaw"), and a move away from constitutional and security issues heralds a return to "normal" politics. Even if these political developments are welcome, does the absence of violence, a functioning devolved power-sharing government, and a "settled" constitutional agreement constitute a sustainable and quality peace in Northern Ireland? This is not to underestimate the significant achievements in reaching this point but instead to ask whether the popular euphoria emanating from the Belfast Agreement (1998), the St. Andrews Agreement (2006), the Agreement reached at Hillsborough Castle in 2010, the Stormont House Agreement (2014), and the Fresh Start Agreement (2015) have translated into so-called "peace dividends" or the improvement in the quality of people's lives?

The editors' hypothesis is that at least five variables may promote and/or frustrate a stable peace (in no particular order): the role of civil society; economic reconstruction; post-agreement security; transitional justice and reconciliation; negotiations; and governance. This chapter will therefore explore these factors and consider what progress has been made, through these variables, to embed a quality peace in the context of Northern Ireland.

The role of civil society

Civil society groups have a long history of involvement in Northern Ireland linked directly to the political, constitutional, and security problems they faced. The most recent available statistics indicate that there are 4,836 voluntary and community sector organizations, employing around 27,773 individuals representing 4 percent of the total Northern Ireland workforce. The primary purpose of civil society groups is: community development (15 percent); children and families (14 percent); health and well-being (8 percent); and, education and training (7 percent) (Bloomer et al. 2012). There is no data available to track the functions of civil society prior to the Belfast Agreement, but it seems reasonable to suggest that there was a greater emphasis by the sector on issues of human rights, equality, cross-community relations, and criminal justice work.

The prorogation of Stormont and the introduction of direct rule from Westminster in 1972 was an important milestone in the evolution of civil society. Direct rule witnessed the demise of local government and the absence of political accountability for public services. British ministers had no local electoral base in Northern Ireland and were preoccupied with "high" politics—this vested significant powers in the hands of civil servants who paid scant regard to local councilors. The resulting democratic deficit stirred the first signs of self-help in the community. A number of community action groups emerged in response to the trauma of political violence but without government support. As Nolan described it (2000):

All over Northern Ireland there were people trying to help the families that had been burnt out, or establishing food co-operatives, or taking kids from the frontline areas off on holiday, or setting up peoples' assemblies, or trying to get dialogue going between Catholics and Protestants. There was prodigious energy, and an optimism that this ragbag of people could create a sort of counter-culture that would not only challenge the rising sectarianism, but would give expression to a new radical politics.

Increasingly, Northern Ireland Office ministers and senior civil servants recognized the contribution which civil society could make to a wide spectrum of government programs: health and social services, urban renewal, economic development, poverty initiatives, and, importantly, community relations. This, in turn, led to a more professionalized sector that worked with, and accepted more resources from, government in the 1980s and was well placed to support efforts to build a peace process in the 1990s. Self-help and community activism, however, were more evident in Nationalist areas whose history depicted the state as a Unionist oppressor. Fearon observed, "groups were more likely to be found in areas of high economic deprivation and nationalist in hue. Unionist groups still saw community development as a rebellious activity, something that sought to subvert and undermine the state" (2000).

Following the Belfast Agreement some politicians were envious of the privileged access that civil society had to senior civil servants during the period of direct rule. As one Ulster Unionist Member of the Legislative Assembly (MLA) put it, "it is time for the sector to stand aside" (F. Cobain cited in McCall and Williamson 2001). Yet there is also an acknowledgement of the valuable contribution that the sector makes to post-conflict Northern Ireland (Williamson et al. 2000; Cochrane 2001; Hodgett and Johnson 2001; Acheson and Williamson 2007). Consociational arrangements brokered through the Belfast Agreement cannot, in themselves, deliver stability on the ground and require active engagement with civil society as key stakeholders in the community (Byrne 2001). This approach has been described by Taylor as social transformation that "challenges ethno-national group politics in favour of a democratic, non-sectarian future" (2009).

In recognition of the contribution of the role that civil society could play in peacebuilding, the devolved government launched a strategy document entitled *Partners for Change* (Volunteer Sector Compact Team, DSD 2001). Although this was billed as a government strategy, it had been developed collaboratively by the Joint Government/Voluntary and Community Sector Forum. *Partners for Change* undoubtedly gave a firm commitment to collaborative working between the devolved administration and civil society. The Department for Social Development described how the voluntary and community sector had become a key social partner in the processes of government. That involvement, it argued, "reflects a more developed and mature relationship and role within Government than anywhere else in the United Kingdom, Ireland or indeed Europe" (Voluntary and Community Unit, DSD 2002). The contribution of civil society to the Northern

Ireland Executive's *Programme for Government 2008–11* emphasized the importance of "the Executive working together with the Assembly and harnessing the talents of all the sectors—public, private, voluntary and community" (2008). The follow-on *Programme for Government 2011–15* reinforced the concept of partnership working between government and civil society and made a firm commitment to "invest in the growth of social enterprise to increase the sustainability of civil society" (2011a). The devolved government has also provided substantial funds to support the development of civil society and its activities, as well as purchasing services from it. Government funding has moved from being primarily grants made to the sector toward purchasing public services (earned income). Over half of civil society income (£392 million) derives from government purchasing goods and services (Bloomer et al. 2012). One manifestation of the growing strength of the relationship between civil society and the devolved government is a joint Concordat described as a "shared vision to work together as social partners to build a participative, peaceful, equitable and inclusive community in Northern Ireland" (Northern Ireland Executive 2011a).

A report by the Public Accounts Committee (PAC) of the Northern Ireland Assembly carried out a review of the voluntary and community sector, concluding: "the public sector's relationship with the Sector is complex. This has contributed to over-bureaucratic, disproportionate and risk-averse approaches to monitoring of funding and lack of focus on what is actually being delivered" (2012). The PAC concluded that the Concordat between Government and the Sector offered another opportunity for a fresh start. However, it argued that there needed to be a concerted effort by all public bodies and Sector organizations to actively implement and live by its values and principles.

In response, the Department of Social Development led the establishment of a cross-departmental "Addressing Bureaucracy Project." Therein, government acknowledged that the voluntary and community sector "makes an important and valued contribution to all aspects of community life in Northern Ireland" (Northern Ireland Executive 2013a). It highlighted the partnership role between executive departments and the Sector in delivering key priorities in the Programme for Government and concluded: "In many instances the voluntary and community sector takes responsibility on behalf of Government (through a grant funding arrangement) for the delivery of important and vital services to often marginalised and disadvantaged communities" (Northern Ireland Executive 2008). Government claimed a common purpose with the voluntary and community sector in "the delivery of high quality services that make a real difference to our society." Recommendations in the report were aimed at delivering greater proportionality of administration, reducing duplication of effort, and delivering better value for money. A Joint Forum between the government and the Sector exists to oversee the implementation of the Concordat and the reports outlined above. The joint forum noted:

> All members recognise that a good working relationship between Government and the Sector is vital to the overall well-being of the people of Northern

Ireland and that this is a unique opportunity to make a positive contribution to society. Particularly notable is the enthusiasm of members to address the long-standing issues that have impacted on this relationship and to take a different perspective at ways and means of taking matters forward.

(Donnelly and O'Reilly 2014)

So, while not without problems in terms of the practicalities of work between government and the third sector, there appears to be a willingness to acknowledge both the role played by civil society and the valuable support that it offers in a post-conflict Northern Ireland.

The first baseline data available on civil society in Northern Ireland was constructed in 2006 using an index developed by CIVICUS and comprising 74 indicators to measure four dimensions of civil society including structure, environment, values, and impact on a scale of 0–3 (a score of 3 is the highest achievable) (McCarron 2006). Figure 15.1 shows the performance of civil society in Northern Ireland. The key findings on the state of civil society based on the index were:

- Most of the elements of civil society's *structure* in NI are well developed but there is quite low participation in collective community and non-partisan political actions (score of 1.8).
- The *environment* for support of civil society is well developed but tolerance of differences within society is relatively low and constitutes an area of weakness (score of 2.4).
- Civil society *values* within Northern Ireland are quite strong but practices and campaigns to support and promote these values are lacking (score of 2.1).

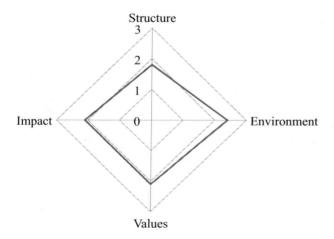

FIGURE 15.1 Civil society in Northern Ireland

Source: CIVICUS—Civil Society in Northern Ireland.

- CSOs are quite active in society but they do not have a strong *impact* on the national budgeting process and are weak when it comes to holding state and private corporations accountable (score of 2.1) (NICVA 2006).

These civil society indicators therefore reflect the divisiveness of Northern Ireland society at a point in time (2006) that preceded power-sharing arrangements and a working devolved government. Since then, civil society has been actively involved in issues such as education, health, and welfare reforms on a unified platform that has cross-cut traditional cleavages and contributed toward a more inclusive shared society. These functions are well articulated and developed in a companion chapter by Paffenholz in this volume.

Economic reconstruction

Following the Belfast Agreement, better economic prospects of the so-called "peace dividend" were heralded. An underlying theme in this economic reconstruction was that a peaceful Northern Ireland would attract international investment from companies that previously regarded it as too unstable for business. Typical of this international "open-for-business" endorsement was (then) New York Mayor, Michael Bloomberg, who addressed an investment conference in Belfast (2008) at which he highlighted American support in four key areas: infrastructure, small business development, tourism, and private investment. He noted, "I would be willing to bet that a decade from now, the Dublin-London-Belfast triangle could be one of the largest and most competitive financial hubs in the world if the political situation continues to improve," although he qualified his remarks with reference to demolition of the "peace" walls (2008). The US has been consistently supportive of Northern Ireland, both in terms of the peace process and efforts to encourage and grow private investment. For example, the region has been able to attract American investment from companies such as Terex, Seagate, Dupont, NYSE Technologies, Allstate, Caterpillar, and Citi. More recently Northern Ireland has attracted further US investment in the form of technology companies and in television and film production (HM Treasury 2011).

Despite international support and gestures of good will, Northern Ireland's economic fortunes since 1998 have been, at best, mixed. The EU, for example, has supported Northern Ireland over several decades through structural funds, four phases of PEACE funding and via the International Fund for Ireland (with match funding from the USA). In May 2007, a European Commission Task Force was set up to support efforts to create change and improve competitiveness by helping Northern Ireland become more integrated into European networks. Northern Ireland's regional priorities are consistent with Europe's response to the global economic and financial crisis—sustainable and inclusive economic growth that will deliver high levels of employment, productivity, and social cohesion (Northern Ireland Executive 2011b).

Until the beginning of the economic downturn in 2008, Northern Ireland experienced a period of comparatively strong economic growth. For example, between 1997 and 2007, the average rate of growth was marginally above the UK (5.6 percent compared to 5.4 percent). However, little progress was made in improving living standards (measured by the Gross Value Added), which remained around 80 percent of the UK average. Northern Ireland's living standards are below other parts of the UK except for two regions (North East England and Wales). The rate of economic growth was reflected in increased levels of employment. For example, the Northern Ireland economy created 124,000 jobs between December 1997 and 2007—an increase of 20.5 percent, in excess of the growth in employee jobs in the UK, which grew by 10.7 percent over the same period. Despite the growth in employment, the local economy continued to experience a relatively low employment rate and high level of economic inactivity. The unemployment rate had fallen to one of the lowest within the UK by 2007 (Table 15.1).

With the onset of the economic recession, Northern Ireland, along with the rest of the UK, has faced significant economic pressures—some 34,000 employee jobs have been lost since the peak of employment in June 2008, at which point 773,150 people were in employment compared to 699,650, at June 2011—a decrease of 4.6 percent. The majority of the losses were in manufacturing, construction, retail, and business and finance—unemployment increased by 158 percent from 23,600 people (February 2008) to 60,900 (September 2011). The latest (2015) Northern Ireland seasonally adjusted unemployment rate (5.8 percent) is the same as the overall UK average rate (5.8 percent) and was the sixth lowest rate among the 12 UK regions. The Northern Ireland rate was below the EU (10 percent) and Republic of Ireland (10.9 percent).

The rise in job losses has been reflected in an increased number of people claiming unemployment benefits with the majority of claimants from lower wage occupations. The claimant count has fallen 14,600 since its most recent peak in December 2012. It stands at 50,200 (5.7 percent of the workforce) in December 2014. Although all age groups have been impacted by the recession, 16–24 year olds have been hit hardest and there is a growing number of long-term unemployed. Moreover, future

TABLE 15.1 Key economic indicators

Rate (%)	1997 NI	1997 UK	2007 NI	2007 UK	2011 NI	2011 UK	2015 NI	2015 UK
Employment	65.5	71.2	67.9	72.9	67.9	70.3	67.8	73
Unemployment	8.8	6.5	4.3	5.2	6.9	8.3	5.8	5.8
Economically inactive	28.1	23.8	29.0	23.1	26.9	23.2	27.9	22.4

Sources: Northern Statistics and Research Agency; Office for National Statistics.[1]

1. Northern Ireland Statistics and Research Agency, 2015, available at: www.nisra.gov.uk/publications/default.asp5.htm.

prospects are pessimistic. Economic growth prospects globally have been downgraded. The Eurozone faces huge challenges, and Northern Ireland's traded sector has significant exposure in this market. Invest Northern Ireland, the agency charged with regional development, has attracted high-quality inward investments especially in finance, technology, and business services but under EU rules the state financial aid that incentivized these deals ended in 2013/2014. In 2010–2011 there was a £128 million net reduction in funding available for public services in Northern Ireland, and the UK public spending review resulted in a loss to the Northern Ireland block grant of £4 billion over the period 2011–2015, from an overall annual budget of approximately £10 billion. These budget cuts will clearly impact public sector jobs and services in an economy that is heavily reliant on public sector jobs (210,000) with 29.3 percent of employees in Northern Ireland (in 2015).

The worst of this economic downturn is felt in socially deprived areas of Northern Ireland, which also suffered most from sectarian violence. As one former MLA put it, "Why is it that 13 years on from the Good Friday Agreement, while we have settled into political stability, we haven't addressed long-term unemployment, life expectancy, and low educational attainment?" (Butler 2011). Some Unionist/Loyalist community activists accuse politicians of abandoning the grassroots, "when you look at areas such as the greater Shankill there has been no peace dividend, no investment, and no improvement in the lives of people who live there" (Irvine 2011). Serious street rioting in East Belfast during the summer of 2011 was attributed by some to the widespread feeling of alienation because of the extent of deprivation among the local working class Unionist community. Others dismiss this completely:

> These (deprivation and street rioting) are two separate issues and care should be taken not to conflate them. Doing so partly excuses the inexcusable, reinforces a sense of self-pitying helplessness, heightens resentment, lets paramilitaries off the hook, and signals that violence is a way to gain sympathetic publicity for social problems. Never mind monetary gain from the peace process, the overriding benefit that has followed to all of us in equal measure is the peace it has delivered.
>
> (Adams 2011)

The difficulty in tracking economic development in Northern Ireland since the Agreement is threefold: first, can we attribute the improving economic prospects directly to the peace dividend up until 2007/2008 or would it have happened in any case (the counterfactual problem)?; second, given Northern Ireland's reliance on public sector jobs (approximately 32 percent of the employment base) and faced with public expenditure cuts, future economic prospects are more dependent on the size of the public purse than political stability; and third, external factors such as exit from the European Union and global downturn may put at risk local efforts at economic reconstruction.

Post-agreement security

Given the highly contested nature of the former security forces (Royal Ulster Constabulary—RUC) and the centrality of human rights and equality principles to any durable political settlement at the signing of the Belfast Agreement, decisions were taken to "hive-off" controversial issues on policing, reviewing the criminal justice system, and establishing new independent human rights and equality institutions to independent commissions. In other words, an assessment was made "to park" these contentious problems and secure agreement on the constitutional issues around which the main political parties could agree. An independent commission chaired by Chris Patten published its report entitled *A new beginning: Policing in Northern Ireland* (Independent Commission on Policing for Northern Ireland 1999) with radical proposals for change that were subsequently endorsed by the British Secretary of State. The report included the creation of a new independent Policing Board to hold the Chief Constable and police service to account; downsizing police numbers with generous severance arrangements; a new 50:50 recruitment policy of Catholics and Protestant to address a significant imbalance; a change in the name and symbols associated with the police; a new emphasis on community policing; and an oversight commissioner to monitor the implementation of the changes (1999). The new Police Service of Northern Ireland (PSNI) came into existence in November 2001. Independent accountability mechanisms are now in place through the Northern Ireland Policing Board and the Police Ombudsman for Northern Ireland.

Two of the most obvious sources of evidence to track the effectiveness of post-agreement security are statistics on the levels of crime associated with the security situation and public perceptions of the police. In a probability survey of around 1,200 people, participants were asked, "how much confidence do you have in the PSNI's ability to provide an ordinary day-to-day service for all the people of Northern Ireland?" Given the highly negative perceptions of the RUC in Nationalist/Republican communities, confidence in its successor is clearly important to a sustainable peace. Sinn Féin, for example, refused to join the Policing Board until 2007, because it was not satisfied that the recommendations of the Patten report had been implemented in full. The results of survey findings are set out Table 15.2.

What is interesting about these statistics on perceptions of the PSNI is that Catholic confidence in the police has grown over the 13-year period, yet Protestants are now less confident (than in 2001) that the police can provide a policing service for all the people of Northern Ireland. This could be a reaction, in part, to the 50:50 recruitment process that has now resulted in more Catholic police officers in the PSNI, currently: 67.15 percent Protestant and 30.73 percent Catholic (at January 2015—the remainder are "not determined"). The 50:50 quota policy ended in March 2011.

Notwithstanding the public perceptions about the PSNI, levels of violence directly linked to the security situation have improved significantly. Compare, for

TABLE 15.2 Confidence in PSNI's ability to provide a service for all people of NI

Rating	2001 Catholic (%)	2001 Protestant (%)	2001 Total (%)	2010 Catholic (%)	2010 Protestant (%)	2010 Total (%)	2014 Catholic (%)	2014 Protestant (%)	2014 Total (%)
A lot or total confidence	28	60	47	39	46	42	43	52	49
Some confidence	41	30	35	39	37	38	46	36	40
Little or no confidence at all	29	9	18	21	16	18	10	12	11

Sources: Compiled from Omnibus Surveys—Northern Ireland Policing Board.

example, the fact that in 2014 there were two deaths due to terrorism with 470 in 1972 at the height of the conflict. There is a similar trend for security-related incidents (shootings by terrorists and the security services). There were 73 shooting incidents in 2014 compared with 10,631 in 1972 (Police Service of Northern Ireland 2015). Figure 15.2 shows trends in security-related incidents (deaths, shootings, and bombing incidents) since 1998 onwards. Officially however, the level of security threat from terrorism, according to MI5 Security Service, is considered "severe" defined as "an attack is highly likely," principally from Republican terrorist groups (Continuity IRA and Real IRA).

Policing, however, remains a highly sensitive area in Northern Ireland. A report by the Criminal Justice Inspectorate was very critical of the Office of the Police

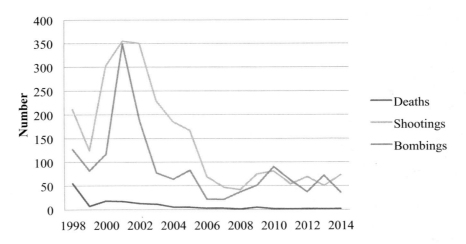

FIGURE 15.2 Security-related incidents

Source: Compiled from Police Service of Northern Ireland statistics.

Ombudsman over his handling of high-profile historical cases, claiming evidence of flawed investigative processes resulting in the lowering of the standards of independence of the office (2011). Significant political pressure was exerted on the (then) Ombudsman who left the post before his intended retirement date.

Transitional justice and reconciliation

Transitional justice

While the above statistics show that the security situation has improved significantly (although there remains a threat of dissident Republican activity), Northern Ireland's conflict is yet to be resolved. Dealing with the past remains an ongoing issue and attracts diverse opinions. All politicians claim support to see justice for those who have unanswered questions surrounding the deaths of their relatives. Unionists, on the one hand, support the work of the Historical Enquiries Team (HET) (within the PSNI), which, if it finds evidence, may secure convictions through the courts. Nationalists and Republicans support some form of truth recovery process. Sinn Féin, for example, wants to see a fully independent, international truth commission, established by a reputable international body (such as the UN), the equivalent of the TRC in South Africa that had the power to grant protection from prosecution for those who had carried out crimes in the cause of truth recovery. (Then) First Minister, DUP Peter Robinson, has rejected this idea claiming that it would be a "half-truth commission" where state organizations would be forthcoming with information and evidence but paramilitaries would not and, hence, a distortion of the truth would emerge. What has happened to date has been a piecemeal approach of: individual inquiries (such as the Saville Enquiry (2010) on "Bloody Sunday" which exonerated 14 marchers shot dead by British soldiers at a civil rights demonstration in 1972); the publication of a controversial report entitled *Consultative group on the past* (2009); and, ongoing work by the PSNI's HET and the Police Ombudsman's Office.

There is a degree of cynicism about the call for, and support to, any proposed truth commission. As one observer has noted:

> It is tempting to conclude that republicans rhyme on about a commission knowing there isn't going to be one, in the comfortable certainty they will never face moral pressure to follow generals and politicians to the stand. The British authorities are just as determined as Sinn Féin and a host of others ... to keep guilty secrets. Across the barriers of nationality and opposing versions of history, ex-combatants by their demands and protestations secure each other's silence.
>
> (O Connor 2011)

Perhaps this assertion was borne out by the former British Secretary of State's (Owen Paterson) blunt refusal to set up a truth commission, the rejection by ex Prime Minister Cameron of an inquiry into the high-profile Pat Finucane case where there is reported evidence of state collusion (Lord Stevens and retired Judge Peter Cory), and lack of support for any future public inquiries.

The Consultative Group on the Past (chaired by the former Church of Ireland primate Lord Eames and former vice-chair of the Policing Board, Denis Bradley) was established by previous British Secretary of State Peter Hain to try to achieve community consensus on how the legacy of the past might be tackled and, as a result, to help build a shared future. Its overall recommendations were overshadowed by a specific proposal for the government to make a one-off ex-gratia payment of £12,000 to the nearest relative of someone who had died as a result of the conflict. This payment included relatives of Republican and Loyalist paramilitaries or those involved in killings through official state collusion. Hence relatives of some 3,700 people killed in the conflict would receive the payment amounting to £40 million approximately. This recommendation was immediately vetoed by the British government. Unionists rejected the report claiming there could be no moral or legal equivalence between innocent victims of violence and criminal terrorists. The consultative report also recommended the setting up of an independent Legacy Commission with the aim of promoting peace and stability. The British government has simply sat on the report since its publication. The then First Minister proposed to establish a storytelling archive for victims in a conflict resolution center to be built as part of a major development project at the site of the former Maze Prison (H-Blocks) where paramilitaries were held and Republican hunger strikers died. The center had secured an £18 million grant from European PEACE III funds and would be one component of the 350-acre redevelopment project costing £300 million aimed at attracting jobs and inward investment. Funding was reallocated after the First Minister withdrew his support (August 2013), stating it should not proceed without consensus after some Unionist politicians and victims' families feared it could be turned into a "shrine" to IRA terrorism and would not become a shared space.

The HET was established by a former Secretary of State (Paul Murphy) in 2005 with a 6-year timescale, a budget of £24.3 million, and an objective to pursue new evidence in 3,260 murders during 30 years of the conflict between 1968 and 1998 to provide answers to the bereaved. The HET is a special investigative unit attached to the PSNI and accountable to the Chief Constable, which re-examines the deaths of thousands of people in the civil unrest between 1968 and the signing of the Belfast (Good Friday) Agreement in April 1998. The HET works closely with families and aims to provide each with a report based on "maximum permissible disclosure" on the death of their relatives. Maximum disclosure may be restricted because of the role played by informants which could jeopardize national security where Special Branch and MI5 have/had an interest. Not every family engages with the HET, preferring not to know some of the gruesome details of how death occurred but others do, and find comfort in answers to questions that have troubled them. According to one journalist who closely monitors the work of the HET, "it may not uncover all the evidence surrounding an incident, but it can, in most cases, bring closure that no rambling political activist and a cast of highly-paid lawyers will ever achieve" (Moriarty 2013).

Part of the work of the HET involved reviewing 157 killings by the British army between 1970 and 1973. Controversy arose when Ulster University academic (Professor Patricia Lundy) claimed the HET gave former soldiers preferential treatment and did not properly investigate deaths caused by the military (2009, 2010, 2011). The HET and PSNI rejected the claims in her report. Only after a request from the Policing Board, did former Chief Constable Matt Baggott agree to commission a review by Her Majesty's Inspectorate of Constabulary on the matter. The review found that HET's policy was based on a "misrepresentation of the law" and its approach to cases involving the state was inconsistent with the European Convention on Human Rights. Since 2010, there were 39 cases involving 119 killings referred back to the PSNI for potential criminal investigation. However during this time frame, no British military cases were referred to the PSNI for further investigation.

Her Majesty's Inspector of Constabulary, Stephen Otter said:

> We think the HET was acting unlawfully in regard to state cases because it treats them differently in policy terms and in the way that then acts out in practice. So, state cases were less effective as a result. Effectiveness is a key test of whether it is Article 2 Complaint under the European Convention on Human Rights. What is indefensible is that Professor Lundy made these findings in 2009, so for four years nothing was being done to address those findings and I do find that that is very difficult to believe. Historical Enquiries Team risked undermining the confidence of the families of those who died during the Troubles in its effectiveness and impartiality.
>
> (Moriarty 2013)

The Director of the HET stood down, and under pressure to cut its budget (in line with other public bodies), the PSNI moved to close HET although claiming it would continue to meet its legislative responsibilities with regards to the past, including fresh investigations where new and compelling evidence emerged. The Stormont House Agreement (2014) makes clear:

> that legislation will establish a new independent body to take forward investigations into outstanding Troubles-related deaths; the Historical Investigations Unit (HIU). The body will take forward outstanding cases from the HET process, and the legacy work of the Police Ombudsman for Northern Ireland (PONI). A report will be produced in each case.

Reconciliation

The British government and the local politicians have made attempts to promote reconciliation through two key public policy commitments: *A shared future* (2005) and the consultation document *Programme for cohesion, sharing and integration* (2010).

The former was devised by British ministers during the direct rule and the latter has emerged after protracted negotiations between Sinn Féin and the DUP. The "Shared Future" policy document, drawing on extensive public consultation, argued that there was overwhelming support for a shared society in Northern Ireland. Its underpinning principles were rooted in the Belfast Agreement that claimed "an essential aspect of the reconciliation process is the promotion of a culture of tolerance at every level of society, including initiatives to facilitate and encourage integrated education and mixed housing" (Strand Three 1998: 18). The policy document was emphatic in its tone: "separate but equal is not an option." *A shared future* was rejected by the devolved government because of its genesis in British ministers. Northern Ireland politicians launched a consultation document, *Programme for cohesion, sharing and integration*," which set out the Northern Ireland Executive's vision for the future by challenging the assumption that division and segregation is a "normal" pattern of living (Knox 2011). The Executive listed a number of "themes for action." These included:

- ensuring that good relations considerations are embedded within all government policy making;
- reducing and eventually eliminating segregated services; and
- addressing interfaces and encouraging shared neighborhoods.

Responses to the government's proposals were mostly negative and best captured by one political commentator who described them as "aspirational or motherhood and apple pie" (Devenport 2010). This reaction reflected wider criticism that the *Programme for cohesion, sharing and integration* fails to set targets or dates for measurable progress and does not mention any financial commitment on the part of government. As one newspaper editorial described it: "the proposed programme suggests that the Executive has set out to manage, rather than eradicate, sectarianism" (Opinion 2010). Following concerted criticism, the government published a revised strategy entitled *Together: Building a united community* (2013). This represented a much more ambitious document with four priorities and associated aims:

- Children and young people: to continue to improve attitudes among our young people and to build a community where they can play a full and active role in building good relations.
- Shared community: to create a community where division does not restrict the life opportunities of individuals and where all areas are open and accessible to everyone.
- Safe community: to create a community where everyone feels safe in moving around and where life choices are not inhibited by fears around safety.
- Cultural Expression: to create a community that promotes mutual respect and understanding, is strengthened by its diversity, and where cultural expression is celebrated and embraced.

Acutely aware of criticism leveled at previous attempts to develop reconciliation policies, government made explicit commitments to: build ten new shared education campuses; get 10,000 young people, who were not in education, employment, training, or a place on the United Youth volunteering program; establish ten new shared housing schemes; develop four urban villages; develop a significant program of cross-community sporting events; remove interface barriers by 2023; and to pilot 100 shared summer schools (Northern Ireland Executive 2013b). Because a number of these commitments involve several government departments and, in some cases capital projects, there is no guarantee of implementation.

Is Northern Ireland a more reconciled society since the Belfast Agreement? Figure 15.3 traces probability survey responses (n ≈ 1,200) over a 16-year period when members of the public were asked the question: "Would you say that relations between Catholics and Protestants are better than they were 5 years ago, worse, or about the same now as then?" Despite a dip in relations during 2001–2002 (when devolution was in trouble), the overall trend is toward better relations between the two communities, although the contentious issues of parades may well have had a negative impact recently. Notwithstanding, the number of "peace walls" or physical barriers, built as security measures to protect communities from each other (so-called "interface areas"), remain a symbolic reminder of separation (Gormley-Heenan et al. 2013). There are at least 60 walls, gates, or fences dividing communities, most of them in Belfast. There is some political impetus to remove these symbols of a divided society through the Department of Justice, alongside financial support from the International Fund for Ireland to communities living at either side of the barriers aimed at creating dialogue, building trust, and confidence.

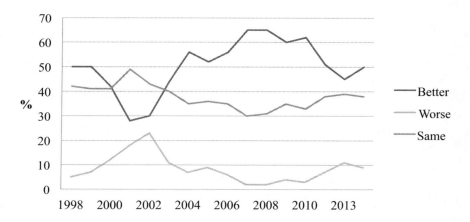

FIGURE 15.3 Relations between Catholics and Protestants

Sources: Compiled from Northern Ireland Life and Times surveys 1998–2014.

Negotiations and governance

Devolution in Northern Ireland followed directly from the Belfast Agreement that provided, *inter alia*, for a democratically elected Assembly "inclusive in its membership, capable of exercising executive and legislative authority, and, subject to safeguards to protect the rights and interests of all sides of the community" (1998). The British government linked the political process and the peace process directly. Peter Mandelson, then Secretary of State for Northern Ireland, argued that the Agreement established the principle that "political stability is best achieved in the absence of violence, but an unbreakable peace can only be built in the context of fair, inclusive, and functioning political institutions" (Mandelson 2000). Hence, long-term political stability and peace are predicated upon violence abatement *and* devolution. Intermittent and faltering spells of devolution delivered a hugely imperfect peace at the start of this process until the St. Andrew's Agreement (October 2006). This resulted in full support for policing and the rule of law across the whole community, the subsequent devolution of policing and justice powers to the Northern Ireland Assembly, and support for power-sharing and the political institutions.[1]

A key element in securing agreement for a power-sharing government was the provision of safeguards to copper-fasten inclusion and avoid regression to Unionist hegemony that characterized the Stormont regime from 1921 to 1972. Wilford outlines how the "consociational bargain" plays out in devolved government in Northern Ireland through four key characteristics or safeguards which are integral to the design and operation of the Assembly and how wider society is organized (2001):

- A partnership within and between the executive and legislature: a four-party coalition (now five) that makes up the executive; the relationship between the Executive and the Assembly; and intra-Assembly arrangements among political parties within statutory committees.
- Proportionality in electoral systems, allocation of public expenditure, and public employment.
- Autonomy over each community's sense of identity—the endorsement of social segregation.
- Mutual veto among political elites—unanimity among decision makers in the form of "key decisions" and "cross-community" consent.

Most decisions taken in the Assembly are agreed by a simple majority of members. Certain key decisions, however, require cross-community support. Issues subject to key decisions are either laid down in legislation or are listed in the standing orders of the Assembly (e.g., exclusion of a minister or members from holding office, a financial vote, a vote on making or amending standing orders). This is to protect against any one political group from dominating the decision-making process or reverting to majoritarianism. This may be done in two ways:

- *Parallel Consent* where over 50 percent of members voting, including over 50 percent of Nationalists and over 50 percent of Unionists voting, all agree to the motion.
- *A Weighted Majority*, which requires the support of 60 percent of those voting, including 40 percent Unionist and 40 percent Nationalist support.

Cross-community voting demands ethnic self-designation. Members of the Legislative Assembly must therefore designate themselves as "Nationalist," "Unionist," or "other" and can only change their community designation between elections if they change political party affiliation. Critics argue that designation reinforces sectarian divisions by accepting the pre-existing order of Northern Ireland society and the system is too rigid and acts as deterrent to non-aligned parties (Farry 2009).

Following the first complete electoral mandate of the Northern Ireland Assembly from 2007–2011, only modest policy successes could be reported: free public transport was made available to everyone aged over 60; local rates (property taxes) were frozen for 3 years; medical prescription charges were abolished; there was investment in infrastructure projects in schools, roads, and hospitals; and water charges were deferred. While these policies have been popular with the electorate, they are predicated on an expanding public sector budget, no longer available. The key achievement is that there is a coalition of the five main political parties that continue to share power and had realistic prospects of its long-term sustainability until the collapse of the Assembly in January 2017.

Politicians, particularly those from the two largest power-sharing parties (DUP and Sinn Féin), are quick to stress what they see as the significant benefits of devolution. The (then) First Minister argued:

> Devolution is good in theory but it has also been good in practice. However, I concede that one area where we have failed has been selling the benefits of devolution. Significantly, devolution provides the foundation for peace and prosperity, but it also allowed us to make a real difference to people's everyday lives.
>
> (Robinson 2009)

The verdict on "making a real difference to people's lives" is perhaps best left to the people of Northern Ireland who have expressed their view through survey data since 2002 on the performance of the Assembly (see Figure 15.4). Survey participants responded to the question: "Overall, do you think that the Northern Ireland Assembly has achieved a lot, a little or nothing at all?" The trend from 2002–2014 is not particularly encouraging with around half of all respondents (n ≈ 1,150) claiming the Assembly had achieved "a little."

252 C. Knox

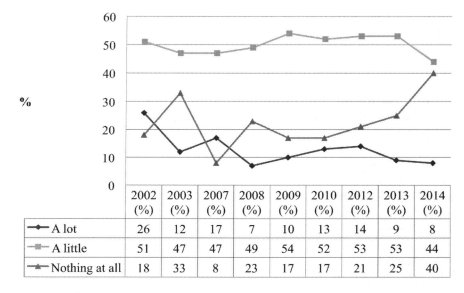

FIGURE 15.4 How much has NI Assembly achieved?
Sources: Compiled from Northern Ireland Life and Times surveys.

Conclusions

The five key variables considered in this chapter to test the quality and stability of peace in Northern Ireland provide evidence of a dynamic civil society with a strong and growing relationship with the devolved government; some early signs of economic reconstruction adversely affected by the global recession and limited peace dividends in socially deprived areas; a significant decline in violence associated with the security situation, although a mixed picture on public confidence in policing; unresolved and contested policy responses to dealing with the past, alongside improving relations between Catholics and Protestants; and, optimism about the political stability of the power-sharing institutions of governance but an unremarkable performance by the Northern Ireland Assembly in policy terms.

If one were to judge the relative contribution of these factors to secure quality peace in Northern Ireland, then security, negotiations, and governance must rank as the most important constituents. Terrence Lyons in Chapter 2 on post-agreement security in this volume emphasizes the importance of managing security-related issues first as a condition for quality peace in the second stage. In this chapter, I came to a similar conclusion. However, the decline in violence and stable political power-sharing governance emerging from a negotiated settlement are necessary but not sufficient requirements for building a future quality peace. Conflict impacts the quality of people's lives whether directly because of violence or indirectly as a consequence of segregated communities living under the control of paramilitaries. People must therefore see the real benefits of a political settlement beyond the absence of violence and political stability, particularly in those socially deprived communities most impacted by the conflict. Hence, economic reconstruction is pivotal to embedding peace, described in the Northern Ireland context as the "peace dividend" (Knox 2016). The absence of violence clearly helps to create more certainty for potential external investors but at a time of a global recession, economic reconstruction is a huge challenge. Yet there are things that can be done by targeting public sector budgets toward those areas blighted by terrorism and social deprivation. Unless people living in these areas experience a difference in the quality of their lives, young unemployed men (largely) become easy targets for recruitment by dissident Republicans and Loyalists. To move forward demands a consensus on dealing with the past alongside reconciliation pathways to the future. Northern Ireland has yet to resolve these issues. A key element of building confidence in the future is a dynamic civil society working in partnership with government and giving voice to community groups that represent the fabric of a more cohesive society. In order of ranking, therefore: post-agreement security; negotiations and governance; economic reconstruction; transitional justice and reconciliation; and a strong civil society represent the path toward quality peace in Northern Ireland, acknowledging that this is not a linear or sequential process.

It is clear to politicians since the elections to the Assembly in May 2011 that the stability of devolution was a given until the events of January 2017 and there is a real need to deliver tangible "bread and butter" public policy issues—in short, the peace process and devolution have to demonstrate an improvement in the quality of people's lives. This demands a different kind of composite index to measure quality peace than those variables described in this chapter although, importantly, they are integral to it. One such index could include a range of measures designed to impact directly on the quality of people's lives and is likely to include variables that capture (in no particular order): community cohesion and involvement; community safety; economic well-being; education and lifelong learning; health and social well-being; the environment; housing; and transportation.[2] Such an index could become the responsibility of local government in Northern Ireland, which in 2015 has statutory powers for community planning, and the power of well-being (Knox and Carmichael 2015). These powers allow local councils (n = 11) to call to account all public service providers delivering functions within their geographical areas and to monitor the impact which these services are having on the quality of life of their residents through some suitably devised metric. For Northern Ireland therefore, the road map to quality peace has included securing a political agreement; an inexorable decline in violence; the creation of stable governance arrangements (yet to be achieved); delivery of public policy gains (limited so far); and an improvement in the quality of people's lives (future goal).

Notes

1. Stand I of the Belfast (Good Friday) Agreement agreed on democratic institutions within Northern Ireland. Strands II and III involved North-South and East-West relationships. The former is operationalized through the North-South Ministerial Council and the latter

via the British-Irish Council and British-Irish Intergovernmental Conference. Coakley (2007) cites their limitations as having an absence of political direction and failing to ignite popular imagination, respectively.
2. See, for example, Audit Commission 2005.

References

Acheson, Nicholas V., and Arthur P. Williamson. "Civil society in multi-level public policy: the case of Ireland's two jurisdictions." *Policy & Politics* 35, no. 1 (2007): 25–44.

Adams, David. "East Belfast flashpoint a result of political failure." *The Irish Times*, June 30, 2011. Accessed October 1, 2017 at www.irishtimes.com/opinion/east-belfast-flashpoint-a-result-of-political-failure-1.610806.

Agreement reached in the multi-party negotiations. Her Majesty's Stationery Office (HMSO), 1998.

Audit Commission. *Local quality of life indicators – supporting local communities to become sustainable.* Audit Commission, 2005.

Bloomberg, Michael. *Mayor Bloomberg's speech at US-Northern Ireland investment conference.* Belfast, May 8, 2008. Belfast: OFMdFM Press Release, 2008.

Bloomer, Stephen, Ciaran Hughes and Andrea Thornbury. *State of the Sector VI.* Belfast, Northern Ireland: Northern Ireland Council for Voluntary Action (NICVA), 2012. Accessed October 1, 2017 at www.nicva.org/sites/default/files/d7content/attachments-resources/stateofthesectorvi-introduction.pdf.

Butler, P. "Quality of life in North's deprived areas worsen – little evidence of peace dividend." *The Irish News*, March 24, 2011: 25.

Byrne, Sean. "Consociational and civic society approaches to peacebuilding in Northern Ireland." *Journal of Peace Research* 38, no. 3 (2001): 327–352.

Coakley, John. "Wider Horizons: Cross-Border and Cross-Channel Relations." In Paul Carmichael, Colin Knox, and Robert Osborne, Eds. *Devolution and constitutional change in Northern Ireland.* Manchester University Press, 2007.

Cochrane, Feargal. "Unsung Heroes? The role of Peace and Conflict Resolution Organizations in Northern Ireland." In John McGarry, Ed. *Northern Ireland and the divided world: The Northern Ireland conflict and the Good Friday Agreement in comparative perspective.* Oxford University Press, (2001): 137–158.

Criminal Justice Inspectorate. *An inspection into the independence of the office of the Police Ombudsman for Northern Ireland.* Belfast: Criminal Justice Inspection Northern Ireland (CJINI), 2011.

Devenport, Mark. "Groundhog day revisited." *BBC: The Devenport Diaries*, July 13, 2010. Accessed October 1, 2017 at www.bbc.co.uk/blogs/legacy/thereporters/markdevenport/2010/07/groundhog_day_revisited.html.

Donnelly, Michael and Anne O'Reilly. *Annual report on the Concordat between the voluntary & community sector and the Northern Ireland Government.* Joint Government/Voluntary and Community Sector Forum. Belfast, Northern Ireland: Department for Social Development, 2014.

Farry, Stephen. "Consociationalism and the Creation of a Shared Future for Northern Ireland." In Ruper Taylor, Ed. *Consociational theory: McGarry and O'Leary and the Northern Ireland conflict.* London: Routledge, (2009): 165–179.

Fearon, Kate. "Life in civic society." *Fortnight* 388 (2000): 26–27.

Gormley-Heenan, Cathy, Jonny Byrne, and Gillian Robinson. "The Berlin Walls of Belfast." *British Politics* 8, no. 3 (2013): 357–382.

Hodgett, Susan, and David Johnson. "Troubles, partnerships and possibilities: A study of the making Belfast work development initiative in Northern Ireland." *Public Administration and Development* 21, no. 4 (2001): 321–332.

HM Treasury. *Rebalancing the Northern Ireland economy*. HM Treasury, March 2011. Accessed October 1, 2017 at www.gov.uk/government/uploads/system/uploads/attachment_data/file/81554/rebalancing_the_northern_ireland_economy_consultation.pdf.

Independent Commission on Policing for Northern Ireland. *A new beginning: Policing in Northern Ireland*. Her Majesty's Stationery Office (HMSO), September 1999. Accessed October 1, 2017 at http://cain.ulst.ac.uk/issues/police/patten/patten99.pdf.

Irvine, William. "People feel let down by politicians." *Belfast Telegraph*, July 27, 2011: 12.

Knox, Colin. "Cohesion, sharing and integration in Northern Ireland." *Environment and Planning C: Government and Policy* 29, no. 3 (2011): 548–566.

Knox, Colin. "Northern Ireland: Where is the peace dividend?" *Policy & Politics* 44, no. 3 (2016): 485–503.

Knox, Colin, and Paul Carmichael. "Local government reform: Community planning and the quality of life in Northern Ireland." *Administration* 63, no. 2 (2015): 31–57.

Lundy, Patricia. "Exploring home-grown transitional justice and its dilemmas: A case study of the Historical Enquiries Team, Northern Ireland." *International Journal of Transitional Justice* 3, no. 3 (2009): 321–340.

Lundy, Patricia. "Commissioning the past in Northern Ireland." *Review of International Affairs* 60, no. 1138–1139 (2010): 101–133.

Lundy, Patricia. "Paradoxes and challenges of transitional justice at the 'local' level: Historical enquiries in Northern Ireland." *Contemporary Social Science* 6, no. 1 (2011): 89–105.

Mandelson, Peter. "Round Table – Secretary of State's Comments." Belfast, Northern Ireland: Information Service Office, March 8, 2000.

McCall, Cathal, and Arthur Williamson. "Governance and democracy in Northern Ireland: The role of the voluntary and community sector after the agreement." *Governance* 14, no. 3 (2001): 363–383.

McCarron, JJ. *Northern Ireland Council for Voluntary Action: CIVICUS Civil Society Index*. 2006. Accessed October 1, 2017 at www.civicus.org/media/CSI_Northern_Ireland_Country_Report.pdf

Moriarty, Gerry. "Northern Ireland's killings review team criticized in report." *The Irish Times*, July 4, 2013: 4. Accessed October 1, 2017 at www.irishnationalcaucus.org/damning-report/.

Nolan, Paul. "The plump Cinderella; or politics without politics." *Fortnight* 388 (2000): 29–30.

Northern Ireland Council for Voluntary Action (NICVA). CIVICUS: Civil society in Northern Ireland. 2006. Accessed October 1, 2017 at www.nicva.org.

Northern Ireland Executive. *Programme for Government 2011–2015: Building a better future*. Belfast, Northern Ireland: Office of the First Minister and Deputy First Minister, 2008.

Northern Ireland Executive. *Concordat between voluntary and community sector and the Northern Ireland Government*. Belfast, Northern Ireland: Office of the First Minister and Deputy First Minister, 2011a. Accessed October 1, 2017 at www.communities-ni.gov.uk/publications/concordat-between-voluntary-and-community-sector-and-ni-government

Northern Ireland Executive. *Northern Ireland Executive economic strategy: Consultation on priorities for sustainable growth and prosperity*. Belfast, Northern Ireland: Office of the First Minister and Deputy First Minister, 2011b.

Northern Ireland Executive. *Addressing bureaucracy: A report on tackling bureaucracy in government funding to the voluntary and community sector*. Belfast, Northern Ireland: Department for Social Development, 2013a.

Northern Ireland Executive. *Together: Building a united community*. Belfast, Northern Ireland: Office of the First Minister and Deputy First Minister, 2013b.

O Connor, Fionnuala. "Ex-combatants secure each other silence." *Irish News*, October 11, 2011: 14.

Opinion. "Executive fails to grasp the nettle." *Irish News*, July 29, 2010: 10.

Police Service of Nothern Ireland. 2015. Accessed on October 1, 2017 at www.psni.police.uk/inside-psni/Statistics/

Public Accounts Committee (NI). *Report on creating effective partnerships between government and the voluntary and community sector*. Belfast: NIA 24/11–15 Public Accounts Committee, 2012.

Robinson, P. "Making devolution work," Speech at the Ulster Hall, Belfast September 8, 2009. Accessed October 1, 2017 at www.dup.org.uk/default.htm.

Strand Three. Rights, Safeguards and Equality of Opportunity, paragraph 13. From Peace Accords Matrix Accessed on October 1, 2017 at https://peaceaccords.nd.edu/sites/default/files/accords/Good_Friday_Agreement.pdf.

Taylor, Rupert. "The Injustice of a Consociational Solution to the Northern Ireland Problem." In Ruper Taylor, Ed. *Consociational theory: McGarry and O'Leary and the Northern Ireland conflict*. Routledge, (2009): 309–330.

Voluntary and Community Unit, DSD. *Voluntary and community research in Northern Ireland*. Belfast, Northern Ireland: Department for Social Development (DSD), 2002.

Volunteer Sector Compact Team, DSD. *Partners for change: Government's strategy for support of the voluntary and community sector, 2001–2004: A consultation document*. Belfast, Northern Ireland: Department for Social Development (DSD), 2001.

Wilford, Rick. "The Assembly and the Executive." In Rick Wilford, Ed. *Aspects of Belfast Agreement*. Oxford University Press, 2001.

Williamson, Arthur, Duncan Scott, and Peter Halfpenny. "Rebuilding civil society in Northern Ireland: The community and voluntary sector's contribution to the European Union's Peace and Reconciliation District Partnership Programme." *Policy & Politics* 28, no. 1 (2000): 49–66.

16
MOZAMBIQUE
A credible commitment to peace

Carrie Manning and Chipo Dendere

Background

Why did a strategy of negotiated peace succeed in Mozambique for more than 20 years? And what explains the return to sporadic low-intensity armed conflict in 2013 and again in 2016? To analyze the outcomes of Mozambique's peace process, we explore the effect of five factors on the construction of quality peace in Mozambique: post-accord security, the political settlement, economic reconstruction, civil society, and transitional justice. In so doing, we distinguish between the two separate processes that comprise peacemaking: one is stopping the war and the other is building a peace agreement that all relevant actors can accept and implement. We find that the political settlement and economic reconstruction process were critical to building quality peace in the first instance. However, both came under increasing strain as Mozambique's natural resource economy heated up, raising the stakes of political power at the same time as power was being concentrated in the ruling Frelimo party and specifically in the hands of its president, Armando Emilio Guebuza. During Guebuza's tenure, some of the commitments from the initial peace settlement, particularly around the integration of Renamo personnel into defense and security forces and around inclusive governance of election administration processes, were rolled back. These developments led to the gradual unraveling of peace and ultimately a return to armed conflict.

In the following section of this chapter, we briefly trace the factors that contributed to the war between the Frelimo (Front for Liberation of Mozambique) government and the rebel group, Renamo (Mozambique National Resistance Movement). This provides the necessary backdrop for the primary focus of this chapter—the factors that contributed to a successful peace. The chapter then describes the conditions leading up to the agreement of the two sides to engage in talks, the resulting agreement signed in Rome in 1992, the involvement of international third parties, implementation issues, and the current state of Mozambique's politics and economy. The conclusion discusses the recent return to violence and offers lessons learned from the Mozambican case.

Mozambique, ruled for nearly five centuries by Portugal, achieved independence on June 24, 1975, following Portugal's return to democracy and a decade of guerrilla warfare by Frelimo. The newly independent country, one of the poorest in the world, had a turbulent start. Frelimo came to power vowing to transform social and economic relations in Mozambique. By 1977, under the leadership of President Samora Machel, the party declared itself a Marxist-Leninist single-party state. The effects of draconian economic and social policies, combined with the 1974 worldwide recession and South Africa's use of economic means (as well as covert military support to Renamo) to destabilize its neighbors, brought Mozambique to the brink of economic collapse. Between 1981 and 1986, Mozambique's national production fell by 30 percent, per capita income was cut in half, and exports fell by 60 percent.[1] Additionally, Mozambique was drawn into liberation movements in neighboring countries: it provided support for the Zimbabwe African National Union (ZANU) and South Africa's ANC. The governments of Zimbabwe and South Africa, in turn, armed and financed a Mozambican armed opposition group, the Resistência Nacional de Moçambique (Renamo),[2] led by Afonso Dhlakama.

Frelimo faced an armed insurgency within 2 years of independence. After more than a decade of internal conflict, by the late 1980s economic conditions provided incentives to both the government and the Renamo rebels to explore ways to bring the war to an end. A severe drought that began in the early 1980s made it harder for Renamo to sustain itself by living off the local population. The looming end of the apartheid regime in South Africa threatened to cut off remaining external aid for the rebel movement. In combination with the dramatic economic decline resulting from external shocks and disastrous policy decisions, the drought also forced Frelimo to turn toward the West for economic support, culminating in a World Bank austerity program begun in 1987.

In return, Mozambique was able to reschedule its debt on the most favorable terms ever offered by the Paris Club, and to receive more than $100 million in annual balance-of-payments loans from the IMF and World Bank. Western donors also pledged substantial amounts of new aid (Manning 2002: 123). With this new influx of aid came a large number of international aid agencies and NGOs. This influx of aid agencies would prove significant to the success of the peace process. Through their involvement in aid provision during the humanitarian emergency, the country's major donors gained an extensive familiarity with local conditions and political actors. They also garnered experience in working together in small ad hoc groups to address discrete tasks, in part because, in the view of these donors, the UN had failed to provide adequate direction and coordination to meet the exigencies of the crisis.[3] Many of these same donors became major contributors to the peace process. At the formal talks, and later at meetings of the country's major donors, these donors in particular would commit additional resources beyond those of the UN peace operation.

It was in this economic context that Frelimo moved to abandon its official Marxist-Leninist approach. At its Fifth Congress in July 1989, Frelimo opened party membership to religious leaders, business owners, and others who had previously been excluded. A number of younger party members were brought into the leadership, many of them doctors, lawyers, and other professionals who had been to university in Western Europe. The party congress also officially endorsed the idea of pursuing peace with Renamo (Vines 1991: 123).

Meanwhile, in June 1989, Renamo held its first party congress in Gorongosa, in central Mozambique. Renamo leader Afonso Dhlakama called openly for peace talks with Frelimo, with no specific preconditions. He called upon Frelimo to engage in "genuine negotiation leading to national reconciliation and constitutional reform," and called for "the creation of a government of national reconciliation that within two years will institutionalize democracy in Mozambique" (quoted in Vines 1991: 123).

When the Frelimo government drafted a new constitution in 1990 abolishing the one-party state and ushering in an era of democracy, it undermined Renamo's remaining justification for continuing the war—that it was fighting for democracy and economic freedom in Mozambique. In the fall of 1989, Frelimo broached the idea of constitutional reform to bring multiparty politics to Mozambique.

Peace talks

The changes within the ruling party and the constitution paralleled quiet exploration of the possibilities for peace talks. The earliest overtures toward Renamo aimed at bringing about a negotiated peace came from Mozambican religious leaders. This was essentially the only formal part that Mozambican civil society played in the peace process. As early as 1984, the Catholic bishops in Mozambique had called for talks between the government and Renamo. In 1987, a group of Protestant clergy from the Christian Council of Mozambique (CCM) sought and received permission from President Chissano to contact Renamo. This group invited the Catholic Archbishop of Maputo to join them in contacting Renamo leaders. The first official "talks about talks" were held in Nairobi in 1989 between a Renamo delegation and this group of clergy, which called itself the "Peace and Reconciliation Commission."

Direct peace talks began in Rome in July 1990 and were hosted by the Italian government and by Sant'Egidio, a Catholic lay community based in Rome. Sant' Egidio's leadership had strong ties with the Archbishop of Beira, Don Jaime Gonçalves, who was sympathetic to Renamo. Sant'Egidio had been among the first outside organizations to deliver humanitarian aid to Renamo-held zones in the mid-1980s.

The offer by Sant'Egidio to host peace talks with the support of the Italian government helped strengthen the confidence of Renamo's leadership that a peace agreement could be enforced, and that Renamo could survive and succeed in a new, post-conflict political system. The first major step was taken when the Sant'Egidio community offered to host peace talks in Rome with the support of the Italian government.[4] The Italian government footed the bill for the Renamo delegation's stay in Rome during the entire 2-year negotiation process, paying for everything from the hotel bill to new suits for Renamo officials to wear to the signing ceremony. Personal relationships between members of the Sant'Egidio community in Rome and individuals trusted by Renamo, such as Archbishop Don Jaime Gonçalves, urged flexibility by Renamo. US diplomats also stepped in at crucial times during the talks to offer moral and logistical support, as well as promises of financial support for the implementation process (Bartoli 1999: 258–259). A key part of this promise was the creation of the donor-financed trust fund for Renamo's transition from rebel group to political party.

The peace talks were also marked by a decision to invite individuals to mediate the talks, rather than mediators who officially represented governments. This was an innovation born of the inability of Renamo and the government of Mozambique to agree on any states as mediators. The four individuals chosen: Mario Rafaelli, an Italian Member of Parliament; Jaime Gonçalves, Archbishop of Beira; and Andrea Riccardi and Matteo Zuppi of Sant'Egidio, had been instrumental up to that point in bringing the two sides together. Cameron Hume, a US State Department official who observed the talks, viewed the decision not to rely on individual mediators as a crucial one. These individual mediators, he wrote,

> having no leverage to apply, relied on the skills and qualities of any good mediators: competence, a positive relationship with both parties, creativity, patience, and determination. They persuaded the parties simply by encouraging dialogue, reducing their fears, and making reconciliation seem possible.
> (1994: 145)

In addition, a number of countries, led by the US and Italy, and the UN played crucial roles as observers and facilitators at the talks, pledging resources for various elements of the implementation process and offering consensus drafts at key points in the negotiations.

After initial movement on the structure of the post-war political settlement (competitive elections, the acceptance of Renamo as a political party, and design of the electoral system), talks bogged down as the stakes of the issues addressed and the risks associated with compliance increased. Decisions about the DDR process of military forces and the reconstitution of a national army and police force, for example, were repeatedly delayed.

In an effort to move talks forward, President Mugabe announced that he would host a summit for Dhlakama and Chissano in August 1992 to address the remaining issues. At that meeting—the first ever between Dhlakama and Chissano—they committed to signing a final agreement in early October of the same year. The UN, the US, Portugal, and South Africa, among others, offered expertise, resources, and reassurances that agreements would be enforced. However, they did not impose a structure or an agenda on the peace talks; that was left to the mediators, who represented neither states nor intergovernmental organizations. "The mediators concentrated on developing mutual recognition and respect," writes Hume, "rather than relying on outside leverage to push the parties together" (1994: 146).

However, the mediators resorted to ambiguity in order to get an agreement. The General Peace Agreement (GPA), signed October 1992, left substantial issues open to interpretation during the implementation phase. This proved an effective strategy for securing a formal agreement. However, it increased the risk of failure in the implementation period. "Despite the efforts of the mediators and the observers, especially their military experts, the parties never seriously discussed the practical elements of these documents," Hume noted, going on to say:

> They had little idea how to set up, let alone operate, the complex set of commissions, committees, and subcommittees they insisted on creating to manage these arrangements. They had stipulated a timetable that they could not possibly keep to, even in the first weeks after a ceasefire.
> (1994: 138)

Substance of the agreement

The GPA's seven protocols addressed both the formal resolution of Mozambique's civil war and the establishment of the post-war political system. Essential to the agreement was the prior establishment of a competitive multiparty democracy, structured along majoritarian lines, defined in the 1990 constitution. The agreement called for the demobilization of Renamo's armed forces and the integration of some of these troops into a new, unified national army; the reform or dismantling of a number of government security forces and the restructuring of the police force; the reintegration of Renamo-held territory into a unified state administration; and the holding of the country's first multiparty elections. Provisions for transitional justice— such as a special tribunal or truth commission—were never formally raised by either side, and they are absent from the peace accord. Nor has the question of transitional justice at a national level been an issue of public concern in the years since the end of the war. On a local scale however, customary healing and cleansing practices were often used to reintegrate returning fighters back into their own communities.[5]

The GPA called for the completion of all tasks outlined in the agreement by October 1993, culminating in the country's first multiparty elections that same month. This deadline was later extended to October 1994 due to delays in the early stages of the implementation process.

The agreement was to be overseen and supported by the 6,800-strong UN observation mission (UNOMOZ), with substantial participation by Mozambique's key donor countries: The US, the UK, Portugal, Italy, France, and Germany. The GPA's implementation plan also called for the creation of a series of peace commissions, staffed by representatives of various donor countries and UNOMOZ, and corresponding to the tasks outlined in the peace agreement.

The GPA, however, did not specify a process for police reform or for the reintegration of territories that Renamo held at the end of the war in which it had set up a rudimentary "parallel administration."[6] "The Rome text on civil administration had papered over the problem [of territorial reintegration] with a complicated procedural mechanism, not solved it," Hume notes (1994: 143). The committees on police and state security were slow to be established and accomplished little. Disagreements between the government and Renamo festered for months and stalled implementation, but the ceasefire held. UN Secretary General, Boutros Boutros-Ghali, arrived in Mozambique in October 1993 to convene a meeting between Dhlakama and Chissano, at which they agreed to set aside their differences in the interest of the implementation process. However, security and police force reform satisfactory to both sides remained an unfulfilled goal of the GPA. Thus, while donors provided essential financial and logistical support for the DDR (disarmament, demobilization, and reintegration) of *military* forces, the thorny issues involved in reforming police and paramilitary forces were left to be addressed at a later date. Though neglect of comprehensive security sector reform slowed the reassertion of state authority in a few districts where Renamo's main wartime bases were located, and resulted in a few clashes between government paramilitary police and Renamo supporters, the overall effect on durable peace was minimal for more than 20 years. Yet this issue became one of the sparks that reignited conflict in 2013.

Given extensive involvement by external actors in the peace process during the early 1990s, it is worth asking whether that involvement helped compensate for trust problems that might otherwise have arisen. Beginning with the peace talks in Rome, external actors proved crucial, first as mediators, and then as financial and "moral" guarantors of the process, helping to ensure that each side delivered on its commitments. External actors involved in Mozambique's peace process—mediators who were trusted although partial to one side or the other, a UN peacekeeping operation, and bilateral donors—together successfully played the role of external guarantor for the peace process.

Finally, in part because of the long-standing commitment of major donors to the country, and in part because of the desire by the UN and by major donors involved in Mozambique and elsewhere in "second-generation" peacekeeping operations, external actors had a strong commitment to making Mozambique a success story. This led external actors to commit more resources than they otherwise might have and to monitor implementation of key aspects of the peace agreement closely. In addition, because many of the donors involved in the peace process were also involved in providing long-term economic development aid, external actors remained attentive and proactive in monitoring the terms of Mozambique's peace well beyond the transitional elections in 1994.

Implementation

Post-accord security

Mozambique benefited from the experience of the international community in Cambodia and especially in Angola (1991–1995). In light of the debacle in Angola (when transitional elections were immediately followed by a return to war), the international intervention in Mozambique was larger and costlier. More effort was put into ensuring that demobilization was completed and the new joint army established prior to elections. This supports Lyons' argument in Chapter 2 in this volume regarding the importance of prioritizing demilitarization of politics in the early phase of a peace implementation process. More than 300 military observers and 5,500 troops were sent to Mozambique to monitor and verify the ceasefire; to demobilize and disarm troops from both the government and Renamo armies; and to provide security for the transition process.[7] The mission also included more than 1,000 police observers.

During the implementation period, Renamo enjoyed a wide range of support from international actors, including direct financial support in the form of a UN-administered and donor-funded trust fund to support Renamo's transformation into a political party, with logistical and financial support for Renamo's relocation to Maputo, and the establishment of functioning party offices (the Renamo trust fund). International support also included financial, logistical, and technical support for DDR; training in vocational skills for ex-combatants not integrated into the army, into positions within the party, or into the party as candidates; and political skills training, focused on contesting and monitoring elections.

Mozambique's transition marked a number of precedents in international financial support for war termination. Financial incentives for the troops were accompanied by a hefty trust fund to support Renamo's transformation into a political party, as well as a more modest trust fund to support campaign costs of smaller opposition parties. Renamo's trust fund had a target amount of $19 million, with actual contributions amounting to $17 million. The use of Renamo's trust fund was overseen and audited by the UN. Aldo Ajello, the Special Representative of the UN Secretary General (UN SRSG) in Mozambique, administered the fund and certified on a monthly basis that Renamo was spending it appropriately.[8] Expenditures included substantial cash payments to Dhlakama as leader of Renamo, in exchange for his ongoing participation in the peace process (Synge 1997: 60). For example, out of Renamo's trust fund, $300,000 per month was allocated directly to Dhlakama during the 13 months leading up to the 1994 transitional elections. Ajello viewed these cash payments as essential: "We realized it was critical to keep Dhlakama strongly in control of his organization," Ajello noted, going on to say:

> Any splintering of Renamo into factions would have produced a warlord scenario and severely jeopardized peace. We therefore had to ensure that Dhlakama maintained his status as an African leader. Hence, when his supporters needed help, he needed the ability to dispose of some funds independently; he would have lost face if he had to tell them to approach the UN administrator.
>
> (1999: 637)

Donor support for the formal DDR processes in Mozambique was considered, at the time, both unusually generous and risky. Contrary to usual practice, UNOMOZ did not rely exclusively on UN military observers to oversee disarmament and demobilization. Instead, it created a "Technical Unit," comprising civilians drawn from various donor governments and NGOs, to work with both sides to plan the assembly, registration, and reintegration processes. The creation of the Technical Unit gave UNOMOZ access to people with both substantial technical expertise drawn from experiences elsewhere with DDR and knowledge of local conditions. The Technical Unit also helped facilitate buy-in and coordination from the NGOs and donor governments that delivered some of the essential services for DDR, such as relocation of demobilized soldiers.[9] The use of side payments by conflict mediators is widespread. In Mozambique's peace process, "purchase" was used to elicit cooperation from both Renamo and the government. However, this was a novel role for the UN.[10]

The financial support package created for DDR—ultimately worth $50 million—was also important. The government provided 6 months' salary for each demobilized soldier. This was supplemented by another 18 months' salary paid by a UN trust fund, which was administered by the UNDP and funded by donors. In addition to their salaries, demobilized soldiers were given a 3-month supply of food, seed and tool packages, and access to various vocational training programs, and micro-credit schemes. These support packages would create incentives for individual soldiers to come forward for demobilization even if the parties sought to withhold some troops for contingency purposes.[11] While critics argued that "buying off" soldiers with a compensation package was a costly initiative that would address only the symptoms of the problem, not its root cause, financial incentives to demobilize did take the possibility of unrest by demobilized soldiers out of the equation for the first 2 years of the post-war period.

Suggesting that disarmament and demobilization could not be separated from reintegration, Renamo withheld participation in demobilization until donors followed through, in April 1993, on commitments made in Rome to help fund its transition to a political party.[12] The trust fund was only part of the support package for Renamo's transition, however. There was also the question of the logistics of this transition. According to Protocol III of the GPA, the government, with support from the international community and especially from Italy, would provide support for Renamo's emergence from the bush and its installment in Maputo as a functioning political party.[13]

Renamo and the government interpreted this protocol differently. Roughly 2 weeks after the GPA was signed in October 1992, Renamo members of the Supervision and Control Commission (CSC, the peace commission that had oversight responsibility for the peace process as a whole) had failed to report for duty in Maputo because they lacked transport to Maputo from Renamo's base in the provincial town of Maringue, and lacked acceptable accommodation in Maputo. The government had offered a plane and housing, but Renamo had rejected the latter as inadequate and beneath the status of the group representing the main opposition. Italy had initially provided a house for the Renamo delegation, but Renamo leaders objected to the fact that they were being accommodated by a donor country rather than by the government, as if they were guests in their own country. On December 3, 1992, Boutros-Ghali in his monthly report to the Security Council noted that the absence of an official Renamo delegation in Maputo was seriously impeding the start of the peace process. This seemingly marginal logistical problem was a major impediment to the initial establishment of the monitoring and verification machinery (UN Secretary General 1992).

SRSG Ajello intervened and brokered a compromise: the government provided Renamo with six more houses and paid for transportation and communication. Renamo eventually accepted this offer, along with food, rent and expense money from the Italian government—$65,000 for the month of March 1993 alone—as well as $28,000 worth of office equipment from the British (Mozambiquefile, April 1993). While Renamo's needs were genuine, it is difficult to avoid the conclusion that the organization exploited the issue of poor logistical conditions to gain time while it struggled to find loyal, trusted, and competent personnel to fill its positions on the peace commissions, and to attract legislative candidates to run on the party slate.

Renamo also received ad hoc support from donors to help secure housing, jobs, and transportation for members who had not been incorporated into the formal demobilization and reintegration program, or who were not involved in any of the commissions or selected as candidates. These included, in particular, a number of Renamo's military officers.[14] After the departure of UNOMOZ in 1995, key donors, including the US and the EU, continued to provide reassurances and small-scale financial support to Renamo and intervened often in the political process and to prevail upon both sides to compromise, particularly in the run-up to later elections. Donors provided training programs for parliamentary candidates and for party poll-watchers, funded programs for the development of domestic observer groups, and continued to provide financial support for Renamo.[15] Key bilateral donors, including the Nordic countries, Netherlands, the US, as well as the World Bank, worked closely with the Mozambican government, offering both financing for key transition tasks (including elections, demobilization and reintegration), and more generous terms of support for macro-economic policy reform.[16]

Political settlement

The post-war political settlement was built on the establishment of a multiparty democracy. Like the external actors discussed earlier, the leading domestic political actors considered making the political settlement work a top priority. Moreover, each was relatively well-positioned to act on that basis. In addition to believing that peace was preferable to continued war, Renamo leader, Dhlakama, and Mozambican President, Joaquim Chissano, each had the ability to deliver their followers and to fulfill commitments made at the negotiating table. Renamo was a highly centralized organization that revolved around the personal authority of Afonso Dhlakama. Frelimo was a comparatively well-institutionalized party with a tradition of internal dissent and self-criticism whose history as an armed movement had given it a hierarchical authority structure in which the decisions of the party leader, once made, were not opposed. Neither party faced the problem of divided authority; each party's delegation to the peace talks coordinated closely with its party's leader and had the leader's full confidence. Each party had used support for democracy to bolster its own legitimacy. Toward the end of the war, Renamo sought to portray itself as the democratic, market alternative to a socialist, autocratic Frelimo. The Frelimo government's embrace of multiparty politics in 1990 undermined this claim and wedded both parties to a pro-democracy stance.

In October 1994, Mozambique held its first multiparty elections, marking the final step in the formal transition from war to peace. Frelimo, Renamo, and 12 other parties and coalitions participated. Turnout was close to 90 percent. President Joaquim Chissano was elected to office with 53.3 percent of the vote. Renamo's Afonso Dhlakama trailed, pulling in 33.7 percent. No other candidate polled more than 3 percent. Frelimo also won the most seats in the legislature with 129 of 250 seats. Renamo won 112 seats. Over the next two general elections, in 1999 and 2004, Frelimo would increase its margin of victory in parliament, winning 160 seats to Renamo's 90 in 2004. The vote share for Frelimo presidential candidates also increased with each election. In 2004, Joaquim Chissano stepped down as leader of his party, and Armando Emilio Guebuza became the party's leader and its presidential candidate. He won with 63.7 percent of the vote in 2004. Frelimo and Renamo are still the two major parties. Other opposition parties took only five seats in the legislative election of 2004, and those five had been elected as part of a coalition with Renamo (Manning 2008: 51).

In 2009, the ruling party further entrenched itself in power, winning three-quarters of the legislative and presidential votes. Mozambique's credentials as an "electoral democracy" slipped as the election was marked by a lack of transparency in electoral administration and decisions by purportedly independent electoral authorities that clearly favored the ruling party.[17] In 2013, Renamo's leader, Afonso Dhlakama, took his armed supporters back to the bush, where they began attacking road and rail traffic in the center of the country. Rail transport of coal between Tete and the port at Beira dropped by half, and Rio Tinto, one of the major coal mining concerns operating in the region, briefly suspended coal shipments due to security concerns. The government and Renamo signed a peace agreement in August 2014, but important issues were left unresolved. Among these was the demobilization of Renamo's "residual forces," as they are known, who remain armed in the bush in the central part of the country. Reintegration of these forces into the armed forces and police has been a political football since 1992. Added to that now are nagging questions about provincial autonomy and the distribution of natural resource wealth.

In September 2014, Renamo signed an agreement with the Frelimo government and returned to the democratic process for the 2015 presidential and parliamentary elections. However, tensions continued to simmer as further negotiations between the government and Renamo aimed at integrating Renamo's residual forces into the police and security forces, among other issues, foundered.

Another complicating factor—one fueled by natural resource discoveries in the central provinces from which Renamo draws much of its support—is the question of decentralization. Since 1998 a staged process of decentralization—through the creation of a small number of directly elected municipal governments in selected cities, created at least the theoretical possibility of a diffusion of power between the two main parties and has even given rise to a viable third party, the Movement for Democracy in Mozambique (MDM) (Sitoe and Hunguana 2005). However, the decentralization process has followed a political rather than a technical logic, with opposition forces arguing that cities were selected for municipalization based on the likelihood of an opposition win. And the ruling party has done much to block effective governance in the handful of opposition-ruled municipalities, lending support to this claim. Renamo submitted legislation proposing the creation of elected provincial governments, but this was roundly rejected by the legislature in April 2015.

Armed clashes between Renamo and the government resumed late in 2015. In the early months of 2016, government and Renamo forces repeatedly clashed, driving thousands of refugees across the border into Malawi. The political settlement that contributed to building peace in the first two post-war decades was weakened by, among other things, a failure to fully settle crucial questions about how and to what extent opposition actors—whether as members of the security forces, in political office, or as ordinary citizens—will be able to integrate fully into national life.

Economic reconstruction

Economic recovery played an important part in the construction of a durable peace in Mozambique for two decades. As discussed above, donors helped ease macro-economic reform and austerity requirements attached to aid while they also provided crucial infusions of cash at key points in the process. In the immediate aftermath of the war, Mozambique experienced a dramatic economic recovery, with an average annual economic growth rate of 8 percent between 1996 and 2007.[18] Per capita GDP in 2010 was estimated at US $414, up from the mid-1980s level of US $120.[19] The World Bank reports that, of a total population of 20 million people, 3 million Mozambicans were lifted above the poverty line between 1997 and 2003. Infant and under-five mortality fell by 35 percent in the same period, and primary school enrollment increased by 65 percent. Landmine removal programs, while far from complete, permitted the resumption of transportation networks and agricultural production throughout the country.[20]

In April 2000 and July 2006, the World Bank wrote off $1.3 million of Mozambique's debt. In 2007, the IMF wrote off $153 million of Mozambican debt and the African Development Bank wrote off $370 million.[21] The US and the Paris Club have also repeatedly erased Mozambique's debt, making it easier for the country to borrow more money. While development agencies did not prioritize a development agenda as part of the negotiation strategy as suggested by Wennmann in this volume, donor countries and development agencies played an important role in Mozambique's post-war economic recovery.

More recently, the discovery of significant reserves of coal and gas have driven robust foreign investment in Mozambique. According to the *Financial Times*, foreign direct investment increased 67 percent in 2014 over the previous year, to $9 billion. And the IMF reports that total investment in Mozambique's Rovuma gas fields alone is eventually expected to reach $100 billion. Yet beneath strong economic growth, problems such as poverty, inequality, corruption, and political violence persist. The UNDP Human Development Index ranks Mozambique ninth from the bottom of 187 countries surveyed. Ninety percent of the population still lives on less than $2 per day, and the Multidimensional Poverty Index places Mozambique among the 12 poorest countries in the world. While some argue that early euphoria over the country's natural resource wealth may have been overblown —as gas prices fall, estimated profits are adjusted downwards and investors consider their options—it is nevertheless clear that the prospect of an economic boom fueled by resources located in or near areas that Renamo has tended to claim as its own areas of strong popular support has contributed to the party's decision to try to renegotiate the terms of its inclusion.

Civil society and transnational justice

The role of domestic civil society in securing the peace in Mozambique was limited, due in part to the fact that civil society activity autonomous from the state was only legalized in 1990, just 2 years before the peace agreement was signed. While dozens of organizations mushroomed soon after constitutional reform ended the ruling party monopoly on political and social mobilization, most of these were involved in humanitarian work funded by international donors. However, certain civil society actors were important at distinct points in the peace process. As discussed above, church leaders were influential in urging the government to approach Renamo for talks about peace in the late 1980s. After the war, the CCM and other civil society groups engaged in small projects funded by donors to assist in reintegrating demobilized soldiers into civilian life and to support disabled veterans. In addition, a women's group, Mulheres pela Paz (Women for Peace), organized protests and used their members' network of personal contacts to pressure political actors at certain points when the peace process stalled.

After 1994, as the country settled in to peacetime competitive politics, more rights-oriented groups began to emerge, including AMODEG, the Mozambican Association of Demobilized Soldiers, who sought greater support from the government for reintegration into civilian life. In addition, after the first elections, new electoral legislation enshrined a more robust role for civil society groups in election administration, mandating that the president of the National Elections Commission (CNE) would be drawn from a list of individuals nominated by CSOs. In addition, independent media outlets have proliferated, especially in print media, and independent radio and television outlets have emerged in the capital and some other major cities.

In 2001, the Organization for Conflict Resolution (OREC) was founded by a network of civil society groups. OREC has been instrumental in helping individuals and groups solve conflict in a peaceful manner through mediation and capacity building. Since its founding OREC has mediated in more than 20 various conflicts, including interpersonal, organizational, family, and ex-combatant communities.[22] Beyond mediation OREC has conducted research on the different typologies of violence in different regions. The research has been used by other organizations to improve intervention techniques.

In 2003, fearing a return to violence during the election season, civil society groups formed a partnership called the Election Observatory. The Observatory in coalition with other international agencies such as USAID and the Electoral Institute for Sustainable Democracy in Africa (EISA) was successful in training over 400 civilian election observers to verify election outcomes in the highly contested 2003 local elections.[23] In 2004, they observed the general elections and have continued to do so in every election since. The Observatory has also been very influential in reducing the risk of violence outbreaks in political hot-spots. For example, in Marromeau district, during the 2003 local elections, the National Electoral Commission (NEC) declared the Frelimo candidate the winner and yet independent polling indicated that Renamo had won the seat. The Observatory presented their findings to the NEC who were cooperative and revised their ruling, and in doing so prevented an outbreak of violence. There have been similar incidents in other rural regions. The Observatory has also garnered a reputation of being independent, reliable, and partial with all major political parties, the media, and the general population. Another arm of the Observatory is the Center for Democracy and Development (CEDE) whose main purpose is intervening in elections-related violence. CEDE has been most active in Changara and Montepeuz. These two areas are very important for the survival of quality peace in Mozambique because an outbreak of violence in either area has potential to reignite war in the rest of the country (Mazula and Mbilana 2003).

Though their involvement in the politics of peacemaking was limited initially, CSOs played an important role in social and economic reconstruction. After the war, poverty and disease posed a major threat to the survival of peace especially in rural areas. In response to these challenges, civil society groups led by the church created a wide variety of short and long-term impact projects. For example, the Catholic Church built the Catholic University, which has been made affordable to many low-income students via grants and scholarships from the church. The Catholic Church, in collaboration with the Italian community of Sant'Egidio, also initiated the DREAM project to combat the HIV-AIDS pandemic.

The abundance of small arms among the civilian population in Mozambique posed an additional challenge after the war. The situation in Mozambique was fragile and adding to this instability was the fact that the majority of civilians, including children, remained armed. The UN observation mission (ONUMOZ) had been fairly successful in disarming rebels and assisting their transition into the national army. But more than 190,000 of the collected weapons managed to make their way back into the communities (Forquilha 2005: 623–29). In response to this problem, the CCM launched a disarmament project called Transforming Arms into Ploughshares, or the TAE project in October 1995. The project provided participants with necessities such as food and clothing in exchange for weapons. They also encouraged people to make furniture, for example chairs, and artwork from weapons to generate income that they could then invest in other businesses.

Although the number and engagement of civil society organizations has grown exceptionally since 1992, many challenges remain. According to a Norwegian aid report, the voluntary associations in Mozambique have avoided addressing political processes. The most active organizations are "more likely to disengage the state than seek to hold it responsible" (Rebelo et al. 2002: 9). The spread of social media has given independent newspapers a wider audience and given rise to more open commentary on controversial issues, but internet access remains limited for most people in Mozambique, and print media circulation is also small. Since 2015, intimidation and violence toward those who criticize the government has increased, with a prominent legal scholar assassinated in the street in broad daylight. A leading economist was arrested after posting a letter on Facebook that was critical of the president. All in all, civil society remains weak where it matters—in voicing the political concerns of its constituencies.

Conclusion

What lessons can be drawn from Mozambique for other cases in which external actors seek a negotiated peace? One could argue that the early success of Mozambique was "overdetermined" and that there were so many factors in favor of success that it is impossible to draw generalizations for other cases. This argument is better suited, however, to explaining the end of Mozambique's armed conflict than it is to illuminate why a peace agreement was successfully reached and implemented. Far from being foreordained, the success of the peace agreement rested in large part on the readiness of external actors to be flexible and responsive to problems that arose as the peace process unfolded on the ground, and on capable and committed domestic leadership. While "capable and committed domestic leadership" cannot be replicated in other cases by external actors seeking to promote a negotiated peace, the Mozambican case does yield useful insight into what it takes for external actors to be effective guarantors of peace.

Mozambique offers a clear case where a credible commitment by external actors made a difference, particularly between the end of the war in October 1992 and the transitional elections 2 years later. In addition to providing resources, external actors also maintained a proactive stance that was facilitated, if not required, by the robust mandate of UNOMOZ. In other words, the UN SRSG, Aldo Ajello, along with the ambassadors and other representatives of the US and other key donor countries, the church, and NGOs, served as essential third parties to the peace process. To do so required them to interpret UNOMOZ's mandate liberally; to augment the resources for specific processes, such as elections and DDR; and to coordinate in the provision of resources and monitoring of compliance with the commissions attached to those resources. External actors did not come in with a pre-formed plan that offered resources and security in exchange for a set of actions by the formerly warring parties. Instead, the GPA provided a starting point that left many details to be worked out during the implementation process. Implementing it required external actors to engage in continual innovation, shuttle diplomacy, and resource provision. International actors served on peace commissions, arbitrated disputes about the implementation of the peace accords, and provided assurances, mainly for Renamo, that it was safe to proceed with the demobilization and disarmament of its military wing. In doing so, international actors and especially bilateral donors became directly involved in implementing, funding, and monitoring specific terms of the agreement, and in offering both carrots and sticks to foster compliance.

Also important was the fact that both the government and Renamo had influential and trusted "partial mediators" among the international actors who played a part in securing the peace. These included, for the government, its long-standing donors such as the Nordic countries, as well as newer large donors like the US and the World Bank, who guaranteed financial support for the major tasks the government would have to undertake to fulfill its commitments, such as organizing multiparty elections and integrating Renamo elements into a new armed force. The government also relied upon regional allies, notably the government of Zimbabwe, which offered guarantees of security for the government at different points over the peace process. For Renamo, the Italian Catholic lay community of Sant'Egidio and individuals with links to the Italian government provided Renamo with assurances of material support to help the movement evolve from rebel group to political party. During the implementation period, Renamo looked repeatedly to these donors for guarantees that the donors would not allow the government to back out of its commitments.[24]

In the literature on post-conflict peace operations, there is broad agreement that third-party intervention increases the chances of peace after civil war. In a seminal 1997 article, Barbara Walter applied the concept of the security dilemma, much studied in interstate wars, to the case of civil war. She noted that negotiated agreements to civil war were near impossible without an external guarantor (Walter 1997). In a study of UN peacekeeping operations, Michael Doyle and Nicholas Sambanis noted that "a critical difficulty in negotiating an end to civil wars is that negotiated agreements are often not credible. By that we mean that an agreement must be either self-enforcing or externally enforced so that violators will be punished" (2006: 48). Detailed, formal peace agreements, backed by external actors prepared to guarantee their terms, are most likely to result in definitive peace (Walter 1997; Fortna 2004). Such effective enforcement by international actors is rare, however, due to inadequate information about local context, coordination problems among international actors involved in the intervention, and lack of political will to provide a sufficiently robust and well-resourced mandate for an intervention force.

In Mozambique, the close and continuous involvement of major donors who had local standing with domestic actors, and with resources independent of those allocated for UNOMOZ, allowed the international community in Mozambique to overcome these difficulties. Success in Mozambique required, on the international side, a diversity of actors, each with available resources, monitoring power, and a good working relationship with one or both warring parties. Moreover, these external actors had a stake in the outcome tied to their longer-term interests as donors in Mozambique. The country's aid dependency made both warring parties keenly aware of the "audience costs" that would apply should they renege on the commitments they had made in Rome.[25]

The specifics of the Mozambican case, in sum, tend to confirm research on the conditions that make for effective external guarantors. Effective external guarantors have been, unfortunately, quite rare, because few countries have the combination of committed and capable leaders, together with a diversified community of interational actors willing and able to act in concert, that helped usher Mozambique to peace.

While external actors played an important role to bring peace in Mozambique in 1992, the active role of external actors gradually diminished once the post-conflict elections were held in 1994. In the two decades that followed, Mozambican politics developed a pattern in which elections, won by Frelimo, were followed by opposition allegations of fraud and incompetence, which were in turn followed by face-saving consultations between the leadership of both sides. These tended not to change the outcomes of the political process, but created a sense of inclusion for Renamo in national political life. After 2004, President Guebuza's administration ended this pattern of consultation and negotiation even as the ruling party's electoral advantage grew. By 2009, Frelimo held more than two-thirds of the seats in the legislature and its president was elected with 75 percent of the vote. Increasing political exclusion for the opposition coincided with the onset of significant natural resource discoveries. The result was a return to conflict and a return to demands—like full integration of Renamo fighters—not fully implemented from the last peace process, as well as a quest by Renamo for greater political and economic inclusion.

Notes

1. The history is described in Manning 2002: 55–67.
2. See also Manning 2008.
3. See Barnes 1998.
4. For an account of Sant'Egidio's involvement, see Bartoli 1999: 245–274.
5. The purpose of such ceremonies was not so much reconciliation with former enemies as it was to cleanse and restore the virtue of those who had killed and to placate the spirit of the killer's victims.
6. These territories were concentrated mainly in Manica and Sofala provinces, in the center of the country.
7. For a comparison of the UN missions in Angola and Mozambique, see Jett 2001.
8. See Manning 2002, and Ajello 1999.

9. For details on DDR, see Ajello 1999, Jett 2001, Manning 1997, and Synge 1997.
10. For more on side payments in peace negotiations, see Rothchild 1997.
11. Within months of the establishment of the demobilization camps, "the troops already registered [in the demobilization camps] loudly demanded their benefits, and those held back from assembly became determined not to miss out," notes Richard Synge. "With the help of the Reintegration Support Scheme (RSS), demobilization succeeded in flushing out most of the organized combatants in the country" (1997: 30).
12. See Manning 1997: 193–201.
13. Protocol III.7, General Peace Agreement of Mozambique.
14. The US embassy, for example, provided training for one Renamo general to become a driver. Renamo had a fair number of military officers who either lacked the necessary skills or education to serve in political positions or in high-ranking positions in the Mozambican army, and who were not demobilized prior to the 1994 elections.
15. The European Commission delegation in Mozambique, for example, helped Renamo pay off some of its campaign debt from the 1994 elections. Swiss Cooperation purchased around 25 flats for Renamo in Maputo. See Manning 2002.
16. See Manning and Malbrough 2010.
17. For details, see Manning 2010.
18. Data from IMF on Mozambique, see https://tradingeconomics.com/.
19. Mozambique country report, US Department of State. Accessed at www.state.gov/outofdate/bgn/mozambique/191089.htm on April 13, 2012.
20. World Bank, *Mozambique Country Brief*, September 2008. Accessed at http://web.worldbank.org/WBSITE/EXTERNAL/COUNTRIES/AFRICAEXT/MOZAMBIQUEEXTN/0,,menuPK:382142~pagePK:141132~piPK:141107~theSitePK:382131,00.html on February 13, 2009.
21. https://tradingeconomics.com/mozambique/government-debt-to-gdp?continent=g20.
22. See Murdock and Zunguza 2010.
23. USAID Mozambique news story "Strengthening democracy in Mozambique." Accessed at www.usaid.gov/stories/mozambique/ss_mozambique_election.pdf.
24. See Hume 1994 and Vines 1991.
25. For the impact of "audience costs" on warring parties in interstate conflicts, see Fortna 2004.

References

Ajello, Aldo. "Mozambique: Implementation of the 1991 Peace Agreement." In Chester A. Crocker, Fen Osler Hampson, and Pamela Aall, Eds. *Herding cats: Multiparty mediation in a complex world*. United States Institute for Peace, 1999: 615–642.

Barnes, Sam. *Humanitarian aid coordination during war and peace in Mozambique, 1985–1995*. No. 7. Nordic Africa Institute, 1998.

Bartoli, Andrea. "Mediating Peace in Mozambique: The Role of the Community of Sant'Egidio." In Chester A. Crocker, Fen Osler Hampson, and Pamela Aall, Eds. *Herding cats: Multiparty mediation in a complex world*. United States Institute for Peace, 1999: 245–274.

Doyle, Michael W. and Nicholas Sambanis. *Making war and building peace: United Nations peace operations*. Princeton University Press, 2006.

Forquilha, Albino. "Transforming Arms into Ploughshares: The Christian Council of Mozambique." In Paul Van Tongeren, Malin Brenk, Marte Hellema, and Juliette Verhoeven. *People building peace II: Successful stories of civil society*. Lynne Rienner, 2005.

Fortna, Virginia Page. *Peace time: Cease-fire agreements and the durability of peace*. Princeton University Press, 2004.

Hume, Cameron. *Ending Mozambique's war: The role of mediation and good offices*. US Institute of Peace, 1994.

Jett, Dennis C. *Why peacekeeping fails*. Palgrave Macmillan: 2001.
Manning, Carrie Lynn. *Democratic transition in Mozambique, 1992–1995: Beginning at the end?* University of California, Berkeley, 1997.
Manning, Carrie. *The politics of peace in Mozambique: Post-conflict democratization, 1992–2000.* Praeger, 2002.
Manning, Carrie. *The making of democrats: Elections and party development in postwar Bosnia, El Salvador, and Mozambique*. Palgrave Macmillan, 2008.
Manning, Carrie. "Mozambique's slide into one-party rule." *Journal of Democracy* 21, no. 2 (2010): 151–165.
Manning, Carrie, and Monica Malbrough. "Bilateral donors and aid conditionality in post-conflict peacebuilding: the case of Mozambique." *The Journal of Modern African Studies* 48, no. 1 (2010): 143–169.
Mazula, Brazao and Guilherme Mbilana. "O Papel das Organizacoes da Sociedade Civil na Prevencao, Gestao, e Transformacao de conflictos: A Experiencia de Mocambique." Paper presented at the Catholic University of Angola, November 27, 2003.
"Mozambiquefile, April 1993." *Mozambique Peace Process Bulletin*, no. 2, March 1993.
Murdock, Janet, and A. Zunzuga. "The cumulative impacts of peacebuilding in Mozambique." *Reflecting on peace practice program-cumulative impacts case study*. CDA Collaborative Learning Projects (2010).
Rebelo, Pamela, Nanna Thue, Lise Stensrud and Sissel Idland. *Study of future Norwegian support to civil society in Mozambique*. NORAD Report, 2002. Accessed October 1, 2017 at www.norad.no/en/toolspublications/publications/2009/study-of-future-norwegian-support-to-civil-society-in-mozambique/.
Rothchild, Donald S. *Managing ethnic conflict in Africa: Pressures and incentives for cooperation*. Brookings Institution Press, 1997.
Sitoe, Eduardo and Carolina Hunguana. *Decentralisation and sustainable peace-building in Mozambique: Bringing the elements together again*. Centro de Estudos da Democraçia e Desenvolvimento (CEDE), October 2005. Accessed at http://iepala.es/IMG/pdf/unpan031032.pdf.
Synge, Richard. *Mozambique: UN peacekeeping in action, 1992–94*. US Institute of Peace Press, 1997.
UN Secretary General. "Report of the Secretary-General on UNOMOZ." United Nations: S/24892, December 3, 1992.
Vines, Alex. *Renamo: Terrorism in Mozambique*. Indiana University Press, 1991.
Walter, Barbara F. "The critical barrier to civil war settlement." *International Organization* 51, no. 3 (1997): 335–364.

Conclusion

17
DEVELOPING QUALITY PEACE
Moving forward

Peter Wallensteen and Madhav Joshi

In this book we have demonstrated the value of defining and delimitating the concept of *quality peace* based on theoretical work and thorough investigation. In addition to the framework chapter, this volume consists of 15 empirical contributions, 11 of which focus on the five dimensions that have been identified as contributing to quality peace, and four case studies where the simultaneous operation of the five dimensions are analyzed. In this concluding chapter, we outline the way forward in the study of quality peace.

The definition of quality peace provided in this volume is applied to post-war conditions. All the conflict situations considered here are internal wars (whether about government power or territorial control) that ended through a peace agreement. Following the signing of an agreement, the accord implementation process provides us with a yardstick by which to measure the quality of the resulting peace. If all parties adhere to the peace agreement when the war ended, it is assumed there would be an improvement of post-war conditions. This, then, approaches what we mean by "quality peace": conditions of mutual respect, provisions of security, and an expectation that these conditions are stable enough to be sustained. The five dimensions that we highlight in this volume provide both a theoretical explanation and some empirical evidence of the conditions in which some post-war societies could excel in quality peace measures while others could significantly lag behind.

In the 2015 volume by Peter Wallensteen, *Quality Peace: Peacebuilding, Victory and World Order*, a theoretical background is provided for the discussion about the conditions that might prevent the recurrence of war in relations that ended a conflict through a victory or a peace agreement. It could build this on a systematic comparison of these two outcomes, whichever way the war was ended, and identify the three factors just mentioned as crucial and identifiable for wars within between states and major powers as well (Wallensteen 2015). In this volume, we have focused on the conditions after civil wars that ended with peace agreements, which should be optimal conditions for continued and deepened quality peace.

Thus, this particular volume has a closer focus. It deals with internal wars that largely concern government control. It departs from a theoretical expectation (as outlined in Chapter 1) that there are five crucial dimensions of quality peace. These were identified based on earlier contributions and as well as theoretical considerations. They were illuminated with observations from the data collected by the Uppsala Conflict Data Program (UCDP) at Uppsala University, Sweden, and the Kroc Institute Peace Accords Matrix (PAM) project at the University of Notre Dame, USA, as well as cases studies and personal experiences from peace processes. The five dimensions include post-war security, governance, economic reconstruction, reconciliation and justice, and civil society. The factors were identified one by one, and without a specific assumption or theory about their interconnections. An understanding of their links to one another was meant to arise as part of the writing process. Thus, two workshops were convened at the Kroc Institute, in November 2010 and May 2012, and the studies were updated in 2016.

As expected, the authors' writings in this volume reflect their diverse backgrounds. There are important differences in their analyses. However, there are also basic agreements that need first to be spelled out before looking at these variations. Let us make clear, however, that the diversity that is evident in this volume is what makes it valuable. It stems from the fact that contributors do have different theoretical and empirical perspectives, as well as epistemological starting points, all still compatible within the framework of this book.

Furthermore, there is a fascinating variation in the implementation of agreements. The PAM scores for the conflicts included here demonstrate this very clearly. In the contribution by Manning and Dendere, it is argued that the agreement on Mozambique has a high degree of implementation and that this was due to the commitment of international actors. However, also other agreements have a strong implementation score, according to PAM. For the cases of Northern Ireland, Mozambique and El Salvador the implementation scores are in the range of 90 percent. A contrast is Cambodia with only 73 percent (Joshi et al. 2015).

In addition, there is diversity with respect to the type of conflicts, although they are all internal wars and most are traditional civil wars. The exceptions are nevertheless important, notably the Northern Ireland conflict. In terms of implementation, however, there is not likely to be a difference in this regard. There is also the diversity of the peace agreements themselves, which vary in important respects. The implementation score is but one way to gauge their "quality." It would also be possible to determine if the peace accords actually cover the items that would be important for the future of the peace.

The five dimensions

A first observation is that the 11 contributions dealing with the five dimensions individually find them to be significant in determining quality peace. However, authors presenting case studies provide a more mixed picture. This may be natural when the authors weigh the local factors in the post-war processes. Thus, the case studies provide the real test to the importance of the five dimensions. Contrasting the cases is an instructive way to consolidate findings and point to the future.

The case studies agree on the importance of the political settlement (the governance dimension) and the security situation (reduction in political violence and disarmament measures) in determining quality peace while the other three dimensions have a more varied record. As mentioned, many of the conflicts in this sample deal with governance issue; thus, it makes sense to see that the way this particular dimension is handled gives clues to the future. Obviously many peace agreements regulate relations on an elite level. Mac Ginty points to the importance of also observing governance on the local and everyday level, which remains a challenge.

Also, the matters of security are basic as it means the return to law, order, and predictability in terms of personal physical safety. However, the ways of achieving this varies between cases and in the collected experience. Theoretically, it ranges from complete military integration to full disarmament, under the auspices of international peacekeeping. The variations reported here are less dramatic than the potential suggests.

Thus, these two dimensions emerge in all the cases as important, and that makes the three remaining ones more challenging as they stretch our thinking beyond the traditional and obvious. How do they fare in the general studies and in the case studies?

Surprisingly, the case studies largely find that reconciliation processes are either of lesser importance in determining quality peace or neglected in the peace implementation process. In fact, national reconciliation processes were completely absent in Mozambique, and remain contested in cases, such as Cambodia, El Salvador, and Northern Ireland. Would this imply that the issue of reconciliation is of a global value that is not equally important in all local contexts? Or does it say the opposite: the fact that it was not addressed in some local situations suggests a continued fragility in some of the cases?

The civil society dimension received more emphasis in some of the case studies. The significance of civil society was generally seen to be low in the peace negotiation processes but gained more importance after an agreement and end to fighting. This observation is derived from the four case studies. Furthermore, civil society's role in post-settlement periods is important as Guardado et al. discuss in their chapter's concluding remarks. Although the authors do not directly test the dimension of civil society as a contributing factor for sustaining the peace, their theoretical underpinnings assumes a significant role of civil society actors and organizations at the local level for mediating the relationship between government provision of services and peace in the country. The authors contrast these dimensions with the traditional "top-down" factors associated with power-sharing and peacekeeping. Again, we face a conclusion that seems contradictory and again we need to ask whether it illuminates something regarding the quality of the post-war peace. Certainly, a vigorous civil society would be able to signal early warnings for potential renewed tensions. Furthermore, there could be a temporal difference. Civil society is more important in the 2000s than in the 1990s, which is the period on which our case studies are based (Anheier 2004; Edwards 2011).

The factors of economic reconstruction were obviously significant in the four case studies, and several of them report a remarkable, positive economic growth following the agreements. The most marked example was Mozambique, which had a high and constant growth rate for almost 20 years. Northern Ireland, on the other hand, while faring somewhat better than Britain as such, was badly hit by the recession from 2008 onwards. Cambodia's economic growth took place in ways that were more controlled by the governing circles (going from being "roving" to "stationary bandits," as said in the contribution), which means with a long-term interest in the country's development in ways that would line their pockets. El Salvador's economy also improved and poverty was somewhat reduced, but its progress was hardly on par with other South American countries.

Thus, among the five dimensions, two strongly emerge as significant for *durable* peace: governance and security. Both of them could be described as traditional factors. It still gives us reason to ponder on the *quality* of that peace, which is more likely to emerge from the way the economy is mastered, popular participation can be expressed, and the way recent history is approached. In particular, it raises questions of relative importance as well as sequences: what comes first and with what weight?

Sequences and weight of the dimensions

These investigations suggest that security and governance belong to the primary issues that are tackled after a peace agreement. However, it is hard to say that there is a simple sequence where these dimensions always "come first." On the contrary, many things have to take place almost simultaneously and in ways, which support each other. It is illustrated by the dimension of economic growth, which certainly is significant, but may be particularly important when we discuss *quality* peace; basic material requirements of life get sufficient attention. Several authors underline the importance of the peace dividend and of ensuring that promises of improved living conditions are met. The two chapters on the economic dimension of quality peace differ somewhat on which strategy is preferred for jumpstarting economic development: international assistance or local business entrepreneurship? It may be of less significance, which one is emphasized, as long as there is some success to report. However, during negotiations and in the period immediately following the peace agreement, development funds are more useful and often more readily available, as exemplified in the case of Mozambique.

Examining the contribution of civil society to quality peace is somewhat challenging because there was no vibrant non-governmental society during some of peace processes that were studied. In the post-Cold War period, there has been a remarkable growth in the number of CSOs, whether local, national, or international. Such organizations may raise issues that many governments would prefer to neglect in the political process, such as reconciliation and truth. These are also novel concerns that were not part of peace processes 25 years ago; for example, the importance of justice and the rise of civil society are recent developments that may support each other. Not only has this resulted in the creation of the ICC but has also led to investigations of crimes that occurred many years ago. One example is Kenya, where actions by British soldiers in the war against the uprisings (the Mau-Mau rebellion) in the 1950s have led to court cases in the 2010s that acknowledged wrongdoing. These developments suggest that both civil society and justice/reconciliation should remain part of what we mean by quality peace, despite the fact that they may not have been important in the older peace processes selected for this study.

There are also some challenges for how investigations into war crimes should be carried out. The findings on retraumatization of victims suggest the need for counseling as part of any public reconciliation or truth-telling process. Such a concern can also become an argument against the benefit of such processes. For instance, in the case of Northern Ireland there is a reluctance to allow public access to archives as it may open old wounds. Politically, this may be seen as unproblematic in the short term, particularly as reports suggest that tensions have eased between the two population groups. However, waiting 50 or 60 years for some element of truth and justice, as evidenced by Kenya, is likely to be untenable and increasingly unacceptable. The time has come for political leaders to confront difficult issues such as reconciliation and justice processes, or refusing to undergo such processes, as these may have important effects on the quality of future relations between groups and individuals.

The same may be true for the issue of security equality. None of the case studies have taken up this issue; however, security for men and women should, of course, be a concern for society as a whole. Quality peace cannot be achieved if there is only protection for former warriors and financial incentives for them to find jobs. There must also be concern for security issues in other sectors of society and an effort to address the needs of all soldiers and victims.

Thus, we conclude that all the five dimensions are significant, but that the temporal sequence and the interlinkages need to be explored. Some of them are focusing on agency (e.g., the role of civil society), other on substance (type of economic growth, form of reconciliation), others are more structural (constitutions, disarmament). The complexities abound and should be addressed in further work.

Methodological requirements

The different contributions vary with respect to methodology. This is a necessity for a novel concept like quality peace. For instance, the contribution by Mac Ginty is more conceptual, while Guardado et al. pursues a statistical study of one element with respect to local governance. It points out that the data requirements for dealing with the dimensions of quality peace we have introduced here are more demanding than what is readily available today. Thus, a further development of data collection is necessary for moving deeper into the dimensions of quality peace. And indeed, to demonstrate this is also one of the purposes of this volume: there is more insight today, but the resources available to the scholarly community are still far from meeting such demands.

There are also another methodological challenges. The further down the timeline one goes, the more difficult it becomes to establish a direct (and sometimes even an indirect) connection between events happening in a post-conflict country and the implementation of a peace agreement. Thus, there is a need for theoretical elaboration. An example was just mentioned: the issue of reconciliation. Political and strategic concerns may motivate a postponement of activities to deal with crimes of different sorts, associated with the previous regime or with the war. However, the issues are likely to linger and affect the way the post-war society is constructed. But if there is no return to this issue, the dangers of romanticizing a country's history and its earlier leaders may become apparent. The evils will be overlooked and only achievements considered positive reproduced. For instance, Russia's remembrance of Stalin stands in stark contrast to Germany's approach to the crimes of Hitler. Similarly, Finland continues to have difficulties in confronting the atrocities of the civil war in 1918. It is a methodological challenge, but, as a distinct issue area, matters of reconciliation may have a coherence transcending decades. The study of memory needs to be part of the search for quality peace.

Other dimensions have such coherence across time, such as the dynamics of economics. The time dimension is particularly interesting in view of the time lines suggested for economies to recover discusses in terms of 15–30 years (World Bank 2011). Under which circumstances, one may ask, will it be possible for states to maintain growth during such long periods of time? The results may not be apparent until after many years, giving rise to popular discontent and elite infighting. It points to the problem of regime coherence in the meantime, i.e., the ability of leading circles to maintain sufficient consensus on a particular policy for a sufficiently long time. In Mozambique and Cambodia, for instance, the same party has retained political power for the entire period after the peace agreement. It adds to such an economic coherence. Obviously, this element among the quality peace dimension may, thus, stand in conflict with the one of governance, or at least democratic forms of governance. El Salvador saw a sharp political shift approximately 15 years into its post-war recovery, when a rebel leader was elected. Northern Ireland has had some shifts in the governing coalition. This is a good test of the democratic strength of the society. Mozambique and Cambodia still face such a transition. There are recent events in both countries that challenge the ability of these societies to manage this in a peaceful way. Indeed, having the same party and leaders at the helm for several decades is likely to cement authoritarianism and stimulate corruption—factors that will undermine the legitimacy of a regime, but perhaps also of the entire post-accord political order.

The studies reported in this book demonstrate that the notion of quality peace begs new and important questions, as well as raises challenges of measurement.

Northern Ireland is one of the most researched conflict processes and there is, seemingly, an abundance of data that can be used for studies. However, it is also important to look at other contexts if we want to draw general conclusions.

Forward

To move forward in understanding quality peace, there is a need to sharpen the definitions, evaluate whether the five dimensions comprise the most important elements of quality peace, locate sources of information, and above all, make clear that such information is actually relevant for our purposes, as is pointed out by Mac Ginty in his contribution. Indeed, quality peace may allow more pluralistic thinking about what "quality" could mean in different societies, from The Solomon Islands to Northern Ireland, and from El Salvador to Cambodia.

For how long should a peace process be seen as active? PAM has used the criterion of a 10-year cut-off, but indeed peace agreements are documents with a longer life, even if references to them gradually become more ceremonial than real. If we want to understand and explain the longevity of peace, it might be more important to have qualitative criteria, such as whether the agreement stands the test of dramatic political changes or not, e.g., change of government, new security challenges, discomforting revelations about the past, serious economic crises, etc.

In general, these studies point to a longer time period than 10 years. Economic recovery may take 15–30 years; reconciliation processes may need a similar time horizon. The same is true for governance: a truly anchored political system is one that can withstand repeated changes of government in a substantial way (going from left to right, for instance). Civil society needs time to develop and solidify its legitimacy. Similarly, the sense of security will take time to root, the longer a war has gone on. The revolutionary change is the one when the actors no longer conceive of solving internal political disputes with weapons. This means a transition from a society where power and security is a zero-sum game to one where there is growth for all with security for all. It may be at least a generational matter, perhaps even longer if there are temporary relapses into violence. It has been done, and it can be repeated. In Mozambique, Renamo briefly returned to armed conflict in 2013 out of frustration of Frelimo's dominance in post-accord years. Likewise the 2015 political crisis tested Burundi's peace process as the president targeted violence against opponents that objected to constitutional changes that would allow the incumbent to run for a third term.

Certainly, the building of quality peace needs support. The regional setting is important. Regions with considerable experience of recent violence are likely to be unsettled for a considerable period of time. Regions that have left violence may have a greater chance of not relapsing. An instructive comparison may be Central America versus the Arab World, or East Asia before and after 1980.

The study of quality peace is a large agenda that involves many dimensions. The five we have highlighted here belong to the core. It is also important to have a long-term perspective, even beyond the 20 years applied in some of these studies. This provides for theoretical challenges (how do factors relate to one another?), practical questions (in which sequence should they most appropriately be tackled?), and for historical awareness (what is the time perspectives researchers and practitioners should apply?). The importance of the topic justifies asking large questions and finding at least partial answers.

References

Anheier, Helmut K. *Civil society: Measurement, evaluation, policy*. Earthscan. 2004.
Edwards, Michael (Ed.). *The Oxford handbook on civil society*.Oxford University Press, 2011.
Joshi, Madhav, Jason Michael Quinn, and Patrick M. Regan. "Annualized implementation data on comprehensive intrastate peace accords, 1989–2012." *Journal of Peace Research* 52, no. 4 (2015): 551–562.
Wallensteen, Peter. *Quality peace: Peacebuilding, victory and world order*. Oxford University Press, 2015.
World Bank. *World development report 2011: Conflict, security, and development*. World Bank, 2011.

INDEX

absence of war 4, 8, 197
Aceh (Indonesia) 111
Adams, Gerry (Northern Ireland) 235
Afghanistan 112–113, 166, 169, 174;
  and the United States 65
Africa 37, 84, 87, 122, 166, 263, 267, 269;
  see also specific areas and countries
aggression 121, 131, 132
Ajello, Aldo (Mozambique) 39, 263–265, 270
aid 93, 180, 186, 259, 267, 270, 272;
  foreign 78, 115–116, 169, 179, 258;
  as an incentive 113–114, 182–183, 242;
  military 181
Albania *see* Kosovo Albanians
Americas 84, 87
Amin, Idi (Uganda) 131
Amnesty 19, 123–130, 135, 151, 186, 188–191, 199, 203–204, 227
anarchy 32
ANC (African National Congress, South Africa) 124
Angola 7, 38–39, 262–263; and the United Nations 39
apartheid (South Africa) 68, 124, 129, 258;
  see also South Africa
Arab Spring 172
Appleby, Scott xvi
Arab World 283
ARENA (Alianza Nacional Republicana) 179, 185, 189, 215–216, 223–224, 227
Argentina 123

armed conflict i, xv, 4–20, 31, 35, 44–48, 55, 75–76, 108–110, 112, 137, 169–171, 174, 179, 220;
  outcomes 79, 116, 135, 164–166, 171, 203, 212, 270
armies 197, 198, 263
arms 35–36, 110, 137, 206, 220, 269;
  see also weapons
assassination 123, 181–187
audience costs 272
Australia 49, 137–139
authoritarian regimes 142, 172, 213, 282
autonomy 81–82, 97–100, 106, 199, 250, 266
available resources 272

Baghdad (Iraq) *see* Iraq
balance of power 31, 37, 123, 199
Balkans 4, 64, 68; Balkans War 104, 124
Beira (Mozambique) 259–260, 266
Belfast Agreement (Northern Ireland) 236–237, 240–243, 248–249
BLDP (Buddhist Liberal Democratic Party) 198–199, 203
Bolivia 142
bombs 105, 244
borders 105, 199, 267
Bosnia-Herzegovina 38, 45, 63, 72, 166
boundaries 153
Boutros-Ghali, Boutros (UN) 262, 265
boycotts 199, 203
Britain 138, 280
Burundi 101, 283

business 15, 61, 64, 93–106, 108, 201, 216, 223, 226–227, 235, 240–242, 259, 270, 280

capitulation 168
Caprioli, Mary 45
Carter, Jimmy (USA) 181
Castillo, Graciana del 14
casualties of war 153, 212; see also victims
causes of war 75
CAVR (Commission for Reception, Truth and Reconciliation) 141–3
CBOs (Community-Based Organizations) 204, 206
CCM (Christian Council of Mozambique) 259, 268, 270
CDD (Community-Driven Development) 78
CDR (Community-Driven Reconstruction) 78
CEDE (Center for Democracy and Development) 269
center (of a state) 48, 138, 201, 266
Central America 18, 68, 181, 213, 218–219, 221
Chechnya (Russia) 64
China, People's Republic of 151, 200
Chissano, Joaquim (Mozambique) 259–260, 262, 265–266
CIVICUS 239
civilians 8, 12, 114, 128, 165, 171, 174, 179, 182, 264, 268; and casualties 47, 178, 182, 188, 198; and police 221–223; and political process 121, 123, 190, 213, 269; see also victims
civil rights 152, 245
civil society organizations (CSO) xv, 17, 37, 88, 167–168, 173–174, 204–206, 208, 213, 225–226, 240, 268–269, 280
Clinton, Bill (USA) 64
Cold War xv, 6–8, 72, 76, 84, 178, 197, 202, 212–215, 280
Collier, Paul 8, 77, 95
Colombia 221
Colonialism 139
communism 121, 182
compensation 139–140, 264
CONARA (National Commission for Restoration of Areas) 186
conciliation 149
confidence-building measures 69
conflict dynamics 32
conflict management 63

conflict resolution 21, 55, 63, 76, 80–81, 122–123, 136, 246, 269
conflict termination xv, 8, 75, 78–80, 121, 123–125
confrontation 131, 204
Congo, Democratic Republic 45, 54, 111, 142, 166, 171
consensus 15, 114, 213, 226–227, 246, 253, 260, 282; see also Washington Consensus
COPAZ (Comisión Nacional para la Conslidación de la Paz) 36–37
corruption 3, 97, 106, 108, 189, 208, 217, 219, 268, 282
Costa Rica 182, 188
Côte d'Ivoire see Ivory Coast
coup, military (coup d'état) 123, 137, 139, 200, 206
courts 122, 124, 131, 186, 203, 222, 228, 245
COVAFGA (Cooperative de Valorisation des Fruites de Gakenke) 101, 102
CPA (Comprehensive Peace Agreement) 3, 4, 7
CPDN (National Debate for Peace (El Salvador)) 183–184
CPP (Cambodian People's Party) 198–200, 203–204, 206–208
crime 47, 53, 171, 185, 187–191, 206, 212, 219–223, 243
Croatia 6, 130
CRPs (Community Reconciliation Processes) 141–142
CSC (Supervision and Control Commission (Mozambique)) 264
CSO (Civil Society Organization) 17, 37, 88, 167–168, 173–174, 204–205, 208, 213, 225–226, 240, 268–269, 280
Cyprus 163, 166, 171

Darby, John xv–xvi, 9–11, 16–17, 109, 148
Davenport, Christian 157
DDR (Disarmament, Demobilization, Reintegration) 45, 69, 71, 110, 260, 262–264
debt 223, 258, 267
decentralization 207, 267
de facto/de jure recognition 70, 188, 199, 207
defeat 39, 105, 136, 150, 202, 206; see also victory
defense 257
demilitarization 12, 20, 29, 31, 35–40, 263
demobilization 11, 31, 35, 39, 45, 154, 171, 198, 261–236, 271

Democratic Unionist Party (DUP, Northern Ireland) 152, 156, 235, 245
democratization 6, 37, 122–124, 207, 212–230
development agencies 15, 108–117, 267
devolution 207, 235–236, 249–253
Dhlakama, Afonso (Mozambique) 258–260, 262–266
dialogue 109, 168–170, 174, 179, 182–185, 190–191, 226–227, 237, 249, 260
dictatorship 178
Diehl, Paul 5
dignity 10, 99, 106, 140, 188
diplomacy 66, 109
disarmament 7, 37, 45, 76–78, 81, 83, 139, 171, 198, 264, 270–271, 279, 281
discrimination 44, 55, 70–72, 101, 153
dissidents 130
Doyle, Michael W. 7, 46, 76–77, 271
drought 258
Dublin (Ireland) 240
DUP (Democratic Unionist Party) 152, 156, 235, 245, 248, 251

East Asia 283; *see also* Northeast Asia
Eastern Europe 104, 163
East Timor 6, 48–49, 94, 141
ECCC (Extraordinary Chamber in the Court of Cambodia) 202, 204
economic crises 283
economic development 15, 77–78, 109, 111, 115–116, 128, 171, 179, 184, 207, 242, 262
economic growth 3, 8, 14–15, 19, 93, 96, 101, 185, 197, 201, 205, 208, 224, 240–242, 267–268, 280–281
economic reconstruction xvi, 3, 11, 14–15, 18, 93, 197, 200, 212, 223, 240, 252, 253, 257, 267–269, 278–280
economic recovery 8, 108–117, 267
ECOWAS (Economic Community for West African States) 167
education 69, 95, 99, 102, 111, 154, 169, 188–189, 200, 205–208, 236, 240, 242, 248–249, 253
Egypt 94
EISA (Electoral Institute for Sustainable Democracy in Africa) 269
elites 11, 68, 75–76, 78–85, 116, 129, 184, 188, 201, 223, 250
El Salvador 3–4, 6, 18–19, 36–38, 72, 111, 164, 170, 178–192, 212–230, 278, 282–283; *see also* FMLN
emergency 258

escalation 49
ethnic minorities 15, 71
Europe 84, 122
European Commission 240
European Union (EU) 226
exclusion 71, 110, 113, 183, 185–187, 215, 220, 225, 250, 272
expectations 5, 10, 30–32, 35–39, 62, 76, 81, 109, 113, 115, 122, 127, 129, 136, 143, 145, 153–154, 199, 277–278

facilitators 260
Fearon, James. D. 78, 237
Finland 282
FMLN (Farabundo Martí National Liberation Front, El Salvador) 3, 18, 36, 179, 181–191, 212–216, 222–223, 226–227
fragility 112, 115, 166, 279
France 261
Frelimo (Front for Liberation of Mozambique) 19, 38, 257–259, 266, 269, 272, 283; *see also* Mozambique
FUNCINPEC (Front uni national pour un Cambodge indépendant, neutre, pacifique et coopératif) 198–199, 200, 203, 206
FUSADES (The Salvadoran Foundation for Economic Development) 179, 185

gacaca (Rwanda) 123, 131
Galtung, Johan 9, 13
GDP 97, 102, 201, 267
gender 12–13, 40, 44–48, 54–55, 71, 125, 136–137, 164, 174, 205, 208
gender equality 48, 55, 205
genocide 101–102, 122–124, 131, 204
geography 98
Germany 150, 155, 261, 282
Ghana 94, 129
Globalization 67, 188
Good Friday Agreement (1998) 19, 127, 152, 242
Gonçalves, Don Jaime 259–260
GPA (General Peace Agreement, Mozambique) 261
Great Britain *see* Britain
Guatemala 38, 94, 111, 123, 166–167, 171, 221, 232n32
guilt 3, 47, 150, 204, 245

hegemony 250
HET (Historical Enquiries Team (in Northern Ireland)) 245–247

288　Index

Hitler, Adolf (Germany) 282
Höglund, Kristine 4–5, 10–11, 46
Honduras 94, 182, 221
Honiara (Solomon Islands) 138–139
Hungary 130

ICC (International Criminal Court) 124, 150
ICTY (International Criminal Tribunal for the Former Yugoslavia) 123–124
identity 2, 55, 97, 136, 153, 168, 217, 250
IDPs (Internally Displaced Persons) 102, 183
illegality 126
IMF (International Monetary Fund) 93, 100, 258, 267–268
implementation of peace agreements xv, 110, 115, 174
impunity 16, 122, 125–126, 132, 186–191, 202–203, 218
incompatibility 81, 83–85, 90
independence 49, 51, 93, 130, 138–139, 141, 202, 213–215, 245, 258
indigenous people 71, 138
Indonesia 48–49, 51, 94, 141, 143
injustice 45, 109, 127, 202; social 9
integration 77, 81, 83, 156, 190, 247–248, 257, 261, 272, 279
integrity 100, 157, 206
INTERFET (International Force in East Timor) 49, 51–52, 54
internal conflicts 151, 258
international community 4, 48, 54, 66, 114, 131, 181, 199–204, 223, 235, 262, 264, 272
international organization 86, 167, 226
international relations 156
internet access 270
intervention 4, 61, 65–67, 76–78, 115, 137–139, 148, 168, 170, 184, 263, 269, 271
IRA (Irish Republican Army) 152, 246
Iraq 113
Israel 62–64, 105, 166, 168, 171
Italy 260–261, 264
IUDOP (University Institute for Public Opinion) 182–183, 228, 229
Ivory Coast (Côte d'Ivoire) 4

Japan 48, 138, 150–151, 155
justice, transitional xvi, 11, 15–19, 45, 119–160, 197, 208, 212, 227, 236, 245, 253, 257, 261

Kenya 94, 124, 281
Khmer Rouge (Cambodia) 198–204, 208
Korea *see* North Korea; South Korea
Kosovo 54, 63, 70
Kosovo Albanians 70
Kroc Institute, University of Notre Dame xv–xvi, 4, 278
Kurdish conflict 166

Lebanon 15, 94, 97, 104–105
Lederach, John Paul xvi, 149
legality 190
liberation 220
liberation movement 258
Liberia 7, 36–38, 114, 129
Libya 4, 124
Lithuania 127
local capacity 139
local institutions 75, 77–78, 106
London (UK) 240
Los Angeles (US) 187
LPC (Liberia Peace Council) 38
LRA (Lord's Resistance Army, Uganda) 69

Machel, Samora (Mozambique) 258
mafia 165, 218
McGuinness, Martin (Northern Ireland) 235
majority 30–34, 38, 47, 70, 131, 155, 202–203, 250, 251
major powers 277
Malaita, Malaitans 137–139
mandates 108, 198
Mandela, Nelson (South Africa) 151, 155
Maoist 3, 66, 111, 173
Maputo (Mozambique) 259, 263–265
Marxism-Leninism 213, 258–259
Marxist theory 38
massacres 182–183
mediation 9, 109, 115–116, 122, 163, 183, 199, 269
Mediation Support Unit, UN xv
Melander, Erik xvi, 157
Mexico 167
Middle East 64, 84, 87, 163, 166, 172
militias 35, 38–39, 49, 52, 137
Milosevic, Slobodan (Yugoslavia) 123–124
Mindanao (Philippines) 15, 94, 97–100
minorities 3, 15, 71, 81, 165; *see also* ethnic minorities
Mozambique 4, 18–20, 38–39, 72, 257–272, 278–283
multinational corporations 93, 103–104
Muslims 97, 100

Nairobi (Kenya) 259
Namibia 6, 54
NATO (North Atlantic Treaty Organization) 56n8
NEC (National Electoral Commission) 269
Nepal 3, 6, 38, 66, 71, 111, 166, 168, 171, 173
Netherlands 265
New York (US) 240
NGOs (non-governmental organizations) 103, 167, 170, 172, 206
Nicaragua 94, 182, 213
Nigeria 129, 166
normal political discourse 205
norms 30–32, 36, 67, 69–70, 126, 128, 141, 145, 150
North Africa 163
Northeast Asia 151, 156
Northern Ireland
North Korea 151
Norway, Norwegian 63, 170, 270

occupation 48–51, 127, 141, 143, 197, 241
ODA (Overseas Development Assistance) 200, 205
OHR (Office of the High Representative) 63
OREC (Organization for Conflict Resolution) 269
Oslo Process 170

Paisley, Ian (Northern Ireland) 235
Palestine 166, 171
partnerships 36, 71, 93, 103–104, 106, 205, 238, 250, 253, 269
PCNAs (Post-Conflict Needs Assessments) 113
peace see quality peace
Peace Accords Matrix (PAM) xv–xvi, 6, 278, 283
peace dividend 105, 110, 115, 178, 229, 236, 240, 242, 280
peacekeeping 9, 11, 31, 33, 37, 39, 49, 51–52, 76–77, 81, 83, 85, 262, 271, 279
peacekeeping operations 76, 81–85, 271
peacemaking xv, 62, 64–67, 70–71, 108, 111–116, 174, 257, 269
peace research 6
People's Republic of China (PRC) see China
Philippines 15, 94, 97–99
physical violence 47, 55
PNC (National Civilian Police) 187, 221

Poland 127, 130
polarization 12, 153, 164, 174, 180, 186, 190, 216, 227–8, 230
political institutions 19, 37, 250
political parties 16, 34–35, 38–39, 179, 203, 212, 216, 226, 235, 243, 250–251, 269
political violence 16, 148–149, 156, 206, 236, 279
Pol Pot (Cambodia) 203
Pope Francis 181
Portugal 48–49, 258, 260–261
Post-Cold War period 6–7, 280
poverty 48, 96, 113–114, 185, 201, 220, 225, 229, 237, 267–280
power 11, 13, 31–39, 46, 64–66, 77, 80–83, 86, 105, 111, 123, 130, 139, 164–168, 173, 199–203, 207, 221, 253, 258, 277
power-sharing 9, 14, 19, 30, 33, 76–87, 152, 235–236, 240, 250–252, 279
PPA (Paris Peace Agreement) 197- 204, 206–208
PRIO (Peace Research Institute Oslo) 57n16
PRK (People's Republic of Cambodia) 197, 207, 209n2
predictability 111, 279
privileges 213
protection 12, 44–55, 69–70, 95, 124–130, 165–174, 181, 199, 245, 281
Protestants 152, 237, 243, 249, 252
PSNI (Police Service of Northern Ireland) 243–245, 247
public service 21, 200, 236, 238, 242, 253
punishment 122, 189

quality peace xvi, 4–5, 18–21, 283–284; definition 8–10; dimensions 10–18, 21, 192n2, 278, 281–282; indicators 5, 10–18, 278–280; measurement 18–21, 280–282

RAMSI (Regional Assistance Mission to the Solomon Islands) 137, 139
rebellion 32, 93, 281
recognition 38, 53, 113–115, 128, 153, 155, 183, 188, 237, 261
reconstruction 4, 11, 14–15, 18–19, 63, 67, 71, 135, 152, 179, 185, 200, 212, 223, 225, 252–253, 280
referendum 49, 66, 123, 141
reform 69, 83, 180, 188, 205, 208, 229, 259, 261–262, 267–268; see also DDR; SSR

Index

refugees 18, 105, 166–167, 171, 167
Regan, Patrick M. 5, 31, 157
Renamo (Mozambique) 19, 38, 257–272, 283
reparations 16, 122, 125–128, 151, 186, 189, 191
repression 19, 155, 178–179, 181–184, 189–190, 226, 228
resistance 64, 69, 181, 197
respect 10, 20, 37, 51, 69, 153, 204, 222, 229, 248, 278, 281
responsibility 5, 103, 112, 115, 149, 150, 189, 235, 238, 253, 264
restoration 149
retribution 105, 128
revolt 130
revolutions 163, 213
rewards 32, 35, 94, 96
riots 52, 242
Robinson, Peter (Northern Ireland) 235, 245
Romania 127
Rome (Italy) 257–262, 264, 272
Romero, Oscar (El Salvador) 181, 189
RUF (Revolutionary United Front) 38
rule of law 13, 19, 54, 97, 129, 187, 203, 205–206, 208, 217–218, 222, 229, 250
Russia 64, 282
Rwanda 6, 15, 94, 97, 100–102, 123–124, 130–131, 150

Sambanis, Nicholas 7, 46, 76–77, 135, 271
sanctions 122, 126
Sant'Egidio 259–260, 269, 271
Saudi Arabia 64
Savimbi, Jonas (Angola) 39
secession 63
Second World War *see* World War II
secrecy 199
Security Council, UN 44–45, 49, 55
security dilemma 29, 33, 271
security equality 12, 44–49, 53–56, 281
security sector reform (SSR) 5, 31, 45, 54, 69 122, 262
self-determination 199
self-interest 95, 100, 103–104
Senegal 94
separation 249
Serbia 123, 130
Serbs 70
SICA (Solomon Islands Christian Association) 137, 145n3
Sierra Leone 38, 94, 124, 150

Sinn Féin (Northern Ireland) 152, 156, 235, 243, 245, 248, 251
Sisk, Timothy 152
SIT (Social Identity Theory) 153
small arms 269
SoC (State of Cambodia) 198,
social justice 9, 13, 153, 178, 182
social media
Söderberg Kovacs, Mimmi 46
solidarity movements 179, 181–182
Solomon Islands 16–17, 135–145
Somalia 32, 166
South Africa 6, 130, 151–152, 157, 258, 260; Truth and Reconciliation Commission 4, 15, 124, 129, 137, 149–150, 245; *see also* apartheid
South America 280
South Korea 151, 155, 200
South Pacific 136
South Sudan 3
sovereignty 7
Soviet Union, The 121
Spain 128, 179
spoilers 5, 11–12, 31, 34–36, 38, 123, 125, 129, 180, 198
Srebrenica (Bosnia) 94
Sri Lanka 63, 94, 163, 166, 171
SSR (Security Sector Reform) 5, 31, 45, 54, 69, 75, 122, 262
stalemate 31, 37, 174, 197, 213
Stalin, Joseph (Soviet Union) 282
Stormont (Northern Ireland) 235–236, 247, 250
structural violence 9, 126
Sudan 3, 111, 113, 124
survival 7, 63, 171, 269
Syria 4, 105, 172

Tajikistan 38
Tanzania 131
territory 51, 70, 82, 198, 261
terrorism 244, 246, 253
third parties 32, 63, 66, 79, 111, 153, 258, 270
threats 44, 46, 54–55, 198
Tibet 64
Timor-Leste 13, 45, 48–55, 67, 124, 141, 143
TPA (Townsville Peace Agreement) 138–139
transparency 106, 190, 205, 217, 266
transitional justice *see* justice
TRC (Truth and Reconciliation Commission) 4, 15–17, 124–125,

129–130, 135, 139,140–145, 150–152, 245
truth commissions 16, 122, 124–126, 129, 135–136, 140, 142–145, 155
Turkey 166
Tutsi (Rwanda) 131
Tutu, Desmond (South Africa) 137

UCDP (Uppsala Conflict Data Program) xv–xvi, 76, 78–79, 81, 278
Uganda 15, 69, 94, 97, 102–104, 131, 142
Ukraine 4
ULIMO (United Liberation Movement of Liberia for Democracy, two factions; ULIMO-J and ULIMO-K) 38
UNAMET (United Nations Mission in East Timor) 49
UNDP (UN Development Program) 116, 219, 264, 268
UNITA (Angola) 39
United Kingdom *see* Britain
United Nations (UN) 36, 39, 45, 55, 76, 112, 167, 198–199, 203, 221, 227–228, 258, 260; and East Timor 45, 49, 141; General Assembly 62, 64; Mediation Support Unit xv; and peacebuilding 6, 187–188, 271; Secretary-General 9, 163, 229, 262–263
United States of America (USA) xv, 188, 278
University of Notre Dame xv, 4, 93
UNMISET (United Nations Mission of Support in East Timor) 49
UN OCHA (United Nations Office for the Coordination of Humanitarian) 167
UNOMOZ 261, 264–265, 270, 272
UNOTIL (United Nations Office in Timor-Leste) 49
UN SRSG (United Nations Special Representative of the Secretary General) 263, 265, 270
UNTAC (United Nations Transitional Authority in Cambodia) 198–199, 204, 206

UNTAET (United Nations Transitional Administration in East Timor) 49, 52–54, 142
URNG (La Unidad Revolucionaria Nacional Guatemalteca) 38
Uppsala University xv, 278
USAID (United States Agency for International Development) 179, 185, 187, 188, 192n3, 193n18, n22, 226, 269, 273n23

victims 3, 15–17, 47–48, 51–53, 62, 123, 127–132, 135–145, 180, 186, 191, 204–205, 225–228, 246, 272, 281
victory 6–10, 62–63, 75, 79–80, 86, 213, 266, 277, 284
Vietnam 197–198

Walter, Barbara 6, 8, 11, 13, 33, 40n5, 271
war, causes of 75
warlord 263
Washington Consensus 223
weapons 16, 39, 130, 139, 235, 269–270, 283
welfare 240
Western Europe 259
Westminster (UK) 236
women 3, 12–13, 20–21, 44–55, 71, 78, 102–105, 137–138, 151, 157, 165–168, 173–174, 182, 189, 191–192, 228–230, 268; *see also* gender
World Bank 19, 48, 93, 95, 100, 206, 217, 219, 224, 258, 267, 271
World War II 48, 75, 122, 128, 138, 150, 156

Yemen 4, 64
Yugoslavia 123–124, 142, 150

ZANU (Zimbabwe African National Union) 258
Zartman, I. William 70
Zimbabwe 130, 258, 271

Taylor & Francis eBooks

Helping you to choose the right eBooks for your Library

Add Routledge titles to your library's digital collection today. Taylor and Francis ebooks contains over 50,000 titles in the Humanities, Social Sciences, Behavioural Sciences, Built Environment and Law.

Choose from a range of subject packages or create your own!

Benefits for you
- Free MARC records
- COUNTER-compliant usage statistics
- Flexible purchase and pricing options
- All titles DRM-free.

Benefits for your user
- Off-site, anytime access via Athens or referring URL
- Print or copy pages or chapters
- Full content search
- Bookmark, highlight and annotate text
- Access to thousands of pages of quality research at the click of a button.

REQUEST YOUR FREE INSTITUTIONAL TRIAL TODAY

Free Trials Available
We offer free trials to qualifying academic, corporate and government customers.

eCollections – Choose from over 30 subject eCollections, including:

Archaeology	Language Learning
Architecture	Law
Asian Studies	Literature
Business & Management	Media & Communication
Classical Studies	Middle East Studies
Construction	Music
Creative & Media Arts	Philosophy
Criminology & Criminal Justice	Planning
Economics	Politics
Education	Psychology & Mental Health
Energy	Religion
Engineering	Security
English Language & Linguistics	Social Work
Environment & Sustainability	Sociology
Geography	Sport
Health Studies	Theatre & Performance
History	Tourism, Hospitality & Events

For more information, pricing enquiries or to order a free trial, please contact your local sales team:
www.tandfebooks.com/page/sales

The home of Routledge books

www.tandfebooks.com